ABORTION

AN ETERNAL SOCIAL AND MORAL ISSUE

ISSN 1538-6643

ABORTION
AN ETERNAL SOCIAL AND MORAL ISSUE

Sandra M. Alters

INFORMATION PLUS® REFERENCE SERIES
Formerly Published by Information Plus, Wylie, Texas

THOMSON
™
GALE

Detroit • New York • San Francisco • San Diego • New Haven, Conn. • Waterville, Maine • London • Munich

Abortion: An Eternal Social and Moral Issue
Sandra M. Alters
Paula Kepos, Series Editor

Project Editor
John McCoy

Permissions
Margaret Abendroth, Edna Hedblad,
Emma Hull

Composition and Electronic Prepress
Evi Seoud

Manufacturing
Drew Kalasky

ISBN 0-7876-5103-6 (set)
ISBN 1-4144-0403-4
ISSN 1538-6643

This title is also available as an e-book.
ISBN 1-4144-1043-3 (set)
Contact your Thomson Gale sales representative for ordering information.

Printed in the United States of America
10 9 8 7 6 5 4 3 2 1

TABLE OF CONTENTS

PREFACE vii

CHAPTER 1
Abortion—An Eternal Social and Moral Issue 1

This chapter explains what abortion is, presents a brief historical overview of abortion, and summarizes the positions of various religions on the topic of abortion. Also discussed are pre–*Roe v. Wade* legal decisions on the topic.

CHAPTER 2
Supreme Court Decisions 9

Chapter 2 picks up where Chapter 1 leaves off, describing abortion-related decisions from the Supreme Court, beginning with *Roe v. Wade* (1973), which gave women throughout the United States the right to have legal abortions. Other cases addressing such topics as public funding, state restrictions, parental consent, partial-birth abortion, and abortion clinic protesters are also discussed.

CHAPTER 3
Abortion—A Major Political Issue 21

Ever since *Roe v. Wade*, American political parties have generally taken a strong position on one side or the other of the abortion issue. This chapter examines various political debates, including those over federal and state funding of abortion, funding through Title X for family planning and contraception, international U.S. aid for family planning and contraception, welfare reform and abortion, and the Unborn Victims of Violence Act.

CHAPTER 4
Abortion in the United States: A Statistical Study . . . 37

This chapter compiles various numbers relating to abortions in the United States. Discussed are the number of abortions performed, what types of women typically seek abortions and why they do, where and how abortions are performed, and the average cost of obtaining an abortion.

CHAPTER 5
Teen Pregnancy and Abortion 61

This chapter looks at teen pregnancy and sexual risk behaviors; pregnancy rates, abortion rates, and birth rates among teens; parental involvement in abortion decisions; and teenagers' knowledge of and feelings toward abortion.

CHAPTER 6
Abortion Clinics 81

Abortion clinics, or medical facilities that specialize in performing abortions, are the topic of this chapter. Quality of clinic care is discussed, as is violence and protests against clinics. The last section describes the Freedom of Access to Clinic Entrances Act (FACE).

CHAPTER 7
Medical and Ethical Questions Concerning
Abortion 87

This chapter examines the debate that surrounds abortion as a medical treatment and its potential impact on a woman's physical and mental health. In addition, the ethical implications of issues such as fetal tissue and embryonic stem cell research and the rights of the fetus are also discussed.

CHAPTER 8
Abortion around the World 95

This chapter considers abortion in countries outside the United States by exploring laws and statistics. Snapshots of abortion policies are provided for a number of specific countries, and worldwide conferences on the topic are also discussed.

CHAPTER 9
Public Attitudes toward Abortion 109

Few topics divide the American public more decisively than abortion. This chapter compiles public opinion survey results on when life begins, if abortions should be legal (and if so, under what circumstances), the importance of the abortion issue from a political viewpoint, and late-term ('partial birth') abortion, among others.

CHAPTER 10
It Should Be Illegal for Minors to Cross State Lines for an
Abortion without the Parents' Consent 115

This chapter provides testimony from various people in favor of the "Child Interstate Abortion Notification Act," which would prohibit anyone except a parent from accompanying a minor across state lines to obtain an abortion. Chapter 11 provides counterarguments.

CHAPTER 11

It Should Not Be Illegal for Minors to Cross State Lines for an Abortion without the Parents' Consent 119

This chapter provides testimony from various people opposed to the "Child Interstate Abortion Notification Act," which would prohibit anyone except a parent from accompanying a minor across state lines to obtain an abortion. Chapter 10 provides counterarguments.

CHAPTER 12

The *Roe v. Wade* Decision Should Be Reconsidered . . .123

These statements dating from 1983 to 2005 argue that the *Roe v. Wade* decision should be reexamined. Chapter 13 provides counterarguments.

CHAPTER 13

The *Roe v. Wade* Decision Should Not Be Reconsidered 129

These statements dating from 1983 to 2005 argue that the *Roe v. Wade* decision should stand. Chapter 12 provides counterarguments.

CHAPTER 14

Certain Types of Late-Term Abortions Should Be Illegal 135

This chapter includes statements from political, medical, and judicial figures who argue against the so-called partial-birth abortion procedure that is used in the later stages of pregnancy. Chapter 15 provides counterarguments.

CHAPTER 15

No New Limitations Should Be Placed on Late-Term Abortion Procedures 141

This chapter includes statements from political, medical, and judicial figures who argue that "partial-birth" abortion should not be banned, especially when the life of the mother is at risk. Chapter 14 provides counterarguments.

IMPORTANT NAMES AND ADDRESSES 149

RESOURCES 151

INDEX 153

PREFACE

Abortion: An Eternal Social and Moral Issue is part of the *Information Plus Reference Series*. The purpose of each volume of the series is to present the latest facts on a topic of pressing concern in modern American life. These topics include today's most controversial and most studied social issues: abortion, capital punishment, care for the elderly, crime, the environment, health care, immigration, minorities, national security, social welfare, women, youth, and many more. Although written especially for the high school and undergraduate student, this series is an excellent resource for anyone in need of factual information on current affairs.

By presenting the facts, it is Thomson Gale's intention to provide its readers with everything they need to reach an informed opinion on current issues. To that end, there is a particular emphasis in this series on the presentation of scientific studies, surveys, and statistics. These data are generally presented in the form of tables, charts, and other graphics placed within the text of each book. Every graphic is directly referred to and carefully explained in the text. The source of each graphic is presented within the graphic itself. The data used in these graphics are drawn from the most reputable and reliable sources, in particular from the various branches of the U.S. government and from major independent polling organizations. Every effort has been made to secure the most recent information available. The reader should bear in mind that many major studies take years to conduct, and that additional years often pass before the data from these studies are made available to the public. Therefore, in many cases the most recent information available in 2006 dated from 2003 or 2004. Older statistics are sometimes presented as well if they are of particular interest and no more recent information exists.

Although statistics are a major focus of the *Information Plus Reference Series*, they are by no means its only content. Each book also presents the widely held positions and important ideas that shape how the book's subject is discussed in the United States. These positions are explained in detail and, where possible, in the words of their proponents. Some of the other material to be found in these books includes: historical background; descriptions of major events related to the subject; relevant laws and court cases; and examples of how these issues play out in American life. Some books also feature primary documents or have pro and con debate sections giving the words and opinions of prominent Americans on both sides of a controversial topic. All material is presented in an even-handed and unbiased manner; the reader will never be encouraged to accept one view of an issue over another.

HOW TO USE THIS BOOK

Few topics rouse as much dissension and disagreement as the topic of abortion. While some people assert that it is a woman's right to choose to have an abortion if she wishes, others assert that abortion is tantamount to murder. This book attempts to provide both sides of the divisive argument. Also included is information on the number and types of abortions performed in the United States, abortion clinics, teen pregnancy and abortion, views of abortion from around the world, religious thoughts on abortion, and legal rulings pertaining to abortion.

Abortion: An Eternal Social and Moral Issue consists of fifteen chapters and three appendices. Each of the chapters is devoted to a particular aspect of abortion. For a summary of the information covered in each chapter, please see the synopses provided in the Table of Contents at the front of the book. Chapters generally begin with an overview of the basic facts and background information on the chapter's topic, then proceed to examine subtopics of particular interest. For example, Chapter 5:

Teen Pregnancy and Abortion begins with a discussion of teenage pregnancy in general. This is followed by a section on efforts to lower the teen pregancy rate through various means, the impact of the media on teenage sexuality, and sexual risk factors among teens. Next is a section examining teen pregnancy and birth rates in detail, including breakdowns by age, ethnicity, and region. The remainder of the chapter is devoted to a close examination of abortion among teenagers, including the factors that influence teenagers to get, or not get, an abortion, giving babies up for adoption in lieu of abortion, and studies on what teenagers know about abortion and birth control. Readers can find their way through a chapter by looking for the section and subsection headings, which are clearly set off from the text. They can also refer to the book's extensive Index if they already know what they are looking for.

Statistical Information

The tables and figures featured throughout *Abortion: An Eternal Social and Moral Issue* will be of particular use to the reader in learning about this issue. These tables and figures represent an extensive collection of the most recent and important statistics on abortion and related issues—for example, graphics in the book cover the chronology of major abortion cases, the major political parties' positions on abortion, reported numbers of legal abortions in the United States, teenage birth rates, the number of incidents of violence at abortion clinics, the number of legal and illegal abortions worldwide, and public opinion on when life begins. Thomson Gale believes that making this information available to the reader is the most important way in which we fulfill the goal of this book: to help readers understand the issues and controversies surrounding abortion in the United States and to reach their own conclusions.

Each table or figure has a unique identifier appearing above it for ease of identification and reference. Titles for the tables and figures explain their purpose. At the end of each table or figure, the original source of the data is provided.

In order to help readers understand these often complicated statistics, all tables and figures are explained in the text. References in the text direct the reader to the relevant statistics. Furthermore, the contents of all tables and figures are fully indexed. Please see the opening section of the Index at the back of this volume for a description of how to find tables and figures within it.

Appendices

In addition to the main body text and images, *Abortion: An Eternal Social and Moral Issue* has three appendices. The first is the Important Names and Addresses directory. Here the reader will find contact information for a number of government and private organizations that can provide further information on abortion. The second appendix is the Resources section, which can also assist the reader in conducting his or her own research. In this section the author and editors of *Abortion: An Eternal Social and Moral Issue* describe some of the sources that were most useful during the compilation of this book. The final appendix is the detailed Index, which facilitates reader access to specific topics in this book.

ADVISORY BOARD CONTRIBUTIONS

The staff of Information Plus would like to extend its heartfelt appreciation to the Information Plus Advisory Board. This dedicated group of media professionals provides feedback on the series on an ongoing basis. Their comments allow the editorial staff who work on the project to make the series better and more user-friendly. Our top priority is to produce the highest-quality and most useful books possible, and the Advisory Board's contributions to this process are invaluable.

The members of the Information Plus Advisory Board are:

- Kathleen R. Bonn, Librarian, Newbury Park High School, Newbury Park, California

- Madelyn Garner, Librarian, San Jacinto College— North Campus, Houston, Texas

- Anne Oxenrider, Media Specialist, Dundee High School, Dundee, Michigan

- Charles R. Rodgers, Director of Libraries, Pasco– Hernando Community College, Dade City, Florida

- James N. Zitzelsberger, Library Media Department Chairman, Oshkosh West High School, Oshkosh, Wisconsin

COMMENTS AND SUGGESTIONS

The editors of the *Information Plus Reference Series* welcome your feedback on *Abortion: An Eternal Social and Moral Issue*. Please direct all correspondence to:

Editors
Information Plus Reference Series
27500 Drake Rd.
Farmington Hills, MI 48331-3535

CHAPTER 1
ABORTION—AN ETERNAL SOCIAL AND MORAL ISSUE

WHAT IS ABORTION?

An abortion—also called "induced abortion"—is a procedure performed to end a pregnancy before birth occurs. This is not the same as a spontaneous abortion, a process that occurs when a fetus or embryo dies in the mother's uterus and is expelled by the body. Spontaneous abortion is also called a "miscarriage."

The length of a pregnancy is measured in weeks from the first day of a woman's last menstrual period. A normal human pregnancy lasts about forty weeks. Pregnancy also can be described in "trimesters." There are three trimesters in pregnancy, and each trimester is about three months long. According to the Centers for Disease Control and Prevention (CDC) in "Abortion Surveillance—United States, 2001" (*Morbidity and Mortality Weekly Report, Surveillance Summaries*, vol. 53, no. SS-09, November 26, 2004), 88% of all induced abortions in 2001 were performed during the first twelve weeks, or first trimester, of pregnancy. The later in pregnancy abortion is performed, the higher the risk to the mother. Few reported abortions were provided after fifteen weeks, which is about four months of pregnancy, according to the CDC report. Of abortions in 2001, 4.3% were obtained at sixteen to twenty weeks, and 1.4% were obtained at twenty-one weeks or later.

Induced abortion can be accomplished in several ways. Some abortion procedures are performed with surgery and some with medication. (See Table 1.1.) The type of abortion a woman has depends on her choice, health, and how long she has been pregnant. Early surgical and medical abortions can be done safely in a doctor's office or clinic. Later abortions often are performed in hospitals or in special clinics.

Abortions have been performed since the beginning of recorded history. There have always been women who, for a variety of reasons, wanted to terminate their pregnancies. Today, the abortion issue has developed into a conflict about whether an embryo or fetus is entitled to legal rights, and whether a woman's right to control her life and body includes the right to end an unwanted pregnancy. While abortion has been debated for centuries, motivations to condemn or support it have varied with changing political and social conditions.

ANCIENT TIMES

Abortion is mentioned in the ancient Code of Assyria (in Mesopotamia) of the twelfth century B.C.E. (before the common era). Provision Fifty-three explicitly ordered that any woman who had an abortion should be impaled on stakes without the dignity of burial. If the woman did not survive the abortion, her body was to be similarly impaled, again without burial. Likewise, ancient Jewish law strictly forbade abortion as a method of avoiding childbirth, although it allowed the sacrifice of the fetus to save the life of the mother.

Conversely, in ancient Greece and Rome, abortion often was used to limit family size. It was socially acceptable, as was the practice of disposing of deformed and weak infants through exposure (abandoning babies outdoors with the intent that they die). Males were favored; parents who did not want to have the expense of raising a female infant labeled her as "weak" and resorted to exposure.

Both Plato (c. 428–347 B.C.E.) and Aristotle (384–322 B.C.E.) approved of abortion as a means of population control. They also advocated exposure in the belief that it would ensure the best possible offspring. Plato wrote in *The Republic* that any woman older than forty years (an age when the rate of birth defects increases sharply) should be compelled to abort a pregnancy.

Scholars who credit Hippocrates (c. 460–377 B.C.E.) with the Hippocratic Oath claim that he opposed abortion. (The Hippocratic Oath in its early form prohibited abortion. It has been modified for modern use to be

TABLE 1.1

Methods of abortion

Medical abortion

For a medical abortion, a combination of drugs is taken to end a pregnancy. A medical abortion does not require surgery and can be performed up to 49 days after the first day of the last menstrual period. Two combinations of medications are available for medical abortions:

- Methotrexate and misoprostol—Methotrexate terminates a pregnancy by inhibiting the production of folic acid in the pregnant woman's body. Folic acid is necessary for making the cells that form the brain, spine, organs, skin, and bones of the developing fetus. Misoprostol is then used. This drug causes the uterus to contract and expel its contents.
- Mifepristone (formerly known as RU486) and misoprostol—Mifepristone terminates a pregnancy by blocking the action of progesterone in the pregnant woman's body. Progesterone helps maintain the uterine lining, which is necessary for a pregnancy to be sustained. Misoprostol is then used and works as noted above.

Surgical abortion

Surgical abortions remove the contents of the uterus. They are performed in a few ways, with the procedure depending on the length of the pregnancy:

- Suction curettage (vacuum aspiration)—Suction curettage can be performed during the first trimester—up to 12 weeks— of pregnancy. First, the opening of the uterus (the cervix) is widened, or dilated, by the insertion of small rods or sponges. A thin plastic tube is then inserted through the dilated cervix and into the uterus. The tube is attached to a pump that suctions out uterine contents. After the suctioning, it is sometimes necessary to use a curette (a sharp, spoon-like instrument) to gently scrape the walls of the uterus to be certain that all the fragments of the fetus and placenta have been removed.
- Dilation and Evacuation (D&E)—D&E is generally performed during the second trimester—from 12 to 24 weeks—of pregnancy. The procedure is similar to suction curettage, but the cervix is dilated more. In addition, forceps may be used to grasp larger pieces of tissue.
- Induction—For abortions in the second or third trimester, labor may be started (induced) with drugs. Drugs may be put in the vagina, injected into the uterus, or given intravenously (IV) to start contractions that will expel the fetus. Alternatively, salt water or urea may be injected into the amniotic sac surrounding the fetus. This stops the pregnancy and starts uterine contractions. Taking a large amount of fluid out of the amniotic sac may also be used to stop the pregnancy and start contractions. Some drugs may be given directly to the fetus.

SOURCE: Created by Sandra Alters for Thomson Gale, 2005

a medical code of ethics that states "First do no harm.") Others claim that this prohibition was a reflection of the Pythagorean teaching opposing abortion and that physicians in ancient times generally did not follow this oath.

The consequences of adultery or prostitution were very compelling reasons for a woman or her family to end her pregnancy. In the ancient Roman household, the father was the judge when it came to the ethical life of the family. He alone had the authority to order or forbid an abortion. When abortions were performed, Romans were not concerned with the life of the child but with the health of the mother, because some women were poisoned accidentally by improper mixtures of abortion-inducing drugs. Thus, fathers usually opted for infanticide (killing of an infant after birth) rather than abortion.

CHRISTIAN POSITION ON ABORTION

Christianity is a religion that was founded in Palestine by the followers of Jesus Christ approximately two thousand years ago. There are three broad divisions of Christianity: Roman Catholic, Eastern Orthodox, and Protestant. Within the category of Protestantism, there are a particularly large number of divergent denominations. The Roman Catholic and Eastern Orthodox divisions have existed since the earliest days of Christianity. Protestantism, however, dates back only to the Reformation, a sixteenth-century movement in Western Europe that aimed at reforming some doctrines and practices of the Roman Catholic Church and resulted in the establishment of the Protestant churches. Of adults in America, 52% identify themselves as Protestant, 24.5% as Roman Catholic, and less than one half of one percent as Eastern Orthodox, while 14.1% say they follow no organized religion,

according to the American Religious Identification Survey released in 2001 by the Graduate Center of the City University of New York (http://www.gc.cuny.edu/faculty/ research_studies/aris.pdf, December 19, 2001).

The Eastern Orthodox Church and the Roman Catholic Church consider an induced abortion to be a grave sin. Because Protestantism consists of various denominations and sects, many of which have differing teachings, Protestantism as a whole does not hold one position on abortion.

Abortion in the Christian Era

The first works of the Christian Church hardly mention abortion. The earliest known Christian document that declared abortion a sin was the *Didache* (also known as the *Teachings of the Lord through the Apostles* or the *Doctrine of the Twelve Apostles*), written c. 100 C.E.. *Didache* 2:2 states, "You shall not kill the embryo by abortion and shall not cause the newborn to perish." The early church leaders agreed that if an abortion were performed to hide the consequences of fornication and adultery, then it was a sin that required penance. This sparked the debate as to whether abortion was murder.

According to Dr. Roy Bowen Ward in "Is the Fetus a Person? The Bible's View" (Religious Coalition for Reproductive Choice, Educational Series No. 2., http:// www.rcrc.org/pdf/is%20fetus%20a%20person.pdf), both the Old Testament and New Testament of the Bible are silent on the subject of abortion. John T. Noonan, an antiabortion Roman Catholic scholar, reported in an essay entitled "An Almost Absolute Value in History" (*The Morality of Abortion: Legal and Historical Perspectives*,

Cambridge, MA: Harvard University Press, 1970) that "the Old Testament has nothing to say on abortion."

Roman Catholic Position on Abortion

During the first six centuries of the history of the Roman Catholic Church, theologians theorized and debated about the starting point of human life. St. Augustine (354–430 C.E.), a Doctor of the Church whose teachings helped establish its theological foundation, taught that abortion is not the murder of an infant (infanticide). He wrote, "The law does not provide that the act [abortion] pertains to homicide, for there cannot yet be said to be a live soul in a body that lacks sensation when it is not formed in flesh and so is not endowed with sense." Reflecting a similar viewpoint, the *Irish Canons* (c. 675 C.E.) noted the penalty for illicit intercourse (minimum of seven years on bread and water) as far more severe than the penance for abortion (three and one-half years on the same diet).

St. Thomas Aquinas (1225–1274), generally considered to be one of the greatest Catholic theologians of all time, developed the concept of *hylomorphism*, which defines a human being as the unity of body and soul. This resulted in the belief that there could be no human being without the presence of both elements. The soul, in other words, can exist only in a fully formed body. In *Summa Theologica* (Part I, Question 90, Article 4) St. Thomas Aquinas wrote, "The soul, as part of human nature, has its natural perfection only as united to the body."

However, not all Catholic theologians agreed with the position of St. Thomas Aquinas. Some theologians taught that *hominization* (the point at which a fetus acquires a soul and becomes a human being) occurred at forty days after conception for males and eighty days for females. This also was referred to as the "ensoulment" of the fetus.

In 1312, at the Council of Vienne, the Catholic Church officially adopted St. Thomas Aquinas's hylomorphic theory of human life and upheld this traditional doctrine through the sixteenth century. As a result, priests would not baptize a premature infant unless it had a human form.

Nonetheless, although the Church endorsed St. Thomas Aquinas's theory, theological discussions on abortion and the fetus continued. From the twelfth through the sixteenth centuries, the various popes issued differing pronouncements on abortion and the fetal status depending on their personal beliefs about the moment of ensoulment. In some cases they imposed excommunication (exclusion from Church membership) as a penalty for purposefully aborting a fetus.

In 1869 in *Apostolicae Sedis*, Pope Pius IX declared abortion a homicide and, therefore, grounds for excommunication. This decision was reaffirmed in 1917 with the issuance of the *Code of Canon Law*. Canon 2350,

Paragraph I, explicitly states, "Persons who procure abortion, not excepting the mother, incur, if the effect follows, an automatic excommunication reserved to the Ordinary (nonclergy), and if they be clerics, they are moreover deposed." Recent popes have firmly upheld this canon. Pope Pius XII, deeply concerned about abortion, wrote in his *Allocution to Midwives* in 1951:

> Besides, every human being, even the child in the womb, has the right to life directly from God and not from his parents, not from any society or human authority. Therefore, there is no man, no human authority, no science, no "indication" at all—whether it be medical, eugenic, social, economic, or moral—that may offer or give a valid judicial title for a direct deliberate disposal of an innocent human life, that is, a disposal which aims at its destruction, whether as an end in itself or as a means to achieve the end, perhaps in no way at all illicit. Thus, for example, to save the life of the mother is a very noble act; but the direct killing of the child as a means to such an end is illicit.

The Second Vatican Council (1962–65), the largest Roman Catholic Church gathering in Christian history, declared in *Gaudium Et Spes* that abortion is a "supreme dishonor to the Creator." The Council further observed that "from the moment of its conception, life must be guarded with the greatest care, while abortion and infanticide are unspeakable crimes" (EWTN Catholic Network, *Gaudium Et Spes*, http://www.ewtn.com/library/councils/v2modwor.htm).

In 1968, in the letter *Humanae Vitae* (EWTN Catholic Network, *Humanae Vitae*, http://www.ewtn.com/library/encyc/p6humana.htm), Pope Paul VI stated, "We must once again declare that the direct interruption of the generative process already begun, and, above all, directly willed and procured abortion, even if for therapeutic (medically necessary) reasons, are to be absolutely excluded as licit (legal) means of regulating birth."

In 1995 Pope John Paul II proclaimed his firm stand against contraception, abortion, and euthanasia (mercy killing) in the letter *Evangelium Vitae* (Gospel of Life). The letter claimed that modern society promoted a "culture of death." In November 1998 the National Conference of Catholic Bishops of the United States issued "Living the Gospel of Life: A Challenge to American Catholics" (http://www.usccb.org/prolife/gospel.htm). It stated that "direct abortion is *never* a morally tolerable option. It is *always* a grave act of violence against a woman and her unborn child. This is even so when the woman does not see the truth because of the pressures she may be subjected to, often by the child's father, her parents or friends."

Pope John Paul II died in April 2005. His successor, Pope Benedict XVI, stated shortly after assuming the papacy that he and the Catholic Church will continue to stand firmly against abortion.

Eastern Orthodox Position on Abortion

The Eastern Orthodox position is very similar to the Roman Catholic position: life begins at conception, and abortion is the taking of a human life. Orthodox doctrine maintains that is possible, although difficult, to make a case for abortion in situations involving the rape of a young girl or endangerment of the mother's life.

Protestant Position on Abortion

More than one thousand denominations of Protestantism exist today. Until the late 1960s almost all Protestant churches opposed abortion. However, the changing social climate, as well as the U.S. Supreme Court decision in *Roe v. Wade* in 1973, which legalized abortion in the United States, spurred a change in Protestant positions on abortion.

Since 1970 the Presbyterian Church has supported free and open access to abortion without legal restriction. At about the same time, the United Methodists, the Lutheran Church in America, the United Church of Christ, the Disciples of Christ, and the Southern Baptist Convention adopted policies allowing abortion as a decision of the woman or the couple. In 1980 the Southern Baptist Convention began to reverse its stance, first by opposing the use of tax money to fund abortions. By the late 1980s the Southern Baptist Convention made their opposition to abortion, except to prevent the death of the mother, a firm policy. Many evangelical, fundamentalist, and independent Bible churches are also against abortion. However, many Protestant denominations still support open access to abortion.

ISLAMIC POSITION ON ABORTION

Islam has more than one billion followers worldwide. According to the 2001 American Religious Identification Survey, Muslim and Islamic Americans make up 0.5% of the U.S. population. The Qur'an (Koran), which Muslims believe to contain God's revelations to Muhammad (c. 570–632 C.E.), describes the development of the fetus:

> O Mankind! If ye are in doubt concerning the Resurrection, then lo! We have created you from dust, then from a drop of seed, then from a clot, then from a little lump of flesh shapely and shapeless, that We may make (it) clear for you. And We cause what We will to remain in the wombs for an appointed time, and afterward We bring you forth as infants. (Qur'an 22:5, as translated by Mohammed M. Pickthall in *The Meaning of the Glorious Qur'an*, Beltsville, MD: Amana, 1999)

The Qur'an teaches that fetal development is divided into three stages, each forty days long. At the end of these stages, the soul enters the fetus. Muslims, who belong to various groups, differ in their beliefs as to when—or if—abortion is allowed. Some sects believe it is permissible to have an abortion before ensoulment, whereas others argue that God forbids the killing of both the born and unborn, even those who have not received a soul. They claim the Qur'an specifically teaches, "They are losers who besottedly have slain their children without knowledge, and have forbidden that which Allah bestowed upon them" (6:140). However, the followers of Islam generally agree that abortion is acceptable to save the mother's life.

JEWISH POSITION ON ABORTION

According to the American Religious Identification Survey, Jewish Americans make up 1.3% of the U.S. population. Like Islam, Judaism has no one position on abortion. In the United States most Jews belong to one of three groups: Orthodox, Conservative, or Reform Judaism. Reform and Conservative Jews generally believe that abortion is the choice of the woman. Jewish law does not recognize a fetus, or even an infant younger than thirty days old, as having legal rights. The laws of mourning do not apply to an expelled fetus or a child who does not survive to his thirtieth day. The biblical text that is the basis for this states, "If a man strikes and wounds a pregnant woman so that her fruit be expelled, but no harm befall her, then shall he be fined as her husband shall assess, and the matter placed before the judges. But if harm befall her, then thou shalt give life for life" (Exodus 21:22).

The Mishnah is the code of Jewish law that forms the basis of the Talmud, the most definitive statement of Jewish law. The Mishnah, which dates back to the second century B.C.E., states, "If a woman is having difficulty in giving birth, it is permitted to cut up the child inside her womb and take it out limb by limb because her life takes precedence. However, if the greater part of the child has come out, it must not be touched, because one life must not be taken to save another."

Moses Maimonides (1135–1204), a rabbi, a doctor, and one of the greatest Jewish philosophers, wrote that abortion was permitted if it would ease a mother's illness, even if the illness was not life threatening. Other scholars, however, have differed, saying abortion was permitted only to save the mother's life. During the Holocaust (1939–45) Jewish women who became pregnant were encouraged by their rabbis to abort because the Germans had declared that all pregnant Jewish women would be killed.

Orthodox Judaism takes a restrictive position on abortion, teaching that a fetus is an organic part of the mother and, as such, does not have legal status. Nonetheless, termination of a pregnancy is strongly condemned on moral grounds. Although a mother's life takes precedence over the unborn, Orthodox Jews believe that the fetus, particularly after the fortieth day from conception, has a right to life that cannot be denied. Cases of rape or fetal deformity do not give a mother permission to terminate a pregnancy unless they are a threat to her mental health (for instance, if the mother becomes suicidal as a result of the pregnancy).

THE BRITISH TRADITION

American legal tradition has developed from the British tradition. Until England broke away from the Roman Catholic Church in the fifteenth century, it had observed the Church's laws. Henry de Bracton (c. 1210–68), the father of English common law, was the first to mention abortion in English law. (The English common law was a body of laws based on judicial precedents, or court decisions and opinions, rather than on written laws.) Greatly influenced by Church law and theologians, Bracton wrote in *De Legibus Angliae*, "If there is anyone who has struck a pregnant woman or has given poison to her, whereby he has caused an abortion, if the fetus be already formed or animated and especially if animated, he commits a homicide."

When Sir Edward Coke wrote *The Institutes of the Laws of England* four hundred years later (in the early 1600s), the law had changed. "If a woman be *quick* with a childe," Coke wrote, "and by a potion or otherwise killeth it in her womb or if a man beat her, whereby the child dieth in her body and she is delivered of a dead child, this is a great misprision (misdemeanor) and no murder; but if the child be born alive and dieth of poison, battery, or other cause, this is murder." "Quickening" refers to the first time the mother feels the fetus moving in the womb. It often occurs about the sixteenth to eighteenth week of pregnancy.

A century later Sir William Blackstone, in his *Commentaries on the Laws of England* (1765), upheld Coke's interpretation that it was a serious misdemeanor if the child was killed in the womb and murder if it was killed after birth. Despite the observations of Coke and Blackstone, abortion was not a criminal offense in England from 1327 to 1803.

British Statutes

Nineteenth century British law prohibited abortion. The first written statute in England against abortion was the Miscarriage of Women Act of 1803 (also known as Lord Ellenborough's Act), which affirmed punishment for the administration of drugs to induce abortion. The punishment for abortion before quickening included exile, whipping, or imprisonment. The punishment for abortion after quickening was death. However, after the abolition of the death penalty in 1837, abortion both before and after quickening was considered a felony with similar punishments.

In 1861 Parliament passed the Offences against The Person Act. It stated the following:

> Every woman, being with child, who, with intent to procure her own miscarriage, shall unlawfully administer to herself any poison or other noxious thing, or shall unlawfully use any instrument or other means whatsoever with the like intent, and whosoever, with intent to procure the miscarriage of any woman . . . shall

be guilty of felony, and being convicted thereof shall be liable . . . to be kept in penal servitude for life.

In addition, any person who assisted another in obtaining an abortion was guilty of a misdemeanor and could receive a three-year prison sentence.

In 1929 Parliament enacted the Infant Life Preservation Act, supplementing the Offenses against the Person Act. This Act stated that an abortion, particularly of a viable (able to survive outside the womb) fetus, was unlawful *except* when it could be proved to have been done in good faith to save the mother's life. The passage of the Infant Life Preservation Act was the first time that written English law no longer regarded abortion as a felony if performed to save the life of the mother. In addition, it considered abortion of an inviable fetus to be possibly lawful and stated that twenty-eight weeks was the age at which a fetus must be presumed to be viable.

In 1938 a health exception was added to the Offenses against the Person Act of 1861. A fourteen-year-old girl who was raped and became pregnant went to a London physician, Dr. Aleck Bourne, for an abortion. The doctor performed the abortion free of charge and then reported it to the authorities. In *Rex v. Bourne* Justice MacNaghten noted that the threat to life also involved health and that childbirth might have threatened the young girl's mental health. He instructed the jury to vote for the physician's acquittal if the jurors believed the abortion would preserve the girl's mental health. The jury acquitted. More than a legal precedent, the case became a rallying cry for advocates of liberalizing abortion laws.

In the spring of 1968, following a long and bitter struggle, the Abortion Act of 1967 went into effect. This law permitted abortion if two physicians had determined that the pregnancy threatened the mental and physical health of the mother or that the potential child would suffer serious physical or mental deformities. Thus, the abortion decision was placed in the hands of physicians and not the pregnant woman.

The next change in British abortion laws occurred in 1990. The British House of Commons voted to cut the legal time limit for abortions from twenty-eight to twenty-four weeks of pregnancy, but it also allowed abortions after that upper limit in cases of fetal handicap or "grave permanent injury to the physical and mental health of the pregnant woman." In 1991 the drug mifepristone (also known as RU-486) was approved for medical abortions of up to nine weeks.

There is still debate in England regarding the abortion laws there. Many groups support legal abortion while other groups support reducing the availability of abortion or banning it altogether.

THE AMERICAN EXPERIENCE

In colonial America midwives, not doctors, helped mothers deliver their children. In most cases, however, midwives were forbidden to perform abortions. For example, in 1716, New York City laws licensing midwives required them to swear, among other things, not to "give any Counsel or Administer any Herb, Medicine or Potion, or any other thing to any Woman being with Child whereby She Should Destroy or Miscarry or that she goeth withal before her time."

This and other similar statutes were part of common law. They were enacted to prevent women from dying from the poisons used to terminate pregnancies, and they remained in effect until the American Revolution. In postrevolutionary America, abortion before quickening was legal.

The First Laws

The first abortion laws in the United States were based on English common law, as described by Coke and Blackstone. In 1821 Connecticut passed the first abortion law. Although it was patterned after the British 1803 Miscarriage of Women Act, which addressed all forms of abortion, the Connecticut statute addressed postquickening abortion only, declaring it to be a felony.

In 1828 New York passed a statute with two provisions. The first provision imposed a second-degree manslaughter penalty for a postquickening abortion. A prequickening abortion was considered a misdemeanor. The second provision contained an exception clause permitting "therapeutic" abortion if "necessary to preserve the life of such a mother or shall have been advised by two physicians to be necessary for such a purpose." This New York law served as a model for many statutes prohibiting abortion.

Despite these state statutes regulating abortion, the sale of abortion-inducing drugs continued during the first half of the nineteenth century. The newspapers regularly advertised "Monthly Pills" and new methods to relieve "obstructions of the womb."

In 1871 the *New York Times* called abortion the "Evil of the Age." The newspaper article stated, "The enormous amount of medical malpractice [a euphemism for abortion] that exists and flourishes, almost unchecked, in the city of New York, is a theme for most serious consideration. Thousands of human beings are thus murdered before they have seen the light of this world" (*New York Times*, August 23, 1871).

The American Medical Association

The American Medical Association (AMA), founded in 1847, initially campaigned vigorously against abortion. At that time women did not regularly turn to physicians for questions on childbirth and "women problems," but they went instead to untrained people who pretended to have medical skills ("quacks"), friends, pharmacists, and midwives. The AMA was concerned about the dangers that "quack" abortions posed for the women who received them. In addition, the association argued that abortion providers ignored the portion of the Hippocratic Oath that stated, "I will give no deadly medicine to anyone if asked, nor suggest any such counsel."

The simplest solution to this difficult situation was to make abortion illegal. The medical profession saw this as an opportunity to drive quacks out of the field and bolster their own professional image. In addition, medical science recently had recognized that life existed in the fetus before quickening, and many physicians were morally offended by the act of aborting a live fetus.

The AMA was not motivated to criminalize abortion for moral or professional reasons alone. Physicians were swept up by the growing anti-immigrant sentiments of the time. There were concerns that, because of the uncontrolled use of abortion, the proportion of "good Anglo-Saxon stock" was diminishing in the face of increasing immigration, which was predominantly Catholic at the time.

Antiabortion Laws

Because of the intense lobbying by the AMA, the period from 1860 to 1880 produced the most important proliferation of antiabortion legislation in American history. States and territories enacted more than forty antiabortion statutes. Of these, thirteen outlawed abortion for the first time and twenty-one revised old antiabortion laws by making them more stringent. In 1873 the U.S. Congress passed the Comstock Law (named after its chief supporter, Anthony Comstock). Primarily intended to ban the dissemination of pornography and birth control devices, this legislation also prohibited the use of abortion devices.

Abortion continued despite the laws that banned it. In the early twentieth century as many as one in three pregnancies was terminated. (Other forms of birth control were either unreliable or difficult to obtain.) Wealthy women generally found physicians who lent their own interpretations to the allowable exceptions for "therapeutic," or medically necessary, abortions. Poor women, however, usually had to resort to self-induced or illegal abortions, which resulted in countless mutilations and deaths.

In 1934 Congress held hearings to amend the Comstock Law to allow doctors to provide birth control information and prescribe contraceptive devices. However, support was strong for the Comstock Law; defenders of the law held that allowing doctors to provide birth control information was tantamount to the government supporting population control. The Comstock Law remained in effect for nearly four more decades. On January 8, 1971, President Richard Nixon signed a law overturning the ninety-eight-year-old federal anticontraception law. The law was sponsored by Representative George H. W. Bush of Texas.

CHANGING ATTITUDES

Over time, advances in medicine enabled most women to carry their pregnancies to term uneventfully. Doctors became hard-pressed to diagnose life-threatening complications so that they might prescribe "therapeutic" abortions. In 1959 the American Law Institute proposed a revised Model Penal Code that gave physicians guidelines with which to work. The Model Penal Code proposed that physicians be permitted to terminate a pregnancy if one of the following conditions was met:

- The pregnancy threatened the life of the mother or would critically impair the mother's physical or mental condition.

- The child would be born with a grave physical or mental defect.

- The pregnancy resulted from rape or incest.

The need for the abortion had to be approved by two physicians. The inclusion of the mother's mental condition became a factor for doctors because the definition of health was beginning to include mental health at that time.

By the 1960s all fifty states and the District of Columbia allowed "therapeutic" abortions to save the life of the mother. Colorado and New Mexico also permitted abortions to prevent serious irreparable harm to the mother. Alabama, Oregon, Massachusetts, and the District of Columbia allowed abortions simply to protect the health of the mother.

Thalidomide and Rubella

No sooner were these laws adopted than their restrictions were tested by events that occurred in the early 1960s. In 1962 Sherri Finkbine of Arizona found out that thalidomide, a drug she had been taking during pregnancy, may have caused deformities in the child she was carrying. European women who used the drug to treat morning sickness were reported to be delivering severely deformed babies. Finkbine decided, on her physician's advice, to have a legal abortion.

After Finkbine publicized her dilemma to warn others of the effects of thalidomide, the hospital refused the abortion for fear of criminal liability. An appeal to the Arizona State Supreme Court was unsuccessful, so the Finkbines flew to Sweden, where the abortion was performed. The Swedish doctor confirmed that the embryo was deformed.

During the early 1960s a rubella (German measles) epidemic swept the United States. Many women who had contracted measles during early pregnancy obtained legal abortions because they thought their fetuses might have birth defects. Many others could not have abortions, either because of legal restrictions or lack of funds. Consequently, they either delivered their children with greater risk of disabilities or had illegal abortions.

In 1967 the AMA called for the liberalization of abortion laws and, in 1970, urged that abortion be limited only by the "sound clinical judgment" of a physician.

WOMEN SPEAK OUT

The thalidomide and rubella episodes stimulated interest in the abortion issue and created empathy for the mothers-to-be who had found themselves in these difficult situations. Furthermore, the 1960s were a period of change—a time when many people questioned accepted beliefs. Americans were discussing human sexuality more openly, which made it easier to talk about abortion. Many sought to put a stop to the deaths and mutilations brought on by unqualified abortionists.

The Laws Begin to Change

Increased interest in the abortion issue caused many states to reform their laws, using the Model Penal Code as a guide. In 1967 Colorado, California, and North Carolina became the first states to liberalize their statutes. By 1973 a total of thirteen states had enacted this type of legislation.

In 1970 Alaska, Hawaii, New York, and Washington chose the radical alternative of legalizing all abortions performed by a physician—up to a legally determined time in the pregnancy. Alaska, Hawaii, and Washington also established state residency requirements and shorter time periods during which women could have abortion on demand. By one vote, New York passed the most liberal law of the four states. It permitted abortion for any reason up to twenty-four weeks of pregnancy. Beyond that point, an abortion could only be performed to save the mother's life.

In 1972 the American Bar Association approved the Uniform Abortion Act as a model for all state statutes. It was based on the New York law. That same year the President's Commission on Population Growth and the American Future, headed by John D. Rockefeller III, released its final report, which recommended that "present state laws restricting abortion be liberalized along the lines of the New York statute" (Center for Research on Population and Security, The Rockefeller Commission Report, http://www.population-security.org/rockefeller/017_recommendations.htm).

Meanwhile, as legislatures continued to reexamine their state abortion laws, state and federal courts were beginning to declare state abortion laws unconstitutional because they were vague and interfered with a woman's right to privacy. Many thousands of women traveled to states where abortion had become legal to obtain an abortion. The New York State Department of Health reported that between July 1, 1970, and December 31, 1972, more than three hundred thousand women traveled to New York to get abortions. Many states watched to see what would happen in New York, Alaska, Hawaii, and Washington, and everyone awaited the legal clarification that inevitably would have to come from the U.S. Supreme Court. It came on January 22, 1973, in the historic *Roe v. Wade* decision. Chapter 2 describes that and other U.S. Supreme Court decisions on abortion.

CHAPTER 2
SUPREME COURT DECISIONS

JUDICIAL APPOINTMENTS AND POLITICS

The federal court system is divided into three major types of courts: District Courts, Circuit Courts of Appeals, and the Supreme Court. There is at least one District Court in each state; they serve as trial courts for lawsuits pertaining to federal law that arise in that state. Circuit Courts of Appeals reconsider rulings from the District Courts, usually by a three-judge panel. Federal lawsuits that have passed through the District Courts and Circuit Courts of Appeals may then be appealed to the Supreme Court—the ultimate authority in interpreting federal law.

Federal judges are not elected; they are appointed and serve lifetime terms. Federal judges are nominated by the president of the United States and then must be approved by a majority of the U.S. Senate before they can be officially appointed. When the president and the Senate are controlled by the same political party, and when they are in agreement about the direction public policy should take, confirmation of a nominee is relatively easy, though the opposition party is sometimes able to use procedural practices, such as filibusters, to delay or prevent the confirmation vote.

Since federal judges are appointed for life, each appointment has a long-lasting influence on the court system and on the lives of Americans. Because the judges are appointed by the president, the nominees usually hold political views that are similar to the president's. Thus, if a president is opposed to abortion, it is likely that he will appoint federal judges who are known to be conservative on that issue.

Jeffrey A. Segal, coauthor of *Advice and Consent: The Politics of Judicial Appointments* (Oxford, United Kingdom: Oxford University Press, 2005), notes that "most justices appointed by conservative presidents cast a high percentage of conservative votes.... Likewise, most justices appointed by liberal presidents cast a higher percentage of left-of-center votes than their colleagues seated by more conservative presidents."

However, Segal's coauthor Lee Epstein adds, "During the first four years of justices' tenure, their voting behavior correlates at a rather high level with their appointing president's ideology, but for justices with ten or more years of service, that relationship drops precipitously. In other words, liberal presidents appoint liberal justices who continue to take liberal positions for a while, and the same holds true for conservatives. But as new issues come to the Court, or as the justice for whatever reason makes adjustments in his or her political outlook, the president's influence wanes."

Given their prominent role in interpreting the country's laws, federal judges have had a tremendous impact on the issue of abortion. Nowhere is that more true than in the numerous Supreme Court rulings that have dealt with the topic since the 1970s.

ROE V. WADE

On January 22, 1973, the Supreme Court of the United States handed down a landmark decision in the now famous *Roe v. Wade* legal battle. Their ruling made it legal for a woman and her doctor to choose abortion without restrictions in the earlier months of pregnancy and with restrictions in the later months. The lawsuit was filed on behalf of Norma McCorvey, using the alias "Jane Roe." Her attorneys alleged that the abortion law in Texas (the state in which she lived) violated her constitutional rights and the rights of other women. The defendant was the district attorney of Dallas County, Texas, Henry B. Wade.

Now, more than three decades and many dozens of court decisions later, the essential tenet of the *Roe v. Wade* decision—that abortion is a constitutional liberty—has not been overturned. However, several court decisions have permitted increasing restrictions and preconditions on a woman's right to an abortion. This chapter will examine the major steps in the Supreme Court's interpretation of the *Roe v. Wade* decision from 1973 through mid-2005. The cases are presented by issue. A chronology and a brief explanation of major abortion cases can be found in Table 2.1.

TABLE 2.1

Chronology of major abortion cases, 1973–2004

Roe v. Wade—1973, 410 U.S. 113

Found abortion legal and established the trimester approach of unrestricted abortion in the first trimester, reasonably regulated abortion in relation to the woman's health in the second trimester, and permitted states to prohibit abortion in the third trimester, except when necessary to preserve the woman's life or health.

Doe v. Bolton—1973, 410 U.S. 179

Held unconstitutional Georgia's statute requiring performance of abortions in hospitals, approval by hospital abortion committee, confirmation by two consulting physicians, and restriction to state residents.

Bigelow v. Virginia—1975, 421 U.S. 809

Made invalid the application of a Virginia statute that prohibited the advertisement of abortion services.

Connecticut v. Menillo—1975, 423 U.S. 9

Ruled that states may require that abortions must be performed by physicians. This case was an appeal of a conviction of a nonphysician for performing abortions.

Planned Parenthood of Central Missouri v. Danforth—1976, 428 U.S. 52

Ruled that a state may not require the written permission of a spouse or the consent of a parent, in the case of a minor, for an abortion. Further ruled that the state could not prohibit the use of saline injection abortions, and found the provision requiring the physician to preserve the life of the fetus "unconstitutionally overbroad."

Maher v. Roe—1977, 432 U.S. 464; **Beal v. Doe**—432 U.S. 438; **Poelker v. Doe**—432 U.S. 519

Ruled that, although the state could not ban abortion, it was under no legal obligation to fund nontherapeutic abortions or provide the public facilities for such abortions.

Colautti v. Franklin—1979, 439 U.S. 379

Overturned a Pennsylvania law that required physicians to try to save the fetus even if the fetus was less than six months developed and not yet viable.

Bellotti v. Baird—1979, 443 U.S. 622

Found that a statute requiring a minor to get her parents' consent or to obtain judicial approval following parental notification unconstitutionally burdened the minor's right to an abortion.

Harris v. McRae—1980, 448 U.S. 297

Found that the Hyde Amendment did not impinge on a woman's freedom to terminate a pregnancy but, rather, encouraged alternatives deemed to be in the public interest. This ruling also permitted use of federal Medicaid funds only for abortions necessary to save the life of the pregnant woman.

Williams v. Zbaraz—1980, 448 U.S. 358

Ruled that states do not have to pay for medically necessary abortions for women on Medicaid (as in *Harris* v. *McRae*). This case was a challenge to a version of the Hyde Amendment in Illinois.

H.L. v. Matheson—1981, 450 U.S. 398

Upheld a Utah statute requiring a physician to notify a minor's parents of their daughter's intention to obtain an abortion.

Planned Parenthood of Kansas City, Missouri v. Ashcroft—1983, 462 U.S. 476

Found unconstitutional that all abortions after 12 weeks of pregnancy be performed in a hospital, but upheld a provision requiring pathology reports for every abortion, the presence of a second physician for abortions performed after viability, and parental consent or judicial bypass for minors.

City of Akron v. Akron Center for Reproductive Health, Inc.—1983, 462 U.S. 416

Held unconstitutional the following requirements: that all abortions after the first trimester be performed in a hospital, parental consent or judicial order be required for all minors under 15 years of age, specific information designed to dissuade a woman from abortion be presented, a 24-hour waiting period be observed, and methods for the disposal of fetal tissue be established.

Simopoulos v. Virginia—1983, 462 U.S. 506

Upheld Virginia hospitalization requirement that included outpatient clinics. This case was an appeal of a criminal conviction of a physician for violating a Virginia law that requires all post-first-trimester abortions to be performed in hospitals. Virginia law provides for licensing of freestanding ambulatory surgical facilities as "hospitals." If Dr. Simopoulos's clinic had been licensed, criminal prosecution could have been avoided. The Virginia law is constitutional and not as restrictive as the laws struck down in **City of Akron v. Akron Center for Reproductive Health, Inc.** (1983) and **Planned Parenthood of Kansas City, Missouri v. Ashcroft** (1983)

Thornburgh v. American College of Obstetricians and Gynecologists—1986, 476 U.S. 747

Ruled that the information required under "informed consent," public reports, and disclosure of detailed information about abortions performed were not reasonably related to protecting a woman's health.

Webster v. Reproductive Health Services—1989, 492 U.S. 490

Upheld the Missouri law stating that "the life of each human being begins at conception." Also ruled that the state had the right to require physicians to perform viability tests on any fetus believed to be 20 or more weeks old, to forbid the use of public employees and facilities to perform abortions not necessary to save a woman's life, and to prohibit the use of public funds, employees, or facilities to counsel a woman to have an abortion not necessary to save her life.

Hodgson v. Minnesota—1990, 497 U.S. 417

Upheld a law requiring minors to notify both parents of an abortion decision because there was a provision for judicial bypass within the law.

Ohio v. Akron Center for Reproductive Health, Inc.—1990, 497 U.S. 502

Upheld ruling requiring one-parent notification plus judicial bypass. Also upheld a requirement that the physician personally notify the parent and ruled that states need not guarantee absolute anonymity to the minor seeking bypass.

Rust v. Sullivan—1991, 500 U.S. 173

Prohibited clinics that used Title X funds from counseling regarding abortion or giving abortion referrals.

TABLE 2.1

Chronology of major abortion cases, 1973–2004 [CONTINUED]

Planned Parenthood of Southeastern Pennsylvania v. Casey—1992, 505 U.S. 833

Stopping just short of overturning **Roe v. Wade**, this ruling dropped the trimester framework and adopted an "undue burden" standard. Specifically, it upheld informed consent, a 24-hour waiting period, parental consent, and reporting and recordkeeping requirements. It rejected a requirement for spousal consent.

Bray v. Alexandria Women's Health Clinic—1993, 506 U.S. 263

Found that the anti-abortion protests outside of clinics could not be interpreted as a violation of the Civil Rights Act. Women seeking abortions were not a class of persons qualifying for protection under the law and the protesters' behavior did not show class-based discriminatory ill will against women.

National Organization for Women v. Scheidler—1994, 114 S. Ct. 798

Ruled that the Racketeer-Influenced and Corrupt Organizations Act did not have to include an economic motive and could be used to prosecute the protest activities of anti-abortion groups and any other groups that seek to prevent the operation of legitimate businesses.

Madsen v. Women's Health Center—1994, 114 S. Ct. 2516

Upheld an injunction forbidding anti-abortion protesters from entering a 36-foot fixed buffer zone in front of an abortion clinic, and upheld noise restrictions, which prevented the use of bullhorns and shouting. The Court did not uphold the injunction preventing protesters from approaching patients and staff workers in a 300-foot buffer zone around clinics and staff residences or the prohibition against nonthreatening posters and signs in the 36-foot buffer zone.

Schenck v. Pro-Choice Network of Western New York—1997, 117 S. Ct. 855

Upheld an injunction forbidding anti-abortion protesters from entering a 15-foot fixed buffer zone in front of an abortion clinic. Also upheld the provision of "cease and desist," whereby two protesters at a time could perform "sidewalk counseling." However, the protesters had to stop counseling and leave the buffer zone on request. The Court did not uphold the injunction preventing protesters from coming within a 15-foot floating buffer zone of people entering or leaving an abortion clinic.

Hill v. Colorado—2000, 530 U.S. 703

Ruled that a Colorado statute does not violate the First Amendment by forbidding anyone from knowingly approaching closer than within eight feet of another person who is within 100 feet of the entrance of a health care facility, without that person's consent, to give them a leaflet, display a sign, or engage in protest, education, or counseling. It was found not to violate the First Amendment because it does not regulate speech on the basis of content or viewpoint.

Stenberg v. Carhart—2000, 530 U.S. 914

Upheld by a narrow margin (5–4) the Eighth Circuit Court of Appeals' decision that made Nebraska's ban on "partial-birth" abortion invalid. The court ruled on two components of Nebraska's ban, including the lack of a health exception and the undue burden on a woman's right to abortion created by broad language of the ban.

Scheidler v. NOW—2003, 537 U.S. 393

Held that rights potentially violated by clinic protesters, including a woman's right to seek medical services, clinic doctors' rights to perform their jobs, and clinics' rights to provide medical services and otherwise conduct their business, were not "property" that could be "obtained" within the meaning of the Hobbs Act (a federal antiextortion statute). Thus the Court overturned a jury verdict against clinic protesters, in which jurors had found that the protesters had used improper means to obtain "property" belonging to the plaintiffs (clinics and patients or prospective patients) and therefore had committed extortion.

Planned Parenthood Federation of America v. Ashcroft—2004, C 03-4872 PJH

Ruled that the Partial-Birth Abortion Ban Act of 2003 was unconstitutional in three ways: it places an undue burden on women seeking abortions, its language is vague, and it lacks a required exception for medical actions needed to preserve the woman's health.

SOURCE: Compiled by Information Plus staff and author

The History of *Roe v. Wade*

In 1969 Texas abortion law, dating back to 1857, permitted abortion only when the mother's life was endangered. McCorvey, a pregnant single woman challenged the constitutionality of this law, using the pseudonym "Jane Roe," to protect her privacy. In *Roe v. Wade* (410 U.S. 113, 1973) the Supreme Court, in a 7–2 decision, found that a law that prohibited abortion, except to save the life of the mother and without regard for the state of the pregnancy, violated the "due process" clause of the Fifth Amendment. The due process clause of the Fifth Amendment, ratified in 1791, is the Constitution's guarantee that no level of government can arbitrarily or unfairly deprive individuals of their basic constitutional rights to life, liberty, and property. The Fourteenth Amendment takes this guarantee one step further—ensuring protection against infringement (taking away rights) by state governments as well. The high court said the Fourteenth Amendment protects the right to privacy against state action, including a woman's right to terminate her pregnancy. The Supreme Court based this right to privacy on a 1942 case, *Skinner v. Oklahoma* (316 U.S. 535), which struck down a state law that called for sterilizing people who have been con-

victed two or more times of "felonies involving moral turpitude" (immoral acts).

In the *Roe v. Wade* decision, however, the Court noted that, although the right to abortion is guaranteed, the state has legitimate interests in protecting the health of the pregnant woman and the potentiality of human life. The weight given to each of these interests changes as the pregnancy develops.

The Court divided a normal pregnancy into three-month stages (trimesters):

- First trimester—During approximately the first three months, the decision to abort must be left up to the woman and her physician.

- Second trimester—After the first trimester of pregnancy, the state may regulate the abortion procedure in ways necessary to promote the mother's health.

- Third trimester—After the fetus is "viable" (able to survive outside the womb), the state, to protect the potential life of the fetus, may regulate and even forbid abortion, except where necessary to preserve the life or health of the mother.

DOE V. BOLTON

On the same day that the Supreme Court decided *Roe v. Wade*, it expanded the ruling with *Doe v. Bolton* (410 U.S. 179, 1973), a lawsuit bought against Georgia's attorney general by a pregnant woman, "Mary Doe," and twenty-three others. Doe had applied for a therapeutic abortion under Georgia law and had been turned down. While reiterating their *Roe v. Wade* ruling that states may not prevent abortion by making it a crime, the high court observed that states are not allowed to make abortions hard to obtain by imposing complicated procedural conditions. The Court found unconstitutional the following state requirements:

- All abortions must take place in hospitals accredited by the Joint Committee on Accreditation of Hospitals.

- Abortions must be approved by a hospital abortion committee.

- Two consulting physicians must confirm the judgment of the performing physician.

GOVERNMENT SUPPORT OR NONSUPPORT OF ABORTION

Public Funding of Nontherapeutic Abortions

On June 20, 1977, the Supreme Court ruled on three cases concerning women too poor to afford an abortion. One case involved the Connecticut Welfare Department, which had issued regulations limiting state Medicaid benefits for first-trimester abortions to those that were "medically necessary." An indigent (poor) woman, "Susan Roe," challenged the regulations and sued Edward Maher, the commissioner of social services in Connecticut. In *Maher v. Roe* (432 U.S. 464) the Court held that the Fourteenth Amendment does not require a state participating in Medicaid to pay for needy women's expenses arising out of nontherapeutic (not medically necessary) abortions simply because it pays childbirth expenses. The Court observed that a state may choose to favor childbirth over abortion and is under no obligation to show why it chooses to do so.

Another case, similar to the one in Connecticut, involved the Pennsylvania Department of Public Welfare. A Pennsylvania law restricted Medicaid-funded abortions to indigent women, allowing them only in situations deemed medically necessary by a physician. In *Beal v. Doe* (432 U.S. 438, 1977) the Supreme Court found that states could exclude nontherapeutic abortions from coverage under their Medicaid programs.

The third case involved a St. Louis policy that prohibited nontherapeutic abortions in the city's two publicly run hospitals. In *Poelker v. Doe* (432 U.S. 519, 1977) the high court ruled that St. Louis could refuse to provide publicly financed hospitals for nontherapeutic abortions even though it provided facilities for childbirth. Since the policy did not deny women the right to have an abortion, it was consistent with the Constitution. In summary, the Supreme Court found with these three cases that although the state cannot ban abortions, it is under no legal obligation to fund nontherapeutic abortions or provide public facilities for such abortions.

The Hyde Amendment—Constitutional or Not?

The Hyde Amendment was passed by Congress in 1976 and excludes abortion from the comprehensive health care services provided to low-income people by the federal government through Medicaid. The cases of *Maher*, *Beal*, and *Poelker* did not address the issue of whether federal law, such as the Hyde Amendment, or state laws with similar provisions were constitutional. Because most federal funding for abortion was done through Medicaid, cutting federal monies most directly affected the poor. Not surprisingly, the issue of the constitutionality of the Hyde Amendment soon made its way into the nation's courts.

In June 1980, in a 5–4 decision, the Supreme Court, in *Harris v. McRae* (448 U.S. 297), held that the Hyde Amendment is constitutional. The Court ruled that the funding restrictions of the Hyde Amendment do not infringe on a woman's right to terminate her pregnancy as held in *Roe v. Wade*. The Court stated:

> It simply does not follow that a woman's freedom of choice carries with it a constitutional entitlement to the financial resources to avail herself of the full range of protected choices....: although government may not place obstacles in the path of a woman's exercise of her freedom of choice, it need not remove those not of its own creation. Indigency falls in the latter category.... Abortion is inherently different from other medical procedures, because no other procedure involves the purposeful termination of a potential life.

PUBLIC FUNDING OF THERAPEUTIC ABORTIONS. In *Harris v. McRae* the high court further ruled that a state that participates in the Medicaid program is not required to fund therapeutic abortions if federal reimbursement has been withdrawn under the Hyde Amendment. On that same day the Supreme Court, in three related cases—*Williams v. Zbaraz*, *Miller v. Zbaraz*, and *United States v. Zbaraz* (448 U.S. 358)—held that an Illinois law, with similar funding restrictions as the Hyde Amendment, did not violate the Fourteenth Amendment.

FEDERALLY FUNDED CLINICS CANNOT COUNSEL ABOUT ABORTION AS AN OPTION. The central question of *Rust v. Sullivan* (500 U.S. 173) was whether government regulations violate the First Amendment if they prohibit federally funded projects from engaging in counseling concerning referrals for activities advocating abortion as a means of family planning. In May 1991 the Supreme Court ruled that providing information was included in this prohibition and that rights provided by the First Amendment (free speech) and Fifth Amendment (preventing government from depriving individuals of their basic constitutional rights) were not infringed upon by this prohibition. Chief Justice Rehnquist stated:

> Nothing in them [the Title X regulations] requires a doctor to represent as his own any opinion that he does not in fact hold.... The program does not provide post-conception medical care, and therefore a doctor's silence with regard to abortion cannot reasonably be thought to mislead a client into thinking that the doctor does not consider abortion an appropriate option for her.

Justice Blackmun, in his dissenting opinion, saw the case very differently. He stated: "Whatever may be the Government's power to condition the receipt of its largess [generosity] upon the relinquishment of constitutional rights, it surely does not extend to a condition that suppresses the recipient's cherished freedom of speech based solely upon the content or viewpoint of that speech."

Blackmun's dissent continues: "The Regulations are also clearly viewpoint-based. While suppressing speech favorable to abortion with one hand, the Secretary compels antiabortion speech with the other." (This is a reference to the fact that the clinics are required to give prenatal advice.)

STATE RESTRICTIONS ON ABORTION

Since *Roe v. Wade*, abortion laws generally have been modified by the continual addition of restrictions on the ability to obtain an abortion. Over the years many states have passed statutes stretching the limits of the law, mainly in the areas of informed consent, waiting periods, spousal or parental consent, parental notice, and place of abortions, as well as fetal viability and the disposal of the fetus.

Table 2.2 shows the states that have abortion bans as of 2005. Fifteen states outlaw abortion throughout pregnancy. Twenty-seven states outlaw abortion after twelve weeks with no health exception. These bans contradict 2005 federal law and cannot be enforced.

Informed Consent and Spousal/Parental Consent

Planned Parenthood of Central Missouri v. Danforth (428 U.S. 52, 1976) was the first case heard before the Supreme Court to challenge *Roe v. Wade* and *Doe v. Bolton*. Two Missouri-licensed physicians challenged several restrictions of the Missouri Code, which required the following:

- A woman must sign a written consent to the abortion and certify that "her consent is informed and freely given and is not the result of coercion."

- A woman must get a written consent from her husband for the abortion.

- The attending physician must exercise professional care to preserve the fetus's life and health, failing which he or she would be held guilty of manslaughter and liable for damages.

- An unmarried woman under eighteen must get the written consent of a parent or person in the place of a parent to permit abortion.

The Supreme Court, in *Planned Parenthood v. Danforth*, ruled that during the first twelve weeks of pregnancy an abortion was a matter of interest only to the woman and her physician. The state cannot "delegate to a spouse a veto power that the State itself is absolutely and totally prohibited from exercising during the first trimester of pregnancy," as ruled in *Roe v. Wade*. Similarly, the Court struck down the parental consent requirement. The Court found the provision requiring the physician to preserve the life and health of the fetus "unconstitutionally overbroad," especially because it covered the first three months of pregnancy when the fetus is not able to survive outside the womb. In addition, the majority also ruled that the state could not prohibit the use of saline amniocentesis or any other proven safe abortion method.

PARENTAL CONSENT. In 1979 a Massachusetts law required parental consent for an abortion to be performed on an unmarried woman under the age of eighteen. However, if either or both of the parents refused, a judge of the superior court could rule on the issue. The *Bellotti v. Baird* (443 U.S. 622, 1979) case asked whether the law unconstitutionally restricted the right of a minor to have an abortion. In an 8–1 ruling the Supreme Court observed, "A child, merely on account of his minority, is not beyond the protection of the Constitution." The Court declared the Massachusetts statute unconstitutional on two grounds:

> First, it permits judicial authorization for an abortion to be withheld from a minor who is found by the superior court to be mature and fully competent to make this decision independently. Second, it requires parental consultation or notification in every instance, whether or not in the pregnant minor's best interests, without affording her an opportunity to receive an independent judicial determination that she is mature enough to consent or that an abortion would be in her best interests.

Parental Notification

Two years later the Supreme Court ruled again on whether a minor, who was fully dependent on her parents, had to inform her parents of her decision to have an abortion (that is, to notify them, not to obtain their consent). Referring to *Bellotti v. Baird*, the Court, in *H. L. v. Matheson* (450 U.S. 398), noted the following:

> A statute setting out a mere requirement of parental notice when possible does not violate the constitutional rights of an immature, dependent minor.... whether or

TABLE 2.2

State abortion bans, 2005

	Has unconstitutional and unenforceable bans on abortion

| State | Bans abortion throughout pregnancy | | | | | Broad ban could outlaw abortion after 12 weeks—without health exception |
	Has life exception	Has limited health exception	Has health exception	Has exception for rape/incest	Without exception	
Alabama	X		X			X
Alaska						X
Arizona	X					X
Arkansas					X	X
California						
Colorado	X		X[a]	X		
Connecticut						
Delaware	X	X		X		
District of Columbia						
Florida						X
Georgia						
Hawaii						
Idaho						X
Illinois						X
Indiana						X
Iowa						X
Kansas						
Kentucky						X
Louisiana	X			X		X
Maine						
Maryland						
Massachusetts					X	
Michigan	X	X				X
Minnesota						
Mississippi	X			X		X
Missouri						X
Montana						
Nebraska						X
Nevada						
New Hampshire						
New Jersey						X
New Mexico	X	X		X		
New York						
North Carolina						
North Dakota						X
Ohio						X[b]
Oklahoma	X					X
Oregon						
Pennsylvania						
Rhode Island						X
South Carolina						X
South Dakota						X
Tennessee						X
Texas						
Utah	X	X		X		X
Vermont	X					
Virginia						X
Washington						
West Virginia	X					X
Wisconsin	X					X
Wyoming						
Total	**13**	**4**	**2**	**6**	**2**	**27**

[a]Law contains a full health exception, but requries approval from a three-physician panel.
[b]Ohio's ban on D+X abortion, which includes exceptions to protect a woman's life and a limited health exception, is constitutional.

SOURCE: "Abortion Bans," in *Who Decides? The Status of Women's Reproductive Rights in the United States, 14th ed.*, NARAL Pro-Choice America & NARAL Pro-Choice America Foundation, updated May 27, 2005, http://www.prochoiceamerica.org/yourstate/whodecides/maps/abortion_bans.cfm (accessed September 20, 2005)

not to bear a child…is a grave decision, and a girl of tender years, under emotional stress, may be ill-equipped to make it without mature advice and emotional support.

Similarly, in 1990 the Supreme Court in *Ohio v. Akron Center for Reproductive Health* (497 U.S. 502) upheld a 1985 Ohio statute that requires a physician performing an abortion on a minor to give twenty-four hours' prior notice to at least one parent or guardian. The law provided the minor with a way to bypass her parents (called a judicial bypass) by asking the juvenile court to issue an order that would authorize her to give her own consent. In upholding this part of the statute, the Supreme Court also ruled that states need not guarantee absolute anonymity to the minor seeking judicial bypass.

In 1981 Minnesota passed a law requiring a minor to inform *both* parents forty-eight hours before having an abortion, even if the parents were no longer married and one parent had little or nothing to do with the minor's upbringing (Subdivision 2 of Minn. Stat. 144.343). Subdivision 2 was mandatory except in cases of parental abuse or neglect. The law, however, also created a judicial bypass procedure. Subdivision 6 allowed a minor who did not want to inform either parent to go to court, be supplied with counsel, and be judged whether she was mature enough to make the decision alone or if an abortion was in her best interests.

The Supreme Court in *Hodgson v. Minnesota* (497 U.S. 417, 1990) upheld the law requiring minors to notify both parents of an abortion decision because there was a provision for judicial bypass within the law. The high court ruled that "the constitutional objection to the two-parent notice requirement is removed by the judicial bypass option provided in Subdivision 6 of the Minnesota statute." The decision, however, was divided, with several justices agreeing with some parts of the decision but not others.

Justice Stevens, although the author of the majority opinion, disagreed with the key finding of the Court and thought the law to be unconstitutional. He felt that judicial bypass was being misused in the ruling because it was designed to handle exceptions to a "reasonable general rule, and thereby preserve the constitutionality of that rule," and not as a justification to permit an unconstitutional rule to stand. Justice Marshall, agreeing with Stevens, wrote in his dissent:

> The bypass procedure cannot save those requirements because the bypass itself is unconstitutional, both on its face and as applied. At the very least, this scheme substantially burdens a woman's right to privacy without advancing a compelling state interest. More significantly, in some instances it usurps a young woman's control over her own body by giving either a parent or a court the power effectively to veto her decision to have an abortion.

In 2003 Planned Parenthood of Northern New England sought a ruling against a 2003 New Hampshire law that required written parental notification forty-eight hours prior to any abortion provided to a minor unless "the attending abortion provider certifies in the pregnant minor's medical record that the abortion is necessary to prevent the minor's death and there is insufficient time to provide required notice." There was also a provision for judicial bypass within the law. In *Planned Parenthood of Northern New England, et al. . . . v. Peter Heed, Attorney General of the State of New Hampshire*, the district court found the law unconstitutional because it lacked an explicit exception to protect the health of the pregnant minor and because the exception for abortions necessary to prevent the minor's death was too narrow. An appeals court upheld this ruling in 2004. The Supreme Court heard this case in November 2005 and was expected to issue a decision in 2006.

According to the Planned Parenthood Federation of America, forty-four states have laws requiring parental consent or notification prior to a minor's having an abortion. Of these laws, thirty-three are in effect—not barred due to litigation. Six states and the District of Columbia have no such laws.

Place Restriction, Fetal Development and Viability Discussion, and Fetal Disposal

In 1975 in *Connecticut v. Menillo* (423 U.S.9), the Supreme Court ruled that a state may require that abortions be performed only by physicians. Such restrictions continued in 1978 when the city of Akron, Ohio, enacted an ordinance titled "Regulations of Abortions," which determined how abortions should be performed in the city. Among the restrictions on abortions were the following:

- All abortions performed after the first trimester of pregnancy had to be done in a hospital.

- The attending physician must inform the patient of the status of her pregnancy; the development of the fetus; the date of possible fetal viability; the physical and emotional complications that may result from an abortion; and the availability of agencies to provide her with assistance and information with regard to birth control, adoption, and childbirth. The physician also must tell the patient about the particular risks associated with her pregnancy and the abortion method to be used.

- Physicians performing abortions must ensure that fetal remains were disposed of in a "humane and sanitary manner."

Violation of any provision constituted a criminal misdemeanor. Many antiabortion groups considered the Akron ordinances model legislation to be followed by other communities wishing to regulate abortion within their jurisdictions.

After mixed rulings in the federal district court and in the federal court of appeals, the case was argued before the Supreme Court. In 1983 in *Akron v. Akron Center for Reproductive Health, Inc.* (462 U.S. 416), the Supreme Court, in a 6–3 decision, upheld its earlier ruling in *Roe v. Wade*.

Noting the significant medical improvements in abortion procedures and the concurrent sharp decrease in the number of deaths resulting from late-term abortions, the high court ruled that it was not necessary to have all second-trimester abortions performed in a hospital.

The high court also ruled that the provision regarding what information the physician must give the woman before abortion was unconstitutional:

> [The ordinance provision that] begins with the dubious statement that "abortion is a major surgical procedure" and proceeds to describe numerous possible physical and psychological complications of abortion is a "parade of horribles" intended to suggest that abortion is a particularly dangerous procedure.... By insisting upon recitation of a lengthy and inflexible list of information, Akron unreasonably has placed "obstacles in the path of the doctor upon whom [the woman is] entitled to rely for advice in connection with her decision."

Finally, the Supreme Court invalidated the provision requiring a "humane and sanitary" disposal of the fetal remains because it violated the Fourteenth Amendment. Although Akron claimed the purpose of this provision was to prevent the disposal of aborted fetuses in garbage piles, the city was not clear that this alone was the main reason for the provision. The high court agreed with the appellate court that the provision suggested a possible regulation on "some sort of 'decent burial' of an embryo at the earliest stages of formation." The high court concluded that this unclear provision is "fatal" where a physician could be criminally held liable for disposing of the fetal remains.

Dissenting from the majority, Justice O'Connor observed that the trimester concept established in *Roe v. Wade* now had become virtually unworkable and should be thrown out because the high court was extending the rules that applied in the first trimester well into the second trimester:

> Just as improvements in medical technology inevitably will move forward the point at which the State may regulate for reasons of maternal health, different technological improvements will move backward the point of viability at which the State may proscribe [prohibit] abortions except when necessary to preserve the life and health of the mother....
>
> The *Roe* framework, then, is clearly on a collision course with itself. As the medical risks of various abortion procedures decrease, the point at which the State may regulate for reasons of maternal health is moved further forward to actual childbirth. As medical science becomes better able to provide for the separate existence of the fetus, the point of viability is moved further back toward conception.

O'Connor indicated that potential life exists at any time during the pregnancy. Because the difference between potential life and capable life never has been clearly defined, she stated, "the State's interest in protecting potential human life exists throughout the pregnancy." Although this appeared to be a call for a reversal of *Roe v. Wade*, Justice O'Connor later turned out to be not as eager to overturn *Roe* as this dissent would seem to indicate.

A case in 1983 further challenged such restrictions on abortion. The case of *Planned Parenthood Assn. v. Ashcroft* (462 U.S. 476) concerned a Missouri law requiring the following:

- All abortions after the first trimester must be performed in a hospital.
- Minors must have parental consent or judicial authorization for their abortions.
- Two doctors must be present at the abortion.
- A pathologist's report must be obtained for every abortion.

The Court found the hospitalization requirement to be unconstitutional for the same reasons stated in *Akron v. Akron Center for Reproductive Health, Inc.* (1983), but the Court found the other restrictions constitutional.

Partial-Birth Abortion

Since 1995 thirty states have adopted laws banning so-called "partial-birth" abortions. The term "partial-birth abortion" is favored by those who oppose the procedure and is the "common name" for the medical procedure known as intact dilation and extraction (D&X), which can be used to end pregnancies in the second or third trimester, generally after twenty weeks of gestation. According to the Centers for Disease Control and Prevention in "Abortion Surveillance—United States, 2001" *Morbidity and Mortality Weekly Report, Surveillance Summaries*, vol. 53, no. SS-09, November 26, 2004), in 2001 853,485 abortions were performed. Of these abortions, only 1.4% were performed after twenty weeks of pregnancy.

The partial-birth abortion laws in twenty of the thirty states adopting them were ruled unconstitutional when challenged. Nebraska's law was the first to reach the Supreme Court. In June 2000 in *Stenberg v. Carhart* (530 U.S. 914), the Supreme Court struck down Nebraska's "Partial Birth Abortion Ban" by a narrow margin of 5–4 saying it was unconstitutional because it did not have an exception for protecting a woman's health.

"Partial-birth abortion" is defined in the Nebraska statute as "an abortion procedure in which the person performing the abortion partially delivers vaginally a living unborn child before killing the unborn child and completing the delivery. For purposes of this subdivision, the term 'partially delivers vaginally a living unborn child before killing the unborn child' means deliberately and intentionally delivering into the vagina a living unborn child, or a substantial portion thereof, for the purpose of performing a procedure that the person performing such procedure knows will kill the unborn child and does kill the unborn child."

Attorneys challenging the law as unconstitutional had three arguments:

- These bans are deceptive measures designed to outlaw virtually every type of abortion procedure.

- These laws are unconstitutional because they have no exceptions for women's health, and they criminalize doctors for providing the safest medical care.

- These laws are unconstitutional because they unduly burden a woman's right to choose, thus violating standards set in *Roe v. Wade* and *Planned Parenthood of Southeastern Pennsylvania v. Casey*.

The Court ruled on the last two points—the lack of a health exception (allowing an abortion when "necessary, in appropriate medical judgment, for the preservation of the life or health of the mother") and the undue burden on a woman's right to abortion (created by broad language of the ban, which makes it unclear which methods of abortion are banned). For the majority, Justice Breyer wrote, "Taking account of these virtually irreconcilable points of view, aware that constitutional law must govern a society whose different members sincerely hold directly opposing views, and considering the matter in light of the Constitution's guarantees of fundamental individual liberty, this Court, in the course of a generation, has determined and then redetermined that the Constitution offers basic protection to the woman's right to choose."

For the minority, Justice Thomas wrote, "*Casey* itself noted that States may 'express profound respect for the life of the unborn'.... States may, without a doubt, express this profound respect by prohibiting a procedure that approaches infanticide, and thereby dehumanizes the fetus and trivializes human life. The AMA [in the American Medical Association Board of Trustees "Factsheet" on H.R. 1122, June 1997] has recognized that this procedure is 'ethically different' from other destructive abortion techniques because the fetus, normally twenty weeks or longer in gestation, is killed outside the womb. The 'partial birth' gives the fetus an autonomy which separates it from the right of the woman to choose treatments for her own body."

In 1995 Congress passed the Partial-Birth Abortion Ban Act, which was vetoed by President Bill Clinton in 1996. In 1997 Congress once again passed the Partial-Birth Abortion Ban Act, coming close to a vote that would override a presidential veto, but not achieving it. The legislation was once again vetoed by President Clinton that same year. Congress then passed the Partial-Birth Abortion Ban Act of 2003. On November 5, 2003, President George W. Bush signed it into law, becoming the first U.S. president to ever place a federal ban on abortion. However, within hours of Bush's signing the bill, a federal judge in Nebraska granted a temporary restraining order, making the law ineffective until its constitutionality—according to the 2000 *Stenberg* decision—could be determined.

Lawsuits challenging the constitutionality of the Partial-Birth Abortion Ban Act of 2003 were brought in three states: New York, Nebraska, and California. The federal judge in San Francisco, the first to render a decision, ruled that the Partial-Birth Abortion Ban Act of 2003 was unconstitutional in three ways: it places an undue burden on women seeking abortions, its language is vague, and it lacks a required exception for medical actions needed to preserve the woman's health. In 2004 federal judges in all three states ruled the legislation as unconstitutional. In July 2005 a Federal appeals court in St. Louis upheld the Nebraska ruling. At that time, the Bush administration planned to ask the Supreme Court to uphold the partial-birth abortion ban.

PROTESTERS AT ABORTION CLINICS

In the more than thirty years since the *Roe v. Wade* Supreme Court decision legalized abortion, reproductive health clinics and health care providers across the United States and Canada have been under attack by antiabortion protesters. Physicians and clinic workers have been shot; clinics have been bombed, burned down, invaded, and blockaded; and patients have been abused and intimidated. In 1993 the protests turned deadly for the first time when Dr. David Gunn was shot and killed by an antiabortion protester in Pensacola, Florida. In that same year there were twelve arsons, one bombing, and sixty-six blockades against abortion clinics.

Also in 1993 the U.S. Supreme Court heard *Bray v. Alexandria Women's Health Clinic* (506 U.S. 263), a case in which antiabortion protesters challenged an injunction (ban) against their activities, which included blocking access to health care facilities in the Washington, D.C., area. The injunction being challenged was based on an 1871 civil rights statute that provided protection against private conspiracies, such as the Ku Klux Klan preventing blacks from exercising their freedoms. In this case it was argued that antiabortion activists were preventing women from exercising their freedoms. The judges found that antiabortion protests outside of an abortion clinic were not in violation of the Civil Rights Act because "women seeking abortions" were not a "class of persons seeking protection under the law" and protesters do not show class-based discrimination toward women.

In 1994, to help prevent clinic violence, Congress overwhelmingly passed the Freedom of Access to Clinic Entrances Act (FACE), which was signed into law by President Clinton. FACE is designed to protect both those providing and those receiving reproductive health care services. It forbids the use of "force," "threat of force," or "physical obstruction" to prevent someone from providing or receiving reproductive health services. There are criminal and civil penalties for those who break the law. It is clear that the law has had an effect on certain types of clinic violence (see Chapter 6). However, violence does continue.

Other Supreme Court cases provide for the constitutionality of "buffer zones" between protesters and patients and clinic employees. For instance, in *Madsen v. Women's Health Center* (512 U.S. 753) in 1994, the court upheld an injunction that forbade protesters from entering a thirty-six-foot buffer zone in front of an abortion clinic and upheld noise restrictions. (However, the Court did not uphold an injunction that prevented protesters from getting within three hundred feet of a clinic or staff residence to approach clinic staff and patients. Also, nonthreatening posters within the thirty-six-foot buffer zone were allowed.)

In 1997 in *Schenck, et al., v. Pro-Choice Network of Western New York, et al.* (519 U.S. 357), the Court upheld an injunction that forbade antiabortion protesters from entering a fifteen-foot fixed buffer zone in front of an abortion clinic. The protesters had argued that their right to free speech was being violated, but the high court ruled that their free speech was ensured because they could be heard from a distance. Also, the Court allowed "cease and desist" counseling. This meant that as many as two protesters at a time could perform "sidewalk counseling" within the buffer zone, but if the counselors were asked to stop (to "cease and desist"), they had to honor that request and leave the buffer zone. (The Court did not uphold the injunction preventing protesters from coming within a fifteen-foot floating buffer zone of people entering or leaving an abortion clinic. A floating buffer zone around a person moves as the person moves.)

In 2000 in *Hill v. Colorado* (530 U.S. 703), it was ruled that a Colorado statute does not violate the First Amendment (free speech) and the right to a free press. The statute forbids anyone to knowingly come closer than eight feet to anyone who is within one hundred feet of the entrance of a health-care facility without that person's consent, for the purpose of giving the person a leaflet, offering education or counseling, displaying a sign, or otherwise engaging in protest. The Court concluded that the statute "is not a regulation of speech. Rather, it is a regulation of the places where some speech may occur."

In 2003 the seventeen-year-old *NOW v. Scheidler* case was decided. The parties to the case were the National Organization for Women (NOW) and Joseph Scheidler of the Pro-Life Action League.

In June 1986 NOW and two abortion clinics in Delaware filed a complaint in federal court against Scheidler and the Pro-Life Direct Action League alleging violations of the Sherman and Clayton antitrust laws that are intended to prevent the formation of monopolies. In 1989 NOW added charges that individuals and organizations that oppose legal abortion violated the Racketeer Influenced and Corrupt Organizations Act (RICO) by engaging in a nationwide conspiracy to shut down abortion clinics through "a pattern of racketeering activity" that included acts of extortion in violation of the Hobbs Act.

In 1991 the case was dismissed on grounds that the RICO law requires the defendants to have an economic motive for their crimes, and an appeal by NOW also was unsuccessful. In 1992 NOW asked the Supreme Court for a ruling on the use of the RICO statute. In 1994 the high court ruled in favor of NOW, allowing it to use federal antiracketeering laws against antiabortion activists who organize others for terrorist activities, such as bombing and forcefully blocking abortion clinics. RICO cannot be used against those engaging in peaceful protests.

After numerous delays, the *NOW v. Scheidler* trial took place in 1998. The jury found that the defendants were guilty of racketeering and engaged in a nationwide conspiracy to deny women access to medical facilities. However, in 2002 Scheidler asked the Supreme Court to review the decision. In February 2003 the Supreme Court decided 8–1 in *Scheidler v. NOW* that the RICO statute was used improperly against Scheidler and other antiabortion activists.

RULINGS ON THE FETUS

Saving a "Viable Fetus"

In January 1979, almost six years after the landmark *Roe v. Wade* decision, the issue of the legal identity of the fetus first reached the Supreme Court. In *Colautti v. Franklin* (439 U.S. 379) the plaintiff (person who brings an action in a court of law) challenged the provisions of a Pennsylvania law that gave the state the power to protect an unborn child beginning in the sixth month of pregnancy.

This law required physicians performing abortions to save the fetus if they had grounds to believe that the fetus "may be viable." The Supreme Court held that the provisions of the law were "void for vagueness" because the meanings of "viable" and "may be viable" were unclear and these provisions interfered with the physicians' proper exercise of judgment. The Court also found the law unconstitutional because it could impose criminal liability on physicians if they were thought to have failed to take proper action.

Life Begins at Conception

In 1986 Missouri passed legislation amending a number of laws concerning unborn children and abortion. It placed a number of restrictions on abortions. The new law:

- Declared that life begins at conception

- Required physicians to perform tests to determine the viability of fetuses after twenty weeks of gestational age

- Forbade the use of public employees and facilities for abortions not necessary to save the mother's life

- Prohibited the use of public funds, employees, or facilities for the purpose of counseling a woman to have an abortion not necessary to save her life

Lower courts struck down these restrictions, but the Supreme Court did not. In 1989 the Court upheld the Missouri law in *Webster v. Reproductive Health Services* (492 U.S. 490). This ruling was the first case in which a majority of the justices generally opposed abortion, and it revealed the Court's willingness to adopt a more lenient attitude toward state limitations on abortions.

Writing for the 5–4 majority, Chief Justice Rehnquist (joined by Justices White and Kennedy) found nothing wrong with the preamble of the Missouri law, which stated that "the life of each human being begins at conception." The Court observed that *Roe v. Wade* "implies no limitation on the authority of a State to make a value judgment favoring childbirth over abortion.... The preamble can be read simply to express that sort of value judgment." The Court chose not to rule on the constitutionality of the law's preamble because they considered it to be merely an abstract proposition.

Relying on *Maher*, *Poelker*, and *McRae*, the Court ruled that "a government's decision to favor childbirth over abortion through the allocation of public funds does not violate *Roe v. Wade*." In addition, "Missouri's decision to use public facilities and employees to encourage childbirth over abortion places no governmental obstacle in the path of a woman who chooses to terminate her pregnancy, but leaves her with the same choices as if the State had decided not to operate any hospitals at all."

Perhaps the most controversial aspect of the Missouri law was the requirement that a physician determine the viability of the fetus if she or he thought the fetus might be twenty or more weeks old. There was no debate over whether a fetus is viable at twenty weeks—it is not. The earliest that a fetus is viable is at 23.5–24 weeks of gestational life. However, there could be a four-week error in estimating gestational age. The Court ruled that the testing for fetal viability was constitutional because it furthered Missouri's interest in protecting potential human life.

Chief Justice Rehnquist thought the "rigid" trimester system outlined in *Roe* was no longer useful, if it ever was. Rehnquist felt the *Roe* framework, containing such specific elements as trimesters and viability, is not consistent with the concept of a Constitution that supposedly deals with general principles.

Although they came very close, the majority did not overturn *Roe v. Wade*. Although respecting the preamble of the Missouri law, the chief justice concluded that although the state's interest had been moved back well into the second trimester of pregnancy, *Webster* did not revisit the *Roe* rulings.

Justice Scalia, however, believed *Roe* should have been overturned in this case because most of the justices thought the *Roe* decision was wrong. "It thus appears," Scalia stated, "that the mansion of constitutionalized abortion law, constructed overnight in *Roe v. Wade*, must be disassembled door-jamb by door-jamb, and never entirely brought down, no matter how wrong it may be."

Justice Blackmun (who wrote the *Roe* decision) was equally angry but for the opposite reason. In a dissent joined by Justices Brennan and Marshall, Blackmun observed that the "fundamental constitutional rights of women to decide whether to terminate a pregnancy survive, but are not secure."

Although it did not overturn *Roe*, *Webster* did mark a significant change in the legal landscape related to abortion. It gave the states more latitude in placing restrictions on abortion and weakened the "viability" and trimester framework that had previously been used to help determine the legality of terminating a pregnancy.

ROE V. WADE IS NOT OVERTURNED

From the "Trimester Framework" to "Undue Burden"

Pennsylvania has had a long history of trying to pass restrictive abortion statutes, which began with the Abortion Control Act of 1974. In 1989, having seen how, in *Webster*, a more conservative Supreme Court seemed ready to overturn decisions made by an earlier, more liberal Court, the Pennsylvania legislature passed a new Abortion Control Act, which was an amended version of the 1974 abortion law.

Before the Abortion Control Act took effect, five abortion clinics and one physician (representing himself and a group of physicians who provided abortion services) sued the state of Pennsylvania, represented by Governor Robert Casey. The resulting case was *Planned Parenthood of Southeastern Pennsylvania v. Casey* (505 U.S. 833, June 29, 1992).

The Supreme Court ruling on *Casey* was a 5–4 split decision, with the majority opinion written by Justices O'Connor, Kennedy, and Souter and joined in part by Justices Stevens and Blackmun. The majority reaffirmed the essential holding in *Roe v. Wade*: "A recognition of the right of the woman to choose to have an abortion before [fetal] viability and to obtain it without undue interference from the State." After viability, however, the State may prohibit abortion but only if it provides exceptions for pregnancies that may endanger the woman's life or health.

In addition, the Court rejected the trimester framework, which had strictly limited the state from regulating abortion during early pregnancy, and replaced it with the "undue burden" standard. Under the "undue burden" standard, states may put restrictions on the abortion process (throughout the whole pregnancy) as long as they do not have "the purpose or effect of placing a substantial obstacle in the path of a woman seeking an abortion of a nonviable fetus."

The justices upheld Pennsylvania's proposed restrictions—a twenty-four-hour waiting period, informed consent, parental consent, and reporting and record-keeping requirements—except for the spousal-consent requirement. Chief Justice Rehnquist and Justices Thomas, White, and Scalia agreed with the provisions upheld by the majority decision, but they felt the decision did not go far enough. They proposed that requiring spousal consent was a rational attempt to encourage communication between spouses and should be upheld. Furthermore, they felt that a woman's liberty to abort her unborn child is not a right protected by the Constitution and that the *Roe* decision had been a mistake.

Justice Stevens, however, wrote an opinion supporting the *Roe* decision and rejecting the twenty-four-hour waiting period and the "biased" informed-consent provision (which required "pro-life" information to be given to the woman seeking an abortion). Justice Blackmun rejected all the provisions of the Pennsylvania law and reaffirmed the constitutionality of the *Roe* decision.

THE BASIS FOR MAINTAINING *ROE*. Although conceding that people differ in their beliefs about the morality of terminating a pregnancy, even during its earliest stage, the justices explained that they upheld *Roe*'s essential holding because their duty is "to define the liberty of all," not to impose their own moral standards:

> These matters, involving the most intimate and personal choices a person may make in a lifetime, choices central to personal dignity and autonomy, are central to the liberty protected by the Fourteenth Amendment. At the heart of liberty is the right to define one's own concept of existence, of meaning, of the universe, and of the mystery of human life. Beliefs about these matters could not define the attributes of personhood were they formed under compulsion of the State.

The justices also maintained the following:

> Though abortion is conduct, it does not follow that the State is entitled to proscribe it in all instances. That is because the liberty of the woman is at stake in a sense unique to the human condition, and so, unique to the law. The mother who carries a child to full term is subject to anxieties, to physical constraints, to pain that only she must bear. That these sacrifices have from the beginning of the human race been endured by woman with a pride that ennobles her in the eyes of others and gives to the infant a bond of love cannot alone be grounds for the State to insist she make the sacrifice. Her suffering is too intimate and personal for the State to insist, without more, upon its own vision of the woman's role, however dominant that vision has been in the course of our history and our culture. The destiny of the woman must be shaped to a large extent on her own conception of her spiritual imperatives and her place in society.

The Court also upheld the right to abortion because of its obligation to follow precedent. Under the doctrine of *stare decisis* (literally, to stand by things decided), which requires courts to reach consistent conclusions in cases that raise the same factual and legal issues, a majority of the Court could not justify overthrowing the findings of *Roe*.

CHAPTER 3
ABORTION—A MAJOR POLITICAL ISSUE

On January 22, 1973, the Supreme Court legalized abortion, setting the stage for this politically sensitive issue to become a continuing topic of debate on the floor of Congress and in state legislatures. In general, state Democratic parties support a woman's right to choose abortion, and state Republican parties do not. (See Table 3.1.)

In 2004 the majority of states considered legislation that would place greater limits on a person's right to choose abortion. (See Figure 3.1.) People supporting such measures are sometimes described as being "antichoice." Likewise, those who oppose limitations on abortion rights are often described as "pro-choice." According to the NARAL Pro-Choice America Foundation in *Who Decides? A State-by-State Review of Abortion and Reproductive Rights*, in 2004 a total of 714 antiabortion measures were introduced among all the states, and twenty-nine were enacted; 422 pro-choice measures were introduced, and thirty were enacted. The antichoice legislative measures most frequently considered by states in 2004 were increased counseling (giving "pro-life" information to a woman seeking an abortion) and mandatory delay requirements, refusal to provide medical services, restrictions on young women's access to reproductive health services, targeted regulation of abortion providers, and abstinence-only education. (See Figure 3.2.)

Figure 3.3 shows the choice positions of state governments. In order to be considered either pro-choice or antichoice in this analysis, both the majority of the legislature and the governor of the state must hold that position. Figure 3.4 and Figure 3.5 separate the two. Figure 3.4 shows each governor's position on choice, while Figure 3.5 shows each state legislature's positions on choice.

State restrictions on abortion are varied and numerous. The most common restrictions in effect are parental notification or consent requirements for minors, state-sponsored counseling and waiting periods prior to receiving an abortion, and limitations on public funding ("State Facts about Abortion," New York: Alan Guttmacher Institute, 2003).

The *Roe v. Wade* decision was a catalyst for the right-to-life (or pro-life) movement, which had its beginnings in the late 1960s. Pro-life groups (called antiabortion or antichoice groups by their opponents) consider the *Roe v. Wade* decision to be government-sanctioned mass killing of the unborn. Following the landmark decision, antiabortion activists supported constitutional amendments to overturn the *Roe v. Wade* ruling, but none were passed. A constitutional amendment requires two-thirds approval of each house of Congress and ratification by three-quarters of the state legislatures. Antiabortion groups since have attempted to limit aspects of the *Roe* decision, not only by influencing the appointment of lower court and Supreme Court judges but also by restricting the rights to abortion conferred by the *Roe v. Wade* ruling. Pro-choice groups suggest that other antichoice legislative measures—such as recognizing the embryo and fetus as a person for legal purposes, mandating a waiting period and counseling requirements, and restricting minors' access to abortion—also are attempts to chip away at the *Roe v. Wade* decision.

FEDERAL FUNDING AND ABORTION

The federal government established the Medicaid program in 1965 to pay for medical care for the nation's needy through a federal–state cost-sharing arrangement. During the presidential administration of Richard Nixon (1969–74), the Department of Health, Education, and Welfare (HEW, now the Department of Health and Human Services, or HHS) reimbursed states for abortions for poor women. Following the *Roe v. Wade* decision in 1973, HEW considered abortion a medical procedure funded by Medicaid.

TABLE 3.1

Positions of state Democratic and Republican parties on a woman's right to choose abortion, 2004

State	Democrat				Republican			
	Supports	Opposes	No position	Unknown	Supports	Opposes	No position	Unknown
National	X					X		
Alabama			X					X
Alaska	X					X		
Arizona	X					X		
Arkansas			X					X
California	X					X		
Colorado	X					X		
Connecticut	X						X	
Delaware	X					X		
District of Columbia				X			X	
Florida	X					X		
Georgia			X			X		
Hawaii	X					X		
Idaho	X					X		
Illinois	X					X		
Indiana			X			*		
Iowa	X					X		
Kansas			X			X		
Kentucky	X					X		
Louisiana	X					X		
Maine	X					X		
Maryland	X					X		
Massachusetts	X						X	
Michigan	X					X		
Minnesota	X					X		
Mississippi		X				X		
Missouri	X					X		
Montana	X					X		
Nebraska	X					X		
Nevada	X					X		
New Hampshire	X					X		
New Jersey	X					X		
New Mexico			X			X		
New York	X							X
North Carolina	X					X		
North Dakota			X			X		
Ohio	X					X		
Oklahoma	X					X		
Oregon	X					X		
Pennsylvania				X		X		
Rhode Island	X							X
South Carolina	X					X		
South Dakota			X			X		
Tennessee	X					X		
Texas	X					X		
Utah	X					X		
Vermont	X					X		
Virginia	X					X		
Washington	X					X		
West Virginia	X					X		
Wisconsin	X					X		
Wyoming	X					X		
Total	**41**	**1**	**8**	**2**	**0**	**44**	**3**	**4**

*This party platform does not explicitly oppose a woman's right to choose, but it supports an Indiana law that states, "Childbirth is preferred, encouraged, and supported over abortion."

Notes:

Democratic Party

40 state Democratic Party platforms fully support a woman's right to choose.

8 state Democratic Party platforms do not take a position on a woman's right to choose: AL, AR, GA, IN, KS, NM, ND, SD.

Mississippi is the only state whose Democratic Party platform opposes a woman's right to choose.

Republican Party

44 state Republican Party platforms oppose a woman's right to choose.

2 state and the District of Columbia Republican party platforms do not take a position on a woman's right to choose: CT, MA.

SOURCE: Adapted from "Political Findings: Political Party Platform Information," in *Who Decides? The Status of Women's Reproductive Rights in the United States, 14th ed.*, NARAL Pro-Choice America & NARAL Pro-Choice America Foundation, January 2005, http://www.prochoiceamerica.org/yourstate/ whodecides/trends/2005_key_findings.cfm#political (accessed September 20, 2005)

FIGURE 3.1

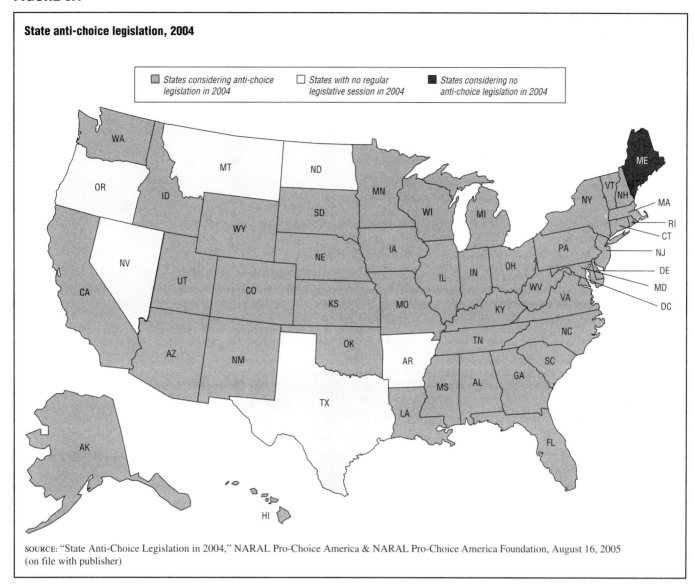

State anti-choice legislation, 2004

Legend:
- ☐ States considering anti-choice legislation in 2004
- ☐ States with no regular legislative session in 2004
- ■ States considering no anti-choice legislation in 2004

SOURCE: "State Anti-Choice Legislation in 2004," NARAL Pro-Choice America & NARAL Pro-Choice America Foundation, August 16, 2005 (on file with publisher)

In 1974 abortion opponents in Congress attached a rider to the annual HEW appropriations (funding) bill. The rider forbade or restricted the use of federal funding for abortion, but it was overwhelmingly defeated.

After the Supreme Court ruling in *Roe v. Wade*, the number of abortions increased rapidly until, by 1976, according to the Centers for Disease Control and Prevention, almost one million abortions were being performed annually. An estimated three hundred thousand of these were federally funded. Abortion foes were angered by what they considered a mass slaughter being partially financed with tax dollars, and they responded by lobbying their senators and representatives to end this practice.

In 1976 then-freshman congressman Henry Hyde (R-IL) introduced an abortion rider to the HEW-Labor appropriations bill. Reflecting changing political attitudes in Congress, it passed. In fact, the 1976 rider, since known as the Hyde Amendment, has become the subject of an annual battle in Congress.

Representative Hyde originally proposed that no federal funding could be used for abortion. Following considerable debate, Congress settled on a compromise, which stated that none of the funds contained in the appropriations bill would be used to perform abortions except "where the life of the mother would be endangered if the fetus were carried to term." (This is a common sticking point for abortion legislation—such as in the case of laws relating to partial-birth abortion.) The Departments of Labor and Health, Education, and Welfare Appropriations Act (PL 94-439), which included the abortion provision, became law in September 1976. However, because of legal challenges, it did not go into effect until almost a year later, in August 1977.

Almost immediately, the Hyde Amendment was challenged in the courts. The U.S. Supreme Court heard

FIGURE 3.2

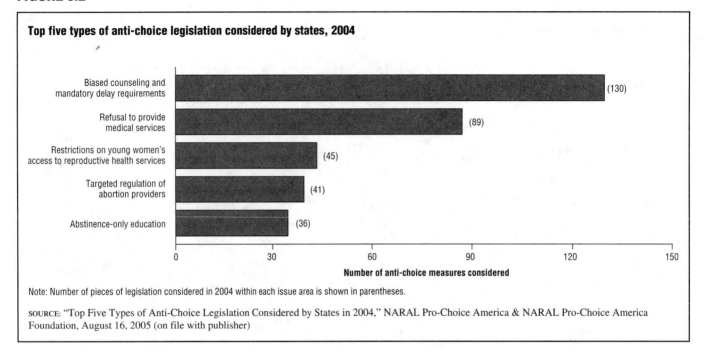

Top five types of anti-choice legislation considered by states, 2004

Note: Number of pieces of legislation considered in 2004 within each issue area is shown in parentheses.

SOURCE: "Top Five Types of Anti-Choice Legislation Considered by States in 2004," NARAL Pro-Choice America & NARAL Pro-Choice America Foundation, August 16, 2005 (on file with publisher)

and ruled on public funding cases involving funding limitations both for therapeutic (medically necessary) and nontherapeutic (elective, or not medically necessary) abortions.

Funding Compromise

Over the years the language of the Hyde Amendment has changed occasionally. The conflict usually has involved the House demanding strict control over the use of federal monies for abortion and the generally more liberal Senate trying to modify House demands. In 1977 the House passed an amendment calling for Hyde's original proposal that no federal funds be used for any abortion, even one necessary to save the life of the mother. However, after lengthy debate and political maneuvering, the final compromise prohibited the use of federal funds to pay for abortions except:

• For victims of rape or incest if the occurrence was reported promptly to the proper authorities

• If justified to save the mother's life

• In instances where two doctors determined that "severe and long-lasting physical health damage to the mother" may result

Congress began applying the Hyde Amendment to Medicare and Medicaid in 1988. Although Medicare is a medical insurance program for people over the age of sixty-five, it does provide for some disabled persons younger than sixty-five. Under the Hyde Amendment, all federally funded abortions for disabled women were banned except in cases of life endangerment, rape, or incest.

STATE FUNDING AND ABORTION

Medicaid is a federal assistance program for low-income people. Medicaid is implemented by the states, but with federal funds and federal guidelines. As of 2005, thirty-two states plus the District of Columbia allowed the funding of abortion under Medicaid in cases of life endangerment, rape, and incest. (See Table 3.2.) One state (South Dakota), in violation of federal law, provided Medicaid funding for abortion only if a woman's life was in danger. Seventeen states funded abortion in all or most circumstances, using state funds when Medicaid would not pay.

Abortion Funding and Managed Care

For the first time since the *Roe v. Wade* decision, the 1996 congressional elections resulted in a pro-life majority in both the House and the Senate. Pro-life lawmakers pointed out that, because states are increasingly contracting with managed-care organizations to provide Medicaid recipients with health services, the Hyde Amendment had to be revised. Representative Hyde sought to forbid health plans from offering abortion coverage when they contracted with states under Medicaid. He claimed that in cases where states used their own funds to pay for abortions beyond the federally mandated cases of rape, incest, and life endangerment, purchasing a health plan using a "co-mingling" of federal and state monies presented the possibility of an indirect federal abortion subsidy.

Hyde's proposed change met with great opposition from pro-choice Democrats. They protested that the new law would negatively affect privately insured women whose insurance companies contracted with the states.

FIGURE 3.3

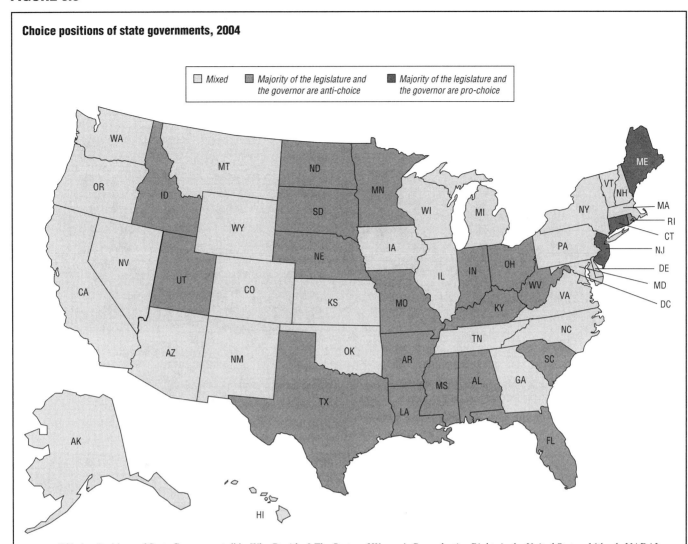

Choice positions of state governments, 2004

☐ Mixed ▨ Majority of the legislature and the governor are anti-choice ■ Majority of the legislature and the governor are pro-choice

SOURCE: "Choice Positions of State Governments," in *Who Decides? The Status of Women's Reproductive Rights in the United States, 14th ed.*, NARAL Pro-Choice America & NARAL Pro-Choice America Foundation, January 2005, http://www.prochoiceamerica.org/yourstate/whodecides/about/loader .cfm?url=/commonspot/security/getfile.cfm&PageID=15441 (accessed September 20, 2005)

It also would affect Medicaid recipients in those states where abortions were subsidized. In the end the revised version passed with the provision that federal funds would not be used to purchase managed-care packages that included coverage of abortion. States that covered abortion with their own funds would be able to continue doing so under a separate program. In November 1997 President Clinton signed the FY (fiscal year) 1998 Departments of Labor, Health and Human Services, and Education, and Related Agencies Appropriations Act (PL 105-78) with the abortion provision.

Abortion Funding and the State Children's Health Insurance Program

In August 1997 the Balanced Budget Act (PL 105-33) amended the Social Security Act (PL 89-97) by adding Title XXI (State Children's Health Insurance Program, or CHIP) to allocate funds to states to provide child health assistance to uninsured, low-income children who are not eligible for Medicaid. Under CHIP, state funds may be used for abortion only to save the life of the mother or if the pregnancy resulted from rape or incest.

How Much Do States Pay?

According to the Alan Guttmacher Institute (AGI), in 2001 about 14% of all abortions in the United States were paid for with public, mainly state, funds. About 74% of abortions were paid with personal funds, and the remaining 13% were paid for by private health insurance. Table 3.3 shows that, among the abortions paid for with public funds, state governments reported spending $72 million in 2001 to provide 168,518 abortion procedures. The federal government spent $233,000 for eighty-three abortion procedures. The eighteen states with nonrestrictive policies used their own funds to pay for most or all of the medically necessary abortions provided to Medicaid

FIGURE 3.4

Choice positions of state governors, 2005

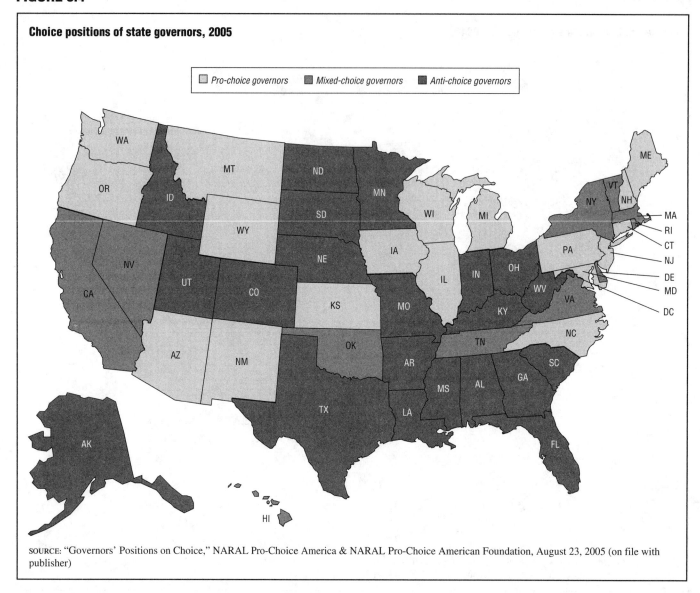

SOURCE: "Governors' Positions on Choice," NARAL Pro-Choice America & NARAL Pro-Choice American Foundation, August 23, 2005 (on file with publisher)

recipients. These funds accounted for well over 99% of the total expenditures and procedures paid for with public funds.

ABORTION SERVICES FOR MILITARY PERSONNEL

Before 1970 the armed forces of the United States did not have any official policy regarding the provision of abortion. Individual commanders had unwritten policies, which lower-rank personnel followed. Military medical facilities followed the laws in the states in which they were located, and it was up to individual physicians whether to offer abortion services.

According to "Abortion Services and Military Medical Facilities" (University of Maryland School of Law, Thurgood Marshall Law Library, http://www.law.umaryland.edu/marshall/crsreports, November 24, 2002), in 1970 the Department of Defense (DOD) issued an order

that "military hospitals perform abortions when it is medically necessary or when the mental health of the mother is threatened." Military physicians, however, were not required to perform abortions.

After the 1973 Supreme Court decision in *Roe v. Wade*, the DOD funded abortions for women eligible for military health care. To perform an abortion, two physicians had to satisfy the above stipulation of "medical necessity" or "risk to mental health." In addition, the funding had to fall within the state regulations concerning abortions.

During the rest of the 1970s, varying abortion language was added to the DOD appropriations acts, with the exceptions ranging from saving the mother's life, rape, and incest, to severe, long-lasting physical damage to the mother. Women whose condition did not satisfy the law paid for their abortions at the military medical facilities.

FIGURE 3.5

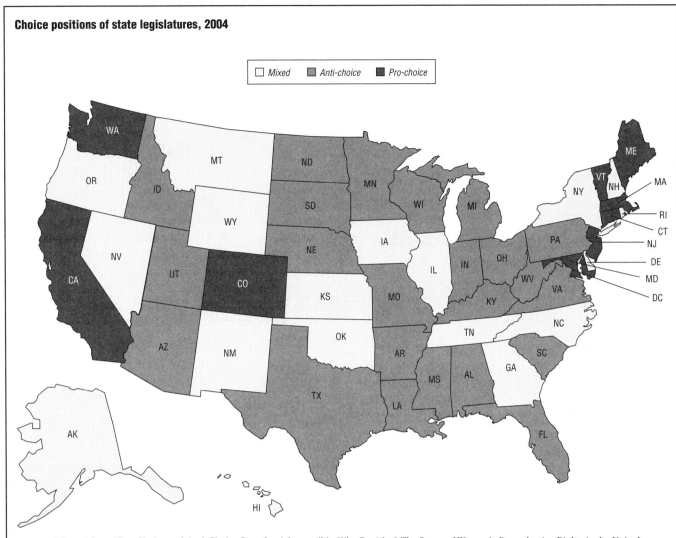

Choice positions of state legislatures, 2004

☐ *Mixed* ▧ *Anti-choice* ■ *Pro-choice*

SOURCE: Adapted from "Pro-Choice and Anti-Choice State Legislatures," in *Who Decides? The Status of Women's Reproductive Rights in the United States, 14th ed.*, NARAL Pro-Choice America & NARAL Pro-Choice America Foundation, January 2005, http://www.prochoiceamerica.org/yourstate/ whodecides/about/loader.cfm?url=/commonspot/security/getfile.cfm&PageID=15441 (accessed September 20, 2005)

By 1981 abortion was allowed only to save the life of the mother. In 1988 the DOD began banning all abortions at military medical facilities overseas, even if the woman was willing to pay for the procedure herself. In 1993, following his inauguration, President Clinton issued a memorandum to "permit abortion services to be provided [at U.S. military facilities], if paid for entirely with non-DOD funds" (quoted in "Abortion Services and Military Medical Facilities"). However, in 1996, after Republicans took control of Congress, the National Defense Authorization Act (PL 104-106) again banned the performance of abortions in U.S. military medical facilities except in cases of endangerment to the mother's life, rape, or incest.

At subsequent sessions of Congress, proposed amendments to PL 104-106, allowing privately paid abortions, were defeated. Currently, women in the U.S.

armed forces wanting an abortion must return to the United States or have the procedure performed at a private overseas facility.

AVOIDING ABORTION: FUNDING THROUGH TITLE X FOR FAMILY PLANNING/CONTRACEPTION

In 1970, with broad bipartisan support, Congress enacted Title X of the Public Health Service Act (Family Planning Program, PL 91-572), which provides federal assistance to family planning clinics for contraception, infertility, and basic gynecologic services. The law specifically prohibits abortion as a method of family planning and forbids the use of any program monies to perform or advocate abortion. The program is intended to primarily benefit low-income women and adolescents. According to the AGI in "Fulfilling the Promise: Public

TABLE 3.2

Low-income women's access to abortion, 2005

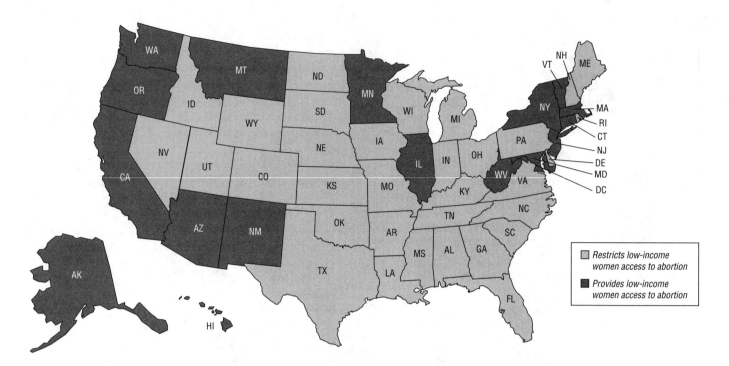

| State | State prohibits low-income women's access to abortion except in* | | Low-income women's access to abortion allowed | State | State prohibits low-income women's access to abortion except in* | | Low-income women's access to abortion allowed |
	Life endangerment only	Cases of life endangerment, rape, or incest			Life endangerment only	Cases of life endangerment, rape, or incest	
Alabama		X		Nebraska		X	
Alaska			X	Nevada		X	
Arizona		X		New Hampshire		X	
Arkansas		X		New Jersey			X
California		X		New Mexico			X
Colorado		X		New York			X
Connecticut		X		North Carolina		X	
Delaware		X		North Dakota		X	
District of Columbia		X		Ohio		X	
Florida		X		Oklahoma		X	
Georgia		X		Oregon			X
Hawaii		X		Pennsylvania		X	
Idaho		X		Rhode Island		X	
Illinois		X		South Carolina		X	
Indiana		X		South Dakota	X		
Iowa		X		Tennessee		X	
Kansas		X		Texas		X	
Kentucky		X		Utah		X	
Louisiana		X		Vermont			X
Maine		X		Virginia		X	
Maryland		X		Washington			X
Massachusetts		X		West Virginia			X
Michigan		X		Wisconsin		X	
Minnesota		X		Wyoming		X	
Mississippi		X		**Total**	**1**	**33**	**17**
Missouri		X					
Montana			X				

*This information is not conclusive as some states allow abortion in select other circumstances such as substantial and irreversible impairment of a major bodily function, medical emergency, and/or some cases of fetal anomaly.

SOURCE: "Low-Income Women's Access to Abortion," in *Who Decides? The Status of Women's Reproductive Rights in the United States, 14th ed.*, NARAL Pro-Choice America & NARAL Pro-Choice America Foundation, updated May 27, 2005, http://www.prochoiceamerica.org/yourstate/whodecides/maps/low_income.cfm (accessed September 20, 2005)

TABLE 3.3

Public funding for abortion services, 2001

State	Expenditures [in thousands]			Number of abortions		
	Total	Federal	State	Total	Federal	State
U.S. total	**$72,707**	**$233**	**$72,473**	**168,601**	**83**	**168,518**
Nonrestrictive policy						
Voluntary policy	32,722	0	32,722	51,852	0	51,852
Hawaii	nr	0	nr	nr	0	nr
Maryland	2,300	0	2,300	3,324	0	3,324
New York	23,090	0	23,090	36,131	0	36,131
Washington	7,332	0	7,332	12,397	0	12,397
Court ordered policy	39,735	11	39,724	116,651	26	116,625
Alaska	277	3	274	541	5	536
California	27,183	0	27,183	84,381	0	84,381
Connecticut	u	u	u	3,913	5	3,908
Idaho	27	5	22	39	5	34
Illinois	6	0	6	u	0	u
Indiana	0	0	0	0	0	0
Massachusetts	2,391	0	2,391	5,874	0	5,874
Minnesota	856	3	853	3,241	11	3,230
Montana	100	0	100	u	0	u
New Jersey	6,000	0	6,000	11,514	0	11,514
New Mexico	451	0	451	1,265	0	1,265
Oregon	1,930	0	1,930	4,371	0	4,371
Vermont	181	0	181	469	0	469
West Virginia	334	0	334	1,043	0	1,043
Restrictive policy						
Life, rape, incest	231	220	10	81	56	25
Alabama	1	1	0	5	5	0
Arizona	0	0	0	0	0	0
Arkansas	0	0	0	0	0	0
Colorado	nr	0	nr	nr	0	nr
Delaware	0	0	0	0	0	0
District of Columbia	0	0	0	0	0	0
Florida	nr	0	nr	nr	0	nr
Georgia	13	5	8	23	5	18
Kansas	u	0	u	u	0	u
Kentucky	13	13	0	8	8	0
Louisiana	0	0	0	0	0	0
Maine	3	3	nr	u	u	nr
Michigan	0	0	0	0	0	0
Missouri	1	1	0	1	1	0
Nebraska	nr	0	nr	nr	0	nr
Nevada	0	0	0	0	0	0
New Hampshire	nr	0	nr	nr	0	nr
North Carolina	37	37	0	6	6	0
North Dakota	2	2	0	1	1	0
Ohio	42	42	0	6	6	0
Oklahoma	0	0	0	0	0	0
Pennsylvania	0	0	0	0	0	0
Puerto Rico	nr	0	nr	nr	0	nr
Rhode Island	2	0	2	7	0	7
South Carolina	114	114	0	20	20	0
Tennessee	nr	0	nr	nr	0	nr
Texas	2	2	0	3	3	0
Utah	0	0	0	0	0	0
Wyoming	1	1	0	1	1	0

Policy and U.S. Family Planning Clinics" (2000), each year more than four million women receive health care services at family planning clinics funded by Title X. These women are mainly young, poor, and uninsured, and most have never had a child. Of women using Title X-funded clinics, 71% are twenty years or older and 65% are white. Approximately 65% have incomes at or below the federal poverty level (which means they earn less than $15,020 per year for a family of three). It is estimated that these clinics are the only source of family planning services for more than 80% of the women they serve. Fewer than 5% of Title X fund recipients are

abortion providers, according to the National Abortion Federation in "Abortion and Title X: What Health Care Providers Need to Know" (2003).

According to the AGI study "Fulfilling the Promise," Title X-supported clinics enable one million women each year to avoid unintended pregnancy and have helped prevent almost twenty million pregnancies over the last twenty years. Of these pregnancies, nine million would have ended in abortion, according to the report. Services are also available to men; about 2% of Title X clients are adult and adolescent males.

TABLE 3.3

Public funding for abortion services, 2001 [CONTINUED]

State	Expenditures [in thousands]			Number of abortions		
	Total	Federal	State	Total	Federal	State
Life only	0	0	0	0	0	0
Mississippi	0	0	0	0	0	0
South Dakota	0	0	0	0	0	0
Broader than life, rape, incest	19	2	16	17	1	16
Iowa	17	2	15	9	1	8
Virginia	2	0	2	2	0	2
Wisconsin	u	0	u	6	0	6

Notes: States with nonrestrictive policies use their own funds to pay for most or all medically necessarily abortions provided to Medicaid recipients; the policy may have been adopted either voluntarily or because of a court order. States with restrictive policies pay for abortions only in a few circumstances: when necessary to save the life of the woman or when the pregnancy is the result of rape or incest (which is federal policy); only to save the life of the woman (a violation of federal policy); or "broader than life, rape, incest" which means that states use their own funds to pay for abortions under additional rare circumstances such as in cases of fetal abnormality.
nr=no response or not available.
u=unknown.

SOURCE: Adam Sonfield and Rachel Benson Gold, "Table 9. Reported Public Expenditures for Abortions (in 000s of dollars) and Number of Publicly Funded Abortions, by Funding Source, According to State and State Funding Policy (as of October 1, 2001), FY2001," in *Public Funding for Contraceptive, Sterilization and Abortion Services, FY 1980–2001: National and State Tables and Figures*, The Alan Guttmacher Institute (AGI), 2005, http://www.guttmacher.org/pubs/fpfunding/tables.pdf (accessed September 20, 2005)

Guidelines instituted under the presidential administration of Jimmy Carter (1977–81) indicated that federally funded clinics could not advise a pregnant woman to have an abortion, and the clinic could not pay for the abortion should a woman choose to have one. However, the clinics "are to" inform her in a "nondirective" manner that her options include keeping the baby, giving the child up for adoption, or ending the pregnancy by having an abortion. In September 1986 the Reagan administration changed the wording in the guidelines from "are to"—which implied a mandatory requirement—to "may"—which was subject to individual judgment. Should the woman want an abortion, the federally funded agency had to provide her with a list of abortion clinics that operated without federal funding.

Male Involvement in Family Planning

Since 1996 the Title X program has provided additional funds for an adolescent male initiative that employs male high school students as interns in the clinics. The students receive training in clinic operation and peer education, assistance in identifying possible careers in health and health-related occupations, and use of services in a family planning setting. The program also has awarded research grants to organizations that include social and educational services to males, enabling these organizations to evaluate the addition of reproductive health and family planning services to their existing program.

Confidential Family Planning Services for Adolescents

Of the four million people receiving reproductive health and family planning services each year at family planning clinics funded by Title X, about one-third are younger than twenty years old. Although the law requires Title X clinics to encourage parental participation in teenage reproductive health decisions, they have to respect a teenager's wish not to involve his or her parents. Courts have recognized the importance of confidential services for teenagers. In *Planned Parenthood Association of Utah v. Matheson* (582 F. Supp. 1001, 1009 [D. Utah 1983]), a U.S. District Court prohibited a "blanket parental notification requirement" for minors seeking contraceptives. The court observed that adolescents who seek contraceptives are usually already sexually active. Therefore, these same adolescents would continue engaging in sexual activity even if they could not obtain contraceptives, thereby exposing themselves to "the health risks of early pregnancy and venereal disease" (quoted in "Government-Mandated Parental Involvement in Family Planning Services Threatens Young People's Health," NARAL Pro-Choice America Foundation, http://www.prochoiceamerica.org/facts/parental.cfm).

Funding for Private Family Planning Clinics

Besides providing monies to more than four thousand family planning clinics run by state and local governments, Title X also provides grants to private nonprofit groups that provide family planning services. In 1988 the HHS, acting on President Ronald Reagan's recommendation, issued regulations revising their interpretation of Section 1008, the longstanding statutory prohibition against using Title X funds to "promote abortion." The guidelines reaffirmed that Congress intended Title X funds "to be used only to support preventive family planning services."

The Reagan administration further prohibited counselors at federally funded clinics from discussing abortion as an alternative in an unintended pregnancy and from referring pregnant women to an abortion provider even if patients ask for such assistance and it is paid for with private funds. This prohibition against discussing abortion in Title X clinics became known as the "gag rule."

TITLE X CLINICS AND THE "GAG RULE." About thirty-six state health departments and seventy-eight national organizations opposed the gag rule because they said it violated the clinics' First Amendment right to free speech and infringed on the doctor–patient relationship. In May 1991 in *Rust v. Sullivan* (500 U.S. 173), the Supreme Court, voting 5–4, upheld the gag rule.

The American Medical Association (AMA) attacked the ruling, not only because it interfered with the doctor–patient relationship but because it exposed doctors to the risk of medical malpractice lawsuits for not informing a woman with a high-risk pregnancy of all her options. Pregnancy can be a risk to the health of a woman with diabetes, cancer, AIDS, hypertension, renal (kidney) disease, sickle cell anemia, malnutrition, or other serious illnesses. Some of these diseases particularly affect African-American women who, because of their greater rates of poverty, are more likely than white women to use federally funded clinics for health care.

Some federally funded clinics, including Planned Parenthood, chose, at the risk of having to close down, to turn down federal support rather than comply with the gag rule. The then-deputy assistant secretary of the HHS, William Archer, responded that if clinics would not comply, HHS simply would find other clinics to replace them. There were areas of the country, however, where there were no other existing health care providers ready to step in, leaving women who depended on subsidized health care with no source for prenatal care and contraceptive services.

In Congress those opposing *Rust v. Sullivan* fought to overturn the Title X gag rule by placing a rider blocking it on an appropriations bill for the HHS. In November 1991 when President George H. W. Bush received the appropriations bill, he vetoed it due to the rider.

Supporters of the bill tried to garner the two-thirds vote in Congress needed to overturn the presidential veto but failed. In August 1992 a federal appeals court ruled that the HHS could move forward with implementation of the regulations. On January 22, 1993, the twentieth anniversary of *Roe v. Wade*, newly elected President Bill Clinton repealed the gag rule.

The Adequacy of Title X Funding

Although the authorizing law (PL 91-572) for the Title X family planning program expired on September 30, 1985, annual appropriations legislation has continued its funding. During the years of the Reagan administration (1981–89) and the George H. W. Bush administration (1989–93), funding was less than it had been in prior years. Funding rose dramatically during the years of the

Clinton administration (1993–2001). In Clinton's last year in office almost $254 million Title X funds were appropriated. Funding has also increased under the George W. Bush administration, which began in 2001. In 2003 $275 million was funded, and in 2005 $288 million was funded. (See Table 3.4.) Nevertheless, according to the National Family Planning and Reproductive Health Association (http://www.nfprha.org/pac/wac/index.asp?step=2=2956), if Title X funding kept up with inflation since fiscal year 1980, it would have be funded at more than $600 million in 2003.

ATTEMPTS TO "DEFUND" TITLE X. Each year anti-abortion lawmakers try to "defund," or eliminate, federal monies from the Title X program. Although the law prohibits Title X funds from being used for abortion, opponents of Title X argue that organizations such as the Planned Parenthood Federation of America, which provide abortions, should not receive Title X funds. They believe clinic clients might think abortion is a method of family planning. In addition, critics feel that instead of preventing teen pregnancy by providing adolescents with contraceptives, more efforts should be made in encouraging abstinence before marriage. (Title X clinics do offer adolescents abstinence counseling and education.)

INTERNATIONAL U.S. AID FOR FAMILY PLANNING/CONTRACEPTION

The Foreign Assistance Act

In 1961 Congress passed the Foreign Assistance Act (FAA), which reorganized the U.S. foreign assistance programs and mandated the creation of an agency to administer them—the U.S. Agency for International Development (USAID). USAID offered direct support to the developing nations of the world.

The FAA contained few restrictions on how assistance was to be provided and contained only general guidelines on the kinds of factors to be taken into account prior to providing assistance. In 1973 Congress amended the FAA, forbidding the use of American foreign aid funding "to pay for the performance of abortions as a method of family planning or to motivate or coerce any person to practice abortions."

Thus, in 1984 the Reagan administration cut U.S. funding to the International Planned Parenthood Federation because it included abortion among the options recommended for controlling family size. In July 1985 the administration indicated that the United States would provide monies to organizations that advocated only "natural" or noncontraceptive methods of family planning.

The following year, the Reagan administration withheld $10 million in aid to the United Nations Fund for Population Activities (UNFPA). Now called the United

TABLE 3.4

Funding for the Office of Family Planning, fiscal years 1971–2005

Fiscal year	Total funds appropriated
1971	$6,000,000
1972	61,815,000
1973	100,615,000
1974	100,615,000
1975	100,615,000
1976	100,615,000
1977	113,000,000
1978	135,000,000
1979	135,000,000
1980	162,000,000
1981	161,671,000
1982	124,176,000
1983	124,088,000
1984	140,000,000
1985	142,500,000
1986	136,372,000
1987	142,500,000
1988	139,663,000
1989	138,320,000
1990	139,135,000
1991	144,311,000
1992	149,585,000
1993	173,418,000
1994	180,918,000
1995	193,349,000
1996	192,592,000
1997	198,452,000
1998	203,452,000
1999	215,000,000
2000	238,885,000
2001	253,932,000
2002	265,000,000
2003	275,000,000
2004	280,000,000
2005	288,000,000

SOURCE: "Funding History FY 1971–2005," U.S. Department of Health and Human Services, Office of Population Affairs, Office of Family Planning, http://opa.osophs.dhhs.gov/titlex/ofp-funding-history.html (accessed September 20, 2005)

Nations Population Fund, UNFPA was dedicated to limiting the world's population increase. The Reagan administration charged UNFPA with helping the government of the People's Republic of China to carry out forced abortions and sterilizations. The $10 million was roughly equal to the UNFPA's annual spending in the People's Republic of China. Funding for UNFPA has been debated in Congress every year since 1985.

The Mexico City Policy/Global Gag Rule

At the United Nations population conference in Mexico City in 1984, President Reagan announced that the United States would no longer support private family planning groups overseas that, with their own funds, performed or promoted abortion. In June 1991 the Supreme Court upheld the policy by refusing to hear the case *Planned Parenthood Federation of America v. Agency for International Development* (cert. denied, 498 U.S. 933).

When the International Planned Parenthood Federation (IPPF) refused to implement the Reagan restriction on their affiliates in developing countries, the administration withdrew U.S. funds from the IPPF. The Reagan restriction, although never enacted into law, was enforced as an executive order for almost a decade. When President Clinton took office in 1993, he revoked the "Mexico City Policy" and restored the U.S. contribution to the UNFPA.

Many Americans agreed with this decision. A 1992 poll commissioned for the Population Crisis Committee (a nonprofit organization dedicated to providing international contraception and reproductive health care, later renamed Population Action International) found that 58% of Americans supported the use of U.S. funds for family planning in developing countries. About 65% said that family planning aid should not be denied to organizations that provided information about abortion, and 67% indicated that foreign aid should not be used to promote antiabortion policies internationally.

Since 1994, antiabortion advocates have introduced abortion-related clauses to a number of foreign aid measures. These lawmakers, led by Representative Christopher Smith (R-NJ), have sought to restrict U.S. aid to family planning groups that provide legal abortion services or advocate abortion rights in their countries. Pro-choice advocates liken this effort to the Mexico City Policy, calling it the "Global Gag Rule" because, they say, it limits free speech and the provision of abortion services.

For the first time, the Global Gag Rule was written into law for a year in the omnibus appropriations bill for FY 2000. In exchange for the release by Congress of $926 million in dues owed the United Nations, President Clinton agreed to restrictions on the $385 million appropriated for international family planning. Private organizations that performed or promoted abortion could not receive U.S. funds, as was the case under the Mexico City Policy.

On January 22, 2001, on the first business day of President George W. Bush's presidency and the twenty-eighth anniversary of *Roe v. Wade*, the new U.S. president issued a memorandum reinstating the Mexico City Policy, which had been rescinded since January 22, 1993. President Bush wrote in the memo, "It is my conviction that taxpayer funds should not be used to pay for abortions or advocate or actively promote abortion, either here or abroad. It is therefore my belief that the Mexico City Policy should be restored." He stated that he was reviving the rule in the belief that "it will make abortion more rare."

Although the reinstated Global Gag Rule is identical to that implemented two decades ago, the trend in abortion law worldwide has been toward making laws less strict. Since the Global Gag Rule was first implemented, twenty-six countries have made their abortion laws less strict, and five countries have tightened their laws. (See Table 3.5.) In 1999 41% of all women worldwide lived in

TABLE 3.5

Countries changing their abortion laws since the initial imposition of the "Global Gag Rule," 1985–2004

26 countries have liberalized their abortion laws since the initial imposition of the global gag rule

Albania	(1991, 1996)	Ghana	(1985)
Algeria	(1985)	Greece	(1986)
Belgium	(1990)	Guinea	(2000)
Botswana	(1991)	Malaysia	(1989)
Benin	(2003)	Mali	(2002)
Bulgaria	(1990)	Mongolia	(1989)
Burkina Faso	(1996)	Nepal	(2002)
Cambodia	(1997)	Pakistan	(1990)
Canada	(1988)	Romania	(1989)
Chad	(2002)	Slovakia	(1986)
Czech Republic	(1986)	South Africa	(1996)
Ethiopia	(2004)	Spain	(1985)
France	(2001)	Switzerland	(2002)

Five countries have tightened their laws

El Salvador	(1998)	Russian Federation	(2003)
Hungary	(2000)	United States	(2003)
Poland	(1997)		

SOURCE: Compiled by Sandra Alters with data from The Alan Guttmacher Institute and the Center for Reproductive Rights for Thomson Gale

FIGURE 3.6

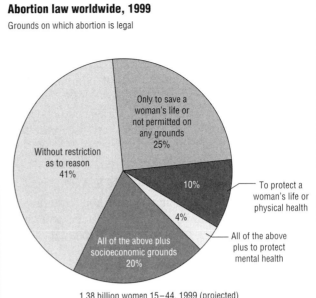

Abortion law worldwide, 1999

Grounds on which abortion is legal

Only to save a woman's life or not permitted on any grounds 25%

Without restriction as to reason 41%

10% — To protect a woman's life or physical health

4%

All of the above plus socioeconomic grounds 20%

All of the above plus to protect mental health

1.38 billion women 15–44, 1999 (projected)

SOURCE: S. Cohen, "Nepal Reforms Abortion Law to Reduce Maternal Deaths, Promote Women's Status," in "For the Record," *The Guttmacher Report on Public Policy*, no. 2, 2002, http://www.guttmacher.org/pubs/tgr/05/2/gr050213.pdf (accessed September 20, 2005)

countries where abortion is legal without restriction. Another 34% lived in countries where abortion is legal with restriction. (See Figure 3.6.) With the more recent implementation of the gag rule, the possibility of conflict arose because more countries that receive U.S. population assistance allowed abortions than during the past implementation. By June 2004, however, the 1999 percentages shown in Figure 3.6 remained relatively unchanged. See Table 8.1 in Chapter 8 for a comparison.

In September 2003 President Bush issued an executive order preventing the State Department from giving family planning grants to international groups that provide abortion-related counseling, effectively extending the Global Gag Rule, which previously applied only to the USAID. The new order exempts agencies in Africa and the Caribbean that would benefit from President Bush's five-year, $15 billion global AIDS initiative, however.

In April 2005 the U.S. Senate passed an amendment to the Foreign Affairs Authorization Act brought forward by Senators Barbara Boxer (D-CA) and Olympia Snowe (R-ME) that would repeal the Global Gag Rule. As of August 2005 no more action had been taken on the legislation.

WELFARE REFORM AND ABORTION

In 1995, as Congress worked to overhaul the nation's welfare system, the legislators were split on issues concerning teen pregnancy and abortion. Some believed that discontinuing federal cash assistance to the needy would help discourage out-of-wedlock childbearing. According to Lisa Kaeser's "Washington Memo" (Alan Guttmacher Institute, August 7, 1996), these members regarded out-of-wedlock births, especially among adolescents, as

"both a central cause of welfare dependency and a direct result of the 'culture' it creates." Others feared that limiting welfare cash benefits would lead poor women to choose abortion.

In 1996 the sixty-year-old federal cash assistance program, Aid to Families with Dependent Children (AFDC), was eliminated, and President Clinton signed the new welfare reform law, the Personal Responsibility and Work Opportunity Reconciliation Act of 1998 (PL 104-193), which created the Temporary Assistance for Needy Families (TANF) program. TANF provides assistance and work opportunities to needy families by granting states the federal funds and wide flexibility to develop and implement their own welfare programs.

The new welfare reform law outlined specific provisions for reducing out-of-wedlock and teen pregnancies. Although it allowed states to spend a portion of their TANF funds on "prepregnancy family services," it prohibited funding of other medical services, such as abortions.

Although most out-of-wedlock births are to women not on welfare, Congress used the welfare reform law to stress the issue of illegitimacy. To encourage the states to develop effective solutions for reducing out-of-wedlock births, PL 104-193 provided for a performance incentive called "Bonus to Reward Decrease in Illegitimacy Ratio." Under the new law the federal government would award up to $100 million annually to a maximum of five states that reduced nonmarital births while decreasing their abortion rates below 1995 levels.

Table 3.6 shows the ranking of the states based on the decline in the percentage of nonmarital births. Table 3.6 shows that the District of Columbia and four states (New York, Maryland, New Hampshire, and Connecticut) had a reduction in their ratio of nonmarital births. The ratio also declined in American Samoa—a decline that was larger than any of the state-specific declines. Table 3.6 does not show whether states decreased their abortion rates below 1995 levels.

UNBORN VICTIMS OF VIOLENCE ACT

Currently, thirty-two states have homicide laws that recognize unborn fetuses as victims at some point before birth. (See Figure 3.7.) On April 1, 2004, the federal Unborn Victims of Violence Act was enacted and covers unborn victims of federal and military crimes; it does not override existing state laws. The legislation states that anyone who causes the death or bodily injury of a fetus is "guilty of a separate offense" and that "the punishment for that separate offense is the same as the punishment provided under Federal law for that conduct had that injury or death occurred to the unborn child's mother." The law makes exceptions for legal medical procedures, including abortion, and acts on behalf of a pregnant woman. Opponents of the law, however, consider it a sneak attack on abortion rights because, in effect, it considers a fetus to be a person. They also state that pro-life groups are attempting to label the fetus as a person to change public perception about the nature of abortion.

TABLE 3.6

Percentage of births to unmarried women, by state and territory, 1999–2000 and 2001–02

| State | Percent unmarried 2001–2002 | Percent unmarried 1999–2000 | Percent change in percent unmarried, 1999–2000 to 2001–2002 | State | Rank order of states by largest decline in percent unmarried, 1999–2000 to 2001–2002 | | |
					Rank	State	Percent change
United States[a]	33.739%	33.120%	1.869%	United States[a]		United States[a]	1.869%
Alabama	34.577%	33.797%	2.308%	Alabama	1	District of Columbia	−6.680%
Alaska	33.399%	33.086%	0.946%	Alaska	2	New York	−2.359%
Arizona	39.940%	39.021%	2.355%	Arizona	3	Maryland	−0.334%
Arkansas	36.629%	35.460%	3.297%	Arkansas	4	New Hampshire	−0.331%
California	32.867%	32.788%	0.241%	California	5	Connecticut	−0.062%
Colorado	25.883%	25.224%	2.613%	Colorado		California	0.241%
Connecticut	29.116%	29.134%	−0.062%	Connecticut		Massachusetts	0.818%
Delaware	40.272%	38.385%	4.916%	Delaware		Alaska	0.946%
District of Columbia	56.946%	61.022%	−6.680%	District of Columbia		Illinois	0.982%
Florida	39.153%	37.864%	3.404%	Florida		Oregon	1.266%
Georgia	37.566%	36.777%	2.145%	Georgia		Mississippi	1.615%
Hawaii	33.292%	32.528%	2.349%	Hawaii		Virginia	1.647%
Idaho	21.969%	21.606%	1.680%	Idaho		Idaho	1.680%
Illinois	34.643%	34.306%	0.982%	Illinois		Utah	1.754%
Indiana	35.913%	34.565%	3.900%	Indiana		New Jersey	1.782%
Iowa	29.059%	27.750%	4.717%	Iowa		Missouri	1.889%
Kansas	30.502%	28.803%	5.899%	Kansas		North Dakota	1.986%
Kentucky	32.443%	30.713%	5.633%	Kentucky		South Carolina	2.017%
Louisiana	46.662%	45.240%	3.143%	Louisiana		Georgia	2.145%
Maine	32.169%	31.162%	3.231%	Maine		Alabama	2.308%
Maryland	34.617%	34.733%	−0.334%	Maryland		Washington	2.335%
Massachusetts	26.750%	26.533%	0.818%	Massachusetts		Hawaii	2.349%
Michigan	34.210%	33.190%	3.073%	Michigan		Arizona	2.355%
Minnesota	26.883%	25.853%	3.984%	Minnesota		Rhode Island	2.388%
Mississippi	46.700%	45.958%	1.615%	Mississippi		Wisconsin	2.424%
Missouri	34.997%	34.348%	1.889%	Missouri		Pennsylvania	2.462%
Montana	32.095%	30.402%	5.569%	Montana		Ohio	2.598%
Nebraska	28.144%	26.513%	6.152%	Nebraska		Colorado	2.613%
Nevada	37.312%	36.045%	3.515%	Nevada		Texas	2.679%
New Hampshire	24.359%	24.440%	−0.331%	New Hampshire		New Mexico	2.761%
New Jersey	29.249%	28.737%	1.782%	New Jersey		Michigan	3.073%
New Mexico	46.595%	45.343%	2.761%	New Mexico		West Virginia	3.094%
New York	35.728%	36.591%	−2.359%	New York		Louisiana	3.143%
North Carolina	34.467%	33.289%	3.539%	North Carolina		Maine	3.231%
North Dakota	28.448%	27.894%	1.986%	North Dakota		Arkansas	3.297%
Ohio	35.271%	34.378%	2.598%	Ohio		Florida	3.404%
Oklahoma	35.813%	33.713%	6.229%	Oklahoma		Nevada	3.515%
Oregon	30.647%	30.264%	1.266%	Oregon		North Carolina	3.539%
Pennsylvania	33.625%	32.817%	2.462%	Pennsylvania		Wyoming	3.773%
Rhode Island	35.721%	34.888%	2.388%	Rhode Island		Tennessee	3.854%
South Carolina	40.216%	39.421%	2.017%	South Carolina		Indiana	3.900%
South Dakota	34.276%	32.632%	5.038%	South Dakota		Minnesota	3.984%
Tennessee	35.947%	34.613%	3.854%	Tennessee		Iowa	4.717%
Texas	31.730%	30.902%	2.679%	Texas		Delaware	4.916%
Utah	17.286%	16.988%	1.754%	Utah		South Dakota	5.038%
Vermont	31.428%	28.530%	10.158%	Vermont		Montana	5.569%
Virginia	30.300%	29.809%	1.647%	Virginia		Kentucky	5.633%
Washington	28.790%	28.133%	2.335%	Washington		Kansas	5.899%
West Virginia	32.691%	31.710%	3.094%	West Virginia		Nebraska	6.152%
Wisconsin	29.962%	29.253%	2.424%	Wisconsin		Oklahoma	6.229%
Wyoming	30.004%	28.913%	3.773%	Wyoming		Vermont	10.158%
Puerto Rico	51.497%	48.921%	5.266%	Puerto Rico		American Samoa	−14.973%
Virgin Islands	67.030%	66.893%	0.205%	Virgin Islands		Virgin Islands	0.205%
Guam	55.534%	55.349%	0.334%	Guam		Guam	0.334%
American Samoa	30.165%	35.477%	−14.973%	American Samoa		Puerto Rico	5.266%
Northern Marianas	58.269%	b	b	Northern Marianas		Northern Marianas	b

Note: Calculations for all states and territories were done on the basis of data files provided by each state to the Centers for Disease Control and Prevention's National Center for Health Statistics (NCHS), which has tabulated the entire national birth file by mother's place of residence.
[a]Excludes data for the territories.
[b]Data not available.

SOURCE: "Percent of Births to Unmarried Women, 1999–2000 Average and 2001–2002 Average, and Percent Change in the Percent of Births to Unmarried Women, 1999–2000 to 2001–2002, and Rank Order of States with Respect to Their Change (in order of largest decline to largest increase) and Rank Order of Territories (ranked separately from States)," Centers for Disease Control and Prevention, National Center for Health Statistics, http://www.cdc.gov/nchs/data/welfare/bonint04.pdf (accessed September 20, 2005)

FIGURE 3.7

States with laws regarding fetuses as victims, June 2005

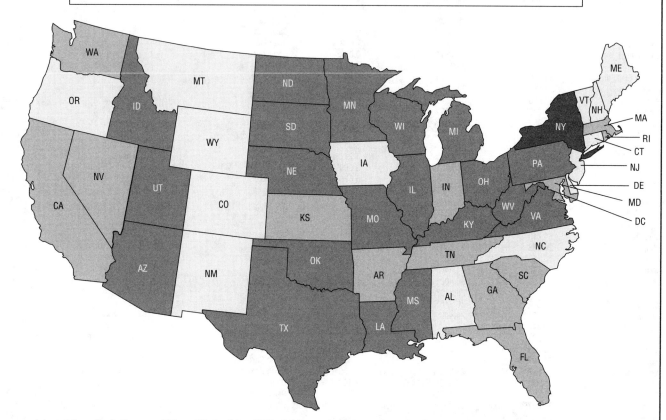

These states have homicide laws that regard fetuses as victims at any stage of prenatal development.

These states have homicide laws that regard fetuses as victims but only at certain stages of prenatal development.

These states do not recognize the killing of an unborn child as homicide.

New York has conflicting laws. One statute dictates that the killing of a fetus after 24 weeks of pregnancy is homicide. Yet a different statute defines a "person" as "a human being who has been born and is alive."

SOURCE: Adapted from "Full-Coverage Unborn Victim States," "Partial-Coverage Unborn Victim States," and "Conflicting Statutes," in *State Homicide Laws That Recognize Unborn Victims*, National Right to Life Committee, June 8, 2005, http://www.nrlc.org/Unborn_Victims/Statehomicidelaws092302 .html (accessed August 17, 2005)

CHAPTER 4
ABORTION IN THE UNITED STATES: A STATISTICAL STUDY

WHO COLLECTS ABORTION DATA?

There are two major sources for abortion statistics. The Centers for Disease Control and Prevention (CDC) of the U.S. Department of Health and Human Services collects abortion statistics for the U.S. government. The Alan Guttmacher Institute (AGI), a private organization that studies reproductive health issues and strongly supports the position that abortion is an acceptable option, conducts periodic surveys of abortions performed in the United States and throughout the world.

The CDC compiles abortion information collected by state health departments, hospitals, and other medical facilities. This data comes from fifty-two reporting areas—the fifty states, the District of Columbia, and New York City. The AGI, in contrast, directly contacts all known abortion providers for its periodic surveys and follows up its inquiries by letter and telephone. Thus, the AGI data is considered to be the most accurate data available.

The total number of abortions reported to the CDC by the individual states generally is lower than that collected by the AGI. The CDC believes that the number of abortions performed in physicians' offices probably is underreported more often than are those done in hospitals and other medical facilities. Because most abortions in physicians' offices usually are performed in the early stages of pregnancy, the CDC's early-abortion counts are very likely less than the actual numbers.

HOW MANY ABORTIONS?

CDC Data

The latest CDC survey data of legal induced abortions are compiled in "Abortion Surveillance—United States, 2001" (*Morbidity and Mortality Weekly Report, Surveillance Summaries*, vol. 53, no. SS-09, November 26, 2004). There has been a consistent decrease in the number of abortions per year since 1996. For 2001, 853,485 abortions were reported. It is difficult to compare this number with years prior to 1998, because the more recent data lacks information from certain states, as noted. (See Figure 4.1 and Table 4.1.)

The CDC began its abortion surveillance in 1969, two years after Colorado became the first state to liberalize its abortion statute. From 1970 through 1982 the reported number of abortions increased each year, with the largest percentage of increase occurring between 1970 and 1971. From 1976 through 1982 the annual increase slowed and then dropped slightly in 1983. From 1983 through 1990 the number of abortions increased again, with year-to-year fluctuations of 5% or less. The annual number of abortions has decreased since 1990 (the year in which the number of abortions was the highest reported by the CDC). (See Figure 4.1 and Table 4.1.)

The *abortion ratio* is the number of legal abortions for every one thousand live births in a given year. In 2001 the abortion ratio was 246 legal abortions per one thousand live births, or about one abortion for every four babies born alive. (See Table 4.1.)

The abortion ratio increased steadily from 1970 through 1980 and then remained somewhat stable for most of the next decade. The CDC reported the highest ratio (364 per one thousand live births) in 1984. Since 1987 the abortion ratio has declined steadily, appearing to increase slightly in 1996. However, the source of birth data changed that year. The ratio for 2000 was the lowest recorded since 1974. (See Figure 4.1 and Table 4.1.)

The *abortion rate* refers to the number of abortions performed per one thousand women ages fifteen to forty-four years (the primary childbearing years). The abortion rate rose from five abortions per one thousand women in 1970 to twenty-five per one thousand in 1980. From 1981 through 1993 the rate remained stable at twenty-three to

FIGURE 4.1

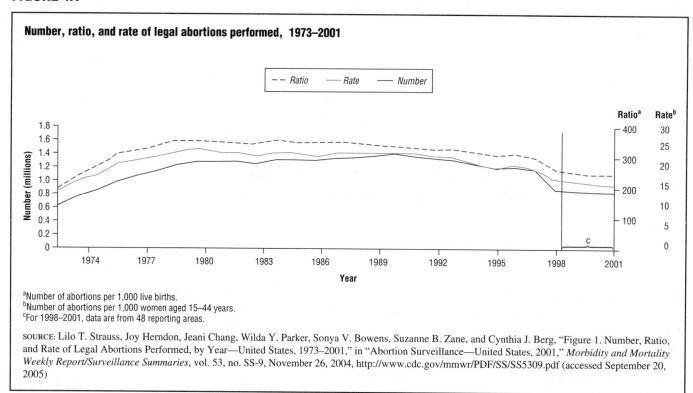

Number, ratio, and rate of legal abortions performed, 1973–2001

[a]Number of abortions per 1,000 live births.
[b]Number of abortions per 1,000 women aged 15–44 years.
[c]For 1998–2001, data are from 48 reporting areas.

SOURCE: Lilo T. Strauss, Joy Herndon, Jeani Chang, Wilda Y. Parker, Sonya V. Bowens, Suzanne B. Zane, and Cynthia J. Berg, "Figure 1. Number, Ratio, and Rate of Legal Abortions Performed, by Year—United States, 1973–2001," in "Abortion Surveillance—United States, 2001," *Morbidity and Mortality Weekly Report/Surveillance Summaries*, vol. 53, no. SS-9, November 26, 2004, http://www.cdc.gov/mmwr/PDF/SS/SS5309.pdf (accessed September 20, 2005)

twenty-four abortions per one thousand women. The abortion rate declined to twenty-one in 1994 and to twenty in 1995. From 1995 to 1997 the rate remained stable at around twenty abortions performed per one thousand women. Since then the rate further declined to seventeen in 1998 and 1999, and then to sixteen in 2000 and 2001. (See Figure 4.1 and Table 4.1.)

The CDC suggests that the overall decreasing abortion rates may be the result of several factors:

- A shift in the age distribution of women of child-bearing age toward the older and, subsequently, less fertile ages

- A decreased number of unplanned pregnancies

- A reduced access to abortion services

- Changes in birth control practices, including an increased use of contraception, particularly in the use of long-acting hormonal methods and condoms by young women

Alan Guttmacher Institute Data

The AGI started collecting data on abortion in 1973, the year of the *Roe v. Wade* ruling. Because the AGI directly surveys abortion providers, its abortion counts generally have been higher than those reported by the CDC. For instance, the total number of abortions reported to the CDC in 1997 was 12% lower than the number AGI reported. According to the AGI, the abortion rate for women

ages fifteen to forty-four was 20.9 in 2002 and 21.1 in 2001. (See Figure 4.2.) The CDC's most recent data, from 2001, calculated the rate at sixteen abortions per one thousand women in the same age group. (See Table 4.1.)

CHARACTERISTICS OF WOMEN SEEKING ABORTION

According to the CDC's "Abortion Surveillance—United States, 2001," slightly more than half (51.5%) of the women who had abortions in 2001 were younger than twenty-five years of age. Most were white (55.4%), unmarried (81.6%), and in the first two months of pregnancy (59.1%). (See Table 4.2.)

Age

Women in the twenty- to twenty-four-year-old age group obtained the greatest proportion of abortions in 2001—one-third (33.6%) of the total. Nearly one-quarter (22.8%) were obtained by those ages twenty-five to twenty-nine, and slightly more than one-sixth (17.0%) were obtained by women ages fifteen to nineteen years. Less than 1% were obtained by women younger than fifteen years. Women ages thirty to thirty-four had 14.7% of abortions in 2001, and women thirty-five years and older had 11.3%. (See Table 4.3.)

In 2001 the majority of abortions (nearly 60%) were early abortions—those obtained during the first eight weeks of pregnancy. The percentage of early abortions had grown rather steadily over the previous twenty-eight

TABLE 4.1

Number, ratio, and rate of legal abortions, 1970–2001

Year	Number of legal abortions	Ratio[a]	Rate[b]	No. of areas reporting Central health agency[c]	No. of areas reporting Hospitals/ facilities[d]
All reporting areas					
1970	193,491	52	5	18	7
1971	485,816	137	11	19	7
1972	586,760	180	13	21	8
1973	615,831	196	14	26	26
1974	763,476	242	17	37	15
1975	854,853	272	18	39	13
1976	988,267	312	21	41	11
1977	1,079,430	325	22	46	6
1978	1,157,776	347	23	48	4
1979	1,251,921	358	24	47	5
1980	1,297,606	359	25	47	5
1981	1,300,760	358	24	46	6
1982	1,303,980	354	24	46	6
1983	1,268,987	349	23	46	6
1984	1,333,521	364	24	44	8
1985	1,328,570	354	24	44	8
1986	1,328,112	354	23	43	9
1987	1,353,671	356	24	45	7
1988	1,371,285	352	24	45	7
1989	1,396,658	346	24	45	7
1990	1,429,247	344	24	46	6
1991	1,388,937	338	24	47	5
1992	1,359,146	334	23	47	5
1993	1,330,414	333	23	47	5
1994	1,267,415	321	21	47	5
1995	1,210,883	311	20	48	4
1996	1,225,937	315[e]	21	48	4
1997	1,186,039	306	20	48	4
1998[e]	884,273	264	17	48	0
1999[e]	861,789	256	17	48	0
2000[g]	857,475	245	16	49	0
2001[g]	853,485	246	16	49	0
48 reporting areas[h]					
1995	908,243	277	18	47	1
1996	934,549	285[e]	18	47	1
1997	900,171	274	17	46	2
1998	884,273	264	17	48	0
1999	861,789	256	17	48	0
2000	850,293	246	16	48	0
2001	846,447	247	16	48	0

[a]Number of abortions per 1,000 live births.
[b]Number of abortions per 1,000 females aged 15–44 years.
[c]State health departments and the health departments of New York City and the District of Columbia.
[d]Hospitals or other medical facilities in state.
[e]Beginning in 1996, the ratio was based on births reported by the National Center for Health Statistics, CDC.
[f]Without estimates for Alaska, California, New Hampshire, and Oklahoma, which did not report number of legal abortions.
[g]Without estimates for Alaska, California, and New Hampshire, which did not report number of legal abortions.
[h]Without estimates for Alaska, California, and New Hampshire, which did not report number of legal abortions for 1998–2001, and for Oklahoma, which did not report for 1998–1999.

SOURCE: Lilo T. Strauss, Joy Herndon, Jeani Chang, Wilda Y. Parker, Sonya V. Bowens, Suzanne B. Zane, and Cynthia J. Berg, "Table 2. Number, Ratio, and Rate of Legal Abortions and Source of Reporting for All Reporting Areas and for the 48 Areas That Reported in 2000, by Year—United States, 1970–2001," in "Abortion Surveillance—United States, 2001," *Morbidity and Mortality Weekly Report/Surveillance Summaries*, vol. 53, no. SS-9, November 26, 2004, http://www.cdc.gov/mmwr/PDF/SS/SS5309.pdf (accessed September 20, 2005)

years, from slightly over 36% in 1973. (See Table 4.2.) As Figure 4.3 shows, the percentage of women who obtained an early abortion in 2001 increased with age. Approximately 66% to 67% of women ages thirty and over obtained early abortions.

In 2001 although less than 1% of all abortions were obtained by teenagers younger than fifteen years of age (see Table 4.3), their abortion ratio (number of abortions per one thousand live births) was the highest. (See Figure 4.4.) Put simply, within this age group the percentage of abortions was small, but of those adolescents who got pregnant, most chose abortion.

In 2001 the abortion ratio was lowest for women ages thirty to thirty-four years (147 per one thousand live births). (See Table 4.4.) Women ages thirty-five to thirty-nine and women twenty-five to twenty-nine had the second- and third-lowest ratio of abortions to live births (180 and 200 per one thousand live births, respectively).

FIGURE 4.2

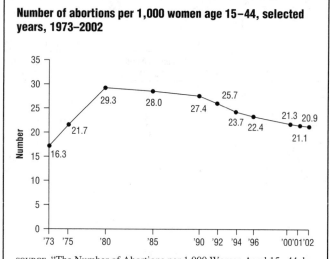

Number of abortions per 1,000 women age 15–44, selected years, 1973–2002

SOURCE: "The Number of Abortions per 1,000 Women Aged 15–44, by Year," in "Induced Abortion in the United States" in *Facts in Brief*, The Alan Guttmacher Institute (AGI), May 2005, http://www.agi-usa.org/pubs/fb_induced_abortion.pdf (accessed September 20, 2005)

With the exception of the thirty-five- to thirty-nine-year-old age group, the abortion ratio increased from 1974 through the early 1980s. It declined thereafter, especially for the youngest and oldest groups, with abortion ratios for the twenty- to thirty-four-year-old age group remaining relatively stable since the mid-1980s. (See Figure 4.5.)

Race and Ethnicity

In 2001 more than half (54.1%) of women in the United States who had an abortion were white, about one-third (35.7%) were African-American, and 7.8% were of other races. (See Table 4.5.) The abortion ratio for African-American women (491 per one thousand live births) was approximately three times the ratio for white women (165 per one thousand live births). Similarly, the abortion rate for African-American women (twenty-nine per one thousand women) was also approximately three times the rate for white women (ten per one thousand women).

The abortion ratio for Hispanic women in 2001 was only slightly lower than that for non-Hispanic women (230 versus 232 respectively per one thousand live births). However, the abortion rate for Hispanic women was considerably higher than that for non-Hispanic women (twenty-two versus fourteen abortions, respectively, per one thousand women). (See Table 4.6.)

For women in all age groups, fertility was higher for Hispanic women at eighty-two births per one thousand women than for non-Hispanic women: 61.0 for white women, 56.5 for white, non-Hispanic women, 64.6 for African-American women, and 55.4 for Asian and Pacific Islander women. (See Table 4.7.)

Marital Status

In 2001, as in past years, unmarried women (divorced, widowed, or never married) comprised the greatest proportion of those who had an abortion (81.6%). Married women, including those who are separated from their husbands, comprised only 18.4% of those who had an abortion in 2001. (See Table 4.2.)

Contraceptive Use Prior to Pregnancy

Rachel K. Jones, Jacqueline E. Darroch, and Stanley K. Henshaw, in "Contraceptive Use among U.S. Women Having Abortions in 2000–2001" (*Perspectives on Sexual and Reproductive Health*, vol. 34, no. 6, November/December 2002), reported that 46.3% of women receiving abortions in 2000 had not used a contraceptive method in the month they conceived, primarily due to perceived low risk of pregnancy (33% of nonusers) and concerns about contraception (32% of nonusers). More than half of women receiving abortions (53.7%) did use a contraceptive method in the month of conception, however. Of these women, most used the male condom (27.6%) followed by the pill (13.6%). (See Table 4.8.) Some women using the condom and the pill (14% and 13%, respectively) believed that they had used the method perfectly, yet had become pregnant. Nevertheless, most women cited inconsistent use of the method as the reason for becoming pregnant—49% of condom users and 76% of pill users gave this reason.

Previous Live Births and Previous Abortions

In 2001 more than half of all women who had an abortion had never obtained one before (54.6%), whereas about one-fourth (25.5%) had obtained one previous abortion and 18.3% had obtained two or more abortions. (See Table 4.9.)

WHY DO WOMEN HAVE ABORTIONS?

The AGI, in "Induced Abortions in the United States: Facts in Brief," (http://www.agi-usa.org/pubs/fb_induced_abortion.html, May, 18, 2005), notes that each year almost half (49%) of the 6.3 million pregnancies in the U.S. are unplanned. Half of the women with unplanned pregnancies obtain an abortion. On average, women give at least three reasons for choosing abortion:

- About three-quarters say that having a baby would interfere with their work, school, or other responsibilities.

- About two-thirds say they cannot afford a child.

- About one-half say they do not want to be a single parent or are having problems with their husband or partner.

TABLE 4.2

Characteristics of women who obtained legal abortions, selected years, 1973–2001

Characteristic	1973	1976	1979	1982	1985	1988	1991	1994	1997	2000	2001
Reported no. of legal abortions	615,831	988,267	1,251,921	1,303,980	1,328,570	1,371,285	1,388,937	1,267,415	1,186,039	857,475	853,485
Reported no. of legal abortions excluding AK, CA, NH, OK[a]									900,171	850,293	846,447
						Percentage distribution[b]					
Residence											
In-state/area	74.8	90.0	90.0	92.9	92.4	91.4	91.7	91.5	91.8	91.3	91.3
Out-of-state/area	25.2	10.0	10.0	7.1	7.6	8.6	8.3	8.5	8.2	8.7	8.7
Age (years)											
<19	32.7	32.1	30.0	27.1	26.3	25.3	21.0	20.2	20.1	18.8	18.1
20–24	32.0	33.3	35.4	35.1	34.7	32.8	34.4	33.5	31.7	32.8	33.4
>25	35.3	34.6	34.6	37.8	39.0	41.9	44.6	46.3	48.2	48.4	48.5
Race[c]											
White	72.5	66.6	68.9	68.5	66.7	64.4	63.9	60.6	58.4	56.6	55.4
Black	27.5	33.4	31.1	31.5	29.8	31.1	32.5	34.7	35.9	36.3	36.6
Other[d]	—[e]	—	—	—	3.5	4.5	3.6	4.7	5.7	7.1	8.0
Ethnicity											
Hispanic	—	—	—	—	—	—	13.2	14.1	15.6	17.2	17.1
Non-Hispanic	—	—	—	—	—	—	86.8	85.9	84.4	82.8	82.9
Marital status											
Married	27.4	24.6	24.7	22.0	19.3	20.3	21.4	19.9	19.0	18.7	18.4
Unmarried	72.6	75.4	75.3	78.0	80.7	79.7	78.6	80.1	81.0	81.3	81.6
Number of live births[f]											
0	48.6	47.7	58.1	57.8	56.3	52.4	47.8	46.2	42.2	40.0	45.2
1	18.8	20.7	19.1	20.3	21.6	23.4	25.3	25.9	27.6	27.7	25.2
2	14.2	15.4	13.8	13.9	14.5	16.0	17.5	17.8	19.1	20.1	18.4
3	8.7	8.3	5.5	5.1	5.1	5.6	6.4	6.7	7.3	7.9	7.3
>4	9.7	7.9	3.5	2.9	2.5	2.6	3.0	3.4	3.8	4.3	3.9
Type of procedure											
Curettage	88.4	92.8	95.0	96.5	97.5	98.6	99.0	99.1	98.3	97.9	95.5
Suction curettage	74.9	82.6	91.3	90.7	94.6	95.1	96.5	96.5	97.3	95.6	92.8
Sharp curettage	13.5	10.2	3.7	5.8	2.9	3.5	2.5	2.6	1.0	2.3	2.7
Intrauterine instillation	10.3	6.0	3.3	2.5	1.7	1.1	0.6	0.5	0.4	0.4	0.6
Hysterotomy/hysterectomy[g]	0.7	0.3	0.1	0	0.8	0.3	0.4	0.4	1.3	1.7	3.9
Other[g]	0.6	0.9	1.6	1.0							
Weeks of gestation											
<8	36.1	47.0	52.1	50.6	50.3	48.7	52.4	53.7	55.4	58.1	59.1
<6	—	—	—	—	—	—	—	15.7[h]	17.6[i]	23.3[j]	24.9[j]
7	—	—	—	—	—	—	—	16.5[h]	18.1[i]	17.8[j]	17.9[j]
8	—	—	—	—	—	—	—	21.6[h]	22.0	19.8	19.0
9–10	29.4	228.1	26.9	26.7	26.6	26.4	25.1	23.5	22.0	19.8	19.0
11–12	17.9	14.4	2.5	12.4	12.5	12.7	11.5	10.9	10.7	10.2	10.0
13–15	6.9	4.5	4.2	5.3	5.9	6.6	6.1	6.3	6.2	6.2	6.2
16–20	8.0	5.1	3.4	3.9	3.9	4.5	3.8	4.3	4.3	4.3	4.3
>21	1.7	0.9	0.9	1.1	0.8	1.1	1.1	1.3	1.4	1.4	1.4

[a]With one exception, no characteristics were available for the excluded states in years before 1998. Oklahoma data available for 2000 and 2001.
[b]Based on known values in data from all areas reporting a given characteristic with ≤15% unknowns. The number of areas adequately reporting a given characteristic varied. For 2001, the number of areas included for residence was 46; age, 48; race, 39; ethnicity, 32; marital status, 39; number of live births, 41; type of procedure, 45; and weeks of gestation, 42. Early numbers might differ (by 0.1%) from numbers previously published because of adjusting percentages to total 100.0%.
[c]Black race reported as black and other races through 1984. For 1990–1997, one state included "other" races with blacks.
[d]Includes all other races.
[e]Not available.
[f]For 1973 and 1976, data indicate number of living children.
[g]Hysterotomy/hysterectomy included in "other" beginning in 1985. "Other" also includes procedures reported as "other" and medical (nonsurgical) procedures beginning in 1997. For 2001, a total of 20,093 medical (nonsurgical) procedures were reported.
[h]Data for 38 of 40 areas reporting weeks of gestation.
[i]Data for 40 of 42 areas reporting weeks of gestation.
[j]Data for 41 of 43 areas reporting weeks of gestation.

SOURCE: Adapted from Lilo T. Strauss, Joy Herndon, Jeani Chang, Wilda Y. Parker, Sonya V. Bowens, Suzanne B. Zane, and Cynthia J. Berg, "Table 1. Characteristics of Women Who Obtained Legal Abortions—United States, 1973–2001," in "Abortion Surveillance—United States, 2001," *Morbidity and Mortality Weekly Report/Surveillance Summaries*, vol. 53, no. SS-9, November 26, 2004, http://www.cdc.gov/mmwr/PDF/SS/SS5309.pdf (accessed September 20, 2005)

TABLE 4.3

Legal abortions, by demographic characteristics, selected states, 2001

Characteristics	White		Black		Other		Total	
	Number	Percent (%)	Number	Percent (%)	Number	Percent (%)	Number	Percent (%)
Age groups (years)								
<15	1,475	(0.5)	1,879	(0.9)	160	(0.4)	3,514	(0.6)
15–19	54,135	(17.9)	32,654	(16.3)	5,567	(13.8)	92,356	(17.0)
20–24	102,072	(33.8)	68,136	(34.0)	12,053	(30.0)	182,261	(33.6)
25–29	64,397	(21.3)	49,766	(24.8)	9,592	(23.8)	123,755	(22.8)
30–34	43,232	(14.3)	29,422	(14.7)	6,945	(17.3)	79,599	(14.7)
35–39	26,713	(8.8)	14,446	(7.2)	4,216	(10.5)	45,375	(8.4)
≥40	10,049	(3.3)	4,064	(2.0)	1,691	(4.2)	15,804	(2.9)
Total[a]	302,073	(100.0)	200,367	(100.0)	40,224	(100.0)	542,664	(100.0)
Marital status								
Married	58,627	(20.5)	21,421	(11.8)	13,578	(35.5)	93,626	(18.5)
Unmarried	227,187	(79.5)	160,729	(88.2)	24,706	(64.5)	412,622	(81.5)
Total[b]	285,814	(100.0)	182,150	(100.0)	38,284	(100.0)	506,248	(100.0)

[a]Data from 36 states and New York City; excludes five states from which race was reported as unknown for >15% of women. Percentages might not add to 100.0 because of rounding.
[b]Data from 33 states and New York City; excludes five states from which race or marital status was reported as unknown for >15% of women.

SOURCE: Lilo T. Strauss, Joy Herndon, Jeani Chang, Wilda Y. Parker, Sonya V. Bowens, Suzanne B. Zane, and Cynthia J. Berg, "Table 14. Reported Legal Abortions, by Known Race, Age Group, and Marital Status of Women Who Obtained an Abortion—Selected States, United States, 2001," in "Abortion Surveillance—United States, 2001," *Morbidity and Mortality Weekly Report/Surveillance Summaries*, vol. 53, no. SS-9, November 26, 2004, http://www.cdc.gov/mmwr/PDF/SS/SS5309.pdf (accessed September 20, 2005)

FIGURE 4.3

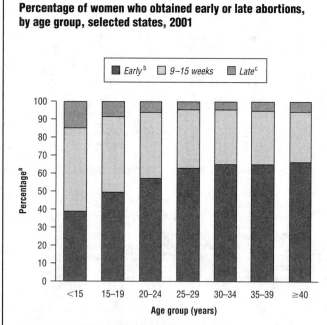

Percentage of women who obtained early or late abortions, by age group, selected states, 2001

Legend: ■ Early[b] □ 9–15 weeks ▨ Late[c]

(Y-axis: Percentage[a], 0 to 100; X-axis: Age group (years): <15, 15–19, 20–24, 25–29, 30–34, 35–39, ≥40)

Note: Data are for 39 states and New York City; excludes three states where gestational age was unknown for >15% of women.
[a]Based on total known weeks of gestation.
[b]≤8 weeks of gestation.
[c]≥16 weeks of gestation.

SOURCE: Lilo T. Strauss, Joy Herndon, Jeani Chang, Wilda Y. Parker, Sonya V. Bowens, Suzanne B. Zane, and Cynthia J. Berg, "Figure 4. Percentage of Women Who Obtained Early or Late Abortions, by Age Group of Women—Selected States, United States, 2001," in "Abortion Surveillance—United States, 2001," *Morbidity and Mortality Weekly Report/Surveillance Summaries*, vol. 53, no. SS-9, November 26, 2004, http://www.cdc.gov/mmwr/PDF/SS/SS5309.pdf (accessed September 20, 2005)

WHERE DO WOMEN GO FOR AN ABORTION?

In 2001, as in previous years, the largest reported numbers of abortions were performed in New York City (91,792), Florida (85,589), and Texas (77,409). New York and Texas are two of the most populated states; California, which is the most populous state and in previous years had the largest numbers of abortions performed there, did not report the number of abortions for 1999 or 2001. The fewest abortions were performed in Idaho (738), South Dakota (895), and North Dakota (1,216). (See Table 4.10.)

Abortion rates by state of occurrence do not necessarily reflect the number of abortions obtained by residents. Many women travel out of state for abortions because of a lack of providers or because of restrictive laws, such as required parental notification and consent (see chapters 10 and 11), waiting periods, and required counseling that involves more than one visit to the provider. See Table 4.11 for a list of states that require a waiting period before an abortion can be obtained and for those that require biased counseling. Biased counseling means that the woman is counseled in a way that promotes choices other than abortion.

For women obtaining an abortion in 2001 whose state of residence was reported, 90.3% had their abortion in the state where they lived. That is, 8.7% of reported abortions (on average) were obtained by out-of-state residents, with a wide range from 0.3% in Hawaii to 56% in the District of Columbia. (See Table 4.10.)

FIGURE 4.4

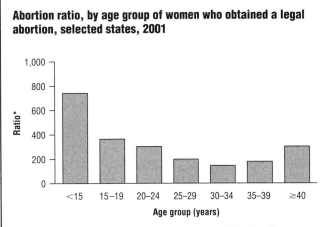

Abortion ratio, by age group of women who obtained a legal abortion, selected states, 2001

Note: Data are from 46 states, the District of Columbia, and New York City.
*Number of abortions per 1,000 live births.

SOURCE: Lilo T. Strauss, Joy Herndon, Jeani Chang, Wilda Y. Parker, Sonya V. Bowens, Suzanne B. Zane, and Cynthia J. Berg, "Figure 2. Abortion Ratio, by Age Group of Women Who Obtained a Legal Abortion—Selected States, United States, 2001," in "Abortion Surveillance—United States, 2001," *Morbidity and Mortality Weekly Report/Surveillance Summaries*, vol. 53, no. SS-9, November 26, 2004, http://www.cdc.gov/mmwr/PDF/SS/SS5309.pdf (accessed September 20, 2005)

AVAILABILITY OF ABORTION PROVIDERS

The AGI notes that in 2000, 87% of U.S. counties had no abortion providers, up from 86% in 1996 and 77% in 1978. About one-third (34%) of women of childbearing age (fifteen to forty-four years old) lived in counties with no known providers. In North Dakota, South Dakota, West Virginia, Mississippi, and Wyoming, approximately four of five women of reproductive age lived in counties with no abortion providers. (See Table 4.12.) Nearly one-third of the country's metropolitan areas lacked abortion services, and for many women in rural areas, obtaining an abortion entailed traveling hundreds of miles from their residence.

According to the AGI, the number of abortion providers in the United States has decreased from a high of 2,908 in 1982 to about 2,000 in 1996 to 1,819 in 2000—11% fewer than in 1996. (See Table 4.12.) To compare, this is less of a decline than from the years 1992 to 1996, which saw a 14% decline in the number of abortion providers. The number of providers in 2000 was 37% lower than the high in 1982.

Between 1996 and 2000 nine states had an increase in the number of providers and thirty-eight states and the District of Columbia saw a decrease. The number of providers did not change in the three remaining states. (See Table 4.12.) A survey conducted in 1997 of obstetricians and gynecologists who perform abortions revealed that more than half of the providers were ages fifty or older, which some believe indicates that the

number of providers will decline as current providers retire. However, according to the AGI in "Abortion Incidence and Services in the United States in 2000" (Stanley K. Henshaw and Lawrence B. Finer, *Perspectives on Sexual and Reproductive Health*, vol. 35, no. 1, January/February 2003), the approval and use of medical abortion (abortion pills) began to play a "small but significant role in abortion provision."

Finer and Henshaw also reported that clinics, including physicians' offices, perform most (93%) of the abortions in the United States, an increase of 3% from 1996. Of the 1,819 providers in 2000, 46% were clinics. Hospitals made up one-third of abortion providers in 2000, nearly the same as in 1996. However, the proportion of abortions performed in hospitals decreased from 7% to 5% from 1996 to 2000. One-fifth (21%) of providers were physicians' offices, down from 23% in 1996. In contrast, in 1973, the year of the *Roe v. Wade* decision, hospitals made up 81% of all providers. In 2000 physicians' offices (23% of providers) accounted for only 2% of the abortions performed, a steady decline from 4% in 1992 and 3% in 1996.

Abortion Medical Training

Abortion continues to be the most frequently performed surgical procedure in the United States. The AGI states, "Traditionally, residency programs in obstetrics and gynecology have been the only programs to formally train residents in abortion procedures and in the management of complications from spontaneous and elective abortions." The legalization of abortion in 1973 did not bring about any marked increase in obstetrics and gynecology resident training in abortion. In fact, from the late 1970s the number of residents trained in abortion was on a steady decline, which caused a major shortage of abortion providers. However, this decades-long trend seems to have changed, and opportunities for training have increased.

In 1998 the National Abortion Federation (NAF), the professional association of abortion providers in the United States and Canada, conducted a survey, asking the 261 accredited U.S. residency programs in obstetrics and gynecology about the opportunities available to medical students for first- and second-trimester abortion training. The results were published in a report, "Abortion Training in U.S. Obstetrics and Gynecology Residency Programs, 1998," by Rene Almeling, Laureen Tews, and Susan Dudley (*Family Planning Perspectives*, vol. 32, no. 6, 2000). Of the 179 programs that responded to the survey, 81% reported that they offer first-trimester abortion training—46% offer it routinely and 34% offer it as an elective. (See Table 4.13.) Second-trimester training is offered by 74% of programs—44% routinely and 29% as an elective. Some programs that do not offer training

TABLE 4.4

Abortion ratio, by age group of women who obtained a legal abortion and state of occurrence, selected states, 2001

State	≤15 Number	(%)	15–19 Number	(%)	20–24 Number	(%)	25–29 Number	(%)	30–34 Number	(%)	35–39 Number	(%)	≥40 Number	(%)	Unknown Number	(%)	Total Number	(%)[a]
Alabama	104	(0.8)	2,407	(18.0)	4,904	(36.6)	3,037	(22.7)	1,683	(12.6)	933	(7.0)	313	(2.3)	1	(0)	13,382	(100.0)
Arizona	47	(0.6)	1,488	(17.9)	2,650	(31.9)	1,708	(20.6)	1,111	(13.4)	605	(7.3)	228	(2.7)	465	(5.6)	8,302	(100.0)
Arkansas	54	(0.9)	1,130	(19.1)	2,046	(34.5)	1,301	(22.0)	781	(13.2)	440	(7.4)	147	(2.5)	25	(0.4)	5,924	(100.0)
Colorado	30	(0.6)	976	(21.1)	1,511	(32.6)	891	(19.2)	587	(12.7)	443	(9.6)	183	(3.9)	12	(0.3)	4,633	(100.0)
Connecticut	67	(0.5)	2,739	(20.6)	4,322	(32.6)	2,712	(20.4)	1,839	(13.9)	1,090	(8.2)	386	(2.9)	110	(0.8)	13,265	(100.0)
Delaware[b]	40	(1.1)	708	(20.3)	1,239	(35.5)	724	(20.8)	446	(12.8)	245	(7.0)	87	(2.5)	0	(0)	3,489	(100.0)
Dist. of Columbia	46	(0.9)	1,107	(20.6)	1,892	(35.1)	1,187	(22.0)	669	(12.4)	363	(6.7)	120	(2.2)	1	(0)	5,385	(100.0)
Georgia	305	(0.9)	5,176	(15.6)	11,116	(33.4)	7,880	(23.7)	5,160	(15.5)	2,724	(8.2)	887	(2.7)	0	(0)	33,248	(100.0)
Hawaii	23	(0.6)	884	(22.1)	1,266	(31.7)	764	(19.1)	548	(13.7)	358	(9.0)	156	(3.9)	0	(0)	3,999	(100.0)
Idaho	4	(0.5)	168	(22.8)	220	(29.8)	145	(19.6)	95	(12.9)	71	(9.6)	34	(4.6)	1	(0.1)	738	(100.0)
Illinois[c]	349	(0.7)	8,867	(19.0)	14,923	(32.1)	10,432	(22.4)	6,649	(14.3)	3,692	(7.9)	1,282	(2.8)	352	(0.8)	46,546	(100.0)
Indiana	68	(0.6)	1,970	(16.6)	4,309	(36.3)	2,595	(21.9)	1,538	(13.0)	854	(7.2)	331	(2.8)	210	(1.8)	11,875	(100.0)
Iowa[b]	38	(0.7)	1,122	(19.6)	2,035	(35.6)	1,146	(20.0)	756	(13.2)	454	(7.9)	171	(3.0)	0	(0)	5,722	(100.0)
Kansas	81	(0.7)	2,350	(19.1)	4,271	(34.8)	2,588	(21.1)	1,693	(13.8)	973	(7.9)	328	(2.7)	0	(0)	12,284	(100.0)
Kentucky	28	(0.7)	613	(16.3)	1,295	(34.4)	862	(22.9)	500	(13.3)	323	(8.6)	116	(3.1)	27	(0.7)	3,764	(100.0)
Louisiana	85	(0.8)	1,868	(17.1)	4,001	(36.6)	2,611	(23.9)	1,378	(12.6)	700	(6.4)	251	(2.3)	38	(0.3)	10,932	(100.0)
Maine	8	(0.3)	544	(21.6)	834	(33.2)	494	(19.6)	302	(12.0)	226	(9.0)	89	(3.5)	18	(0.7)	2,515	(100.0)
Maryland[b]	96	(0.8)	2,170	(17.1)	4,358	(34.3)	2,918	(23.0)	1,910	(15.0)	968	(7.6)	281	(2.2)	0	(0)	12,701	(100.0)
Massachusetts	78	(0.3)	3,735	(14.2)	8,163	(31.0)	5,676	(21.6)	3,926	(14.9)	2,479	(9.4)	1,037	(3.9)	1,199	(4.6)	26,293	(100.0)
Michigan	150	(0.5)	5,034	(17.8)	9,375	(33.2)	6,510	(23.1)	4,096	(14.5)	2,176	(7.7)	728	(2.6)	151	(0.5)	28,220	(100.0)
Minnesota	63	(0.4)	2,450	(16.5)	5,053	(34.1)	3,252	(21.9)	2,182	(14.7)	1,342	(9.0)	490	(3.3)	0	(0)	14,832	(100.0)
Mississippi	38	(1.1)	633	(17.8)	1,326	(37.2)	839	(23.5)	426	(11.9)	224	(6.3)	76	(2.1)	4	(0.1)	3,566	(100.0)
Missouri	46	(0.6)	1,249	(16.0)	2,631	(33.7)	1,739	(22.3)	1,167	(15.0)	703	(9.0)	260	(3.3)	2	(0)	7,797	(100.0)
Montana	13	(0.6)	526	(22.4)	794	(33.8)	410	(17.4)	286	(12.2)	220	(9.4)	93	(4.0)	8	(0.3)	2,350	(100.0)
Nebraska	19	(0.5)	808	(20.3)	1,360	(34.2)	844	(21.2)	510	(12.8)	316	(7.9)	125	(3.1)	0	(0)	3,982	(100.0)
Nevada	52	(0.5)	1,796	(17.8)	2,965	(29.3)	2,227	(22.0)	1,523	(15.1)	949	(9.4)	297	(2.9)	301	(3.0)	10,110	(100.0)
New Jersey[d]	242	(0.7)	5,978	(17.8)	11,090	(33.0)	7,613	(22.7)	4,836	(14.4)	2,794	(8.3)	966	(2.9)	87	(0.3)	33,606	(100.0)
New Mexico	29	(0.6)	1,089	(21.1)	1,752	(33.9)	1,029	(19.9)	659	(12.8)	394	(7.6)	172	(3.3)	42	(0.8)	5,166	(100.0)
New York	773	(0.6)	22,512	(17.7)	38,578	(30.4)	28,574	(22.5)	20,233	(15.9)	11,982	(9.4)	3,998	(3.1)	452	(0.4)	127,102	(100.0)
City	564	(0.6)	14,999	(16.3)	27,100	(29.5)	21,549	(23.5)	15,376	(16.8)	8,981	(9.8)	2,922	(3.2)	301	(0.3)	91,792	(100.0)
State	209	(0.6)	7,513	(21.3)	11,478	(32.5)	7,025	(19.9)	4,857	(13.8)	3,001	(8.5)	1,076	(3.0)	151	(0.4)	35,310	(100.0)
North Carolina	186	(0.6)	4,996	(16.4)	10,184	(33.5)	6,977	(22.9)	4,079	(13.4)	2,333	(7.7)	735	(2.4)	929	(3.1)	30,419	(100.0)
North Dakota	4	(0.3)	285	(23.4)	451	(37.1)	217	(17.8)	129	(10.6)	96	(7.9)	32	(2.6)	2	(0.2)	1,216	(100.0)
Ohio	286	(0.8)	6,485	(17.3)	12,710	(33.9)	8,531	(22.8)	5,299	(14.1)	2,956	(7.9)	1,178	(3.1)	19	(0.1)	37,464	(100.0)
Oklahoma	49	(0.7)	1,317	(18.7)	2,436	(34.6)	1,541	(21.9)	954	(13.6)	505	(7.2)	198	(2.8)	38	(0.5)	7,038	(100.0)
Oregon	64	(0.4)	2,622	(18.4)	4,922	(34.5)	3,064	(21.5)	2,024	(14.2)	1,158	(8.1)	403	(2.8)	15	(0.1)	14,272	(100.0)
Pennsylvania	285	(0.8)	6,463	(17.6)	12,212	(33.2)	8,156	(22.2)	5,467	(14.8)	3,192	(8.7)	1,044	(2.8)	1	(0)	36,820	(100.0)
Rhode Island	26	(0.5)	943	(17.3)	1,935	(35.5)	1,117	(20.5)	795	(14.6)	461	(8.5)	178	(3.3)	0	(0)	5,455	(100.0)
South Carolina	50	(0.7)	1,335	(19.0)	2,294	(32.7)	1,539	(21.9)	980	(14.0)	613	(8.7)	203	(2.9)	0	(0)	7,014	(100.0)
South Dakota	4	(0.4)	190	(21.2)	294	(32.8)	190	(21.2)	120	(13.4)	67	(7.5)	30	(3.4)	0	(0)	895	(100.0)
Tennessee	131	(0.8)	2,994	(17.2)	6,114	(35.1)	4,109	(23.6)	2,334	(13.4)	1,283	(7.4)	420	(2.4)	20	(0.1)	17,405	(100.0)

TABLE 4.4

Abortion ratio, by age group of women who obtained a legal abortion and state of occurrence, selected states, 2001 [CONTINUED]

	Age group (years)																	Total	
	≤15		15–19		20–24		25–29		30–34		35–39		≥40		Unknown				
State	Number	(%)	Number	(%)	Number	(%)	Number	(%)	Number	(%)	Number	(%)	Number	(%)	Number	(%)	Number	(%)[a]
Texas	313	(0.4)	11,170	(14.4)	26,940	(34.8)	18,415	(23.8)	11,443	(14.8)	6,186	(8.0)	2,356	(3.0)	586	(0.8)	77,409	(100.0)
Utah	16	(0.4)	595	(16.6)	1,236	(34.4)	780	(21.7)	512	(14.2)	290	(8.1)	97	(2.7)	68	(1.9)	3,594	(100.0)
Vermont	6	(0.4)	323	(21.3)	532	(35.0)	280	(18.4)	179	(11.8)	138	(9.1)	60	(3.9)	1	(0.1)	1,519	(100.0)
Virginia	143	(0.6)	3,961	(16.1)	7,985	(32.5)	5,492	(22.3)	3,814	(15.5)	2,275	(9.3)	762	(3.1)	154	(0.6)	24,586	(100.0)
Washington	138	(0.5)	5,043	(19.7)	8,469	(33.1)	5,288	(20.6)	3,718	(14.5)	2,088	(8.1)	835	(3.3)	41	(0.2)	25,620	(100.0)
West Virginia	11	(0.5)	451	(19.3)	889	(38.1)	461	(19.8)	296	(12.7)	152	(6.5)	47	(2.0)	25	(1.1)	2,332	(100.0)
Wisconsin[b]	76	(0.7)	1,965	(18.4)	3,734	(34.9)	2,333	(21.8)	1,419	(13.3)	854	(8.0)	322	(3.0)	0	(0)	10,703	(100.0)
Wyoming	0	(0)	1	(25.0)	0	(0)	1	(25.0)	2	(50.0)	0	(0)	0	(0)	0	(0)	4	(100.0)
Total	**4,764**	**(0.6)**	**133,236**	**(17.4)**	**253,616**	**(33.1)**	**171,199**	**(22.4)**	**111,053**	**(14.5)**	**63,688**	**(8.3)**	**22,532**	**(2.9)**	**5,405**	**(0.7)**	**765,493**	**(100.0)**
Abortion ratio[e]	744		366		304		200		147		180		304				234	
Abortion rate[f]	1		17		32		23		13		7		2				15	

Note: Data from 46 states, the District of Columbia, and New York City.

[a] Percentages might not add to 100.0 because of rounding.

[b] Includes residents only.

[c] Unpublished small numbers distributed as the known numbers by using data from public use tape. Number of procedures for the ≥45 years age group are included with those of the unknown age group because data were not available separately (have been <0.2% in past years); the category of ≥40 years thus represents the 40–44 years group for Illinois.

[d] Numbers do not include procedures performed by private physicians.

[e] Calculated as the number of legal abortions obtained by women in a given age group per 1,000 live births to women in the same age group for these states. For each state, data for women of unknown age were distributed according to the known age distribution for that state.

[f] Calculated as the number of legal abortions obtained by women in a given age group per 1,000 women in the same age group for these states. Adolescents aged 13–14 years were used for the denominator for the <15 years age group, and women aged 40–44 years were used for the denominator for the ≥40 years age group. For each state, data for women of unknown age were distributed according to the known age distribution for that state.

SOURCE: Lilo T. Strauss, Joy Herndon, Jeani Chang, Wilda Y. Parker, Sonya V. Bowens, Suzanne B. Zane, and Cynthia J. Berg, "Table 4. Reported Legal Abortions, by Age Group of Women Who Obtained an Abortion and State of Occurrence—Selected States, United States, 2001," in "Abortion Surveillance—United States, 2001," *Morbidity and Mortality Weekly Report/Surveillance Summaries*, vol. 53, no. SS-9, November 26, 2004, http://www.cdc.gov/mmwr/PDF/SS/SS5309.pdf (accessed September 20, 2005)

FIGURE 4.5

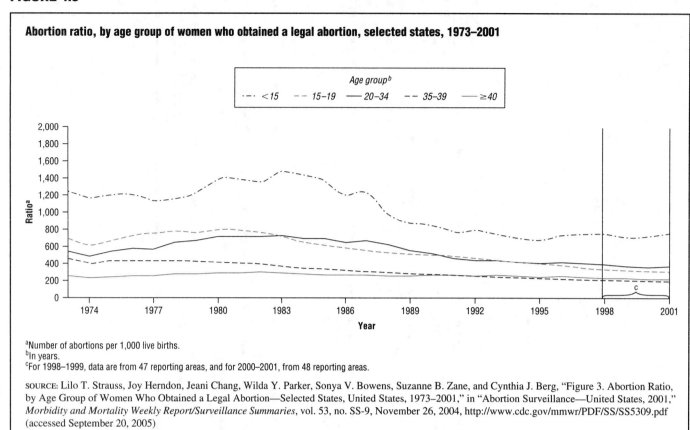

Abortion ratio, by age group of women who obtained a legal abortion, selected states, 1973–2001

[a]Number of abortions per 1,000 live births.
[b]In years.
[c]For 1998–1999, data are from 47 reporting areas, and for 2000–2001, from 48 reporting areas.

SOURCE: Lilo T. Strauss, Joy Herndon, Jeani Chang, Wilda Y. Parker, Sonya V. Bowens, Suzanne B. Zane, and Cynthia J. Berg, "Figure 3. Abortion Ratio, by Age Group of Women Who Obtained a Legal Abortion—Selected States, United States, 1973–2001," in "Abortion Surveillance—United States, 2001," *Morbidity and Mortality Weekly Report/Surveillance Summaries*, vol. 53, no. SS-9, November 26, 2004, http://www.cdc.gov/mmwr/PDF/SS/SS5309.pdf (accessed September 20, 2005)

allow residents to obtain abortion medical training elsewhere. Although 26% of programs indicated that all residents in their programs receive abortion training, 40% said that fewer than half are trained (including 14% that train no residents).

Almeling, Tews, and Dudley note that there is reason to be "cautious" when interpreting the results of the NAF study. Programs that do not offer abortion training may be less likely to respond, or they may feel pressure to report the availability of abortion training because of guidelines from the Accreditation Council for Graduate Medical Education (ACGME). This organization oversees medical education in the United States. It had noticed the trend in the shortage of abortion providers. As a result of the impact of provider shortage on the already dwindling number of abortion services, the ACGME decided that, effective January 1996, induced abortion "must be part of residency training, except for residents with moral or religious objection." Teaching hospitals that did not train or arrange for abortion training risk losing accreditation and, consequently, federal reimbursements of services rendered by medical residents. Under pressure from Catholic bishops and antiabortion groups, the ACGME requirement was amended by Congress. The policy has become a recommendation that elective training in induced abortion be offered in resi-

dency training. So far, no medical school has lost accreditation for failing to do so.

In July 2002 New York City became the first U.S. city to include abortion training as a standard element of obstetrics-gynecology (ob-gyn) residency programs. The plan requires that all ob-gyn residents at the city's eleven public hospitals be trained to provide abortion services, including the administration of mifepristone for medical (nonsurgical) abortion. These residents can refuse the abortion training if they have moral objections to abortion, in accordance with ACGME guidelines.

The American Academy of Family Physicians (AAFP) holds that physicians should work toward decreasing the number of unwanted pregnancies by providing patient education and counseling, as stated in "Reproductive Decisions" (American Academy of Family Physicians, http://www.aafp.org/x7053.xml, March 2005). If a woman becomes pregnant, the AAFP believes that it is her legal right to make reproductive decisions. However, the AAFP also states that a physician shall not be compelled to perform any act that goes against his or her "good judgment or personally held moral principles." The AAFP holds that abortion should be performed only by a "duly-licensed physician in conformance with standards of good medical practice as

TABLE 4.5

Legal abortions, by race of women and state of occurrence, selected states, 2001

State	White		Black		Other		Unknown		Total	
	Number	Percent (%)	Number	Percent (%)	Number	Percent (%)	Number	Percent (%)	Number	Percent (%)[a]
39 reporting areas[b]										
Alabama	6,234	(46.6)	6,827	(51.0)	239	(1.8)	82	(0.6)	13,382	(100.0)
Arkansas	3,536	(59.7)	2,031	(34.3)	285	(4.8)	72	(1.2)	5,924	(100.0)
Colorado	3,682	(79.5)	224	(4.8)	228	(4.9)	499	(10.8)	4,633	(100.0)
Delaware[c]	1,907	(54.7)	1,468	(42.1)	114	(3.3)	0	(0)	3,489	(100.0)
Dist. of Columbia	478	(8.9)	4,047	(75.2)	647	(12.0)	213	(4.0)	5,385	(100.0)
Georgia	13,629	(41.0)	18,153	(54.6)	1,466	(4.4)	0	(0)	33,248	(100.0)
Hawaii	1,044	(26.1)	133	(3.3)	2,590	(64.8)	232	(5.8)	3,999	(100.0)
Idaho	679	(92.0)	13	(1.8)	42	(5.7)	4	(0.5)	738	(100.0)
Indiana	7,466	(62.9)	3,249	(27.4)	267	(2.2)	893	(7.5)	11,875	(100.0)
Iowa[c]	4,603	(80.4)	449	(7.8)	616	(10.8)	54	(0.9)	5,722	(100.0)
Kansas	8,899	(72.4)	2,698	(22.0)	671	(5.5)	16	(0.1)	12,284	(100.0)
Kentucky	2,673	(71.0)	822	(21.8)	190	(5.0)	79	(2.1)	3,764	(100.0)
Louisiana	3,921	(35.9)	5,737	(52.5)	260	(2.4)	1,014	(9.3)	10,932	(100.0)
Maine	2,282	(90.7)	54	(2.1)	106	(4.2)	73	(2.9)	2,515	(100.0)
Maryland[c]	3,844	(30.3)	7,655	(60.3)	791	(6.2)	411	(3.2)	12,701	(100.0)
Massachusetts	14,445	(54.9)	4,766	(18.1)	4,930	(18.8)	2,152	(8.2)	26,293	(100.0)
Minnesota	9,652	(65.1)	2,823	(19.0)	2,078	(14.0)	279	(1.9)	14,832	(100.0)
Mississippi	960	(26.9)	2,574	(72.2)	24	(0.7)	8	(0.2)	3,566	(100.0)
Missouri	4,483	(57.5)	2,953	(37.9)	323	(4.1)	38	(0.5)	7,797	(100.0)
Montana	2,002	(85.2)	8	(0.3)	247	(10.5)	93	(4.0)	2,350	(100.0)
New Jersey[d]	10,111	(30.1)	15,193	(45.2)	8,239	(24.5)	63	(0.2)	33,606	(100.0)
New Mexico	4,342	(84.0)	160	(3.1)	664	(12.9)	0	(0)	5,166	(100.0)
New York City	38,704	(42.2)	45,169	(49.2)	5,706	(6.2)	2,213	(2.4)	91,792	(100.0)
North Carolina	13,419	(44.1)	13,181	(43.3)	3,208	(10.5)	611	(2.0)	30,419	(100.0)
North Dakota	1,035	(85.1)	15	(1.2)	141	(11.6)	25	(2.1)	1,216	(100.0)
Ohio	22,045	(58.8)	13,160	(35.1)	848	(2.3)	1,411	(3.8)	37,464	(100.0)
Oklahoma	4,696	(66.7)	1,249	(17.7)	1,037	(14.7)	56	(0.8)	7,038	(100.0)
Oregon	11,949	(83.7)	821	(5.8)	1,465	(10.3)	37	(0.3)	14,272	(100.0)
Pennsylvania	19,945	(54.2)	15,447	(42.0)	1,376	(3.7)	52	(0.1)	36,820	(100.0)
South Carolina	3,774	(53.8)	3,047	(43.4)	190	(2.7)	3	(0)	7,014	(100.0)
South Dakota	734	(82.0)	21	(2.3)	135	(15.1)	5	(0.6)	895	(100.0)
Tennessee	9,285	(53.3)	7,503	(43.1)	583	(3.3)	34	(0.2)	17,405	(100.0)
Texas	56,008	(72.4)	15,938	(20.6)	3,831	(4.9)	1,632	(2.1)	77,409	(100.0)
Utah	2,752	(76.6)	87	(2.4)	310	(8.6)	445	(12.4)	3,594	(100.0)
Vermont	1,437	(94.6)	30	(2.0)	49	(3.2)	3	(0.2)	1,519	(100.0)
Virginia	12,324	(50.1)	9,320	(37.9)	2,107	(8.6)	835	(3.4)	24,586	(100.0)
West Virginia	2,036	(87.3)	242	(10.4)	48	(2.1)	6	(0.3)	2,332	(100.0)
Wisconsin[c]	7,276	(68.0)	2,642	(24.7)	[e]	NA[f]	785[g]	(7.3)[g]	10,703	(100.0)
Wyoming	4	(100.0)	0	(0)	0	(0)	0	(0)	4	(100.0)
Total	318,295	(54.1)	209,909	(35.7)	46,051	(7.8)	14,428	(2.5)	588,683	(100.0)
Abortion ratio[h]	165		491		376				232	
Abortion rate[i]	10		29		21				13	

[a]Percentages might not add to 100.0 because of rounding.

[b]Data on race/ethnicity from 39 reporting areas (37 states, the District of Columbia, and New York City [NYC]) in which race was classified as white, black, other, and unknown; excludes five states (Nebraska, Nevada, New York [excluding NYC], Rhode Island, and Washington) from which race was reported as unknown for >15% of women.

[c]Includes residents only.

[d]Numbers do not include procedures performed by private physicians.

[e]"Other" included with "unknown."

[f]Not applicable.

[g]Includes "other."

[h]Calculated as the number of legal abortions obtained by women of a given race per 1,000 live births to women of the same race for these states. For each state, data for women of unknown race were distributed according to the known racial distribution for that state.

[i]Calculated as the number of legal abortions obtained by women of a given race per 1,000 females aged 15–44 years of the same race for these states. For each state, data for women of unknown race were distributed according to the known racial distribution for that state. NYC data were excluded because separate population data were not available for NYC.

SOURCE: Adapted from Lilo T. Strauss, Joy Herndon, Jeani Chang, Wilda Y. Parker, Sonya V. Bowens, Suzanne B. Zane, and Cynthia J. Berg, "Table 9. Reported Legal Abortions, by Race of Women Who Obtained an Abortion and State of Occurrence—Selected States, United States, 2001," in "Abortion Surveillance—United States, 2001," *Morbidity and Mortality Weekly Report/Surveillance Summaries*, vol. 53, no. SS-9, November 26, 2004, http://www.cdc.gov/mmwr/PDF/SS/SS5309.pdf (accessed September 20, 2005)

determined by the laws and regulations governing the practice of medicine in that locale."

The organization also recommends that medical students and family practice residents be trained in counseling and referral skills regarding all options available to pregnant women. This would include contraceptive methods (including sterilization), adoption services, abortion services, financial assistance, and other assistance available to the mother or the child.

TABLE 4.6

Legal abortions, by ethnicity of women and state of occurrence, selected states, 2001

State	Ethnicity						Total	
	Hispanic		Non-Hispanic		Unknown			
	Number	Percent (%)	Number	Percent (%)	Number	Percent (%)	Number	Percent (%)[a]
Alabama	346	(2.6)	12,988	(97.1)	48	(0.4)	13,382	(100.0)
Arkansas	101	(1.7)	5,675	(95.8)	148	(2.5)	5,924	(100.0)
Colorado	736	(15.9)	3,336	(72.0)	561	(12.1)	4,633	(100.0)
Delaware[b]	237	(6.8)	3,230	(92.6)	22	(0.6)	3,489	(100.0)
Georgia	1,649	(5.0)	31,217	(93.9)	382	(1.1)	33,248	(100.0)
Hawaii	182	(4.6)	3,459	(86.5)	358	(9.0)	3,999	(100.0)
Idaho	92	(12.5)	641	(86.9)	5	(0.7)	738	(100.0)
Indiana	654	(5.5)	9,551	(80.4)	1,670	(14.1)	11,875	(100.0)
Kansas	869	(7.1)	11,320	(92.2)	95	(0.8)	12,284	(100.0)
Kentucky	1	(0)	3,684	(97.9)	79	(2.1)	3,764	(100.0)
Maine	28	(1.1)	2,159	(85.8)	328	(13.0)	2,515	(100.0)
Minnesota	791	(5.3)	13,895	(93.7)	146	(1.0)	14,832	(100.0)
Mississippi	23	(0.6)	3,540	(99.3)	3	(0.1)	3,566	(100.0)
Missouri	163	(2.1)	7,602	(97.5)	32	(0.4)	7,797	(100.0)
New Jersey[c]	7,370	(21.9)	26,165	(77.9)	71	(0.2)	33,606	(100.0)
New Mexico	2,514	(48.7)	2,649	(51.3)	3	(0.1)	5,166	(100.0)
New York	32,549	(25.6)	87,379	(68.7)	7,174	(5.6)	127,102	(100.0)
City	29,684	(32.3)	60,013	(65.4)	2,095	(2.3)	91,792	(100.0)
State	2,865	(8.1)	27,366	(77.5)	5,079	(14.4)	35,310	(100.0)
North Dakota	34	(2.8)	1,062	(87.3)	120	(9.9)	1,216	(100.0)
Ohio	1,010	(2.7)	36,355	(97.0)	99	(0.3)	37,464	(100.0)
Oklahoma	376	(5.3)	6,284	(89.3)	378	(5.4)	7,038	(100.0)
Oregon	1,421	(10.0)	12,833	(89.9)	18	(0.1)	14,272	(100.0)
Pennsylvania	1,848	(5.0)	34,952	(94.9)	20	(0.1)	36,820	(100.0)
South Carolina	210	(3.0)	6,804	(97.0)	0	(0)	7,014	(100.0)
South Dakota	40	(4.5)	838	(93.6)	17	(1.9)	895	(100.0)
Tennessee	566	(3.3)	16,735	(96.2)	104	(0.6)	17,405	(100.0)
Texas	29,022	(37.5)	46,755	(60.4)	1,632	(2.1)	77,409	(100.0)
Utah	548	(15.2)	2,748	(76.5)	298	(8.3)	3,594	(100.0)
Vermont	22	(1.4)	1,491	(98.2)	6	(0.4)	1,519	(100.0)
West Virginia	16	(0.7)	2,313	(99.2)	3	(0.1)	2,332	(100.0)
Wisconsin[b]	835	(7.8)	9,868	(92.2)	0	(0)	10,703	(100.0)
Wyoming	2	(50.0)	2	(50.0)	0	(0)	4	(100.0)
Total	**84,255**	**(16.7)**	**407,530**	**(80.6)**	**13,820**	**(2.7)**	**505,605**	**(100.0)**
Abortion ratio[d]	230		232				232	
Abortion rate[e]	22		14				15	

Note: Data from 31 states and New York City; excludes nine areas (District of Columbia, Massachusetts, Montana, Nebraska, Nevada, North Carolina, Rhode Island, Virginia, and Washington) from which ethnicity was reported as unknown for >15% of women.

[a]Percentages might not add to 100.0 because of rounding.

[b]Includes residents only.

[c]Numbers do not include procedures performed by private physicians.

[d]Calculated as the number of legal abortions obtained by women of a given ethnicity per 1,000 live births to women of the same ethnicity for these states. For each state, data for women of unknown ethnicity were distributed according to the known ethnicity distribution for that state.

[e]Calculated as the number of legal abortions obtained by women of a given ethnicity per 1,000 women of the same ethnicity for these states. For each state, data for women of unknown ethnicity were distributed according to the known ethnicity distribution for that state.

SOURCE: Lilo T. Strauss, Joy Herndon, Jeani Chang, Wilda Y.Parker, Sonya V. Bowens, Suzanne B. Zane, and Cynthia J. Berg, "Table 10. Reported Legal Abortions, by Ethnicity of Women Who Obtained an Abortion and State of Occurrence—Selected States, United States, 2001," in "Abortion Surveillance—United States, 2001," *Morbidity and Mortality Weekly Report/Surveillance Summaries*, vol. 53, no. SS-9, November 26, 2004, http://www.cdc.gov/mmwr/PDF/SS/SS5309.pdf (accessed September 20, 2005)

They also support language in the "Program Requirements for Residency Training in Family Practice" of the Residency Review Committee for Family Practice that calls for providing opportunities for residents to learn skills they think will be part of their future practices.

HOW MUCH DOES AN ABORTION COST?

Abortion fees vary, depending on the stage of pregnancy, where the abortion is performed, the kind of procedure, and the anesthetic used. There may be other costs if the abortion cannot be done locally. Expenses might include travel costs, costs for overnight stays, or lost wages in states that require a waiting period between counseling and the abortion.

In "Get 'In the Know': Questions about Pregnancy, Contraception and Abortion—Cost of Abortion" (http://www.guttmacher.org/in-the-know/cost.html), the AGI noted that, in 2001, the average charge for an abortion performed at ten weeks of pregnancy in a clinic was $468. The AGI noted, however, that most abortions in the U.S. are performed at low-cost clinics, and the

TABLE 4.7

Fertility indicators for women age 15–44, by age, race, and Hispanic origin, June 2002

Characteristic	Number of women	Percent childless	Women who had a child in the last year		First births per 1,000 women	Children ever born per 1,000 women
			Number with a birth	Births per 1,000 women Rate		
Age						
Total	**61,361**	**43.5**	**3,766**	**61.4**	**23.1**	**1,211**
15 to 19 years	9,809	91.2	549	55.9	27.7	140
20 to 24 years	9,683	67.0	872	90.0	45.3	525
25 to 29 years	9,221	45.2	897	97.2	33.2	1,050
30 to 34 years	10,284	27.6	859	83.6	26.4	1,543
35 to 39 years	10,803	20.2	452	41.9	7.9	1,849
40 to 44 years	11,561	17.9	137	11.9	3.6	1,930
Race and ethnicity						
White						
Total	**48,481**	**43.9**	**2,958**	**61.0**	**22.9**	**1,196**
15 to 19 years	7,699	91.9	394	51.1	24.7	129
20 to 24 years	7,604	69.5	631	83.0	42.8	473
25 to 29 years	7,151	46.6	723	101.1	34.7	1,018
30 to 34 years	8,057	27.2	717	88.9	29.5	1,530
35 to 39 years	8,658	20.2	374	43.2	7.9	1,842
40 to 44 years	9,313	17.9	120	12.8	4.2	1,917
White, Non-Hispanic						
Total	**40,017**	**45.6**	**2,262**	**56.5**	**21.3**	**1,130**
15 to 19 years	6,296	93.0	289	45.8	21.7	116
20 to 24 years	6,138	73.2	437	71.1	37.4	406
25 to 29 years	5,599	51.1	555	99.2	37.4	881
30 to 34 years	6,544	29.9	576	88.0	28.7	1,413
35 to 39 years	7,281	21.5	300	41.2	7.7	1,755
40 to 44 years	8,160	18.5	106	13.0	4.2	1,842
Black						
Total	**8,846**	**39.0**	**571**	**64.6**	**22.3**	**1,354**
15 to 19 years	1,535	86.7	125	81.4	38.0	214
20 to 24 years	1,497	51.1	193	128.9	61.2	828
25 to 29 years	1,351	31.6	98	72.7	18.6	1,392
30 to 34 years	1,440	23.9	95	66.1	10.1	1,790
35 to 39 years	1,506	19.7	52	34.2	5.0	1,942
40 to 44 years	1,518	19.2	8	5.6	*	1,991
Asian and Pacific Islander						
Total	**3,267**	**50.8**	**181**	**55.4**	**27.3**	**994**
15 to 19 years	447	94.2	23	51.1	34.9	86
20 to 24 years	481	81.0	22	45.1	29.5	297
25 to 29 years	608	60.7	66	109.1	45.2	631
30 to 34 years	632	41.2	40	62.5	31.3	1,124
35 to 39 years	530	23.3	21	40.6	17.7	1,605
40 to 44 years	568	16.8	9	15.7	4.8	1,974
Hispanic (of any race)						
Total	**9,141**	**35.8**	**750**	**82.0**	**30.4**	**1,511**
15 to 19 years	1,517	87.8	105	69.3	35.4	172
20 to 24 years	1,574	52.9	226	143.7	70.8	768
25 to 29 years	1,682	29.5	176	104.6	25.8	1,522
30 to 34 years	1,620	15.6	152	93.7	32.6	2,043
35 to 39 years	1,481	13.4	77	52.1	8.1	2,287
40 to 44 years	1,266	13.1	14	10.9	3.8	2,437

Note: Numbers in thousands.
*Represents zero or rounds to zero.

SOURCE: Barbara Downs, "Table 1. Fertility Indicators for Women 15 to 44 Years Old by Age, Race, and Hispanic Origin: June 2002," in "Fertility of American Women: June 2002, Population Characteristics," in *Current Population Reports*, U.S. Census Bureau, U.S. Department of Commerce, Economics and Statistics Administration, October 2003, http://www.census.gov/prod/2003pubs/p20-548.pdf (accessed September 20, 2005)

procedure cost, on average, $372. The fees generally cover the examination, laboratory tests, local anesthesia, the procedure, and the follow-up visit. In clinics offering medical abortions, the average cost was $487. In most cases medical abortions (those using abortion pills) cost slightly more than other first-trimester abortions because of the cost of mifepristone and the follow-up required.

TABLE 4.8

Percentage distribution of women obtaining abortions, by contraceptive method used in the month of conception, 2000

Method	Women having abortions, 2000
Any method	53.7
Long-acting	1.1
Sterilization	0.1
IUD	0.1
Implant/injectable	0.9
Pill	13.6
Male condom	27.6
Withdrawal	7.3
Periodic abstinence	2.2
Other*	1.9
No method	46.3
Never used	8.1
Previously used	38.2
Total	**100.0**

*Female condom, diaphragm, foam, sponge, suppository or any other method.

SOURCE: Adapted from Rachel K. Jones, Jacqueline E. Darroch, and Stanley K. Henshaw, "Table 1. Percentage Distribution of Women Obtaining Abortions in 2000, by Contraceptive Method Used in the Month of Conception, and of Women At Risk of Unintended Pregnancy in 1995, by Contraceptive Method Used," in "Contraceptive Use Among U.S. Women Having Abortions in 2000–2001," *Perspectives on Sexual and Reproductive Health*, vol. 34, no. 6, December 2002 http://www.guttmacher.org/pubs/journals/3429402.pdf (accessed September 20, 2005)

The cost of an abortion increases after the first trimester. Hospital abortions cost more than those performed in abortion clinics and doctors' offices. In addition to the fees of the surgeon and anesthesiologist, costs include the hospital stay, anesthesia, tests, and medications.

The "Cost of Abortion" fact sheet notes that in 2001 about 74% of women funded their own abortions (but may be reimbursed by their insurance provider), 13% were covered by Medicaid (in cases of life endangerment, rape, and incest), and 13% had private insurance that paid abortion costs directly. The fact sheet noted, however, that as of March 2004, seventeen states used their own funds to subsidize abortion for poor women.

WHEN ARE ABORTIONS PERFORMED?

Table 4.2 shows that in 2001 well over half (59.1%) of abortions were performed at eight weeks or less of development. Figure 4.6 shows that in that same year 59.1% of abortions were performed at nine weeks or less. (Such data can differ slightly depending on the source of the data and how the data was calculated.) Both sources show that 19% of abortions were performed at nine to ten weeks of pregnancy. Both sources also show that few abortions were performed after fifteen weeks of gestation—4.3% at sixteen to twenty weeks and 1.4% at or after twenty-one weeks of pregnancy.

As in past years, in 2001 a larger percentage of women ages nineteen years and younger obtained abortions later in pregnancy than did older women. In addition, a larger percentage of African-American women obtained abortions later in pregnancy than did white women and women of other races. (See Table 4.14.)

ABORTION METHODS

Abortion can be performed using surgical or medical (drug) methods. The type of abortion a woman obtains depends on her choice of method, her health, and the gestational age of the fetus. Methods of abortion are described in Table 1.1 in Chapter 1.

Percentages of Methods Used

The CDC has collected data since 1973 on the types of procedures used each year to perform abortions. The CDC has determined that there has been a shift in the proportion of which procedures are used. From 1973 to 1991 the percentage of abortions performed by curettage (which here includes dilation and evacuation) increased from 88.6% to 99.1%. The percentage then dropped somewhat during the 1990s, and more sharply in 2000 and 2001 to 97.9% and then to 95.5%. Nevertheless, the percentage of curettage performed has increased dramatically since 1973. Conversely, the percentage of abortions performed by instillation (induction) declined sharply from 10.3% in 1973 to 0.2% in 1999. This figure increased slightly to 0.4% in 2000 and to 0.6% in 2001. The CDC suggests that the increased use of curettage over induction is likely due to the decreased risk of complications using curettage. In addition, a greater proportion of women obtain abortions earlier in their pregnancy now than in past decades, thus allowing curettage over induction. (See Table 4.2.) Hysterectomy (removal of the woman's uterus), hysterotomy (an incision, or cut, to the uterus, usually to deliver a fetus), and medical (nonsurgical) procedures, which were included in the "Other" procedure category, were used in 3.9% of abortions. For 2001 the CDC reports a total of 20,093 medical abortions performed.

Deaths from Abortion

As Table 4.15 shows, the fatality rate from abortion procedures has dropped from 4.1 deaths per one hundred thousand reported legal induced abortions in 1972 to its lowest point of 0.3 in 1995. (See Table 4.15.) In 1997 the rate was 0.6. Fatality rates are not shown for years 1998–2000 due to missing data. The CDC reported that in 2002 the death rate related to pregnancy and childbirth was 0.1.

Although abortion-related deaths are rare, legal abortions are still surgical procedures and entail some risk. An abortion performed at or before eight weeks of pregnancy is the safest. Similarly, the abortion method used also has a bearing on risk. Vacuum aspiration, used

TABLE 4.9

Legal abortions, by number of previous abortions and state of occurrence, selected states, 2001

State	Number of previous induced abortions											
	0		1		2		≥3		Unknown		Total	
	Number	Percent (%)	Number	Percent (%)	Number	Percent (%)	Number	Percent (%)	Number	Percent (%)	Number	Percent (%)[a]
Alabama	8,943	(66.8)	3,193	(23.9)	891	(6.7)	344	(2.6)	11	(0.1)	13,382	(100.0)
Arkansas	3,848	(65.0)	1,477	(24.9)	431	(7.3)	111	(1.9)	57	(1.0)	5,924	(100.0)
Colorado	2,955	(63.8)	1,145	(24.7)	298	(6.4)	129	(2.8)	106	(2.3)	4,633	(100.0)
Delaware[b]	1,997	(57.2)	852	(24.4)	405	(11.6)	234	(6.7)	1	(0)	3,489	(100.0)
Georgia	19,795	(59.5)	8,686	(26.1)	3,069	(9.2)	1,549	(4.7)	149	(0.4)	33,248	(100.0)
Hawaii	2,508	(62.7)	840	(21.0)	343	(8.6)	262	(6.6)	46	(1.2)	3,999	(100.0)
Idaho	597	(80.9)	96	(13.0)	29	(3.9)	14	(1.9)	2	(0.3)	738	(100.0)
Indiana	7,113	(59.9)	3,083	(26.0)	922	(7.8)	422	(3.6)	335	(2.8)	11,875	(100.0)
Iowa[b]	3,505	(61.3)	1,553	(27.1)	442	(7.7)	212	(3.7)	10	(0.2)	5,722	(100.0)
Kansas	7,560	(61.5)	3,100	(25.2)	1,094	(8.9)	529	(4.3)	1	(0)	12,284	(100.0)
Kentucky	2,137	(56.8)	925	(24.6)	405	(10.8)	297	(7.9)	0	(0)	3,764	(100.0)
Maine	1,662	(66.1)	639	(25.4)	159	(6.3)	55	(2.2)	0	(0)	2,515	(100.0)
Maryland[b]	3,638	(28.6)	4,384	(34.5)	2,602	(20.5)	2,077	(16.4)	0	(0)	12,701	(100.0)
Michigan	14,804	(52.5)	7,501	(26.6)	3,440	(12.2)	2,475	(8.8)	0	(0)	28,220	(100.0)
Minnesota	8,809	(59.4)	3,705	(25.0)	1,370	(9.2)	948	(6.4)	0	(0)	14,832	(100.0)
Mississippi	2,301	(64.5)	961	(26.9)	233	(6.5)	69	(1.9)	2	(0.1)	3,566	(100.0)
Missouri	4,357	(55.9)	2,170	(27.8)	806	(10.3)	462	(5.9)	2	(0)	7,797	(100.0)
Montana	1,291	(54.9)	650	(27.7)	249	(10.6)	160	(6.8)	0	(0)	2,350	(100.0)
Nebraska	2,771	(69.6)	809	(20.3)	256	(6.4)	146	(3.7)	0	(0)	3,982	(100.0)
Nevada	5,577	(55.2)	2,619	(25.9)	1,068	(10.6)	758	(7.5)	88	(0.9)	10,110	(100.0)
New Jersey[c]	21,629	(64.4)	6,501	(19.3)	3,034	(9.0)	2,338	(7.0)	104	(0.3)	33,606	(100.0)
New Mexico	3,635	(70.4)	1,059	(20.5)	299	(5.8)	157	(3.0)	16	(0.3)	5,166	(100.0)
New York	54,666	(43.0)	30,908	(24.3)	17,960	(14.1)	16,564	(13.0)	7,004	(5.5)	127,102	(100.0)
City	37,157	(40.5)	23,721	(25.8)	14,697	(16.0)	14,307	(15.6)	1,910	(2.1)	91,792	(100.0)
State	17,509	(49.6)	7,187	(20.4)	3,263	(9.2)	2,257	(6.4)	5,094	(14.4)	35,310	(100.0)
North Dakota	874	(71.9)	248	(20.4)	68	(5.6)	26	(2.1)	0	(0)	1,216	(100.0)
Oklahoma	4,450	(63.2)	1,686	(24.0)	546	(7.8)	257	(3.7)	99	(1.4)	7,038	(100.0)
Oregon	8,030	(56.3)	3,733	(26.2)	1,480	(10.4)	982	(6.9)	47	(0.3)	14,272	(100.0)
Pennsylvania	20,257	(55.0)	9,890	(26.9)	4,135	(11.2)	2,533	(6.9)	5	(0)	36,820	(100.0)
Rhode Island	2,977	(54.6)	1,468	(26.9)	589	(10.8)	386	(7.1)	35	(0.6)	5,455	(100.0)
South Carolina	4,356	(62.1)	1,814	(25.9)	614	(8.8)	230	(3.3)	0	(0)	7,014	(100.0)
South Dakota	682	(76.2)	145	(16.2)	49	(5.5)	19	(2.1)	0	(0)	895	(100.0)
Tennessee	9,203	(52.9)	4,688	(26.9)	2,058	(11.8)	1,431	(8.2)	25	(0.1)	17,405	(100.0)
Texas	45,545	(58.8)	20,950	(27.1)	7,077	(9.1)	3,604	(4.7)	233	(0.3)	77,409	(100.0)
Utah	2,414	(67.2)	736	(20.5)	235	(6.5)	209	(5.8)	0	(0)	3,594	(100.0)
Vermont	926	(61.0)	379	(25.0)	130	(8.6)	81	(5.3)	3	(0.2)	1,519	(100.0)
Virginia	13,328	(54.2)	6,904	(28.1)	2,731	(11.1)	1,307	(5.3)	316	(1.3)	24,586	(100.0)
Washington	13,858	(54.1)	6,771	(26.4)	2,900	(11.3)	1,993	(7.8)	98	(0.4)	25,620	(100.0)
West Virginia	1,762	(75.6)	427	(18.3)	89	(3.8)	54	(2.3)	0	(0)	2,332	(100.0)
Wyoming	3	(75.0)	1	(25.0)	0	(0)	0	(0)	0	(0)	4	(100.0)
Total	**314,763**	**(54.6)**	**146,696**	**(25.5)**	**62,506**	**(10.8)**	**43,424**	**(7.5)**	**8,795**	**(1.5)**	**576,184**	**(100.0)**

Note: Data from 38 states and New York City; excludes five areas (Arizona, District of Columbia, Massachusetts, North Carolina, and Ohio) from which number of previous induced abortions was reported as unknown for >15% of women.
[a] Percentages might not add to 100.0 because of rounding.
[b] Includes residents only.
[c] Numbers do not include procedures performed by private physicians.

SOURCE: Lilo T. Strauss, Joy Herndon, Jeani Chang, Wilda Y. Parker, Sonya V. Bowens, Suzanne B. Zane, and Cynthia J. Berg, "Table 13. Reported Legal Abortions, by Number of Previous Legal Induced Abortions and State of Occurrence—Selected States, United States, 2001," in "Abortion Surveillance—United States, 2001," *Morbidity and Mortality Weekly Report/Surveillance Summaries*, vol. 53, no. SS-9, November 26, 2004, http://www.cdc.gov/mmwr/PDF/SS/SS5309.pdf (accessed September 20, 2005)

during the first trimester of pregnancy, carries the least risk of the surgical methods.

Do Physicians Offer Medical Abortion?

A survey of health care providers conducted before mifepristone was approved by the FDA asked obstetricians/gynecologists and family practice physicians about their views on medical abortion ("A National Survey: Views of Women's Health Care Providers on Abortion," The Henry J. Kaiser Family Foundation, June 13, 2000). Most of the physician respondents in the survey were familiar with mifepristone—91% of obstetricians/gynecologists and 67% of family practice physicians reported that they were familiar with the drug. However, in a survey conducted by the Kaiser Family Foundation almost one year later and after the drug had been approved for use ("National Survey of Women's Health Care Providers on Reproductive Health: Views and Practices on Medical Abortion," May 15–August 28, 2001), a smaller percentage of physicians in these two groups were familiar with the drug: 82% of obstetricians/gynecologists and 61% of general practice physicians. (See

TABLE 4.10

Number, ratio, and rate of legal abortions, by state, and percentage of legal abortions obtained by out-of-state residents, 2001

State	Residence[d] Number of legal abortions[a]	Ratio[b]	Rate[c]	Occurence Number of legal abortions[a]	Ratio[b]	Rate[c]	Percentage of legal abortions obtained by out-of-state residents
Alabama	11,882	197	12	13,382	221	14	18.1
Alaska[e]	—[f]	—	—	—	—	—	—
Arizona[g]	8,601	100	8	8,302	97	8	0.9
Arkansas	5,687	154	10	5,924	160	11	15.9
California[e]	—	—	—	—	—	—	—
Colorado	3,977	59	4	4,633	69	5	16.7
Connecticut	13,251	311	18	13,265	311	19	3.3
Delaware[h]	3,690	343	21	4,869	453	28	28.3
Dist. of Columbia	2,947	386	21	5,385	706	37	56.0
Florida[i]	431	2[i]	0[i]	85,589	416	26	—
Georgia	30,190	226	16	33,248	249	17	10.5
Hawaii	4,003	234	16	3,999	234	16	0.3
Idaho	1,491	72	5	738	36	3	3.5
Illinois	42,427	231	15	46,546	253	17	9.8
Indiana	13,607	157	10	11,875	137	9	4.2
Iowa[h]	6,354	169	10	5,722	152	9	—
Kansas	6,430	165	11	12,284	316	21	48.9
Kentucky	6,266	115	7	3,764	69	4	14.8
Louisiana[i]	676	10[i]	1[i]	10,932	167	11	—
Maine	2,462	179	9	2,515	183	9	2.9
Maryland[h]	16,397	224	14	13,502	184	11	5.9
Massachusetts[g]	25,082	309	18	26,293	324	18	6.3
Michigan	27,534	206	13	28,220	212	13	3.6
Minnesota	13,971	207	13	14,832	220	14	9.3
Mississippi	6,983	165	11	3,566	84	6	4.3
Missouri	15,602	207	13	7,797	103	6	9.1
Montana	2,093	191	11	2,350	214	13	12.2
Nebraska	3,447	139	9	3,982	160	11	15.8
Nevada	9,356	298	21	10,110	322	23	7.3
New Hampshire[e]	—	—	—	—	—	—	—
New Jersey[l]	34,565	299	19	33,606	290	19	3.7
New Mexico	5,692	210	15	5,166	190	13	4.5
New York	122,997	484	29	127,102	500	30	—
City	86,460	723	—	91,792[k]	767	—	6.4[l]
State	36,537[m]	272	—	35,310	263	—	7.7[l]
North Carolina	27,199	230	15	30,419	257	17	13.8
North Dakota	847	111	6	1,216	159	9	38.3
Ohio	35,059	231	14	37,464	247	15	8.7
Oklahoma	7,546	151	10	7,038	140	10	4.3
Oregon	12,752	281	18	14,272	315	20	12.6
Pennsylvania	37,498	261	15	36,820	257	14	4.9
Rhode Island	4,170	328	18	5,455	429	23	24.8
South Carolina	10,774	193	12	7,014	126	8	5.3
South Dakota	1,045	100	7	895	85	6	15.2
Tennessee	15,490	198	12	17,405	222	14	19.2
Texas	74,237	203	15	77,409	212	16	3.9

Figure 4.7.) The 2000 survey found that, if the FDA approved mifepristone, 54% of obstetricians/gynecologists and 31% of family practice physicians would offer mifepristone abortions. However, in the 2001 survey, only 6% of gynecologists and 1% of general practice physicians reported that they had provided mifepristone to a patient since its approval. (See Figure 4.8.)

Only 27% of obstetricians/gynecologists and 1% of family practice physicians surveyed in 2001 provided surgical abortions to their patients; among that 27%, 12% of providers have used mifepristone since its approval. (See Figure 4.9.)

OPPONENTS AND PROPONENTS OF MIFEPRISTONE. The nation's largest pro-life group, the National Right to Life Committee (NRLC), threatened to boycott any drug company that sells mifepristone. In the early 1980s the NRLC successfully pressured the Upjohn Company to discontinue developing an abortion-inducing drug through a two-year boycott of its products. On FDA approval of mifepristone, Laura Echevarria, spokeswoman for the NRLC, said, "The Clinton–Gore Administration, which claimed it wanted to make abortion rare, has embraced an abortion pill that will result in more abortions and new risks to women" ("F.D.A. Approves Sale of Abortion Pill," National Right to Life, http://www.nrlc.org/press_releases_new/Release092800. html). Pro-life groups argue that "chemical" abortion would leave serious intangible scars on women who would experience real labor pains and see their aborted fetuses.

Pro-choice activists, in contrast, approved of the medical-abortion drug. Gloria Feldt, president of Planned

TABLE 4.10

Number, ratio, and rate of legal abortions, by state, and percentage of legal abortions obtained by out-of-state residents, 2001 [CONTINUED]

State	Residence[d]			Occurence			Percentage of legal abortions obtained by out-of-state residents
	Number of legal abortions[a]	Ratio[b]	Rate[c]	Number of legal abortions[a]	Ratio[b]	Rate[c]	
Utah	3,512	73	7	3,594	75	7	6.2
Vermont	1,320	207	10	1,519	239	12	14.2
Virginia	25,649	259	16	24,586	249	15	6.1
Washington	26,028	327	20	25,620	322	20	4.9
West Virginia	2,739	134	7	2,332	114	6	10.9
Wisconsin[h]	12,279	178	11	10,925	158	9	2.0
Wyoming	737	121	7	4[n]	[n]	0	
Other residence[o]	4,414	—	—	NA[p]	NA	NA	NA
Total known	**752,283**			**853,485**	**246**	**16**	**8.7**
Unknown residence[q]	4,681						
Not reported by residence[r]	96,521						
Total	**853,485**	**246**	**16**				

[a]Abortion data reported by central health agencies.
[b]Number of abortions per 1,000 live births.
[c]Number of abortions per 1,000 females aged 15–44 years.
[d]Based on number of abortions for which residence of women was known.
[e]State did not report abortions.
[f]Not available.
[g]Reported numbers of abortions for in-state residents without detailed information regarding out of-state residents.
[h]Reported for own residents only.
[i]State did not report abortions by residence; therefore, no information regarding in-state residents is available.
[j]Numbers do not include procedures performed by private physicians.
[k]Reported by the New York City Department of Health.
[l]Percentage based on number of abortions reported as "out-of-reporting area."
[m]Abortions for women whose state of residence was listed as New York.
[n]Ratio and rate not provided because of limited numbers.
[o]Women whose residence was listed as Canada, Mexico, or "other."
[p]Not applicable.
[q]Residence reported as unknown (2,821) or out of state, but not specified (1,860).
[r]Total for states that did not report abortions by residence.

SOURCE: Lilo T. Strauss, Joy Herndon, Jeani Chang, Wilda Y. Parker, Sonya V. Bowens, Suzanne B. Zane, and Cynthia J. Berg, "Table 3. Reported Number, Ratio, and Rate of Legal Abortions, by Residence and Occurrence, and Percentage of Abortions Obtained by Out-of-State Residents, by State of Occurrence—United States, 2001," in "Abortion Surveillance—United States, 2001," *Morbidity and Mortality Weekly Report/Surveillance Summaries*, vol. 53, no. SS-9, November 26, 2004, http://www.cdc.gov/mmwr/PDF/SS/SS5309.pdf (accessed September 20, 2005)

Parenthood, stated, "Mifepristone, or the early abortion pill, is as significant a technological advance for women's health as the birth control pill was 40 years ago" ("Food and Drug Administration Approves 'Abortion Pill'," CNN.com, http://archives.cnn.com/2000/HEALTH/women/09/28/abortion.pill/, September 28, 2000). The American Civil Liberties Union issued a statement by Catherine Weiss, director of the group's Reproductive Freedom Project. She

stated, "Mifepristone represents a significant breakthrough in reproductive health care by offering women, especially those who live far from an abortion provider, better access to a safe, private, and early option for ending a pregnancy" ("ACLU Hails FDA Approval of Safe, Early-Option Abortion Pill," American Civil Liberties Union, http://www.aclu.org/ReproductiveRights/ReproductiveRights.cfm?ID=8134&c=143, September 28, 2000).

TABLE 4.11

Mandatory state waiting periods and biased counseling for abortion, 2005

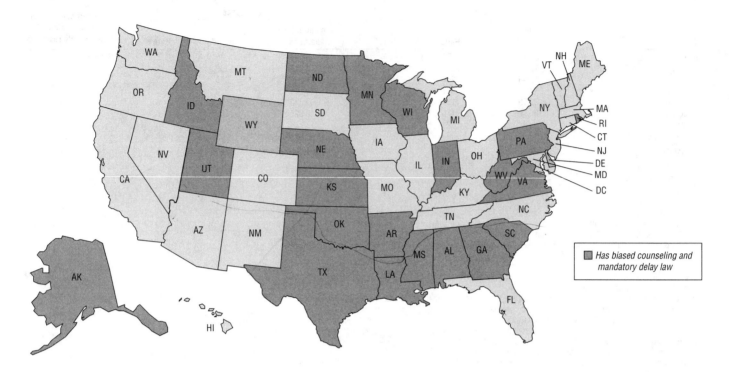

State	State subjects women seeking abortion to		Law enjoined or not enforced	State	State subjects women seeking abortion to		Law enjoined or not enforced
	Biased counseling	Mandatory delay			Biased counseling	Mandatory delay	
Alabama	X	X		Nebraska	X	X	
Alaska	X			Nevada			
Arizona				New Hampshire			
Arkansas	X	X		New Jersey			
California				New Mexico			
Colorado				New York			
Connecticut				North Carolina			
Delaware	X	X[a]		North Dakota	X	X	
District of Columbia				Ohio	X	X	
Florida	X		X	Oklahoma	X	X	
Georgia	X	X		Oregon			
Hawaii				Pennsylvania	X	X	
Idaho	X	X		Rhode Island	X		
Illinois				South Carolina	X	X	
Indiana	X	X		South Dakota	X	X	X
Iowa				Tennessee	X	X	X
Kansas	X	X		Texas	X	X	
Kentucky	X[b]	X		Utah	X	X	
Louisiana	X	X		Vermont			
Maine				Virginia	X	X	
Maryland				Washington			
Massachusetts	X	X[a]		West Virginia	X	X	
Michigan	X	X		Wisconsin	X	X	
Minnesota	X	X		Wyoming			
Mississippi	X	X		**Total**	**31**	**28**	**5**
Missouri	X	X	X				
Montana	X	X	X				

[a]The law is unconstitutional & unenforceable only with respect to the mandatory delay.
[b]The law is unconstitutional & unenforceable only with respect to the in-person receipt of the state-mandated information and materials provision.

SOURCE: "Biased Counseling & Mandatory Delay," in *Who Decides? The Status of Women's Reproductive Rights in the United States, 14th ed.*, NARAL Pro-Choice America & NARAL Pro-Choice America Foundation, updated June 24, 2005, http://www.prochoiceamerica.org/yourstate/whodecides/maps/biased_counseling.cfm (accessed September 20, 2005)

TABLE 4.12

Number of abortion providers in 1992, 1996, and 2000, and percentage of counties and women without an abortion provider, by state, 2000

Region and state	Number of providers				Counties, 2000		
	1992	1996	2000	% change 1996–2000	Total	Without a provider	
						% of counties	% of women*
U.S. total	2,380	2,042	1,819	−11	3,141	87	34
Northeast	620	562	536	−5	217	50	16
Connecticut	43	40	50	25	8	25	9
Maine	17	16	15	−6	16	63	45
Massachusetts	64	51	47	−8	14	21	7
New Hampshire	16	16	14	−13	10	50	26
New Jersey	88	94	86	−9	21	10	3
New York	289	266	234	−12	62	42	8
Pennsylvania	81	61	73	20	67	75	39
Rhode Island	6	5	6	20	5	80	39
Vermont	16	13	11	−15	14	43	23
Midwest	260	212	188	−11	1,055	94	49
Illinois	47	38	37	−3	102	90	30
Indiana	19	16	15	−6	92	93	62
Iowa	11	8	8	0	99	95	64
Kansas	15	10	7	−30	105	96	54
Michigan	70	59	50	−15	83	83	31
Minnesota	14	13	11	−15	87	95	58
Missouri	12	10	6	−40	115	97	71
Nebraska	9	8	5	−38	93	97	46
North Dakota	1	1	2	100	53	98	77
Ohio	45	37	35	−5	88	91	50
South Dakota	1	1	2	100	66	98	78
Wisconsin	16	11	10	−9	72	93	62
South	620	505	442	−12	1,425	91	45
Alabama	20	14	14	0	67	93	59
Arkansas	8	6	7	17	75	97	79
Delaware	8	7	9	29	3	33	17
District of Columbia	15	18	15	−17	1	0	0
Florida	133	114	108	−5	67	70	19
Georgia	55	41	26	−37	159	94	56
Kentucky	9	8	3	−63	120	98	75
Louisiana	17	15	13	−13	64	92	61
Maryland	51	47	42	−11	24	67	24
Mississippi	8	6	4	−33	82	98	86
North Carolina	86	59	55	−7	100	78	44
Oklahoma	11	11	6	−45	77	96	56
South Carolina	18	14	10	−29	46	87	66
Tennessee	33	20	16	−20	95	94	56
Texas	79	64	65	2	254	93	32
Virginia	64	57	46	−19	136	84	47
West Virginia	5	4	3	−25	55	96	83
West	880	763	653	−14	444	78	15
Alaska	13	8	7	−13	27	85	39
Arizona	28	24	21	−13	15	80	18
California	554	492	400	−19	58	41	4
Colorado	59	47	40	−15	63	78	26
Hawaii	52	44	51	16	4	0	0
Idaho	9	7	7	0	44	93	67
Montana	12	11	9	−18	56	91	43
Nevada	17	14	13	−7	17	82	10
New Mexico	20	13	11	−15	33	88	48
Oregon	40	35	34	−3	36	78	26
Utah	6	7	4	−43	29	93	51
Washington	65	57	53	−7	39	74	17
Wyoming	5	4	3	−25	23	91	88

*Population counts are for April 1, 2000.
Note: Numbers of abortions are rounded to the nearest 10.

SOURCE: Lawrence B. Finer and Stanley K. Henshaw, "Table 3. Number of Providers, 1992, 1996 and 2000, and Percentage Change Between 1996 and 2000; and Number of Counties, Percentage of Counties Without an Abortion Provider and Percentage of Women Aged 15–44 Living in a County Without a Provider, 2000—All by Region and State," in "Abortion Incidence and Services in the United States in 2000," *Perspectives on Sexual and Reproductive Health*, vol. 35, no. 1, January/February 2003, http://www.guttmacher.org/pubs/journals/3500603.pdf (accessed September 20, 2005)

TABLE 4.13

Percentage distribution of obstetrics and gynecology residency programs, by availability of first-trimester abortion training, 1985, 1992, and 1998

Year	Offered routinely	Offered as elective	Not offered*	Total
1998				
Assumption A	46	34	19	100
Assumption B	31	23	44	100
1992	12	58	30	100
1985	23	50	28	100

*Includes programs where residents may obtain training elsewhere.
Notes: Under assumption A, nonrespondents offer abortion training at the same rate as respondents. Under assumption B, all nonrespondents, who make up 31% of the survey universe, do not offer abortion training. Percentages do not add to 100 because some respondents did not indicate whether training is routine or elective.

SOURCE: Rene Almeling, Laureen Tews, and Susan Didley, "Table 6. Percentage Distribution of Obstetrics and Gynecology Residency Programs, by Availability of First-Trimester Abortion Training, According to Year of Survey," in "Abortion Training in U.S. Obstetrics and Gynecology Residency Programs, 1998," *Family Planning Perspectives*, vol. 32, no. 6, November/December 2000, http://www.agi-usa.org/pubs/journals/3226800 .pdf (accessed September 20, 2005)

FIGURE 4.6

Timing of abortions, 2001

[In number of weeks of pregnancy]

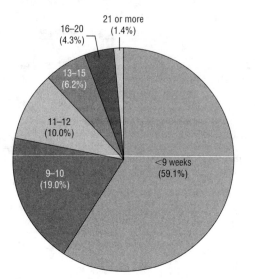

Eighty-eight percent of abortions occurred during the first 12 weeks of pregnancy.

SOURCE: "When Women Have Abortions (in weeks)," in "Induced Abortion in the United States," in *Facts in Brief*, The Alan Guttmacher Institute (AGI), May 2005, http://www.agi-usa.org/pubs/fb_induced_ abortion.pdf (accessed September 20, 2005)

TABLE 4.14

Legal abortions, by length of gestation, and demographic characteristics of women who obtained abortions, selected states, 2001

Characteristics	Weeks of gestation												Total	
	≤8		9–10		11–12		13–15		16–20		≥21			
	Number	Percent (%)	Number	Percent (%)	Number	Percent (%)	Number	Percent (%)	Number	Percent (%)	Number	Percent (%)	Number	Percent (%)[a]
Age group (years)														
<15	1,435	(38.9)	742	(20.1)	556	(15.1)	407	(11.0)	353	(9.6)	192	(5.2)	3,685	(100.0)
15–19	49,795	(49.5)	21,212	(21.1)	12,611	(12.5)	8,470	(8.4)	6,186	(6.1)	2,390	(2.4)	100,664	(100.0)
20–24	112,320	(57.4)	38,334	(19.6)	20,739	(10.6)	13,049	(6.7)	8,528	(4.4)	2,753	(1.4)	195,723	(100.0)
25–29	83,504	(63.0)	24,277	(18.3)	11,849	(8.9)	7,035	(5.3)	4,494	(3.4)	1,394	(1.1)	132,553	(100.0)
30–34	56,046	(65.2)	14,965	(17.4)	7,066	(8.2)	4,029	(4.7)	2,879	(3.3)	1,027	(1.2)	86,012	(100.0)
35–39	32,016	(65.2)	8,418	(17.1)	3,890	(7.9)	2,276	(4.6)	1,875	(3.8)	624	(1.3)	49,099	(100.0)
≥40	11,555	(66.6)	2,816	(16.2)	1,287	(7.4)	740	(4.3)	726	(4.2)	224	(1.3)	17,348	(100.0)
Total[b]	**346,671**	**(59.3)**	**110,764**	**(18.9)**	**57,998**	**(9.9)**	**36,006**	**(6.2)**	**25,041**	**(4.3)**	**8,604**	**(1.5)**	**585,084**	**(100.0)**
Race														
White	169,695	(61.2)	51,287	(18.5)	26,165	(9.4)	15,510	(5.6)	10,711	(3.9)	3,810	(1.4)	277,178	(100.0)
Black	96,581	(54.7)	35,910	(20.3)	19,831	(11.2)	12,509	(7.1)	8,866	(5.0)	3,004	(1.7)	176,701	(100.0)
Other	23,068	(63.7)	6,069	(16.8)	2,792	(7.7)	2,075	(5.7)	1,653	(4.6)	545	(1.5)	36,202	(100.0)
Total[c]	**289,344**	**(59.0)**	**93,266**	**(19.0)**	**48,788**	**(10.0)**	**30,094**	**(6.1)**	**21,230**	**(4.3)**	**7,359**	**(1.5)**	**490,081**	**(100.0)**
Ethnicity														
Hispanic	47,653	(59.6)	14,892	(18.6)	7,420	(9.3)	5,296	(6.6)	3,643	(4.6)	1,102	(1.4)	80,006	(100.0)
Non-Hispanic	215,238	(58.5)	70,433	(19.1)	37,355	(10.1)	22,810	(6.2)	16,529	(4.5)	5,858	(1.6)	368,223	(100.0)
Total[d]	**262,891**	**(58.7)**	**85,325**	**(19.0)**	**44,775**	**(10.0)**	**28,106**	**(6.3)**	**20,172**	**(4.5)**	**6,960**	**(1.6)**	**448,229**	**(100.0)**

[a]Percentages might not add to 100.0 because of rounding.
[b]Data from 39 states and New York City; excludes three areas from which gestational age was reported as unknown for >15% of women.
[c]Data from 33 states and New York City; excludes six areas from which gestational age or race was reported as unknown for >15% of women.
[d]Data from 29 states and New York City; excludes eight areas from which gestational age or ethnicity was reported as unknown for >15% of women.

SOURCE: Lilo T. Strauss, Joy Herndon, Jeani Chang, Wilda Y. Parker, Sonya V. Bowens, Suzanne B. Zane, and Cynthia J. Berg, "Table 16. Reported Legal Abortions, by Known Weeks of Gestation, Age Group, Race, and Ethnicity of Women Who Obtained an Abortion—Selected States, United States, 2001," in "Abortion Surveillance—United States, 2001," *Morbidity and Mortality Weekly Report/Surveillance Summaries*, vol. 53, no. SS-9, November 26, 2004, http://www.cdc.gov/mmwr/PDF/SS/SS5309.pdf (accessed September 20, 2005)

TABLE 4.15

Number of deaths and fatality rates for abortion-related deaths reported to CDC, by type of abortion, 1972–2000

| Year | Type of abortion | | | Total | Case-fatality rate[a] |
| | Induced | | Unknown[b] | | |
	Legal	Illegal			
1972	24	39	2	65	4.1
1973	25	19	3	47	4.1
1974	26	6	1	33	3.4
1975	29	4	1	34	3.4
1976	11	2	1	14	1.1
1977	17	4	0	21	1.6
1978	9	7	0	16	0.8
1979	22	0	0	22	1.8
1980	9	1	2	12	0.7
1981	8	1	0	9	0.6
1982	11	1	0	12	0.8
1983	11	1	0	12	0.9
1984	12	0	0	12	0.9
1985	11	1	1	13	0.8
1986	11	0	2	13	0.8
1987	7	2	0	9	0.5
1988	16	0	0	16	1.2
1989	12	1	0	13	0.9
1990	9	0	0	9	0.6
1991	11	1	0	12	0.8
1992	10	0	0	10	0.7
1993	6	1	2	9	0.5
1994	10	2	0	12	0.8
1995	4	0	0	4	0.3
1996	9	0	0	9	0.7
1997	7	0	0	7	0.6
1998	10	0	0	10	—[c]
1999	4	0	0	4	—[c]
2000	11	0	0	11	—[c]
Total	**362**	**93**	**15**	**470**	**1.1[d]**

Note: Numbers might differ from those in previously published reports because additional information has been reported to CDC (Centers for Disease Control and Prevention).
[a] Legal induced abortion-related deaths per 100,000 reported legal induced abortions for the United States.
[b] Unknown whether induced or spontaneous abortions.
[c] Case-fatality rates for 1998–2000 cannot be calculated because a substantial number of abortions occurred in nonreporting states, and the total number of abortions (the denominator) is unknown.
[d] Case-fatality rates computed for 1972–1997 only.

SOURCE: Lilo T. Strauss, Joy Herndon, Jeani Chang, Wilda Y. Parker, Sonya V. Bowens, Suzanne B. Zane, and Cynthia J. Berg, "Table 19. Number of Deaths and Case-Fatality Rates for Abortion-Related Deaths Reported to CDC, by Type of Abortion—United States, 1972–2000," in "Abortion Surveillance—United States, 2001," *Morbidity and Mortality Weekly Report/Surveillance Summaries*, vol. 53, no. SS-9, November 26, 2004, http://www.cdc.gov/mmwr/PDF/SS/SS5309.pdf (accessed September 20, 2005)

FIGURE 4.7

Percent of physicians surveyed who say they are familiar with mifepristone, May 15–August 28, 2001

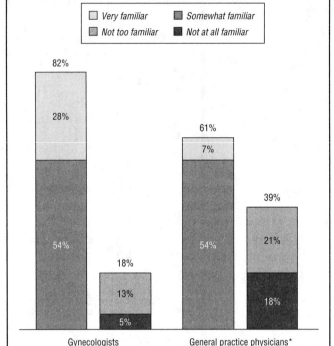

*Includes family practitioners, internists and general practitioners

SOURCE: "Chart 1. Familiarity with Mifepristone," in *Chartpack: National Surveys of Women's Health Care Providers and the Public: Views and Practices on Medical Abortion*, The Henry J. Kaiser Family Foundation, September 24, 2001, http://www.kff.org/womenshealth/loader.cfm?url=/commonspot/security/getfile.cfm&PageID=13852 (accessed September 20, 2005)

FIGURE 4.8

Percent of physicians surveyed who provide mifepristone, and percent who have not yet used mifepristone but will likely provide it in the coming year, May 15–August 28, 2001

PERCENT OF PHYSICIANS WHO HAVE PROVIDED MIFEPRISTONE SINCE ITS APPROVAL...

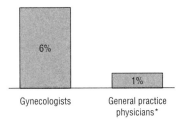

PERCENT OF PHYSICIANS WHO HAVE NOT YET USED MIFEPRISTONE WHO SAY THEY ARE LIKELY TO PROVIDE IT IN THE COMING YEAR...

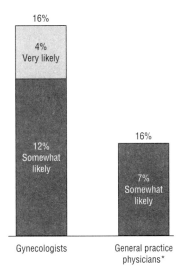

*Includes family practitioners, internists and general practitioners

SOURCE: "Chart 3. Who is Providing Medical Abortion? And Who Will Provide It in the Next Year?" in *Chartpack: National Surveys of Women's Health Care Providers and the Public: Views and Practices on Medical Abortion*, The Henry J. Kaiser Family Foundation, September 24, 2001, http://www.kff.org/womenshealth/loader .cfm?url=/commonspot/security/getfile.cfm&PageID=13852 (accessed September 20, 2005)

FIGURE 4.9

Abortion practices among physicians surveyed, May 15– August 28, 2001

SURGICAL ABORTION PRACTICES AMONG PHYSICIANS...

AMONG THE 27 PERCENT OF GYNECOLOGISTS WHO CURRENTLY PERFORM SURGICAL ABORTIONS, THE PERCENT WHO HAVE PROVIDED MIFEPRISTONE SINCE ITS APPROVAL...

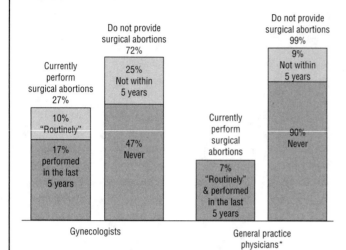

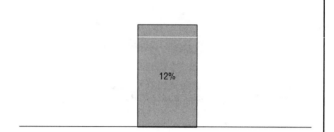

*Includes family practitioners, internists and general practitioners

SOURCE: "Chart 4. Surgical and Medical Abortion Practices," in *Chartpack: National Surveys of Women's Health Care Providers and the Public: Views and Practices on Medical Abortion*, The Henry J. Kaiser Family Foundation, September 24, 2001, http://www.kff.org/womenshealth/loader.cfm?url/=/ commonspot/security/getfile.cfm&PageID=13852 (accessed September 20, 2005)

CHAPTER 5
TEEN PREGNANCY AND ABORTION

TEEN PREGNANCY

Teen pregnancy is a serious concern in America. According to the Alan Guttmacher Institute (AGI), a non-profit corporation that engages in reproductive health research, policy analysis, and public education, 841,450 teens became pregnant in 2000. (See Figure 5.1.) The United States has the highest rate of teen pregnancies, births, and abortions among Western industrialized countries.

Figure 5.2 compares pregnancy and abortion rates of several countries in the mid-1990s. For the United States, for example, the teenage pregnancy rate in the mid-1990s was about eighty-five pregnancies per one thousand teenage girls. The birth rate is read at the end of the dark bar. Thus, in the mid-1990s, the teenage birth rate in the United States was about fifty-five. The rest of the pregnancies were aborted (the light part of the bar), by either induced abortion or spontaneous abortion (miscarriage). Thus, in the mid-1990s the teenage abortion rate in the United States (including miscarriages) was about thirty abortions per one thousand teenage girls. Note the higher numbers for all three rates for the United States compared with Sweden, France, Canada, and Great Britain.

The AGI reported these figures as part of a study conducted to see what the United States can learn from countries with lower teen pregnancy rates. In its report "Can More Progress Be Made?: Teenage Sexual and Reproductive Behavior in Developed Countries" (Alan Guttmacher Institute, http://www.guttmacher.org/pubs/euroteens_summ.html, 2001), the AGI revealed that sexually active teens in the United States are less likely to use contraceptives, especially highly effective ones such as hormonal methods, primarily because they tend to have shorter sexually intimate relationships than do teens in other developed countries. American teens also are more likely to have had multiple sex partners (more than four) than teens in the other study countries: Sweden, France, Canada, and Great Britain.

The report suggests that the U.S. approach to reducing teen pregnancy focuses on telling teens that it is wrong to start childbearing early, and that this pronouncement is not a great enough deterrent to teens. In addition, the report suggests that the United States does not provide sufficient resources to help teens make responsible choices. The study attributes the other countries' lower rates of teenage pregnancy to parental and governmental support of teenagers by providing information about and access to effective contraception and adequate health services. In addition, the AGI found that government agencies and parents in these countries help teenagers make responsible decisions about sexual relationships, the use of birth control, and the prevention of sexually transmitted diseases (STDs).

Results of the Henry J. Kaiser Family Foundation's (KFF) 2003 "National Survey of Adolescents and Young Adults: Sexual Health Knowledge, Attitudes and Experiences" survey (http://www.kff.org/youthhivstds/3218-index.cfm) appear to support the AGI findings. The results reveal that more than 75% of the teens surveyed want to know more about how to use condoms, how to recognize the signs of STD and human immunodeficiency virus (HIV) infection, what STD and HIV testing involves, and where they can go to get tested for either.

Another AGI report—"Socioeconomic Disadvantage and Adolescent Women's Sexual and Reproductive Behavior: The Case of Five Developed Countries," (Susheela Singh, Jacqueline E. Darroch, Jennifer J. Frost, and the Study Team, *Family Planning Perspectives*, vol. 33, no. 6, November/December 2001)—suggests that U.S. teens have higher birth rates and pregnancy rates than

FIGURE 5.1

Number of teen pregnancies, 2000

[Per age group]

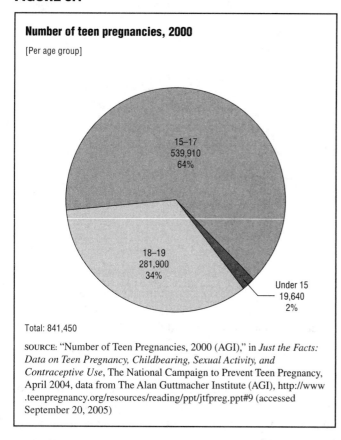

15–17
539,910
64%

18–19
281,900
34%

Under 15
19,640
2%

Total: 841,450

SOURCE: "Number of Teen Pregnancies, 2000 (AGI)," in *Just the Facts: Data on Teen Pregnancy, Childbearing, Sexual Activity, and Contraceptive Use*, The National Campaign to Prevent Teen Pregnancy, April 2004, data from The Alan Guttmacher Institute (AGI), http://www.teenpregnancy.org/resources/reading/ppt/jtfpreg.ppt#9 (accessed September 20, 2005)

FIGURE 5.2

Pregnancy rate, birth rates, and abortion rates among teenagers in the United States and other developed countries, mid-1990s

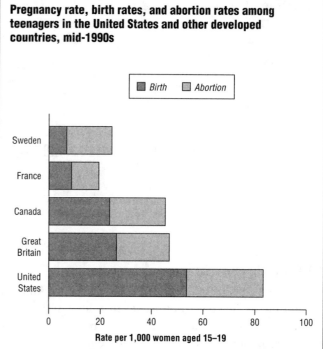

■ Birth   □ Abortion

Sweden
France
Canada
Great Britain
United States

0   20   40   60   80   100

Rate per 1,000 women aged 15–19

SOURCE: Jacqueline E. Darroch, Jennifer Frost, and Susheela Singh, "Chart 2. U.S. Teenagers Have Higher Pregnancy Rates, Birthrates and Abortion Rates Than Adolescents in Other Developed Countries," in *Teenage Sexual and Reproductive Behavior in Developed Countries: Can More Progress Be Made?* The Alan Guttmacher Institute (AGI), 2001, http://www.guttmacher.org/pubs/summaries/euroteens_summ.pdf (accessed September 20, 2005)

those in other developed countries because many American teens are "disadvantaged." To improve U.S. teens' sexual and reproductive behavior, the report suggests, strategies are needed to reduce the numbers of young people growing up in disadvantaged conditions and to help those who are disadvantaged overcome the obstacles they face.

Changes in Teen Pregnancy Rates

Teen pregnancy rates vary with age. As Figure 5.3 shows, in 2000 young women ages eighteen to nineteen had a pregnancy rate more than twice as high as those ages fifteen to seventeen. The pregnancy rates for all teenage groups declined dramatically from 1990–91 to 2000: 35% for young women ages fifteen to seventeen, 28% for those ages fifteen to nineteen, and 21% for those ages eighteen to nineteen.

Teen pregnancy rates also vary among the three major racial/ethnic groups in the United States. (See Figure 5.4.) In 2000 pregnancy rates were highest for non-Hispanic African-American teens, and lowest for non-Hispanic whites. The rates for both groups fell between 1990 and 2000: 32% for African-American teens and 37% for white teens. The rates for Hispanic teens (any race) rose from 1990 to 1992 but then declined to 2000 by 19%.

As the map in Figure 5.5 shows, teen pregnancy rates vary dramatically across the United States, from forty-

two pregnancies per one thousand female teens in North Dakota to 113 per one thousand female teens in Nevada. Figure 5.6 shows the change in teen pregnancy rates from 1992 to 2000. Although rates declined during that period in all states, the declines ranged from 4.9% in Wyoming to 39.6% in California.

Possible Reasons for Changes in Teen Pregnancy Rates

Some analysts suggest factors that may account for the decline in teen pregnancy include an increase in condom use (perhaps to prevent contracting HIV or other STDs); decreased sexual activity reflecting changing attitudes toward sex before marriage; and the use of newer methods of birth control, such as hormonal implants and injectables.

Conservative analysts discount the increasing use of contraception as being responsible for the lower pregnancy rates. Instead, they attribute the drop in teen pregnancy to the increasing practice of abstinence (not having sex). Some observers note that young people have become more conservative in their attitudes toward casual sex.

Survey research conducted jointly by KFF and *Seventeen* magazine, the results of which were published

FIGURE 5.3

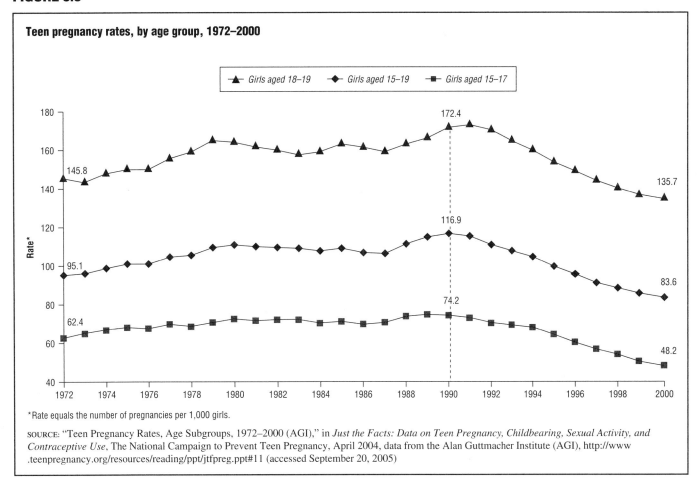

Teen pregnancy rates, by age group, 1972–2000

▲ Girls aged 18–19   ◆ Girls aged 15–19   ■ Girls aged 15–17

*Rate equals the number of pregnancies per 1,000 girls.

SOURCE: "Teen Pregnancy Rates, Age Subgroups, 1972–2000 (AGI)," in *Just the Facts: Data on Teen Pregnancy, Childbearing, Sexual Activity, and Contraceptive Use*, The National Campaign to Prevent Teen Pregnancy, April 2004, data from the Alan Guttmacher Institute (AGI), http://www.teenpregnancy.org/resources/reading/ppt/jtfpreg.ppt#11 (accessed September 20, 2005)

in the October 2003 article "SexSmarts," revealed that the large majority of teens surveyed saw "value in waiting" to have sex. Almost all (92%), including those who were sexually active, said that being a virgin in high school was a "good thing" and that teens who choose not to have sex were "supported" in that decision. Teens also acknowledged that delaying sex had a variety of benefits including respect, control, and freedom from worry about sexual health risks such as pregnancy and STDs. Of teens ages fifteen to seventeen who had not yet had sex, 94% said they had not done so for fear of becoming pregnant; 59% report that it was because they did not have access to contraception.

The 2003 KFF survey "National Survey of Adolescents and Young Adults: Sexual Health Knowledge, Attitudes and Experiences" appeared to mirror these sentiments. Most young people responded that there was pressure to have sex by a certain age and that if you have been "seeing someone for a while," then sex generally was expected. Almost two-thirds thought that waiting to have sex might be a "nice idea, but nobody really does"; more than half agreed that once you do have sex it is harder to say "no" the next time. (See Table 5.1.) Compared with whites and Asians, African-American and Hispanic (Latino) teens more frequently

reported that abstinence is not a realistic option for young people.

Life Consequences of Teen Pregnancy

Douglas Kirby, in "Emerging Answers: Research Findings on Programs to Reduce Teen Pregnancy" (National Campaign to Prevent Teen Pregnancy, http://www.teenpregnancy.org/resources/data/pdf/emeranswsum.pdf, May 2001), pointed out the serious consequences that high teen pregnancy rates have on teenagers, their children, and society at large. According to Kirby:

> When teens give birth, their future prospects become more bleak. They become less likely to complete school and more likely to be single parents, for instance. Their children's prospects are even worse— they have less supportive and stimulating home environments, poorer health, lower cognitive development, worse educational outcomes, more behavior problems, and are more likely to become teen parents themselves.

In "Facts & Stats 17: What Happens to Teen Mothers" (http://www.teenpregnancy.org/resources/teens/facts/fact17.asp), the National Campaign to Prevent Teen Pregnancy reports that only 41% of teen mothers earn a high school diploma and just 1.5% earn a college degree by age thirty. They also are more likely to be on welfare and more likely to

FIGURE 5.4

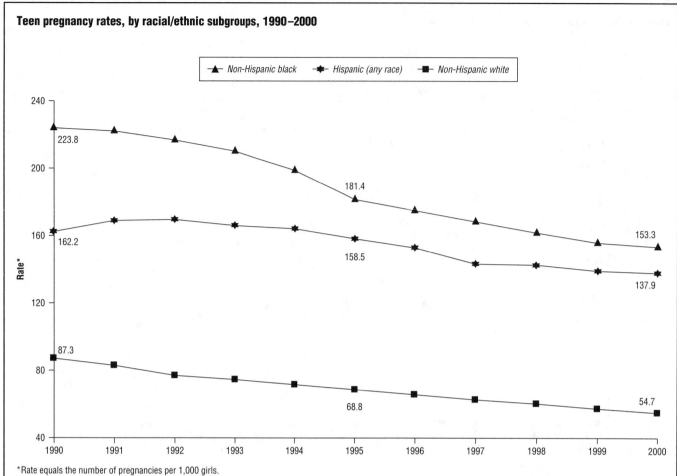

Teen pregnancy rates, by racial/ethnic subgroups, 1990–2000

Legend: ▲ Non-Hispanic black   ★ Hispanic (any race)   ■ Non-Hispanic white

*Rate equals the number of pregnancies per 1,000 girls.

SOURCE: "Teen Pregnancy Rates, Racial/Ethnic Subgroups, 1990–2000 (AGI)," in *Just the Facts: Data on Teen Pregnancy, Childbearing, Sexual Activity, and Contraceptive Use*, The National Campaign to Prevent Teen Pregnancy, April 2004, data from The Alan Guttmacher Institute (AGI), http://www.teenpregnancy.org/resources/reading/ppt/jtfpreg.ppt#15 (accessed September 20, 2005)

be single moms. Another publication by the same organization, "Not Just Another Single Issue" (http://www.teenpregnancy.org/resources/data/pdf/notjust.pdf, February 2002), notes that the children of teenage mothers have lower birth weights, increasing the risk of infant death, blindness, deafness, chronic respiratory problems, mental retardation, mental illness, and cerebral palsy. Low birth weight also doubles the chances that a child will be diagnosed with dyslexia, hyperactivity, or another disability. They also are more likely to be abused and neglected and to perform poorly in school. The Campaign also reports that the sons of teenage mothers are 13% more likely to end up in prison, and daughters of teen mothers are 22% more likely to become teen mothers themselves.

An Overview of Teen Pregnancy Outcomes

According to the National Campaign to Prevent Teen Pregnancy, as of May 2005, 34% of young women became pregnant at least once before they reached the age of twenty ("General Facts and Stats," http://www.teenpregnancy.org/resources/data/genlfact.asp), resulting in about 820,000 teen pregnancies per year. Eight in ten teen pregnancies were unintended and 81% involved unmarried teens. According to the Centers for Disease Control and Prevention (CDC), almost one-third of unintended pregnancies end in abortion. In addition, as Figure 5.7 shows, more pregnancies of girls under age fifteen ended in abortion than those of older teens in 2000. Nearly 44% of pregnant teens under age fifteen terminated their pregnancies with induced abortion. About 13% of pregnancies in this age group terminated naturally with miscarriage. About 43% of under-fifteen pregnant teens carried the pregnancy to term and gave birth in 2000. Figure 5.8 shows that the percentage of pregnancies to teens fifteen to nineteen ending in birth decreased in the 1970s and remained slightly below 50% through most of the 1980s. The period from 1990 to 2000 saw an increase in the percentage of teenagers in this age group carrying their pregnancies to term.

FIGURE 5.5

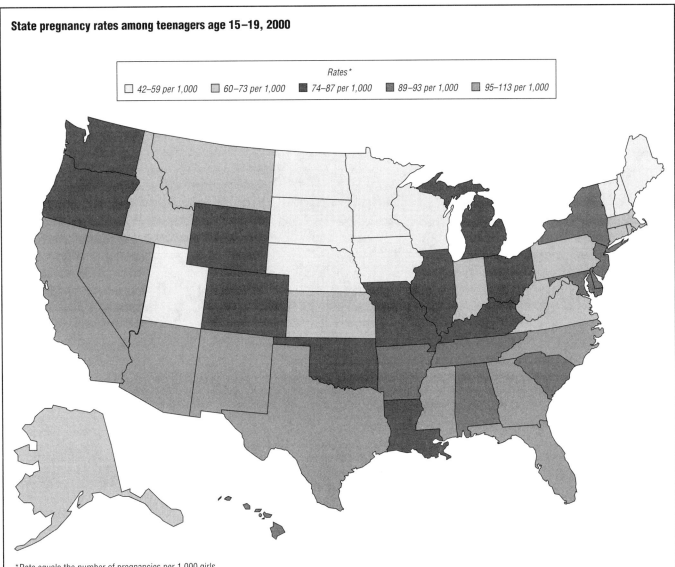

State pregnancy rates among teenagers age 15–19, 2000

Rates*

☐ 42–59 per 1,000   ☐ 60–73 per 1,000   ■ 74–87 per 1,000   ■ 89–93 per 1,000   ■ 95–113 per 1,000

*Rate equals the number of pregnancies per 1,000 girls.

SOURCE: "State Teen Pregnancy Rates, 2000 (AGI)," in *Just the Facts: Data on Teen Pregnancy, Childbearing, Sexual Activity, and Contraceptive Use*, The National Campaign to Prevent Teen Pregnancy, April 2004, data from The Alan Guttmacher Institute (AGI), http://www.teenpregnancy.org/resources/reading/ppt/jtfpreg.ppt#26 (accessed September 20, 2005)

PREVENTING TEEN PREGNANCY

Most people begin having sex in their mid- to late teens, and in 2001 6.6% of teens reported first having sex before age thirteen. In that year the median age at first intercourse was 16.5 years; 61% of twelfth graders had participated in sexual intercourse, as had 35% of ninth graders ("Teen Sexual Activity," Henry J. Kaiser Family Foundation, January 2003). By the time they are eighteen years old, six in ten female teens and nearly seven in ten male teens have had sex ("Sexuality Education: Facts in Brief," Alan Guttmacher Institute, http://www.guttmacher.org/pubs/fb_sex_ed02.html, 2002).

There is little agreement on how to prevent teen pregnancy from occurring as a result of these sexual encounters and what the role of sex education and the availability of contraception should be. Whereas countries such as France, Germany, and the Netherlands try to prevent teenage pregnancy through education about sexuality and safe sex, the United States places more emphasis on preventing teenage sex by encouraging abstinence. Many Americans consider the promotion of birth control as an encouragement to teens to be promiscuous and advocate abstinence instead.

Sex Education/Abstinence Education

The 1996 federal welfare reform law, the Personal Responsibility and Work Opportunity Reconciliation Act (PL 104-193), provided an annual $50 million allocation over a five-year period (1998–2002) to states for abstinence education programs. The purpose of these

FIGURE 5.6

Changes in state pregnancy rates among teenagers age 15–19, 1992–2000

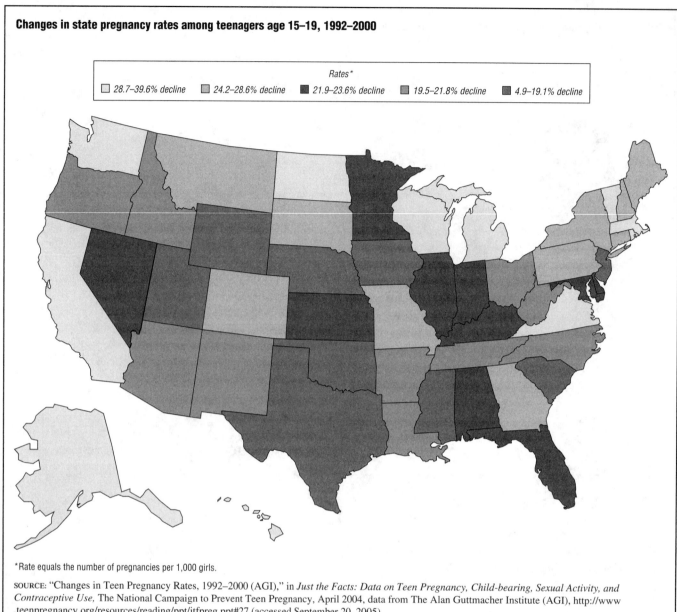

*Rate equals the number of pregnancies per 1,000 girls.

SOURCE: "Changes in Teen Pregnancy Rates, 1992–2000 (AGI)," in *Just the Facts: Data on Teen Pregnancy, Child-bearing, Sexual Activity, and Contraceptive Use,* The National Campaign to Prevent Teen Pregnancy, April 2004, data from The Alan Guttmacher Institute (AGI), http://www.teenpregnancy.org/resources/reading/ppt/jtfpreg.ppt#27 (accessed September 20, 2005)

programs was "to enable the State to provide abstinence education, and at the option of the State, where appropriate, mentoring, counseling, and adult supervision to promote abstinence from sexual activity, with focus on those groups which are most likely to bear children out of wedlock." Funded programs are prohibited from teaching birth control, although students requesting information may be given referrals. In addition, the law included an incentive provision, allotting $50 million to be distributed to the top five states that reduce their out-of-wedlock births without increasing abortions during the previous two years. In mid-2003 Congress passed the "Welfare Reform Extension Act of 2003," which reauthorizes the abstinence education program exactly as under the 1996 law. In addition, $5 million

is provided annually to support a national teen pregnancy prevention resource center, which would offer technical assistance and work with the media to discourage teen pregnancies.

In a review of thirty-five abstinence-based programs, the World Health Organization found that these programs were less effective in reducing risky sexual practices in teens than programs that promoted delaying first intercourse and safer sex practices. According to Douglas Kirby of the National Campaign to Prevent Teen Pregnancy, there is no evidence that abstinence-only education delays teenage sexual activity. Also, research shows that abstinence-only strategies may discourage contraceptive use among teens who are sexually active. A study by Kirby found that comprehensive sex education programs that provide

TABLE 5.1

Attitudes among adolescents and young adults about relationships and sexual activity, November 13, 2001–February 27, 2002

PERCENT OF ADOLESCENTS AND YOUNG ADULTS WHO SAY THEY "STRONGLY" OR "SOMEWHAT" AGREE WITH EACH OF THE FOLLOWING

	Total 15–24	Age		Gender		Race/ethnicity				Sexual status	
		15–17	18–24	Male	Female	White	African American	Latino	Asian	Sexually active	Not sexually active
Waiting to have sex is a nice idea but nobody really does	61%	63%	61%	64%	60%	59%	71%	66%	54%	65%	55%
There is pressure to have sex by a certain age	58%	59%	57%	61%	54%	57%	61%	57%	54%	59%	54%
Once you have had sex it is harder to say no the next time	55%	52%	57%	62%	48%	61%	45%	46%	47%	58%	50%
If you have been seeing someone for a while it is expected that you will have sex	47%	39%	51%	55%	38%	47%	49%	40%	42%	54%	32%
Oral sex is not as big of a deal as sexual intercourse	42%	46%	40%	49%	35%	46%	33%	34%	36%	44%	38%
Number of respondents	1,552	483	1,069	737	815	699	287	336	149	1,014	538

SOURCE: Kaiser Family Foundation, Tina Hoff, Liberty Greene, and Julia Davis, "Table 7. Adolescents and Young Adults: Attitudes about Relationships and Becoming Sexually Active," in *National Survey of Adolescents and Young Adults: Sexual Health Knowledge, Attitudes and Experiences*, The Henry J. Kaiser Family Foundation, May 19, 2003, http://www.kff.org/youthhivstds/loader.cfm?url=/commonspot/security/getfile.cfm&PageID=14269 (accessed September 20, 2005)

FIGURE 5.7

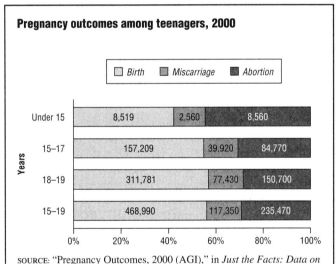

Pregnancy outcomes among teenagers, 2000

SOURCE: "Pregnancy Outcomes, 2000 (AGI)," in *Just the Facts: Data on Teen Pregnancy, Childbearing, Sexual Activity, and Contraceptive Use*, The National Campaign to Prevent Teen Pregnancy, April 2004, data from The Alan Guttmacher Institute (AGI), http://www.teenpregnancy.org/resources/reading/ppt/jtfpreg.ppt#20 (accessed September 20, 2005)

information about both abstinence and contraception "do not accelerate the onset of sex, increase the frequency of sex or increase the number of partners—as critics of sex education have long alleged—but can increase the use of contraception when teens become sexually active" (as summarized by Cynthia Dailard in "Abstinence Promotion and Teen Family Planning: The Misguided Drive for Equal Funding," *The Guttmacher Report on Public Policy*, vol. 5, no. 1, February 2002). These findings were underscored in "Call to Action to Promote Sexual Health and Responsible Sexual Behavior," issued by Surgeon General David Satcher in June 2001.

On February 10, 2005, the Responsible Education about Life Act (the REAL Act) (H.R. 768 and S. 368) was introduced in Congress. This bill would provide funding to states for so-called abstinence-plus programs in schools that would provide medically accurate, age appropriate, comprehensive sex education that includes instruction in both abstinence and contraception. The House of Representatives and the Senate referred the bill to committee. As of September 1, 2005, no action had been taken yet on the bill.

As of August 1, 2005, twenty-two states and the District of Columbia mandated sex education in public schools, and thirty-eight states and the District of Columbia mandated STD/HIV education. Twenty-two states required that abstinence be stressed when taught as part of sex education, and eight states required that it be only "covered." Only fourteen states and the District of Columbia required that sex education programs cover contraception, while seventeen states required that STD/HIV programs cover contraception. No state required that contraception be stressed in either sex education classes or STD/HIV prevention classes ("Sex and STD/HIV Education," *State Policies in Brief*, Alan Guttmacher Institute, August 1, 2005).

Parents and Sex Education

Parental consent requirements or "opt-out" clauses, which allow parents to remove students from instruction the parents find objectionable, may restrict the information adolescents receive. AGI statistics show that as of August 1, 2005, three states required parental consent for students to participate in sex or STD/HIV education, and thirty-six states and the District of Columbia allowed parents to remove their children from these classes.

FIGURE 5.8

Pregnancy outcomes among teenagers age 15–19, 1972–2000

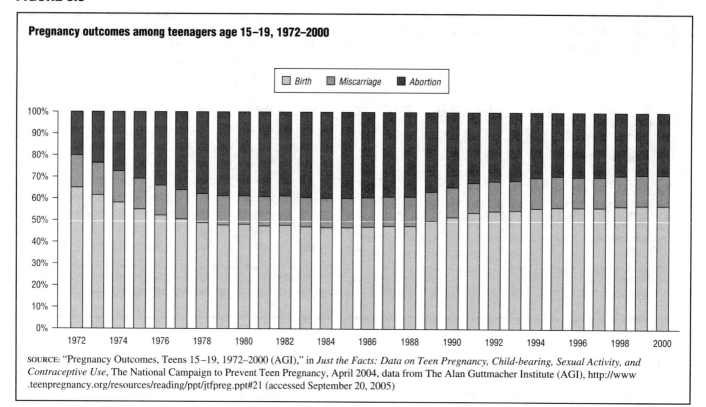

SOURCE: "Pregnancy Outcomes, Teens 15–19, 1972–2000 (AGI)," in *Just the Facts: Data on Teen Pregnancy, Child-bearing, Sexual Activity, and Contraceptive Use*, The National Campaign to Prevent Teen Pregnancy, April 2004, data from The Alan Guttmacher Institute (AGI), http://www .teenpregnancy.org/resources/reading/ppt/jtfpreg.ppt#21 (accessed September 20, 2005)

In the "National Survey of Adolescents and Young Adults," released in 2003, the KFF reported that "sex education in school is also a cornerstone of sexual health information for young people—68% have learned at least 'some,' including 45% who say they have learned a lot, from sex education."

In January 2004 the results of a survey jointly sponsored by National Public Radio, the Henry J. Kaiser Family Foundation, and the Harvard University John F. Kennedy School of Government, were published. The results of "Sex Education in America" (Kaiser Family Foundation, http://www.kff.org/kaiserpolls/pom-r012904oth.cfm, January 29, 2004) revealed that 15% of adult Americans believe that schools should use an abstinence-only approach in sex education classes. Nearly half—46%—believe that abstinence-plus is best. That is, schools should teach that abstinence is a primary goal, but they should also teach about condoms and other forms of contraception. Slightly over one-third (36%) believe that abstinence is not the most important thing, and that sex education classes should focus on helping teens learn how to make responsible decisions about sex.

Characteristics of Effective Sex Education Programs

For many years Douglas Kirby was chairperson of the Effective Programs and Research Task Force for the National Campaign to Prevent Teen Pregnancy. In 2001 he completed a study that surveyed the effectiveness of sex education programs across the United States. At that time Kirby noted that more research needed to be conducted because very few sex education programs have been evaluated as to their impact in delaying sexual intercourse among adolescents. Kirby observed that curricula with the most effective sex and HIV education programs share ten important characteristics. In his words, these programs do the following:

- Focus on reducing one or more sexual behaviors that lead to unintended pregnancy or HIV/STD infection

- Are based on theoretical approaches that have been demonstrated to influence other health-related behavior and identify specific important sexual antecedents to be targeted

- Deliver and consistently reinforce a clear message about abstaining from sexual activity and/or using condoms or other forms of contraception. This appears to be one of the most important characteristics that distinguishes effective from ineffective programs

- Provide basic, accurate information about the risks of teen sexual activity and about ways to avoid intercourse or use methods of protection against pregnancy and STDs

- Include activities that address social pressures that influence sexual behavior

- Provide examples of and practice with communication, negotiation, and refusal skills

- Employ teaching methods designed to involve participants and have them personalize the information

- Incorporate behavioral goals, teaching methods, and materials that are appropriate to the age, sexual experience, and culture of the students

- Last a sufficient length of time (i.e., more than a few hours)

- Select teachers or peer leaders who believe in the program and then provide them with adequate training

The National Campaign to Prevent Teen Pregnancy also suggests that successful programs should emphasize activities that instill teens with confidence and a sense of hope for the future. According to Daniel J. Whitaker, Kim S. Miller, and Leslie F. Clark in "Reconceptualizing Adolescent Sexual Behavior: Beyond Did They or Didn't They?" (*Family Planning Perspectives*, vol. 32, no. 3, May/June 2000), teen sex prevention efforts "must be tailored to the specific needs of teens with varying sexual experiences and expectations, and must address the social and psychological context in which sexual experiences occur." The authors contend that prevention efforts that focus only on delaying sexual onset in teens who have not had sex, and encouraging condom use among teens who already are sexually active, leave out many teens.

Media Influences on Teenage Sex

The number of television shows with sexual content increased significantly from 1998 to 2000. Only one in ten shows that contain sexual content included a reference to safer sex or to the possible risks and responsibilities that go along with having sex. However, there is a trend toward including more of these messages according to the third "Sex on TV: Content and Context" report (Kaiser Family Foundation, http://www.kff.org/entmedia/20030204a-index.cfm, 2003)—a study of the amount and nature of sexual material on television. The report found that the amount of sex on television remains high, but TV programs are more likely to include some reference to issues such as waiting to have sex, using contraception, or the possible consequences of unprotected sex.

The RAND Corporation, a nonprofit research organization, released a study on television and adolescent sexuality in November 2003. Results of this study revealed that teenagers in the United States absorb sex education messages from television programs, and watching and discussing television programs with an adult reinforces the sex education messages. A RAND senior behavioral scientist and colleagues surveyed 506 twelve- to seventeen-year-old viewers of the NBC series *Friends* about an episode in which the character Rachel tells the character Ross that she became pregnant after they had sex although they used a condom. The episode features two mentions that condoms are only 97% effective at preventing pregnancy when used correctly. Most teen viewers reported that they felt the message of the episode was that "lots of times condoms don't prevent pregnancy." The 40% of teen viewers who watched this particular show with an adult were more likely to accurately remember condoms' effectiveness (97%) in preventing pregnancy than teens who did not watch the episode with an adult.

In a special analysis by KFF of the top twenty shows teen viewers watch, almost half (45%) of the episodes that included a reference to sex also included a reference to a safer sex topic. The study also revealed that safer sex messages were more common in shows that have characters involved in sexual intercourse (26%) and teens in sexual situations (34%)—both nearly twice the rate found four years ago.

When the report was released, KFF Vice President Victoria Rideout said, "From a public health perspective, it's encouraging to see this trend toward greater attention to safer sex issues on TV.... This generation is immersed in the media, so when Hollywood makes safer sex sexier, whether it's abstinence or protection, that's all to the good" ("Study Finds Sex Getting Safer on American TV," Dr. Bob Martin, http://www.doctorbob.com/2003k_02_05news03.html, February 5, 2003).

RAND Corporation researchers published a more extensive study on this subject in the journal *Pediatrics* in September 2004: "Watching Sex on Television Predicts Adolescent Initiation of Sexual Behavior" (vol. 114, no. 3, http://pediatrics.aappublications.org/cgi/reprint/114/3/e280). In spite of some of the positive references to safer sex and sexual responsibility on television, a major conclusion of the authors of the report was that "watching sex on TV predicts and may hasten adolescent sexual initiation. Reducing the amount of sexual content in entertainment programming, reducing adolescent exposure to this content, or increasing references to and depictions of possible negative consequences of sexual activity could appreciably delay the initiation of coital and non coital activities. Alternatively, parents may be able to reduce the effects of sexual content by watching TV with their teenaged children and discussing their own beliefs about sex and the behaviors portrayed." In this and their previous studies on sex on television and its influence on adolescents, the RAND Corporation notes that:

- Of all shows, 64% have some sexual content, including one in three (32%) containing sexual behaviors (the rest have talk about sex). This rate of sexual content is similar to that found two years before (68%), up from about half of all shows (56%) four years before.

- One in seven shows (14%) include actual sex, either depicted or strongly implied, which is a 4% increase from two years before and a 7% increase from four years before.
- Overall, the percentage of shows with any sexual content—including more modest content such as talk about sex, kissing, or touching—that also included a safer sex reference was 15%, up from 10% two years before and 9% four years before.

Other television programming, some magazines, and some Web sites targeted to teens provide positive, educational messages regarding teen sex and pregnancy. For example, the Black Entertainment Television (BET) cable show *Teen Summit* features regular programs on teen sexuality. The *Channel One News*, a nationwide school-based news program involving more than eight million students and four hundred thousand educators, covers issues affecting America's teens. *Teen People* magazine and the National Campaign to Prevent Teen Pregnancy sponsor a contest each year asking teens to create a magazine advertisement with a message about preventing teen pregnancy. *Teen People* also has continuing editorial coverage of issues surrounding teen pregnancy, and *Sports Illustrated* and BET's *Heart and Soul* magazine have featured teen pregnancy prevention in their public service messages. Kiwibox.com has featured discussions on what it's like to be a teen mother, how to know when you're ready to have sex, and how to prevent pregnancy and STDs.

TRENDS IN SEXUAL RISK BEHAVIORS

Unprotected sexual intercourse and multiple sex partners place young people at risk for pregnancy as well as for HIV infection and other STDs. In "Trends in Sexual Risk Behaviors among High School Students—United States, 1991–2001" (*Morbidity and Mortality Weekly Report*, vol. 51, no. 38, September 27, 2002), the CDC reported that in the decade 1991–2001 the number of high school students who reported having sex decreased 16% and that those who had multiple sex partners (more than four) decreased 24%. The overall prevalence of current sexual activity did not change.

Among currently sexually active female students, condom use at last sexual intercourse increased from 38% in 1991 to 51.3% in 2001. For males it was 54.5% in 1991, compared with 65.1% in 2001. (See Table 5.2.) The percentage of these students who used alcohol or drugs before their last sexual intercourse, however, increased by 18%.

TEEN BIRTH RATES

In 2001 the CDC reported that the U.S. teen birth rate of 48.7 in 2000 was the highest of twenty-three developed countries ("Births to Teenagers in the United States, 1940–2000," *National Vital Statistics Reports*, vol. 49, no. 10, September 25, 2001). Of these countries, the Netherlands and Japan had the lowest teen birth rates; the U.S. rate was nine times higher. The Russian Federation had the second-highest birth rate with 44.7 births per one thousand teens in 1995. Figure 5.9 shows teenage birth rates in the United States from 1970 to 2000 compared with the birth rates of teens in England and Wales, Canada, France, and Sweden. American teen birth rates have been much higher for decades than those of the other developed countries shown.

Although teen birth rates are relatively high in the United States compared with other developed countries, there are positive statistics: the birth rate for teens ages fifteen to nineteen years decreased 33% between 1991 and 2003. In 2003 the birth rate for this age group was 41.7. The birth rate also declined dramatically for younger teens ten to fourteen years—down 57% since 1991. In 2003 the birth rate for this age group was 0.6. (See Table 5.3.)

Births to Unmarried Teenagers

Most teens who give birth were unmarried—81.6% overall in 2003, with 343,908 babies born to unmarried teens in that year. (See Table 5.4.) From 2002 to 2003 the number of births to unmarried women of any age increased by 0.6% (from 34% to 34.6%), and births to unmarried teens rose by 1.4% (from 80.2% to 81.6%). Within age subgroups of teens, the largest increase in the number of births to unmarried teens was in the eighteen to nineteen age group.

Race and Ethnicity

In the ten to fourteen age group the largest decline in birth rate was among Asian or Pacific Islanders (API teens). In the eighteen to nineteen age group the largest decline was among Native American teens. Rates in 2003 were highest for Hispanic teenagers and lowest for API teens.

According to the CDC, non-Hispanic African-American teens in the fifteen to nineteen age group experienced the largest drop in birth rates since 1991—a 45% decline from 1991 to 2003. (See Table 5.3.) Figure 5.10 shows the decline in teen birth rates from 1990 to 2002 by racial/ethnic group. The dramatic decline in birth rates of African-American teens is evident, although the birth rate of all groups declined.

Hispanic ("Latina") teens had the highest teen birth rates among the major racial or ethnic groups in the United States from 1995 to 2002, according to the National Campaign to Prevent Teen Pregnancy. (See Figure 5.10.) The 2002 birth rate for Hispanic fifteen- to nineteen-year-olds was 82.9 per one thousand, which was nearly double the national rate of 42.9 per one thousand ("Teen Sexual Activity, Pregnancy and Childbearing among Latinos in the United States," *Fact Sheet*, National Campaign to

TABLE 5.2

Percentage of high school students who reported sexual risk behaviors, by selected characteristics, selected years 1991–2003

Characteristic	Ever had sexual intercourse	≥4 sex partners during lifetime	Currently sexually active[a]	Condom use during last sexual intercourse[b]	Alcohol or drug use before last sexual intercourse[b]
	%	%	%	%	%
Sex					
Female					
1991	50.8	13.8	38.2	38.0	16.8
1993	50.2	15.0	37.5	46.0	16.6
1995	52.1	14.4	40.4	48.6	16.8
1997	47.7	14.1	36.5	50.8	18.5
1999	47.7	13.1	36.3	50.7	18.6
2001	42.9	11.4	33.4	51.3	20.7
2003	45.3	11.2	34.6	57.4	21.0
Male					
1991	57.4	23.4	36.8	54.5	26.3
1993	55.6	22.3	37.5	59.2	25.7
1995	54.0	20.9	35.5	60.5	32.8
1997	48.8	17.6	33.4	62.5	30.5
1999	52.2	19.3	36.2	65.5	31.2
2001	48.5	17.2	33.4	65.1	30.9
2003	48.0	17.5	33.8	68.8	29.8
Grade					
9					
1991	39.0	12.5	22.4	53.3	20.9
1993	37.7	10.9	24.8	61.6	22.4
1995	36.9	12.9	23.6	62.9	29.7
1997	38.0	12.2	24.2	58.8	33.2
1999	38.6	11.8	26.6	66.6	25.6
2001	34.4	9.6	22.7	67.5	24.0
2003	32.8	10.4	21.2	69.0	24.4
10					
1991	48.2	15.1	33.2	46.3	22.3
1993	46.1	15.9	30.1	54.7	24.2
1995	48.0	15.6	33.7	59.7	28.6
1997	42.5	13.8	29.2	58.9	22.9
1999	46.8	15.6	33.0	62.6	23.1
2001	40.8	12.6	29.7	60.1	27.7
2003	44.1	12.6	30.6	69.0	26.8
11					
1991	62.4	22.1	43.3	48.7	22.2
1993	57.5	19.9	40.0	55.3	22.0
1995	58.6	19.0	42.4	52.3	24.3
1997	49.7	16.7	37.8	60.1	23.1
1999	52.5	17.3	37.5	59.2	28.6
2001	51.9	15.2	38.1	58.9	24.7
2003	53.2	16.0	41.1	60.8	24.7

Prevent Teen Pregnancy, http://www.teenpregnancy.org/resources/reading/pdf/latinofs.pdf, May 2004). In 2002 30% of the births to women ages fifteen to nineteen years were to Hispanic teens. This birth rate is higher than that for African-American teens, although Hispanic teens have a lower pregnancy rate, because African-American teens are more likely than Hispanic teens to have an abortion.

State-Specific Birth Rates

In 2002 birth rates for teens ages fifteen to nineteen years ranged from a low of 20.0 births per one thousand female teens in New Hampshire to a high of 64.7 in Mississippi. Although a city, so not directly comparable, the District of Columbia had the highest teen birth rate at 69.1. (See Table 5.5.)

In 2000 in every state, the District of Columbia, the Virgin Islands, and Guam, birth rates for teens ages fifteen to nineteen declined from the rates in 1991. (See Figure 5.11.) Declines ranged from less than 16% in Texas, Arizona, Colorado, Nebraska, Arkansas, Mississippi, Alabama, Georgia, North Carolina, and Rhode Island to 25% or more in Washington, California, Alaska, Hawaii, Michigan, Massachusetts, Vermont, New Hampshire, Maine, and the District of Columbia.

TEEN ABORTION

Abortion rates for teens ages fifteen to nineteen years decreased 40% from 1990 to 2000—from 40.3 per one thousand to 24.0 per one thousand. (See Table 5.6.) The

TABLE 5.2

Percentage of high school students who reported sexual risk behaviors, by selected characteristics, selected years 1991–2003 [CONTINUED]

Characteristic	Ever had sexual intercourse %	≥4 sex partners during lifetime %	Currently sexually active[a] %	Condom use during last sexual intercourse[b] %	Alcohol or drug use before last sexual intercourse[b] %
12					
1991	66.7	25.0	50.6	41.4	20.8
1993	68.3	27.0	53.0	46.5	19.1
1995	66.4	22.9	49.7	49.5	20.3
1997	60.9	20.6	46.0	52.4	23.2
1999	64.9	20.6	50.6	47.9	22.0
2001	60.5	21.6	47.9	49.3	25.4
2003	61.6	20.3	48.9	57.4	25.2

[a]Sexual intercourse during the 3 months preceding the survey.
[b]Among students who are currently sexually active.

SOURCE: N. Brener, R. Lowry, L. Kann, L. Kolbe, J. Lehnherr, R. Janssen, and H. Jaffe, "Table. Percentage of High School Students Who Reported Sexual Risk Behaviors, by Sex, Grade, Race/Ethnicity, and Survey Year—United States, Youth Risk Behavior Survey, 1991, 1993, 1995, 1997, 1999, and 2001," in "Trends in Sexual Risk Behaviors Among High School Students—United States, 1991–2001," *Morbidity and Mortality Weekly Report*, Centers for Disease Control and Prevention, vol. 51, no. 38, September 27, 2002, http://www.cdc.gov/mmwr/PDF/wk/mm5138.pdf (accessed September 20, 2005); with additional data from Jo Anne Grunbaum, Laura Kann, Steve Kinchen, James Ross, Joseph Hawkins, Richard Lowry, William A. Harris, Tim McManus, David Chyen, and Janet Collins, "Table 42. Percentage of High School Students Who Engaged in Sexual Behaviors, by Sex, Race/Ethnicity, and Grade—United States, Youth Risk Behavior Survey, 2003," "Table 44. Percentage of High School Students Who Were Currently Sexually Active and Who Used a Condom During or Birth Control Pills Before Last Sexual Intercourse, by Sex, Race/Ethnicity, and Grade—United States, Youth Risk Behavior Survey, 2003," and "Table 46. Percentage of High School Students Who Had Drunk Alcohol or Used Drugs Before Last Sexual Intercourse; Were Ever Pregnant or Got Someone Pregnant; and Were Taught About Acquired Immunodeficiency Syndrome (AIDS) or Human Immunodeficiency Virus (HIV) Infection in School, by Sex, Race/Ethnicity, and Grade—United States, Youth Risk Behavior Survey, 2003," in "Youth Risk Behavior Surveillance—United States, 2003," *Morbidity and Mortality Weekly Report*, vol. 53, no. SS-2, May 21, 2004, http://www.cdc.gov/mmwr/PDF/SS/SS5302.pdf (accessed September 20, 2005)

FIGURE 5.9

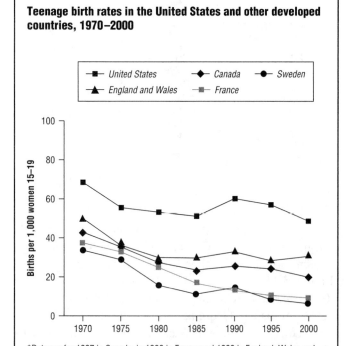

Teenage birth rates in the United States and other developed countries, 1970–2000

Legend:
- United States
- England and Wales
- Canada
- France
- Sweden

*Data are for 1997 in Canada, in 1998 in France and 1999 in England, Wales and Sweden

SOURCE: Jacqueline E. Darroch, Jennifer Frost, and Susheela Singh, "Chart 1. Teenage Birthrates Declined Less Steeply in the United States Than in Other Developed Countries Between 1970 and 2000," in *Teenage Sexual and Reproductive Behavior in Developed Countries: Can More Progress Be Made?* The Alan Guttmacher Institute (AGI), 2001, http://www.guttmacher.org/pubs/summaries/euroteens_summ.pdf (accessed September 20, 2005)

declines in birth and abortion rates during 1990 and 2000 were 23% and 54%, respectively, for non-Hispanic white teens ages fifteen to nineteen years, 32% and 31% for African-American teens, and 13% and 23% for Hispanic teens, according to the CDC in "Estimated Pregnancy Rates for the United States, 1990–2000: An Update" (*National Vital Statistics Report*, vol. 52, no. 23, June 15, 2004).

Figure 5.12 shows the pregnancy, birth, and abortion rates for teens ages fifteen to seventeen years from 1976 to 2003. Since 1990 the pregnancy rate for teens decreased 33%, from 80.3 to 53.5, a record low. The birth rate declined 42%, from its peak of 38.6 in 1991 to 22.4 in 2003. The induced abortion rate declined by 53%, from its peak of 30.7 in 1983 to 14.5 in 2000 ("QuickStats: Pregnancy, Birth, and Abortion Rates for Teenagers Aged 15–17 Years—United States, 1976–2003," *Morbidity and Mortality Weekly Report*, vol. 54, no. 4, http://www.cdc.gov/mmwr/preview/mmwrhtml/mm5404a6.htm, February 4, 2005).

Race and Ethnicity

"Abortion Surveillance—United States, 2001" (*Morbidity and Mortality Weekly Report, Surveillance Summaries*, vol. 53, no. SS-09, November 26, 2004) reports that in 2001, for females whose age and race were known, white teens ages fifteen to nineteen had a greater percentage of abortions (17.9%) than African-American teens (16.3%) or other races (13.8%). (See Table 4.3 in Chapter 4.)

TABLE 5.3

Birth rates for women under age 20, by age, race, and Hispanic origin, selected years 1991–2003

Age and race and Hispanic origin of mother	1991	2001	2002	2003	Percent change, 1991–2003
10–14 years					
All races[a]	1.4	0.8	0.7	0.6	−57
Non-Hispanic white[b]	0.5	0.3	0.2	0.2	−60
Non-Hispanic black[b]	4.9	2.1	1.9	1.6	−67
American Indian total[b]	1.6	1.0	0.9	1.0	−38
Asian or Pacific Islander total[b]	0.8	0.2	0.3	0.2	−75
Hispanic[c]	2.4	1.6	1.4	1.3	−46
15–19 years					
All races[a]	61.8	45.3	43.0	41.7	−33
Non-Hispanic white[b]	43.4	30.3	28.5	27.5	−37
Non-Hispanic black[b]	118.2	73.5	68.3	64.8	−45
American Indian total[b]	84.1	56.3	53.8	52.6	−37
Asian or Pacific Islander total[b]	27.3	19.8	18.3	17.6	−36
Hispanic[c]	104.6	86.4	83.4	82.2	−21
15–17 years					
All races[a]	38.6	24.7	23.2	22.4	−42
Non-Hispanic white[b]	23.6	14.0	13.1	12.4	−47
Non-Hispanic black[b]	86.1	44.9	41.0	38.8	−55
American Indian total[b]	51.9	31.4	30.7	30.3	−42
Asian or Pacific Islander total[b]	16.3	10.3	9.0	8.9	−45
Hispanic[c]	69.2	52.8	50.7	49.7	−28
18–19 years					
All races[a]	94.0	76.1	72.8	70.8	−25
Non-Hispanic white[b]	70.6	54.8	51.9	50.1	−29
Non-Hispanic black[b]	162.2	116.7	110.3	105.3	−35
American Indian total[b]	134.2	94.8	89.2	86.5	−36
Asian or Pacific Islander total[b]	42.2	32.8	31.5	30.1	−29
Hispanic[c]	155.5	135.5	133.0	131.9	−15

Note: Rates per 1,000 women in specified group.

[a]Includes data for white and black Hispanic women, not shown separately.

[b]Race and Hispanic origin are reported separately on the birth certificate. Race categories are consistent with the 1977 Office of Management and Budget standards. California, Hawaii, Ohio (for December), Pennsylvania, Utah, and Washington reported multiple-race data in 2003. The multiple-race data for these states were bridged to the single race categories of the 1977 Office of Management and Budget standards for comparability with other states. Data for persons of Hispanic origin are included in the data for each race group according to the mother's reported race.

[c]Includes all persons of Hispanic origin of any race.

SOURCE: Brady E. Hamilton, Joyce A. Martin, and Paul D. Sutton, "Table B. Birth Rates for Women Under 20 Years of Age, by Age, Race, and Hispanic Origin: United States, Final 1991, 2001 and 2002, and Preliminary 2003, and Percent Change in Rates, 1991–2003," in "Births: Preliminary Data for 2003," *National Vital Statistics Reports*, Centers for Disease Control and Prevention, National Center for Health Statistics, vol. 53, no. 9, November 23, 2004, http://www.cdc.gov/nchs/data/nvsr/nvsr53/nvsr53_09.pdf (accessed September 20, 2005)

TABLE 5.4

Births to unmarried women, 2002 and 2003

Age of mother	Number		Percent	
	2003	2002	2003	2002
All ages	1,415,804	1,365,966	34.6	34.0
Under 20 years	343,908	347,279	81.6	80.2
Under 15 years	6,471	7,093	97.1	97.0
15–19 years	337,437	340,186	81.3	80.0
15–17 years	120,766	122,791	89.7	88.5
18–19 years	216,670	217,395	77.3	75.8

SOURCE: Brady E. Hamilton, Joyce A. Martin, and Paul D. Sutton, "Table C. Number and Percent of Births to Unmarried Women, All Ages and Women Under 20 Years: United States, Final 2002 and Preliminary 2003," in "Births: Preliminary Data for 2003," *National Vital Statistics Reports*, Centers for Disease Control and Prevention, National Center for Health Statistics, vol. 53, no. 9, November 23, 2004, http://www.cdc.gov/nchs/data/nvsr/nvsr53/nvsr53_09.pdf (accessed September 20, 2005)

Abortion Ratios

An abortion rate is the number of abortions per one thousand women in the age category considered. An abortion ratio, as defined by the AGI, is the number of abortions per one hundred pregnancies that ended in abortion or live birth—that is, per one hundred pregnancies that did not end in miscarriage. Thus, an abortion ratio is really the percentage of abortions in one hundred pregnancies. Table 5.7 shows abortion rates and abortion ratios from 1973 through 2002 for women ages fifteen to forty-four. Since 1995, approximately one-quarter of all pregnancies that did not end in miscarriage were terminated by induced abortion. Also during those years, about twenty-one women out of every one thousand women ages fifteen to forty-four had an abortion.

The abortion ratio varies by age, and was highest for teens in 2001, as Figure 5.13 shows. These data are from

FIGURE 5.10

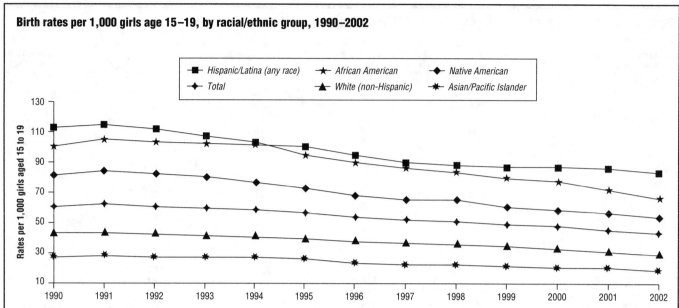

Birth rates per 1,000 girls age 15–19, by racial/ethnic group, 1990–2002

SOURCE: "Figure 3. Since 1995, Latina Teens Have Had the Highest Teen Birth Rate Among the Major Racial/Ethnic Groups in the United States," in *Fact Sheet: Teen Sexual Activity, Pregnancy and Childbearing Among Latinos in the United States*, The National Campaign to Prevent Teen Pregnancy, May 2004, http://www.teenpregnancy.org/resources/reading/pdf/latinofs.pdf (accessed September 20, 2005)

the CDC, which defines abortion ratio as the number of abortions per one thousand live births. The highest abortion ratio in 2001—by far—was that for teens under age fifteen. The next highest abortion ratio was that for teens fifteen to nineteen years old.

Relinquishment for Adoption

A teenager faced with an unintended pregnancy can choose parenthood (often obtaining help from relatives), relinquishing (giving up) the infant for adoption, or abortion. Most women of any age choose to keep their infant or to have an abortion. According to the most recent data published by the CDC, less than 1% of infants born to never-married women under forty-five years of age were relinquished for adoption between 1989 and 1995. This figure is down from 8.7% prior to 1973, 4.1% between 1973 and 1981, and 2% between 1982 and 1988. Relinquishment also occurs among the formerly married and the currently married, but it is very rare ("Adoption, Adoption Seeking, and Relinquishment for Adoption in the United States," *Advance Data from Vital and Health Statistics*, no. 306, Centers for Disease Control and Prevention, http://www.cdc.gov/nchs/data/ad/ad306.pdf, May 11, 1999).

Clearly, there has been a downward trend in relinquishment of births occurring to never-married women. This decline has paralleled a steady increase in the rate of births to unmarried women reported by the CDC during the same period. The CDC suggests that study is needed to determine the reasons why fewer never-married mothers choose to relinquish their babies for

adoption but notes in "Adoption, Adoption Seeking, and Relinquishment for Adoption in the United States" that recent declines in abortion rates suggest that the choice of abortion over relinquishment is not a significant factor in lower prevalence of relinquishment in recent years.

Factors That Affect Pregnancy and Abortion

According to the AGI, factors that affect pregnancy and abortion include the following:

- Marital status—Married teens with unintended pregnancies are less likely than unmarried teens to have an abortion. These teens generally have the support of their spouse and family to carry the pregnancy to term. In addition, married couples are more likely to be employed, have higher incomes, and are more willing to have children. Even so, about one-fourth of married teens with unintended pregnancies obtain an abortion.

- Expectations for the future—In general, teenagers who have a plan for their future are more likely to end their pregnancy. In contrast, teenagers who are ambivalent about their future tend to carry their pregnancy to term.

- Socioeconomic status and parents' education—Teens who come from families that are better off financially and whose parents are more educated tend to have abortions. Those from poor or low-income families and whose parents are less educated tend to choose childbirth.

TABLE 5.5

Teen birth rates per 1,000 girls age 15–19, 2003

[Birth rates are live births per 1,000 estimated population in each area]

State	Rate	Rank
New Hampshire	20.0	1
Massachusetts	23.3	2
Vermont	24.2	3
Maine	25.4	4
Connecticut	25.8	5
New Jersey	26.8	6
North Dakota	27.2	7
Minnesota	27.5	8
New York	29.5	9
Pennsylvania	31.6	10
Wisconsin	32.3	11
Iowa	32.5	12
Washington	33.0	13
Michigan	34.8	14
Maryland	35.4	15
Rhode Island	35.6	16
Montana	36.4	17
Oregon	36.8	18
Utah	36.8	19
Nebraska	37.0	20
Virginia	37.6	21
South Dakota	38.0	22
Hawaii	38.2	23
Idaho	39.1	24
Alaska	39.5	25
Ohio	39.5	26
Wyoming	39.9	27
California	41.1	28
Illinois	42.2	29
Kansas	43.0	30
Missouri	44.1	31
Florida	44.5	32
Indiana	44.6	33
West Virginia	45.5	34
Delaware	46.3	35
Colorado	47.0	36
Kentucky	51.0	37
North Carolina	52.2	38
South Carolina	53.0	39
Nevada	53.9	40
Tennessee	54.3	41
Alabama	54.5	42
Georgia	55.7	43
Oklahoma	58.0	44
Louisiana	58.1	45
Arkansas	59.9	46
Arizona	61.2	47
New Mexico	62.4	48
Texas	64.4	49
Mississippi	64.7	50
United States*	43.0	N/A
Territories and the District of Columbia		
Northern Marianas	42.3	N/A
American Samoa	46.2	N/A
Virgin Islands	56.8	N/A
Puerto Rico	62.2	N/A
District of Columbia	69.1	N/A
Guam	64.7	N/A

*Excludes data for the territories.

SOURCE: Adapted from Joyce A. Martin, Brady E. Hamilton, Paul D. Sutton, Stephanie J. Ventura, Fay Menacker, and Martha L. Munson, "Table 10. Number of Births, Birth Rates, Fertility Rates, Total Fertility Rates, and Birth Rates for Teenagers 15–19 Years by Age of Mother: United States, Each State and Territory, 2002," in "Births: Final Data for 2002," *National Vital Statistics Reports*, Centers for Disease Control and Prevention, National Center for Health Statistics, vol. 52, no. 10, December 17, 2003, http://www.cdc.gov/nchs/data/nvsr/nvsr52/nvsr52_10_table10.pdf (accessed September 20, 2005)

- The age of the teen's partner—Teenagers with partners who are older are more likely to bear a child.

- Race and ethnicity—White teenagers whose pregnancies are unintended are more likely to have an abortion than are African-American and Hispanic teens.

- Medicaid coverage—Teenagers whose health care is covered by Medicaid are less likely to have an abortion. Most states pay for prenatal care and childbirth but not for abortion.

WHAT DO TEENS KNOW ABOUT ABORTION?

Rebecca Stone and Cynthia Waszak of the Center for Population Options, an organization that supports abortion as an alternative, conducted focus-group studies of teens across the country in 1992 (the latest comprehensive data available) to better understand adolescent attitudes on abortion. (In recent years the federal government has withheld funding from researchers studying abortion—including attitudes on abortion. Thus, up-to-date research on such topics is often not available.) The authors wanted to learn where teens got their information; how they formed their opinions on abortion; how they felt about speaking to their parents about the issue or having to turn to them for consent for the procedure; and whether there were gender, ethnic, or cultural differences in attitude. The results of Stone and Waszak's research were published as "Adolescent Knowledge and Attitudes about Abortion" (*Family Planning Perspectives*, vol. 24, no. 2, March/April 1992). The authors found surprising consistency in the responses of the eleven focus groups and identified four major themes.

First, most teens held negative attitudes toward abortion, but they felt that women still needed the right to choose. Data from the Gallup poll "Teens Lean Conservative on Abortion," conducted on November 18, 2003, tend to support these ideas. The Gallup poll revealed that 72% of teenagers think that abortion is morally wrong. However, over half think that abortions should be legal—47% saying that abortions should be legal under certain circumstances and 19% saying that abortion should be legal in all circumstances.

Second, teens did not think that mandatory parental involvement was helpful, no matter how strongly the teenagers opposed abortion. Third, they lacked knowledge about abortion and related laws. They relied on anecdotal evidence and often believed that abortion is medically dangerous, emotionally damaging, and widely illegal. Fourth, teens' attitudes toward abortion were generally shaped by antiabortion views, conservative morality, and religion.

FIGURE 5.11

Percent decline in birth rates for teenagers age 15–19, by state, 1991–2000

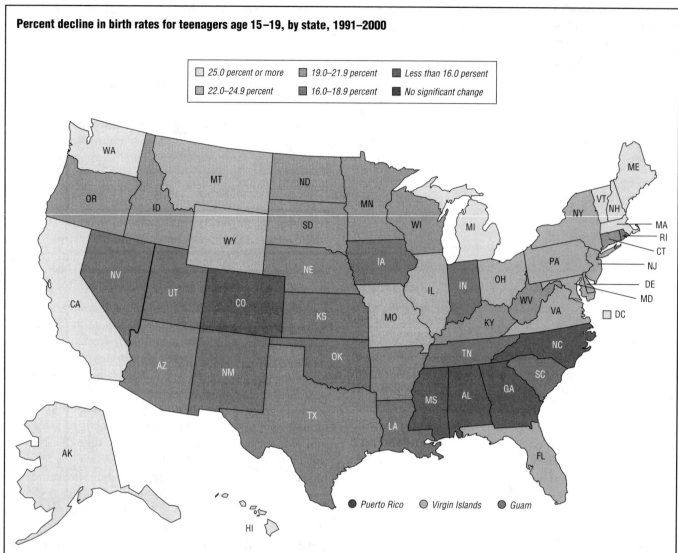

SOURCE: Stephanie J. Ventura, T. J. Mathews, and Brady E. Hamilton, "Figure 2. Percent Decline in Birth Rates for Teenagers 15–19 by State, between 1991 and 2000," in "Teenage Births in the United States: State Trends, 1991–2000, an Update," *National Vital Statistics Reports*, Centers for Disease Control and Prevention, National Center for Health Statistics, vol. 50, no. 9, May 30, 2002, http://www.cdc.gov/nchs/data/nvsr/nvsr50/nvsr50_09.pdf (accessed September 20, 2005)

Teens, regardless of sex, mentioned "murder, killing a baby, or death" when asked about what the word "abortion" brought to mind. Many felt abortion was something done out of fear of being found out. Most of the females agreed that the male had a right to know if his girlfriend was pregnant and to be included in the decision. Although the participants generally disliked abortion, they condoned abortion in cases of rape and incest. Moreover, they approved of keeping abortion legal, either because they felt women would do it anyway and it was better that it was done right, or because they did not feel it was right to dictate ideas to others.

Although the teens generally disapproved of abortion, they did not approve of requiring parental permission for abortion. Even those who reported open relationships with

their parents (mothers in particular) and who claimed they could discuss sex with their parent(s) felt they would have a hard time telling their parents that they wanted an abortion. Even those who felt they could discuss abortion with their parents could imagine circumstances for other teens where it would be very difficult or impossible.

The focus groups revealed teens' lack of understanding about abortion. Teens in the focus groups knew little about the legality of abortion. Only a few were aware of *Roe v. Wade* or its significance. The participants did not know that abortion is legal in all fifty states, although they seemed to know that it is legal in their own state. The teens held misconceptions about the physical and mental effects of abortion. Many believed that abortion, especially multiple abortions, made a

TABLE 5.6

Induced abortion rates by age, race, and Hispanic origin, 1990–2000

[Rates are pregnancy outcomes per 1,000 women in specified group, estimated as of April 1 for 1990 and 2000 and as of July 1 for all other years]

Pregnancy outcome race, and Hispanic origin and year	Total[a]	Under 15 years[b]	Age of woman								
			15–19 years			20–24 years	25–29 years	30–34 years	35–39 years	40–44 years[c]
			Total	15–17 years	18–19 years					
All races[d]										
Induced abortions										
2000	21.3	0.9	24.0	14.5	37.7	46.3	31.6	18.7	9.7	3.2
1999	21.4	0.9	24.7	15.2	38.6	46.4	31.7	18.3	9.7	3.2
1998	21.5	1.0	25.8	16.4	39.9	47.0	31.7	17.9	9.5	3.2
1997	21.9	1.0	27.1	17.2	42.6	48.1	31.9	17.7	9.5	3.1
1996	22.4	1.1	28.6	18.6	44.0	49.3	32.1	17.7	9.7	3.2
1995	22.5	1.2	29.4	19.5	44.8	49.1	31.5	17.5	9.7	3.2
1994	23.7	1.3	31.6	21.0	47.9	51.9	32.1	18.1	9.9	3.2
1993	25.0	1.4	33.9	22.2	51.3	54.9	33.2	18.6	10.2	3.2
1992	25.7	1.4	35.2	22.9	53.3	55.9	33.5	18.9	10.3	3.2
1991	26.2	1.4	37.4	24.2	55.7	56.4	33.4	19.0	10.4	3.0
1990	27.4	1.5	40.3	26.5	57.9	56.7	33.9	19.7	10.8	3.2

Note: Rates for 1990–99 for ages 15–17 and 18–19 years have been revised and may differ from rates previously published.
[a]Rates computed by relating the number of events to women of all ages to women aged 15–44 years.
[b]Rates computed by relating the number of events to women under age 15 years to women aged 10–14 years.
[c]Rates computed by relating the number of events to women aged 40 years and over to women aged 40–44 years.
[d]Includes races other than white and black and origin not stated.

SOURCE: Adapted from Stephanie J. Ventura, Joyce C. Abma, William D. Mosher, and Stanley Henshaw, "Table 1. Pregnancy, Live Birth, Induced Abortion, and Fetal Loss Rates by Age, Race, and Hispanic Origin of Woman: United States, 1990–2000," in "Estimated Pregnancy Rates for the United States, 1990–2000: An Update," *National Vital Statistics Reports*, vol. 52, no. 23, June 15, 2004 http://www.cdc.gov/nchs/data/nvsr/nvsr52/nvsr52_23.pdf (accessed September 20, 2005)

FIGURE 5.12

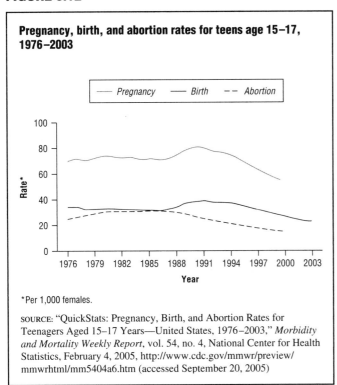

Pregnancy, birth, and abortion rates for teens age 15–17, 1976–2003

*Per 1,000 females.

SOURCE: "QuickStats: Pregnancy, Birth, and Abortion Rates for Teenagers Aged 15–17 Years—United States, 1976–2003," *Morbidity and Mortality Weekly Report*, vol. 54, no. 4, National Center for Health Statistics, February 4, 2005, http://www.cdc.gov/mmwr/preview/mmwrhtml/mm5404a6.htm (accessed September 20, 2005)

Stone and Waszak believed that "from a public health perspective, assessing adolescents' views on abortion is critical to devising effective ways to deliver information and services to teenagers in need of pregnancy prevention or pregnancy option counseling." They further believed that, with the high incidence of pregnancies among American teens, there is a need for educating young people not only about pregnancy prevention but also about early, safe abortion.

PARENTAL INVOLVEMENT IN ABORTION DECISIONS

Most state laws require minors (those under the age of eighteen) to either obtain their parents' consent or notify their parents of their intent to get an abortion before they undergo the procedure. These laws generally include judicial bypass provisions if the young woman does not want to or cannot tell her parents of her decision. In a judicial bypass (waiver), the court decides if the minor is mature enough to make the decision on her own or if the abortion would be in her best interests. A Gallup opinion poll conducted in January 2003 found that 73% of adult respondents favored "a law requiring women under 18 to get parental consent for any abortion."

As of 2005 forty-four states had laws requiring a minor seeking an abortion to obtain the consent of or to

woman sterile and that it was some kind of cutting procedure that hurt. They also thought it was emotionally devastating.

TABLE 5.7

Number of reported abortions, abortion rate, and abortion ratio, 1973–2002

Year	No. (in 000s)	Rate[a]	Ratio[b]
1973	744.6	16.3	19.3
1974	898.6	19.3	22.0
1975	1,034.2	21.7	24.9
1976	1,179.3	24.2	26.5
1977	1,316.7	26.4	28.6
1978	1,409.6	27.7	29.2
1979	1,497.7	28.8	29.6
1980	1,553.9	29.3	30.0
1981	1,577.3	29.3	30.1
1982	1,573.9	28.8	30.0
1983	(1,575)	(28.5)	(30.4)
1984	1,577.2	28.1	29.7
1985	1,588.6	28.0	29.7
1986	(1,574)	(27.4)	(29.4)
1987	1,559.1	26.9	28.8
1988	1,590.8	27.3	28.6
1989	(1,567)	(26.8)	(27.5)
1990	(1,609)	(27.4)	(28.0)
1991	1,556.5	26.3	27.4
1992	1,528.9	25.7	27.5
1993	(1,495)	(25.0)	(27.4)
1994	(1,423)	(23.7)	(26.6)
1995	1,359.4	22.5	25.9
1996	1,360.2	22.4	25.9
1997	(1,335)	(21.9)	(25.5)
1998	(1,319)	(21.5)	(25.1)
1999	1,314.8	21.4	24.6
2000	1,313.0	21.3	24.5
2001	[1,303]	[21.1]	[24.5]
2002	[1,293]	[20.9]	[24.2]

Notes: Figures in parentheses are estimated by interpolation of numbers of abortions; figures in brackets are provisional.

[a]Abortions per 1,000 women aged 15–44 as of July 1 of each year.

[b]Abortions per 100 pregnancies ending in abortion or live birth; for each year, the ratio is based on births occurring during the 12-month period starting in July of that year (to match times of conception for pregnancies ending in births with those for pregnancies ending in abortions).

SOURCE: Lawrence B. Finer and Stanley K. Henshaw, "Table 1. Number of Reported Abortions, Abortion Rate and Abortion Ratio, United States, 1973–2002," in *Estimates of U.S. Abortion Incidence in 2001 and 2002*, The Alan Guttmacher Institute (AGI), May 18, 2005, http://www.guttmacher.org/pubs/2005/05/18/ab_incidence.pdf (accessed September 20, 2005)

FIGURE 5.13

Abortion ratio, by age group of women who obtained a legal abortion, 2001

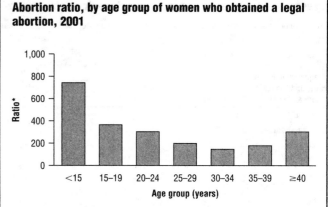

Note: Data are from 46 states, the District of Columbia, and New York City.
*Number of abortions per 1,000 live births.

SOURCE: Lilo T. Strauss, Joy Herndon, Jeani Chang, Wilda Y. Parker, Sonya V. Bowens, Suzanne B. Zane, and Cynthia J. Berg, "Figure 2. Abortion Ratio, by Age Group of Women Who Obtained a Legal Abortion—Selected States, United States, 2001," in "Abortion Surveillance—United States, 2001," *Morbidity and Mortality Weekly Report/Surveillance Summaries*, vol. 53, no. SS-9, November 26, 2004, http://www.cdc.gov/mmwr/PDF/SS/SS5309.pdf (accessed September 20, 2005)

notify an adult, usually a parent. (See Table 5.8.) Thirty-three of these laws were enforceable in that year. Among the states with enforceable consent laws, Maryland and Utah did not provide a judicial bypass to enable a minor to bring her case before the court. Six states (Connecticut, Hawaii, New York, Oregon, Vermont, and Washington) and the District of Columbia do not have any form of parental consent law.

Proponents of parental notification or consent laws suggest that adolescents are at a high risk of physiologi-cal and psychological harm from abortion and that adolescents are not able to make an adequately informed decision about abortion. However, Nancy E. Adler, Emily J. Ozer, and Jeanne Tschann in "Abortion among Adolescents" (*American Psychologist*, vol. 58, no. 3, March 2003) note that abortion carries relatively few medical risks compared with the risks of childbearing. Data from the CDC reveal that overall pregnancy-related death rates in the United States are 9.2 per one hundred thousand live births, whereas overall death rates due to abortion in the United States are 0.3 per one hundred thousand legal abortions. The authors of "Abortion among Adolescents" also note that results of studies of psychological responses following abortion show that the risk of psychological harm is low. After analyzing many studies on the ability of adolescents to make adequate and informed decisions regarding abortion, the authors determined that adolescent abortion patients appear, on the whole, to be competent in their decision-making capabilities. They also note that parental involvement laws aim to promote family communication and functioning but that forcing communication between parents and children about abortion may not have the desired positive effects.

TABLE 5.8

State restrictions on minors' access to abortion, 2005

Twenty-six (26) states restrict young women's access to abortion by requiring parental consent. Eighteen (18) states restrict young women's access to abortion by requiring parental notice.

| | Parental notice/consent in effect |
| | Parental notice/consent unenforceable |

State	State mandates		Consent/notice required from		Law is unconstitutional and unenforceable
	Parental consent	Parental notice	One parent	Two parents	
Alabama	X		X		
Alaska	X		X		X
Arizona	X		X		
Arkansas	X		X		
California	X		X		X
Colorado		X		X	
Connecticut					
Delaware		X	X		
District of Columbia					
Florida		X	X		
Georgia		X	X		
Hawaii					
Idaho	X		X		X
Illinois		X	X		X
Indiana	X		X		
Iowa		X	X		
Kansas		X	X		
Kentucky	X		X		
Louisiana	X		X		
Maine	X		X		
Maryland		X	X		
Massachusetts	X			X*	
Michigan	X		X		
Minnesota		X		X	
Mississippi	X			X	
Missouri	X		X		
Montana		X	X		X
Nebraska		X	X		
Nevada		X	X		X
New Hampshire		X	X		X
New Jersey		X	X		X
New Mexico	X		X		X
New York					
North Carolina	X		X		
North Dakota	X			X	
Ohio		X	X		
Oklahoma		X			
Oregon					
Pennsylvania	X		X		
Rhode Island	X		X		
South Carolina	X		X		
South Dakota		X	X		
Tennessee	X		X		
Texas	X				
Utah		X		X	
Vermont					
Virginia	X		X		
Washington					
West Virginia		X	X		
Wisconsin	X		X		
Wyoming	X		X		
Total	**25**	**19**	**36**	**6**	**9**

Note: Some states allow additional exceptions to these restrictions not included in this chart.
*This statute requires two-parent consent, but a court has issued an order that the law be enforced as requiring the consent of one parent.

SOURCE: "Restrictions on Young Women's Access to Abortion," in *Who Decides? The Status of Women's Reproductive Rights in the United States, 14th ed.*, NARAL Pro-Choice America & NARAL Pro-Choice America Foundation, updated June 24, 2005, http://www.prochoiceamerica.org/yourstate/whodecides/maps/young_women.cfm (accessed September 20, 2005)

CHAPTER 6

ABORTION CLINICS

QUALITY OF ABORTION SERVICES

Clinical Policies Guidelines

The National Abortion Federation (NAF) is the professional association of abortion providers in the United States and Canada. A mission of the NAF is to promote and enhance the quality of abortion services. The organization has developed clinical policies guidelines to help assure safe, high quality abortion care.

The most recent edition of the NAF's *Clinical Policy Guidelines* is available at http://www.guidelines.gov and includes three types of policies: standards, recommendations, and options. Standards are applied rigidly and include directives such as, "Abortions must be performed by licensed physicians, or licensed/certified/registered midlevel clinicians trained in the provision of abortion care, in accordance with state law." Recommendations allow some flexibility in clinical management but must be justified when not followed. Recommendations include items such as, "Appropriate referrals should be available for patients who cannot be cared for at your facility." Options require no justification. For example, the option listed under the standard, "Accurate information must be provided regarding the risks and benefits of abortion," is: "This information may be provided either on an individual basis or in group sessions."

Satisfaction with Quality of Care

In May 1999 the Henry J. Kaiser Family Foundation (KFF) published "From the Patient's Perspective: Quality of Abortion Care" (http://www.kff.org/womenshealth/20010517d-index.cfm), the first large-scale study (and the most recent study available) about the quality of abortion care from the patients' perspective. The KFF commissioned the Picker Institute, a health care assessment and improvement research organization, to interview more than 2,200 abortion patients age eighteen and older from twelve abortion providers in a dozen states

nationwide. The patients were "women who successfully located a provider, could afford the procedure, and were able to get to the clinic."

Of patients, three in five (60%) rated their care as excellent, and nearly two in five (38%) as very good or good. More than half of the patients indicated the information they received and the staff's attention to their privacy were both excellent (56% and 55% respectively). The remaining patients rated these two aspects of their care as very good or good. Three-quarters (78%) of the patients felt "a lot" of confidence and trust in the staff who cared for them, and about one-fifth (18%) reported "some" confidence and trust. Almost all patients (96%) said they would recommend their abortion provider to family or friends.

The adequacy of information about the abortion was the most important issue to the patients. Almost all (98%) of the patients reported that the clinic staff explained the procedure, and 99% thought the explanation was clear. Nearly nine in ten (87%) stated they received all the information they wanted about what to expect during the procedure. More than nine in ten (93%) reported receiving information about emotional or physical reactions that might follow the abortion.

Satisfaction with Method of Abortion

In "Choice of and Satisfaction with Methods of Medical and Surgical Abortion among U.S. Clinic Patients" (*Family Planning Perspectives*, vol. 33, no. 5, September/October 2001), researchers S. Marie Harvey, Linda J. Beckman, and Sarah J. Satre evaluated the medical (nonsurgical) and surgical abortion experience for women. (See Table 1.1 in Chapter 1 for an explanation of these methods.) Among 304 women participating in the clinical trial, 186 received a medical abortion (methotrexate) and 118 were offered a medical abortion but chose to have a surgical abortion. The women completed questionnaires before the abortion procedure and then again during a follow-up visit.

The study participants revealed that both methods of abortion were highly acceptable. Almost half (48%) of the women undergoing a medical abortion reported being very satisfied with the methotrexate-induced method. Slightly more than one-third reported they were somewhat satisfied. Similarly, almost half (43%) of women who had a surgical abortion were very satisfied, and 39% were somewhat satisfied. Most of the women in both groups responded that they would recommend the method they had chosen to a friend, and most (89% of women who had medical abortions and 93% of the surgical group) said they would use the same method again if they terminated another pregnancy.

To determine what characteristics of a particular abortion method women valued most, the researchers asked the women to rate the importance of twenty-one attributes when choosing between the two abortion methods. Women who chose medical abortion differed greatly from the surgical abortion group in their ratings of fourteen of the twenty-one procedure characteristics. The surgical abortion group preferred several features: the procedure is over quickly; it does not have side effects (such as headache, nausea, and diarrhea); the patient does not see blood; it does not cause heavy bleeding or bleeding for longer than a week; it does not cause cramping for more than an hour; it is a technique that has been used for a long time; a doctor or nurse is present for the procedure; and the patient knows when and where the abortion is taking place.

The women who chose medical abortion gave four attributes much more importance than did the surgical abortion group. For the medical abortion group, it is important that the method does not involve surgery; it can take place in private (such as at home); it does not involve surgical instruments; and it is like a "natural miscarriage."

The researchers concluded that women consider numerous factors when deciding on abortion method. They note that abortion providers should supply women with enough information about the characteristics of abortion methods so that they can make informed decisions appropriate for their values and life circumstances.

ACTIONS AGAINST ABORTION CLINICS

Violence and Disruption

Since 1977 the NAF has tracked incidents of violence and disruption against abortion providers across the country. NAF members report incidents on an ongoing basis. Their reports are supplemented with information from newspaper reports, law enforcement agencies, and abortion provider organizations. A year-end survey is conducted to complete each year's presentation.

Over the years many abortion clinics throughout the nation have experienced violence. The most serious instances of clinic violence have been the murder and attempted murder of abortion doctors and clinic workers. The first clinic murder occurred in 1993: Michael Griffin shot and killed Dr. David Gunn in Pensacola, Florida. Four murders occurred the year after, and two happened in 1998. None have occurred since. There have been seventeen attempted murders since 1991.

From 2000 to 2004 there was a decrease in the total number of incidents of extreme violence against abortion providers, specifically bombings, arsons, and attempted bombings and arsons. (See Table 6.1.) The NAF credits the arrest and prosecution of Eric Rudolf, James Kopp, and Clayton Waagner, three antiabortion extremists, as key factors in the decline of severe forms of violence against abortion providers. "Vigorous enforcement of the law" by local, state, and federal officials and "effective vigilance, training, and dedication of clinic staff" also have contributed to the decline, according to the NAF. Overall, in 2004 there were 152 identified acts of violence, down from the record high of 795 in 2001. (The 2001 total was exceptionally high as a result of the 554 hoax anthrax threat letters recorded that year.)

As Table 6.1 shows, during the years 1990 to 2004, 1997 had the highest number of clinic bombings (six). During the same time span, 1992 had the highest number of arson-related fires (nineteen). In more recent years both types of incidents have decreased dramatically. There was one clinic bombing in 2001 and no bombings were reported from 2002 through July 2005. There was one arson-related fire in 2002, three in 2003, and two in 2004.

Incidents of vandalism have remained somewhat stable since 1998, fluctuating from a low of forty-six incidents to a high of sixty-three incidents. Death threats have remained low in recent years: three in 2002, seven in 2003, and four in 2004. There were no death threats to abortion providers between January and July 2005.

Figure 6.1 shows abortion clinic violence by state. The numbers include arsons, bombings, murders, shootings, and butyric acid attacks. (Butyric acid is a liquid with a vomit-like odor. Butyric acid can cause thousands of dollars of damage, requiring clinics to conduct extensive cleanups.) California, Florida, and Texas had the highest number of incidences in the years 1993 to 2004.

The NAF first collected data on stalking (the persistent following, threatening, and harassing of an abortion provider, staff member, or patient *away from* the clinic) in 1993, reporting a record high of 188 cases that year. Stalking cases dropped to about one-third of that amount through the mid-1990s. After 1997 the annual number of

TABLE 6.1

Incidents of violence and disruption against abortion providers in the United States and Canada, 1977–July 2005

Violence	1977–89	1990	1991	1992	1993	1994	1995	1996	1997	1998	1999	2000	2001	2002	2003	2004	2005[d]	Total
Murder[a]	0	0	0	0	1	4	0	0	0	2	0	0	0	0	0	0	0	7
Attempted murder	0	0	2	0	1	8	1	1	2	1	0	1	0	0	0	0	0	17
Bombing[a]	25	1	1	0	1	1	1	2	6	1	1	0	1	0	0	0	0	41
Arson[a]	64	10	8	19	12	11	14	3	8	4	8	2	2	1	3	2	2	173
Attempted bomb/arson[a]	37	3	1	13	7	3	1	4	2	5	1	3	2	0	0	1	4	87
Invasion	247	19	29	26	24	2	4	0	7	5	3	4	2	1	0	0	0	373
Vandalism	244	26	44	116	113	42	31	29	105	46	63	56	58	60	48	49	27	1,157
Trespassing	0	0	0	0	0	0	0	0	0	0	193	81	144	163	66	67	46	760
Butyric acid attacks	0	0	0	57	15	8	0	1	0	19	0	0	0	0	0	0	0	100
Anthrax threats	0	0	0	0	9	0	0	0	0	12	35	30	554	23	0	1	0	655
Assault & battery	58	6	6	9	9	7	2	1	9	4	7	7	2	0	7	8	2	140
Death threats	70	7	3	8	78	59	41	13	11	25	13	9	14	3	7	4	0	365
Kidnapping	2	0	0	0	0	0	0	0	0	1	0	0	0	0	0	0	0	3
Burglary	20	2	1	5	3	3	3	6	6	6	4	5	6	1	9	5	4	89
Stalking[b]	0	0	0	0	188	22	61	52	67	13	13	17	10	12	3	15	1	474
Total	**767**	**74**	**95**	**253**	**452**	**170**	**159**	**112**	**223**	**144**	**336**	**215**	**795**	**265**	**143**	**152**	**86**	**4,441**
Disruption																		
Hate mail/harassing calls	192	21	142	469	628	381	255	605	2829	915	1646	1011	404	230	432	453	79	10692
Email/internet harassment	0	0	0	0	0	0	0	0	0	0	0	0	0	24	70	51	32	177
Hoax device/susp. package	0	0	0	0	0	0	0	0	0	0	0	0	0	41	13	9	3	66
Bomb threats	237	11	15	12	22	14	41	13	79	31	39	20	31	7	17	13	2	604
Picketing	847	45	292	2,898	2,279	1,407	1,356	3,932	7,518	8,402	8,727	8,478	9,969	10,241	11,348	11,640	2,839	92,218
Total	**1,276**	**77**	**449**	**3,379**	**2,929**	**1,802**	**1,652**	**4,550**	**10,426**	**9,348**	**10,412**	**9,509**	**10,404**	**10,543**	**11,880**	**12,166**	**2,955**	**103,757**
Clinic blockades																		
Number of incidents	385	34	41	83	66	25	5	7	25	2	3	4	2	4	10	34	0	731
Number of arrests[c]	24,380	1,363	3,885	2,580	1,236	217	54	65	29	16	5	0	0	0	0	0	0	33,830

Note: All numbers represent incidents reported to or obtained by NAF (National Abortion Federation). Actual incidents are likely much higher. Tabulation of trespassing began in 1999 and tabulation of email harassment and hoax devices began in 2002.
[a]Incidents recorded are those classified as such by the appropriate law enforcement agency. Incidents that were ruled inconclusive or accidental are not included.
[b]Stalking is defined as the persistent following, threatening, and harassing of an abortion provider, staff member, or patient away from the clinic. Tabulation of stalking incidents began in 1993.
[c]The "number of arrests" represents the total number of arrests, not the total number of persons arrested. Many blockaders are arrested multiple times.
[d]Data through July, 2005.

SOURCE: "NAF Violence and Disruption Statistics: Incidents of Violence & Disruption Against Abortion Providers in the U.S. & Canada," National Abortion Federation, July 2005, http://www.prochoice.org/pubs_research/publications/downloads/about_abortion/violence_statistics.pdf (accessed September 20, 2005)

FIGURE 6.1

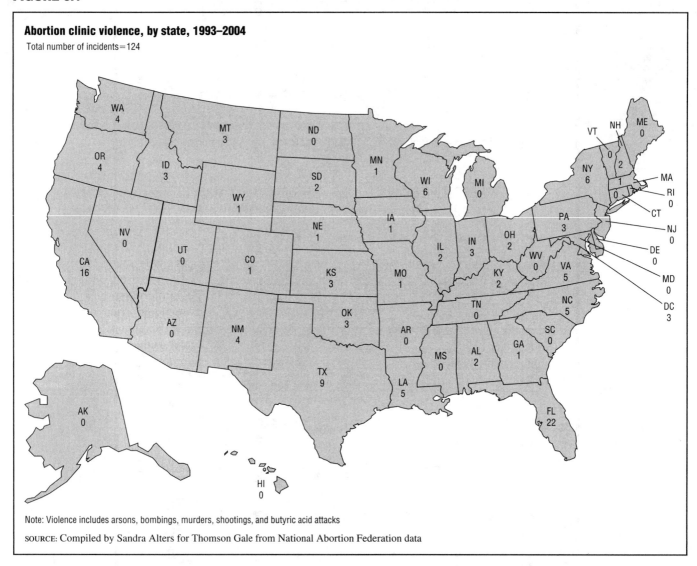

Abortion clinic violence, by state, 1993–2004

Total number of incidents=124

Note: Violence includes arsons, bombings, murders, shootings, and butyric acid attacks

SOURCE: Compiled by Sandra Alters for Thomson Gale from National Abortion Federation data

stalking cases dropped again; in recent years they number in the teens. In 2004 there were fifteen cases of stalking reported. (See Table 6.1.)

After the passage of the Freedom of Access to Clinic Entrances Act in 1994 (FACE, PL 103-259; see later in this chapter), the number of clinic blockades dropped sharply, from twenty-five in 1994 to five in 1995. In general, there have been only a few clinic blockades each year since the mid-1990s (with the exception of 1997). However, clinic blockades increased to ten in 2003 and to thirty-four in 2004. (See Table 6.1.)

Picketing is by far the major activity of pro-life activists. The number of incidents of picketing has increased each year since 2000, peaking at 11,640 incidents in 2004. Picketing and various forms of harassment are becoming more intense, according to reports from abortion clinics.

Many protests at abortion clinics have been under the direction of Operation Save America (formerly Operation Rescue National), an organization that seeks to shut down clinics completely but denies promoting the use of violence. Operation Save America believes that the United States, in permitting abortion, has lost its morality. Demonstrators claim that they are not only saving the lives of the unborn but also preventing the judgment of God from being passed on the United States for murder committed through abortion.

FREEDOM OF ACCESS TO CLINIC ENTRANCES ACT (FACE)

The Freedom of Access to Clinic Entrances Act was signed into law on May 26, 1994, in response to increasing violence against abortion clinic workers and clients. FACE prohibits physical attacks on clinic employees and patient escorts, attempted arson of clinic facilities, blockades of clinic entrances by persons or vehicles, and threats of bodily harm to providers or recipients of services.

The legislation received support from both abortion proponents and opponents. Pro-life advocate Senator Harry Reid (D-NV) said that despite his conviction against abortion, FACE's aim was "not to restrict the rights of people to demonstrate but to protect the rights of people to be free from the fear of violence against them."

Some opponents of FACE, however, have challenged its constitutionality on a number of grounds. Some charge that FACE violates the freedom of speech and religion protections under the First Amendment, whereas others claim that Congress lacks the power to pass such a law under the commerce clause (to regulate interstate commerce) of the Constitution. However, the U.S. Supreme Court has affirmed the constitutionality of FACE by refusing to hear challenges to the law.

For more information on court cases regarding FACE and abortion clinic violence, see "Protesters at Abortion Clinics" in Chapter 2.

The Effectiveness of FACE

According to a 2003 report by NARAL Pro-Choice America, "FACE has proven to be an essential component of the effort to protect access to abortion services." Although violence continues, the frequency of some types of clinic violence has declined since 1994. The federal statute also has spurred enhanced clinic protection by law enforcement and has withstood numerous constitutional challenges. Incidents of extreme violence against abortion providers, however, continue to occur, with two murders and one attempted murder in the United States in 1998 and another attempted murder in 2000.

The U.S. Government Accountability Office (GAO), in "Abortion Clinics: Information on the Effectiveness of the Freedom of Access to Clinic Entrances Act" (Washington, DC: Government Accountability Office, 1998, http://www.gao.gov/archive/1999/gg99002.pdf), studied the occurrence of clinic incidents before and after FACE. The GAO surveyed forty-two clinics that experienced relatively high levels of incidents before FACE was enacted. Most of the clinics (thirty-four) reported experiencing fewer types of incidents during the two years after FACE than they had before FACE became law. Nonetheless, almost all clinics indicated no change in the occurrences of picketing, hate mail, and harassing phone calls before and after FACE. However, thirty-five respondents reported a decrease in the severity of the incidents, particularly of picketing. Overall, most respondents felt that FACE had deterred or reduced clinic incidents.

A survey on clinic violence conducted by the Feminist Majority Foundation (FMF) ("2002 National Clinic Violence Survey Report," http://www.feminist.org/research/cvsurveys/clinic_survey2002.pdf, March 2003) concurred that severe clinic violence decreased since FACE was enacted. Nonetheless, results of the survey revealed that in recent years severe clinic violence was rising; in both 1999 and 2000 it affected 20% of clinics while in 2002 it affected 23% of clinics. Bomb threats, stalking, death threats, and blockades were the most commonly reported types of severe violence in 2002. The number of clinics experiencing three or more forms of violence or harassment also increased—from 5% in 1999, to 11% in 2000, and to 14% in 2002.

CLINIC SATISFACTION WITH LAW ENFORCEMENT OF FACE. Most police departments surveyed by the GAO for its report "Abortion Clinics: Information on the Effectiveness of the Freedom of Access to Clinic Entrances Act" noted that they had taken steps to reduce and better respond to clinic incidents after FACE came into effect. These steps included increasing patrols at clinics during high-risk times (such as at the anniversary of *Roe v. Wade* or on Saturdays, when more protesters were present), training police officers about clinic incidents, and conducting outreach or education with clinic staff.

Most (thirty-five) clinic respondents to the GAO study generally were satisfied with the effectiveness of their local law enforcement in protecting their clinics during the two-year period after FACE; seven were dissatisfied. Five of the seven dissatisfied respondents cited officers' poor response (slow response or lack of response) to incidents.

Three-quarters (75%) of clinic respondents to the 2002 FMF survey rated the law enforcement response to clinic violence as good or excellent. These clinics were less likely than the remaining 25% of clinics to experience antiabortion violence or harassment. Of the clinics that had contact with state law enforcement, and of the clinics that had contact with federal law enforcement, 81% and 82%, respectively, rated their responses as good or excellent.

FACE and the Internet

In February 1999 a federal jury in Portland, Oregon, unanimously ruled that it is illegal for pro-life activists to threaten abortion providers through Wild West-style "wanted posters" and a Web site called the "Nuremberg Files." The "Nuremberg Files" listed the names of abortion doctors accused of committing "crimes against humanity." The list included the doctors' addresses and other family information. Murdered doctors were listed with lines drawn through their names.

The jury ordered the defendants (American Coalition of Life Activists, Advocates for Life Ministries, and twelve individuals) to pay the plaintiffs (Planned Parenthood, the Portland Feminist Women's Health Center, and four abortion doctors) more than $109 million in damages. The jury found all defendants guilty of violating or conspiring to violate FACE and all but two defendants of violating or conspiring to violate the Racketeer Influenced and Corrupt Organizations Act (RICO).

However, in March 2001 a three-judge panel of the Ninth Circuit Court of Appeals unanimously reversed the jury verdict and the injunction against continued publishing of the materials. Then in May 2002 an eleven-judge panel of the Ninth Circuit U.S. Court of Appeals upheld the 1999 trial verdict, stating that the Nuremberg Files Web site and the "wanted" posters amounted to threats and intimidation that violated FACE as well as other laws.

CHAPTER 7
MEDICAL AND ETHICAL QUESTIONS CONCERNING ABORTION

ABORTION AND HEALTH

Abortion was widely practiced during the colonial period and early years of the United States but became less common between the early 1800s and 1973, when—under certain conditions—abortion was considered a criminal offense. After abortion was legally banned, women of means generally were able to find doctors willing to perform supposedly therapeutic (medically necessary) abortions allowed by law. Many poor women, however, died or developed medical complications from self-induced abortions or abortions performed by untrained persons.

Since the 1973 Supreme Court ruling on the legality of abortion in *Roe v. Wade*, a number of studies have been done on the physical, emotional, and psychological impact of abortion on women. In its first major study of abortion (*Legalized Abortion and the Public Health*, Washington, DC: National Academy Press, 1975), the Institute of Medicine concluded that "evidence suggests that legislation and practices that permit women to obtain abortions in proper medical surroundings will lead to fewer deaths and a lower rate of medical complications than [will] restrictive legislation and practices."

In 1987 President Ronald Reagan promised the various right-to-life groups that he would investigate the health effects of abortion. The president instructed Surgeon General C. Everett Koop to prepare such a report. After meetings with experts and thorough reviews of many studies for almost a year and a half, Dr. Koop refused to release a report.

In a January 1989 letter to President Reagan, Dr. Koop reported that "in spite of a diligent review on the part of many in the Public Health Service and in the private sector, the scientific studies do not provide conclusive data about the health effects of abortion on women." Dr. Koop added that the negative physical health effects possible following an abortion—infertility,

a damaged cervix, premature birth, low-birth-weight babies—could also develop if the pregnancy were carried to term. In March 1989, testifying before the U.S. House of Representatives, Dr. Koop reported that, although psychological problems may result from having an abortion, the problem is "minuscule from a public health perspective."

Morbidity and Mortality

In "Safety of Abortion" (National Abortion Federation, http://www.prochoice.org/about_abortion/facts/safety_surgical_abortion.html, revised 2003), Susan Dudley declared, "Surgical abortion is one of the safest types of medical procedures. Complications from having a first trimester abortion are considerably less frequent and less serious than those associated with giving birth." (The National Abortion Federation is the professional association of abortion providers in the United States and Canada.)

However, like any other surgical procedure, surgical abortion carries risks of complications. Major complications from abortions performed before thirteen weeks of pregnancy are rare. About 88% of women who have an abortion are less than thirteen weeks pregnant according to "Induced Abortion in the United States: Facts in Brief" (Alan Guttmacher Institute, http://www.agi-usa.org/pubs/fb_induced_abortion.html, May 18, 2005). Of these women, 97% do not develop complications, 2.5% have minor complications that are treatable at the doctor's office or at the abortion clinic, and less than 0.5% require hospitalization. In general, the earlier in pregnancy the abortion is performed, the less complicated and safer it is.

Besides the length of pregnancy, other factors that determine the likelihood of complications include the physician's skill and training, the use of general anesthesia, the abortion method used, and the woman's overall health. In "Safety of Abortion" Dudley noted that, "although rare, possible complications from an abortion" include the following:

- Blood clots in the uterus, which require a repeat suctioning (occur in less than 1% of cases)

- Infections, most of which are easy to identify and treat if the woman follows the postoperative instructions (occur in less than 3% of cases)

- A tear in the cervix, which may be repaired with stitches (occurs in less than 1% of cases)

- A tear in the uterine wall and/or other organs, which may heal by itself or require surgery or, rarely, hysterectomy (removal of the uterus) (occurs in less than one-half of 1% of cases)

- Missed abortion, which does not terminate the pregnancy and requires a repeat abortion (occurs in less than 1% of cases)

- Incomplete abortion, in which tissue from the pregnancy remains in the uterus and requires a repeat abortion (occurs in less than 1% of cases)

- Too much bleeding, caused by failure of the uterus to contract, which may require a blood transfusion (occurs in less than 1% of cases)

The legalization of abortion has resulted in a significant decrease in abortion-related deaths. According to Dudley's report, one death occurs for every 160,000 women who have legal abortions in the United States. These deaths usually are the result of adverse reactions to anesthesia, embolism (blood clot), infection, or uncontrollable bleeding. In 1989, following Dr. Koop's refusal to release his report and because of his admission of bias against abortion, the House Committee on Government Operations relied instead on research done by the Centers for Disease Control and Prevention (CDC) and concluded that childbirth was seven times more likely to result in the mother's death than was abortion. According to Stanley Henshaw in "Unintended Pregnancy and Abortion: A Public Health Perspective" (*A Clinician's Guide to Medical and Surgical Abortion*, edited by in M. Paul, et al., New York: Churchill Livingstone, 1999), the risk of death is ten times greater for a woman carrying a pregnancy to term and giving birth. Medical abortion, which must be done before nine weeks of pregnancy, also is considered safe.

Post-Abortion Stress Syndrome

Dr. Koop's investigation of the psychological effects of abortion was as inconclusive as his findings of its physical health effects. In the same letter to President Reagan, Koop observed that "the data do not support the premise that abortion does or does not cause or contribute to psychological problems." Many antiabortion groups, however, claim that for many women, having an abortion can lead to serious psychological problems, most notably "post-abortion syndrome." Some have compared this with the post-traumatic stress disorder (PTSD) suffered by many Vietnam veterans.

Following Dr. Koop's findings, an American Psychological Association (APA) expert, Dr. Nancy Adler of the University of California at San Francisco, testified before the Human Resources and Intergovernmental Relations Subcommittee of the House Committee on Government Operations. Dr. Adler reported that an APA expert panel on the psychological effects of abortion found no evidence of the so-called "post-abortion syndrome" of psychological trauma or deep depression. In fact, the APA investigation found "the predominant feelings following abortion to be relief and happiness. Some women report feelings of sadness, regret, anxiety, or guilt, but these tend to be mild." According to the Planned Parenthood Federation of America in "The Emotional Effects of Induced Abortion" (http://www.plannedparenthood.org), "most studies in the last 20 years have found abortion to be a relatively benign procedure in terms of emotional effect—except when pre-abortion emotional problems exist or when a wanted pregnancy is terminated, such as after diagnostic genetic testing."

Henry P. David and Ellie Lee report in "Abortion and Its Health Effects" (*Encyclopedia of Women and Gender*, vol. 1, edited by J. Worrell, San Diego, CA: Academic Press, 2001) that the period of greatest psychological stress occurs immediately before the abortion decision is made and that "legal abortion of an unwanted pregnancy in the first trimester does not pose a severe psychological hazard for the vast majority of women."

According to Nancy Felipe Russo, a leading researcher on abortion and mental health issues in the United Kingdom, "no scientific basis exists for applying a PTSD [post-traumatic stress disorder] framework to understanding women's emotional responses to a voluntarily obtained legal abortion." In "Abortion, Informed Consent, and Mental Health" (Pro-Choice Forum, http://www.prochoiceforum.org.uk/psy_coun11.asp), she and Lisa Rubin report, "Unintended pregnancy, whether resolved by an abortion or by giving birth, is a common life event that is typically perceived as stressful, sometimes profoundly so. In general, however, exercising the option of legal abortion is not 'more dangerous' to physical or mental health than giving birth—indeed many reviews of the scientific literature have established that having a legal abortion, particularly if it is in the first trimester, poses little particular threat to mental health for most women."

In "The Effects of Induced Abortion on Emotional Experiences and Relationships: A Critical Review of the Literature" (*Clinical Psychology Review*, vol. 23, no. 7,

December 2003) Zoe Bradshaw and Pauline Slade obtained similar results. The researchers found that the pre-abortion anxiety experienced by 40% to 45% of women following the discovery of their pregnancy reduces following abortion. About 30% of women still experience emotional problems one month post-abortion, but in the long term they do no worse psychologically than women who give birth.

Others Disagree

Abortion opponents insist that they have ample anecdotal evidence of psychological stress following abortion. According to the Pro-Life Action Ministries in "What They Won't Tell You at the Abortion Clinic" (St. Paul, MN: undated):

> Most often a woman will feel the consequences of her decision within days of her abortion. If they don't appear immediately, they will appear as she gets older. Emotional scars include unexplained depression, a loss of the ability to get close to others, repressed emotion, a hardening of the spirit, thwarted maternal instincts (which may lead to child abuse or neglect later in life), intense feelings of guilt and thoughts of suicide.

Dr. E. Joanne Angelo, an assistant clinical professor of psychiatry at the Tufts University School of Medicine and a psychiatrist in private practice in Boston, has participated in Project Rachel, an outreach program for women and men who have experienced abortion. In "A Special Word to Women Who Have Had an Abortion" (Washington, DC: National Conference of Catholic Bishops, 1999, http://www.usccb.org/prolife/programs/rlp/97rlpang.htm), Dr. Angelo observed:

> Women who have had abortions . . . may turn to alcohol or drugs to get to sleep at night or to deaden the pain of their waking hours, or throw themselves into feverish activity in an attempt to forget their sorrow, guilt and shame. Deep feelings of loneliness and emptiness may lead to binge eating, alternating with purging and anorexia, or intense efforts to repair intimate relationships or develop new ones inappropriately, or to an insatiable need to replace the lost child at any cost.

Project Rachel reports that some who have obtained an abortion, especially young girls, experience negative psychological symptoms soon after the abortion. Yet, according to Project Rachel counselors, it is more common for the symptoms to occur over the course of five to twelve years after the abortion before a woman seeks help. Most studies of post-abortion syndrome do not continue long enough, they contend, often only up to two years after the abortion or less.

ETHICAL QUESTIONS RELATED TO ABORTION

Scientific advances often raise ethical questions. Ethics is a branch of philosophy concerned with evaluating human action. Some distinguish ethics, what is considered right or wrong behavior based on reason, from morals, what is considered right or wrong behavior based on social custom.

Fetal Tissue Transplantation Research

A fetus is a developing animal (in this case human) from the end of eight weeks after conception to birth. The fetus is a rich source of multipotent stem cells. These cells can give rise to a variety of specialized cells, which makes them valuable to scientists who are conducting tissue transplant research. (There is an important difference, however, between the multipotent stem cells and pluripotent stem cells. The multipotent variety can give rise to only certain types of cells; the pluripotent cells—discussed in greater detail below—can develop into any of the more than two hundred types of cells in the body.)

Fetal tissue transplantation involves taking multipotent cells and placing them in a child or adult with the intent of treating certain conditions. Scientists have found that transplanted fetal tissue is less likely to be rejected by the recipient and has the unique ability to take over the functions of some types of diseased tissues. This means that transplanted multipotent cells may be able to replace improperly functioning cells in places such as the pancreas (in order to cure diabetes) or the brain (to cure Parkinson's disease). Fetal tissue transplantation may also prove beneficial in treating neurological disorders such as Alzheimer's disease and Huntington's disease; blood disorders such as leukemia, aplastic anemia, and hemophilia; spinal cord injuries; and stroke.

The ethical controversy of fetal tissue transplantation research has arisen because the source of the fetal tissue is induced abortion. (A tissue is a group of cells that work together to perform a similar function.) Fetal research and the use of fetal tissue in research is not a recent medical development. It dates back to the 1930s and was responsible, in the mid-twentieth century, for the development of vaccines against poliomyelitis and rubella (German measles), as well as the preventive treatment of Rh incompatibility (a condition in which a mismatch between the blood of a pregnant woman and that of her fetus can harm the fetus).

The controversy about the use of aborted fetuses for medical research erupted after the 1973 *Roe v. Wade* decision legalizing abortion. Antiabortion groups oppose fetal research in general and fetal tissue transplantation research in particular because they believe both types of research encourage abortion. For instance, a woman could become pregnant in order to produce fetal tissue that could be transplanted to her father, who has Alzheimer's disease. Or a woman might become pregnant and then obtain an abortion in order to sell her aborted fetus to researchers. Or, to take a less sensational example, a woman might be more inclined to choose abortion because the potential scientific benefits to society might serve to offset the guilt she might feel for ending her pregnancy.

In March 1988 the U.S. Department of Health and Human Services (HHS) imposed a moratorium on the use of federal funds for fetal tissue transplantation research until an expert panel could study the ethical implications of such research. In November 1989, despite the panel's finding that the use of fetal tissue in research is acceptable public policy, Secretary Louis Sullivan of the HHS continued the moratorium. In 1992 President George H. W. Bush vetoed Congress's efforts to restore public funding of fetal tissue research, fearing "its potential for promoting and legitimizing abortion."

When President Bill Clinton took office in 1993, one of his first actions was to lift the ban on federally funded research using fetal tissue from induced abortion. That same year, the National Institutes of Health Revitalization Act (PL 103-43) legalized fetal tissue transplantation research. The law provides ethical guidelines that ensure informed consent, forbid payment for fetal tissue, and forbid altering the timing or method of abortion for the sake of research.

In Vitro Fertilization Research

In vitro fertilization (IVF) is a process by which an egg is fertilized with a sperm in laboratory glassware, and the fertilized egg is then implanted in a woman's uterus for development. The developing organism—from fertilization through eight weeks—is termed an embryo.

In 1995 congress banned the National Institutes of Health from using appropriated funds to create, destroy, discard, or subject to risk of injury or death human embryos for research purposes. Thus, human embryo research, which is legal in the United States, has been conducted by private in vitro fertilization clinics seeking to improve the efficiency of IVF and develop treatments for infertility. IVF researchers rely on embryos donated by couples who no longer need them for implantation or who have abnormal embryos.

Stem Cell Research

Embryos contain pluripotent stem cells—those with the potential to develop into any of various types of cells in the body. Pluripotent stem cells offer the possibility of a renewable source of replacement cells and tissues to treat many types of diseases, conditions, and disabilities, such as repairing spinal cord injuries, treating multiple sclerosis by "regrowing" the degenerating myelin sheath of nerve cells, and curing blindness caused by damage to the cornea. Pluripotent stem cells also could help in the development of more effective drugs to treat diseases. And lastly, scientists can use pluripotent stem cells to study the process of cell differentiation, which is important in the development of diseases such as cancer.

To develop human stem cell lines for research, cells are harvested from the inner cell mass of a week-old embryo. If these stem cells are cultured properly, they can grow and divide indefinitely. The stem cell line is a mass of cells descended from an original stem cell. It shares the original cell's genetic characteristics. Groups of cells can be separated from the cell line and distributed to researchers.

THE ABORTION DEBATE AND STEM CELL RESEARCH. Because one source of stem cells is the human embryo, and because harvesting stem cells destroys the embryo, such research has created a controversy that is similar to the abortion debate. Those opposed to stem cell research say that it destroys human life (in embryo form). Supporters say the embryos were going to be destroyed anyway, and research using the cells may be able to cure debilitating and lifelong diseases. Creating embryos intended for research only raises additional ethical questions.

In January 1999 HHS ruled that stem cell research does not fall within the congressional ban on human embryo research. According to the HHS Office of the General Counsel, because stem cells alone are not capable of developing into a human, they could not be considered embryos. Opponents to stem cell research, however, questioned whether groups of stem cells could congregate to form an entity that is, however briefly, a living organism.

Other opponents of stem cell research noted that, although government-proposed guidelines require that no public monies may be used to destroy an embryo—a necessary step to harvesting stem cells—the rules allow federal researchers to use embryo-derived stem cells created by scientists supported by private funds. They believe that this is an inconsistency in federal policy that should be stopped.

The Clinton administration created rules for funding stem cell research, but they were never implemented. In 2000 the National Institutes of Health announced that it would accept applications for stem cell projects that involved cells taken from frozen embryos developed in fertility treatments that were no longer needed. Shortly after taking office, however, President George W. Bush put that plan on hold and began a review of the policy.

On August 9, 2001, President Bush announced his decision to allow federal funding for experiments involving stem cells already derived from embryos but would not allow federal funding for research that would cause the destruction of further embryos: "Embryonic stem cell research offers both great promise and great peril, so I have decided we must proceed with great care. As a result of private research, more than 60 genetically diverse stem cell lines already exist. They were created from embryos that have already been destroyed, and they have the ability to regenerate themselves indefinitely, creating ongoing opportunities for research," he said. "This allows us to explore the promise and potential of stem cell research without crossing a fundamental moral line, by providing taxpayer funding that would sanction or encourage further destruction of human embryos" ("Remarks by the President on Stem Cell Research," The White House: President George W. Bush, http://www.whitehouse.gov). The decision does not affect private sector embryonic stem cell research.

President Bush placed certain restrictions on the research, however. The embryonic stem cell lines must have been created on or before August 9, 2001, and federal funding is allowed only for experiments involving stem cells already derived from embryos—but not for research that would cause the destruction of additional embryos. One year after President Bush's announcement, there were seventy-eight eligible lines identified in labs around the world, but only about seventeen were available to researchers and only five of them were being used, according to the American Society for Reproductive Medicine (ASRM).

At the same time that he announced his policy on embryonic stem cell research, President Bush created a President's Council on Bioethics to monitor this research, recommend guidelines and regulations, and consider the various "medical and ethical ramifications of biomedical innovation." The council includes scientists, doctors, ethicists, lawyers, and theologians.

Some opposed to embryonic stem cell research supported the idea of using stem cells extracted from human bone marrow for stem cell research. Bone marrow stem cells are those that develop into the various types of blood cells, such as red blood cells and white blood cells, repopulating the blood with these cells as they die. However, in October 2003 the journals *Nature* and *Nature Cell Biology* published two separate studies indicating that only embryonic stem cells—not bone marrow stem cells—can differentiate into new cells of various types and regenerate diseased or dead tissue other than blood. Results of this research suggested that previous studies regarding bone marrow stem cells were "overinterpreted," according to the *Washington Post*. Researchers for the *Nature* article said that the adult stem cells often fused with existing cells in the brain, liver, and heart, but there was no evidence that the cells then differentiated to become new brain, liver, or heart cells.

In 2004 Jeffrey M. Drazen published an editorial in the *New England Journal of Medicine* (vol. 351, no. 17, October 21, 2004), noting that "a critical point has been overlooked" in the embryonic stem cell research debate.

Drazen continued, "Research using this technology is strongly supported in a number of countries, including Australia, Israel, the Czech Republic, Singapore, Korea, and the United Kingdom. Others in the world appreciate the potential of this technology. If we continue to prevent federal funds from being used to support this research in the United States, the ability of our biomedical scientists to compete with other research teams throughout the world will be undermined. No matter how hard we try, we cannot legislate an end to a process of discovery that many in this country and elsewhere in the world consider ethically justifiable. The work will go on—but outside the United States." Drazen concluded, "If we fail to bring the necessary research technology into the mainstream now, our children and grandchildren may need to leave the United States to benefit from treatments other nations are currently developing. Our research scientists must be able to adopt and use embryonic stem-cell technology as they pursue its use in the treatment of many degenerative diseases. Such research has promise, but it must be nurtured to flourish."

Genetic Testing

GENDER SELECTION. Progress in prenatal testing has raised a number of questions about the possible reasons for obtaining an abortion. Ultrasonography (also called ultrasound scanning, in which images of the fetus are made using sound waves) and amniocentesis (removal of a small amount of amniotic fluid to gain information about the fetus) may be able to determine the sex of a fetus.

In some countries of the world, such as China and India, parents often prefer boys and sometimes use abortion to prevent the birth of daughters. In the United States, women generally have not been known to have abortions for reasons of sex preference in a child.

A new technology called "sperm sorting" has become popular with couples who want to choose the sex of a child. The techniques used in sperm sorting were originally developed by the Genetics and I.V.F. Institute, a fertility clinic in Fairfax, Virginia. The original purpose of the technology for human use was to increase significantly the chances of couples, in which the mother is a carrier of 350 X-linked genetic disorders, to produce daughters. Giving the "carrier" X chromosome to a daughter produces another carrier, while giving it to a son produces a child with the affliction. However, sperm sorting is now offered for "family balancing." According to the clinic, more daughters than sons have been selected.

In response to these types of gender selection, the Ethics Committee of the American Society of Reproductive Medicine issued three reports over several years starting in 1994, concluding that "the use of medical technologies to avoid the birth of children with genetic disorders is acceptable. However, the use of these technologies for nonmedical reasons poses a more difficult question."

In 1999 the society's Ethics Committee reported, "The initiation of IVF [in vitro fertilization] with PGD [preimplantation genetic diagnosis] solely for sex selection holds even greater risk of unwarranted gender bias, social harm and the diversion of medical resources from genuine medical need. It therefore should be discouraged."

In May 2001 the committee issued its most recent report on the subject, concluding, "If…methods of preconception gender selection are found to be safe and effective, physicians should be free to offer preconception gender selection in clinical settings to couples who are seeking gender variety in their offspring if the couples (1) are fully informed of the risks of failure, (2) affirm that they will fully accept children of the opposite sex if the preconception gender selection fails, (3) are counseled about having unrealistic expectations about the behavior of children of the preferred gender, and (4) are offered the opportunity to participate in research to track and access the safety, efficacy and demographics of preconception gender selection. Practitioners offering assisted reproductive services are under no legal or ethical obligation to provide nonmedically indicated preconception methods of gender selection."

In April 2004 the Genetics and Public Policy Center of Johns Hopkins University released *Reproductive Genetic Testing: What America Thinks* (Washington, DC: Genetics and Public Policy Center, http://www.dna-policy.org), which contained the results of a study conducted between October 2002 and August 2004. The study included twenty-one focus groups, sixty-two in-depth interviews, and two surveys with a combined sample size of more than six thousand people. The results revealed that most people disapprove of using preimplantation genetic diagnosis for the purpose of having a baby of a particular sex. However, the results also revealed that 61% approve of using the technology to select an embryo that would be a good match to donate cells or tissues to an ailing older sibling.

SCREENING FOR BIRTH DEFECTS AND HEREDITARY DISEASES. Prenatal testing through amniocentesis or ultrasound may reveal severe defects in the fetus, such as anencephaly (congenital absence of part or all of the brain), spina bifida (a condition in which part of the spinal cord protrudes through a gap in the backbone, leading to serious, often fatal, infections and paralysis), and Down syndrome (a genetic disorder that usually includes mental retardation).

In addition, genetic (hereditary) testing has allowed some parents to determine if the child they are carrying

has the gene for certain diseases, such as Huntington's disease, Tay-Sachs syndrome, cystic fibrosis, or the genes *BRCA1* and *BRCA2* that increase a female's risk of breast and ovarian cancer. Women who discover that the fetuses they are carrying are seriously impaired or will develop debilitating diseases may face an agonizing decision about whether or not to have an abortion.

Some people have no problem with genetic testing if it makes possible the use of preventive therapy for a predisposed condition or an acceptance of the child who may be born with abnormalities. However, because most genetic tests are for untreatable disorders, some fear that the screening techniques may be used for eugenic (selective breeding) purposes, preventing the birth of children affected by hereditary defects.

Many people who are handicapped take issue with those who advocate abortions in cases of fetal defects and potential diseases. They argue that had late-term abortions been available to their mothers during pregnancy, they might have never had the chance for life. Many disabled people say they resent those who feel one can mandate a certain quality of life or place an economic value on it. Some observers are also wary that the genetic information obtained from prenatal testing eventually might result in preventing the birth of children with certain traits or behavioral tendencies.

Infertility Treatments

MULTIPLE BIRTHS. Many women who are unable to bear children have turned to assisted reproductive technology (ART). There are several methods of ART, including IVF, gamete intrafallopian transfer, and zygote intrafallopian transfer. IVF is the most widely used method to help women achieve pregnancy. IVF is performed by removing the woman's eggs, fertilizing them in the laboratory, and transferring the resulting embryo or embryos back into her uterus. According to the CDC in "Assisted Reproductive Technology Surveillance—United States, 2002" (*Morbidity and Mortality Weekly Report, Surveillance Summaries*, vol. 54, no. SS02, June 3, 2005), in 2002, 42% of ART transfer procedures resulted in a pregnancy, and 34% resulted in a live-birth delivery. In 2002 45,751 infants were born as a result of ART; 53% were born in multiple-birth deliveries.

The pregnancy success rate in ART decreases as the woman's age increases. Therefore, to increase the chances of success in older women, doctors are likely to implant more embryos. In a number of cases, many well-publicized multiple births have resulted. Table 7.1 shows the outcomes of ART using each technology.

MULTIPLE BIRTHS AND ABORTION. The birth of the McCaughey septuplets in 1997 in Iowa and the Chukwu octuplets in 1998 in Houston brought criticism from

TABLE 7.1

Outcomes of assisted reproductive technology (ART), by procedure type, 2002

ART procedure type	Number of ART procedures started	Number of procedures progressing to retrievals	Number of procedures progressing to transfers	Number of pregnancies	Pregnancies per transfer procedure (%)	Number of live-birth deliveries	Live-birth deliveries per transfer procedure (%)	Number of singleton live births	Singleton live births per transfer procedure (%)	Total number of live-born infants
Patient's eggs used										
Freshly fertilized embryos	85,826	74,519	69,857	29,423	42.1	24,324	34.8	15,723	22.5	33,776
Thawed embryos	16,383	N/Aª	14,598	4,562	31.3	3,620	24.8	2,730	18.7	4,592
Donor eggs used										
Freshly fertilized embryos	9,261	8,647	8,394	4,854	57.8	4,195	50.0	2,416	28.8	6,088
Thawed embryos	3,922	N/A	3,476	1,207	34.7	1,002	28.8	728	20.9	1,295
Total	**115,392ᵇ**	**N/A**	**96,325**	**40,046**	**41.6**	**33,141**	**34.4**	**21,597**	**22.4**	**45,751**

ªNot applicable.
ᵇThis number does not include 146 ART procedures in which a new treatment procedure was being evaluated.

SOURCE: Victoria Clay Wright, Laura A. Schieve, Meredith A. Reynolds, and Gary Jeng, "Table 1. Outcomes of Assisted Reproductive Technology (ART), by Procedure Type—United States, 2002," in "Assisted Reproductive Technology Surveillance, United States, 2002," *Morbidity and Mortality Weekly Report/Surveillance Summaries*, Centers for Disease Control and Prevention, vol. 54, no. SS02, June 3, 2005, http://www .cdc.gov/mmwr/preview/mmwrhtml/ss5402a1.htm#tab1 (accessed September 20, 2005)

many in the medical profession who thought the parents and their fertility doctors had acted irresponsibly. Some believed the mothers had taken a tremendous risk with their health and that of their children. Siblings in multiple births are at a high risk for prematurity, low birth weight, long-term mental and physical disabilities, and death.

Ethicists ask if it is justifiable behavior to abort some fetuses when a woman is pregnant with multiples to reduce the risks to the remaining ones. This process is termed selective reduction. Some people think that the parents of multiples should employ selective reduction. Those who are against selective reduction warn that the acceptance of abortion in cases of multiple births eventually will make it too easy in the future to "selectively reduce" other members of society, such as the elderly or the disabled.

FETAL RIGHTS

"Fetal rights" is the view that the unborn deserve the same legal protections as children. Since its 1973 decision in *Roe v. Wade*, the U.S. Supreme Court consistently has ruled that the woman's right to health and life outweighs the state's interest in the fetus, even after viability. In recent years, however, there have been a number of attempts to elevate the status of the fetus to that of a child.

According to Lynn M. Paltrow in "Punishing Women for Their Behavior during Pregnancy: An Approach That Undermines the Health of Women and Children" (http://www.nida.nih.gov/PDF/DARHW/467-502_Paltrow.pdf), about two hundred women in more than thirty states have been prosecuted for "fetal abuse" for taking drugs while pregnant. However, in most cases courts overturned the convictions on the grounds that a fetus could not be considered a person under criminal child abuse statutes or that the legislature did not intend for an existing criminal statute to apply to a pregnant woman and her fetus. Other courts have found such convictions to be unconstitutional violations of a woman's rights to due process and privacy. In addition, the Supreme Court has ruled that secretive testing of blood taken from a pregnant woman for other tests to which she consents is an unconstitutional search and violates patients' constitutional rights, guaranteed by the Fourth Amendment, to be free from unreasonable search and seizure.

THE FETUS AS A VICTIM OF A CRIME
Unborn Victims of Violence Act of 2004

The Unborn Victims of Violence Act of 2004 (PL 108-212) is the first federal law to recognize the fetus as a victim of a crime. The law makes it "a separate offense" to injure or cause the death of "a child, who is in utero [in the womb] during the commission of a federal crime of violence against a pregnant woman." The act applies only to federal offenses, such as crimes committed on federal properties, against certain federal officials and employees, and by members of the military. It does not apply to crimes prosecuted by the individual states. Although the bill does not seek the prosecution of "conduct relating to an abortion," abortion advocates claim that this bill sets the stage for dismantling the legal right to abortion.

The States and Unborn Victims

As of 2005, twenty states had homicide laws that recognize unborn children as victims throughout the entire prenatal period. Another twelve states had homicide laws that recognize unborn children as victims during part of their prenatal development. (See Figure 3.7 in Chapter 3.)

FETAL RIGHTS VERSUS PARENTS' RIGHTS

Opponents of fetal rights believe that if a fetus is granted the same legal rights traditionally granted to people, the law will be forced to embark on the "slippery slope" of what control the state should have over women (and men). If substance use can be prohibited, then everything a woman does that might potentially harm the fetus could be regulated. Her eating and drinking, her work, or her health habits could all be scrutinized by the courts. Could a woman who inadvertently harmed a fetus before she knew she was pregnant be held liable? Could a woman be criminally prosecuted for failing to seek prenatal care?

Results of medical research have revealed increasing evidence that a woman's behavior is not the only influence on the fetus. Men who smoke, abuse drugs (including marijuana) and alcohol, or work with toxic chemicals may be damaging their sperm, thereby causing genetically defective fetuses. Men, however, have not yet been charged with abuse of the unborn.

CHAPTER 8
ABORTION AROUND THE WORLD

Throughout the world abortion is used regularly as a method of birth control. Because women are fertile for almost half of their lives, many have unwanted pregnancies at one time or another. Regardless of whether abortion is legal, women in all countries and cultures have relied on abortion to control childbirth. Abortion rates around the world generally reflect the religious and political power in the country, the cultural values, and the availability of contraception.

The major organizations that compile international abortion statistics are the Alan Guttmacher Institute (AGI) of New York, an organization that supports a woman's right to choose abortion, and the World Health Organization (WHO) of the United Nations. In countries where abortion is illegal or severely restricted, it is impossible to know how many women get private abortions and how many of those who turn up at the hospital with a "spontaneous abortion" (miscarriage) actually have induced the abortion through a home method. Also, many countries where abortion is legal do not keep complete medical records. The abortion and health data that is available for other countries is often not as current at that for the United States.

The WHO reports that each year, 210 million women throughout the world become pregnant. Of these pregnancies, forty-six million (22%) end in abortion, and twenty million of these abortions are estimated to be "unsafe." A great number of women either do not want any more children or do not want a child at that time. According to the AGI in "Induced Abortion Worldwide: Facts in Brief," (http://www.agi-usa.org/pubs/fb_0599.html), each year in developed countries about half (49%) of the twenty-eight million pregnancies that occur are unwanted. About one-third (36%) end in abortion. In developing countries approximately one-third (36%) of pregnancies are unwanted. One-fifth (20%) end in abortion.

ABORTION LAWS WORLDWIDE

The Center for Reproductive Rights, which supports a woman's right to choose, reported in "The World's Abortion Laws" (June 2004) that 61% of people live in countries where abortion is permitted for a wide range of reasons or without restriction. About one-fourth (26%) of the world's population, however, live in countries that generally forbid abortion. Countries are categorized based on the restrictiveness of abortion laws, as follows (see Table 8.1):

- Prohibited altogether or permitted only to save the woman's life—There are seventy-two countries (26.1% of the world's population) in this category. As the map in Figure 8.1 shows, most countries with highly restrictive laws are in Central and South America, Africa, the Middle East, and Indonesia.

- To preserve the woman's physical health (and to save her life)—Thirty-five countries (9.9%) allow an abortion if it threatens a woman's physical health. These types of laws sometimes require that the potential injury be either serious or permanent.

- To preserve the woman's mental health (and to preserve her physical health and save her life)—Twenty countries (2.7%) allow the termination of pregnancy if continuing it would jeopardize a woman's mental health. However, what constitutes a threat to mental health varies from country to country, from psychological distress caused by rape to mental anguish because the woman is carrying a fetus that might have abnormalities.

- Socioeconomic grounds (also to save the woman's life, physical health and mental health—Fourteen countries (20.7%) permit abortion, but consider a woman's economic resources, her age, whether she is married, and the number of children she already

TABLE 8.1

World abortion laws, June 2004

I. Prohibited altogether or permitted only to save the woman's life
(countries printed in bold make an explicit exception to save a woman's life)

Afghanistan	Iraq	**Papua New Guinea**
Andorra	**Ireland**	**Paraguay**
Angola	**Kenya**	Philippines
Antigua & Barbuda	**Kiribati**	San Marino
Bangladesh	Laos	Sao Tome & Principe
Bhutan–U	**Lebanon**	Senegal
Brazil–R	Lesotho	**Soloman Islands**
Brunei Darussalam	**Libya**–PA	Somalia
Central African Rep.	Madagascar	**Sri Lanka**
Chile–x	**Malawi**–SA	**Sudan**–R
Colombia	**Mali**–R/I	Suriname
Congo (Brazzaville)	Malta	Swaziland
Côte d'Ivoire	Marshall Islands–U	**Syria**–SA/PA
Dem. Rep. of Congo	Mauritania	**Tanzania**
Dominica	Mauritius	Togo
Dominican Republic	**Mexico**◊–R	Tonga
Egypt	Micronesia–U	**Tuvalu**
El Salvador–x	Monaco	**Uganda**
Gabon	**Myanmar**	**United Arab**
Guatemala	**Nicaragua**–SA/PA	**Emirates**–SA/PA
Guinea-Bissau	Niger	**Venezuela**
Haiti	**Nigeria**	**West Bank & Gaza Strip**
Honduras	Oman	**Yemen**
Indonesia	Palau–U	
Iran	**Panama**–PA/R/F	

72 nations, 26.1% of world's population

II. To preserve physical health
(also to save the woman's life)

Argentina–R1	Equatorial Guinea–SA/PA	Peru
Bahamas	Eritrea	Poland–PA/R/I/F
Benin–R/I/F	Ethiopia	Qatar–F
Bolivia–R/I	Grenada	Rep. of Korea–SA/R/I/F
Burkina Faso–R/I/F	Guinea–R/I/F	Rwanda
Burundi	Jordan	Saudi Arabia–SA/PA
Cameroon–R	Kuwait–SA/PA/F	Saint Lucia
Chad–R/I/F	Liechtenstein	Thailand–R
Comoros	Maldives–SA	Uruguay–R
Costa Rica	Morocco–SA	Vanuatu
Djibouti	Mozambique	Zimbabwe–R/I/F
Ecuador– R1	Pakistan	

35 countries, 9.9% of world's population

III. To preserve mental health
(also to save the woman's life and physical health)

Algeria	Liberia–R/I/F	Saint Kitts & Nevis
Botswana–R/I/F	Malaysia	Samoa
Gambia	Namibia–R/I/F	Seychelles–R/I/F
Ghana–R/I/F	Nauru	Sierra Leone
Hong Kong–R/I/F	New Zealand–I/F	Spain–R/F
Israel–R/I/F	Northern Ireland	Trinidad & Tobago
Jamaica–PA	Portugal–PA/R/F	

20 countries, 2.7% of world's population

IV. Socioeconomic grounds
(also to save the woman's life, physical health and mental health)

Australia–◊	Iceland–R/I/F
Barbados–PA/R/I/F	India–PA/R/F
Belize–F	Japan–SA
Cyprus–R/F	Luxembourg–PA/R/F
Fiji	Saint Vincent & Grenadines–R/I/F
Finland–R/F	Taiwan–SA/PA/I/F
Great Britain–F	Zambia–F

14 countries, 20.7% of world's population

V. Without restriction as to reason

Albania	Denmark–PA	Norway–PA
Estonia	Estonia	Romania*
Austria*	France*	Russian Fed.
Azerbaijan	Fmr. Yugoslav Rep.	Serbia &
Bahrain	Macedonia–PA	Montenegro–PA
Belarus	Georgia	Singapore***
Belgium*	Germany*	Slovak Rep.–PA
Bosnia-	Greece–PA	Slovenia–PA
Herzegovina–PA	Guyana†	South Africa
Bulgaria	Hungary	Sweden**
Cambodia*	Italy–ÄPA	Switzerland
Canada◊	Kazakhstan	Tajikistan
Cape Verde	Kyrgyzstan	Tunisia
China◊–S	Latvia	Turkey–‡SA/PA
Croatia–PA	Lithuania	Turkmenistan
Cuba–PA	Moldova	Ukraine
Czech Rep.–PA	Mongolia	United States–◊PA
Dem. People's Rep. of	Nepal–S	Uzbekistan
Korea◊	Netherlands˅	Vietnam˅

54 countries, 40.5% of world's population

A note on terminology: "Countries" listed on the table include independent states and, where populations exceed one million, semi-autonomous regions, territories and jurisdictions of special status. The table therefore includes Hong Kong, Northern Ireland, Puerto Rico, Taiwan, and the West Bank and Gaza Strip.
Note: All countries have a gestational limit of 12 weeks unless otherwise denoted. Gestational limits are calculated from the first day of the last menstrual period, which is generally considered to occur two weeks before conception. Statutory gestational limits calculated from the date of conception have thus been extended by two weeks.

Gestational limits key

†Gestational limit of 8 weeks
‡Gestational limit of 10 weeks
*Gestational limit of 14 weeks
**Gestational limit of 18 weeks
***Gestational limit of 24 weeks
˅=Law does not limit pre-viability abortions
◊=Law does not indicate gestational limit

Key for additional grounds, restrictions and other indications:

R-Abortion permitted in cases of rape
R1-Abortion permitted in the case of rape of a woman with a mental disability
I-Abortion permitted in cases of incest
F-Abortion permitted in cases of fetal impairment
SA-Spousal authorization required
PA-Parental authorization/notification required
◊=Federal system in which abortion law is determined at state level; classification reflects legal status of abortion for largest number of people
x-Recent legislation eliminated all exceptions to prohibition on abortion; availability of defense of necessity highly unlikely
S-Sex selective abortion prohibited
U-Law unclear

SOURCE: "The World's Abortion Laws, June 2004," in *International Factsheets: Abortion*, Center for Reproductive Rights, June 2004, http://www .reproductiverights.org/pub_fac_abortion_laws.html (accessed September 20, 2005)

FIGURE 8.1

Levels of abortion restriction worldwide, June 2004

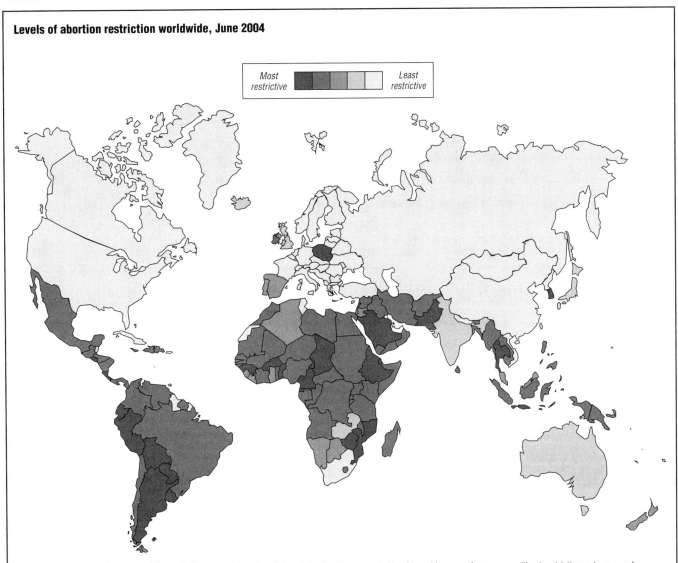

Currently, more than 61% of the world's people live in countries where induced abortion is permitted either for a wide range of reasons or without restriction as to reason. In contrast, 26% of all people reside in countries where abortion is generally prohibited.

SOURCE: "The World's Abortion Laws, June 2004," in *International Factsheets: Abortion*, Center for Reproductive Rights, June 2004, http://www.reproductiverights.org/pub_fac_abortion_laws.html (accessed September 20, 2005)

has. Barbados, Great Britain, India, and Zambia have laws in this category. These laws usually are interpreted liberally.

- Without restriction as to reason—Fifty-four countries, where 40.5% of the world's women live, allow abortion without limiting the reasons for pregnancy termination.

In addition, in some countries a woman may obtain a legal abortion based on "juridical grounds" (rape or incest) or "fetal impairment grounds" (probable genetic defects). Countries that recognize these grounds for legal abortion may be classified under any of the five categories of restrictiveness. Access to abortion also may be limited by spousal or parental consent laws.

Abortion Limitations Even When Laws Are Liberal

In the countries where abortion is not restricted as to reason, and in the countries that allow abortion based on socioeconomic grounds, the laws usually mandate certain conditions for allowing the abortion. According to the Center for Reproductive Rights (*Crafting an Abortion Law That Respects Women's Rights: Issues to Consider*, Briefing Paper, http://www.reproductiverights.org/pdf/pub_bp_craftingabortionlaw.pdf, August 2004), these countries may impose gestational limits; consent, counseling, and waiting-period requirements; fetal-age restrictions; limitations on advertising abortion services; and limitations on the place of abortion and the person performing the procedure. For example, a woman in Turkey needs her husband's permission; in Germany a woman is required to receive counseling that is intended to

TABLE 8.2

Number of legal and illegal induced abortions worldwide, by region and subregion, 1995

Region and subregion	Number of abortions (millions)			% illegal	Rate[1]	Ratio[2]
	Total	Legal	Illegal			
Total	**45.5**	**25.6**	**19.9**	44	35	26
Developed regions	**10.0**	**9.1**	**0.9**	9	39	42
Excluding Eastern Europe	3.8	3.7	0.1	3	20	26
Developing regions	**35.5**	**16.5**	**19.0**	54	34	23
Excluding China	24.9	5.9	19.0	76	33	20
Africa	**5.0**	3	**5.0**	99	33	15
Eastern Africa	1.9	3	1.9	100	41	16
Middle Africa	0.6	3	0.6	100	35	14
Northern Africa	0.6	3	0.6	96	17	12
Southern Africa	0.2	3	0.2	100	19	12
Western Africa	1.6	3	1.6	100	37	15
Asia	**26.8**	**16.9**	**9.9**	37	33	25
Eastern Asia	12.5	12.5	3	4	36	34
South-central Asia	8.4	1.9	6.5	78	28	18
South-eastern Asia	4.7	1.9	2.8	60	40	28
Western Asia	1.2	0.7	0.5	42	32	20
Europe	**7.7**	**6.8**	**0.9**	12	48	48
Eastern Europe	6.2	5.4	0.8	13	90	65
Northern Europe	0.4	0.3	3	8	18	23
Southern Europe	0.8	0.7	0.1	12	24	34
Western Europe	0.4	0.4	3	4	11	17
Latin America	**4.2**	**0.2**	**4.0**	95	37	27
Caribbean	0.4	0.2	0.2	47	50	35
Central America	0.9	3	0.9	100	30	21
South America	3.0	3	3.0	100	39	30
Northern America	**1.5**	**1.5**	3	4	22	26
Oceania	**0.1**	**0.1**	3	22	21	20

[1]Abortions per 1,000 women aged 15–44.
[2]Abortions per 100 known pregnancies. Known pregnancies are defined as abortions plus live births.
[3]Fewer than 50,000.
[4]Less than 0.5%.
Notes: Developed regions include Europe, Northern America, Australia, New Zealand and Japan; all others are considered developing. Regions are as defined by the United Nations (UN). Numbers do not add to totals due to rounding.

SOURCE: Stanley K. Henshaw, Susheela Singh, and Taylor Haas, "Table 1. Estimated Number of Induced Abortions, by Legal Status, Percentage of All Abortions That are Illegal, Abortion Rate and Abortion Ratio, All According to Region and Subregion, 1995," in "The Incidence of Abortion Worldwide," *International Family Planning Perspectives*, vol. 25 (suppl.), January 1999, http://www.guttmacher.org/pubs/journals/25s3099.html (accessed September 20, 2005)

discourage her from having the abortion; and in Belgium the waiting period is six days. Most countries set fetal age limits of seeking an abortion with the least restrictions at an upper limit of twelve to fourteen weeks.

COMPARISONS OF ABORTION STATISTICS WORLDWIDE

Stanley K. Henshaw, Susheela Singh, and Taylor Haas of the AGI reported in "The Incidence of Abortion Worldwide" (*International Family Planning Perspectives*, vol. 25, Supplement, January 1999), that in 1995 an estimated 45.5 million abortions were performed around the world. Nearly 26.0 million were legal and 19.9 million were illegal. The overall worldwide abortion rate was thirty-five abortions per one thousand women ages fifteen to forty-four. About one-quarter (26%) of all pregnancies ended in abortion. (See Table 8.2.)

Regional Estimates

Asia accounted for the largest number of abortions (26.8 million), which corresponds to 59% or three of every five abortions worldwide. Europe was the region with the second most abortions (7.7 million), followed by Africa (5.0 million), Latin America (4.2 million), North America (1.5 million), and Oceania (0.1 million). (See Table 8.2.)

Europe, where abortions are generally legal, had the highest abortion rate of any region—forty-eight abortions per one thousand women ages fifteen to forty-four. In Europe nearly half (48%) of all pregnancies ended in abortion, compared with 15% in Africa. Europe encompassed the two subregions with the highest and lowest rates—eastern Europe, with ninety abortions per one thousand women, and western Europe, with eleven abortions per one thousand women ages fifteen to forty-four.

TABLE 8.3

Measures of legal abortion worldwide, by completeness of data, country, and data year, 1983–97

Completeness and country	Number[1]	Rate[2]	Ratio[3]	Total abortion rate[4]
Believed to be complete				
Australia, 1995–1996	91,900	22.2	26.4	0.57
Belarus, 1996	155,700	67.5	61.9	2.04
Belgium, 1996[5]	14,600	6.8	11.2	0.21
Bulgaria, 1996	89,000	51.3	55.2	1.55
Canada, 1995[6]	106,700	15.5	22.0	0.49
Cuba, 1996	209,900	77.7	58.6	**2.33**
Czech Republic, 1996	46,500	20.7	34.0	0.63
Denmark, 1995	17,700	16.1	20.3	0.48
England & Wales, 1996[7]	167,900	15.6	20.5	0.48
Estonia, 1996	16,900	53.8	56.0	1.63
Finland, 1996	10,400	10.0	14.7	0.31
Germany, 1996	130,900	7.6	14.1	**0.23**
Hungary, 1996	76,600	34.7	42.1	1.07
Israel, 1995	17,600	14.3	13.1	0.43
Kazakhstan, 1996	178,000	43.9	41.3	**1.32**
Latvia, 1996	23,100	44.1	53.9	1.33
Netherlands, 1996[7]	22,400	6.5	10.6	**0.20**
New Zealand, 1995	13,700	16.4	19.1	0.49
Norway, 1996	14,300	15.6	19.1	0.47
Puerto Rico, 1991–1992	19,200	22.7	23.0	**0.68**
Scotland, 1996[8]	12,300	11.2	17.2	0.34
Singapore, 1996	14,400	15.9	22.8	**0.48**
Slovak Republic, 1996	24,300	19.7	28.8	**0.59**
Slovenia, 1996	10,400	23.2	35.7	0.70
Sweden, 1996	32,100	18.7	25.2	0.56
Switzerland, 1996[9]	12,800	8.4	13.3	**0.25**
Tunisia, 1996	19,000	8.6	7.8	**0.26**
United States, 1996	1,365,700	22.9	25.9	**0.69**
Incomplete or of unknown completeness				
Albania, 1996	21,200	27.2	23.7	**0.82**
Armenia, 1996	31,300	35.4	39.4	**1.06**
Azerbaijan, 1996	28,400	16.0	18.0	0.49
Bangladesh, 1995–1996[10]	100,300	3.8	3.1	**0.11**
China, 1995	7,930,000	26.1	27.4	**0.78**
Croatia, 1996	12,300	12.9	18.7	0.38
France, 1995	156,200	12.4	17.7	0.37
Georgia, 1996	26,600	21.9	33.2	0.66
Hong Kong, 1996	25,000	15.1	27.9	0.45
India, 1995–1996	566,500	2.7	2.1	**0.08**
Ireland, 1996[11]	4,900	5.9	8.9	**0.18**
Italy, 1996	140,400	11.4	21.1	**0.34**
Japan, 1995	343,000	13.4	22.4	0.40
Korea (South), 1996[12]	230,000	19.6	24.6	**0.59**
Kyrgyzstan, 1996	24,600	22.4	17.5	**0.67**
Lithuania, 1996	27,800	34.4	41.5	**1.03**
Macedonia, 1996	14,200	28.5	31.1	**0.86**
Moldova, 1996	38,900	38.8	42.7	0.83
Mongolia, 1996	15,600	25.9	18.2	**0.78**
Romania, 1996	394,400	78.0	63.0	**2.34**
Russian Federation, 1995	2,287,300	68.4	62.6	2.56
South Africa, 1997	26,400	2.7	2.4	**0.08**
Spain, 1996	51,000	5.7	12.6	**0.17**
Tadjikistan, 1990[13]	55,500	49.1	21.2	**1.47**
Turkey, 1993[12]	351,300	25.0	20.5	**0.75**

Among the subregions, eastern Europe accounted for the highest proportion (65%) of pregnancies terminated by abortion.

Country Estimates

Table 8.3 illustrates the abortion numbers, rates, and ratios for countries with populations exceeding one million for which the AGI obtained information using available national statistics and surveys. The authors pointed

TABLE 8.3

Measures of legal abortion worldwide, by completeness of data, country, and data year, 1983–97 [CONTINUED]

Completeness and country	Number[1]	Rate[2]	Ratio[3]	Total abortion rate[4]
Turkmenistan, 1990[13]	37,200	44.9	22.9	**1.35**
Ukraine, 1996	635,600	57.2	57.6	**1.72**
Uzbekistan, 1996	63,200	11.8	9.5	**0.35**
Vietnam, 1996[14]	1,520,000	83.3	43.7	**2.50**
Yugoslavia, 1993	119,300	54.6	45.8	**1.64**
Zambia, 1983	1,200	0.4	0.4	**0.01**

[1]Rounded to the nearest 100.
[2]Abortions per 1,000 women aged 15–44.
[3]Abortions per 100 known pregnancies.
[4]The number of abortions that would be experienced by the average woman during her reproductive lifetime, given present age-specific abortion rates. Numbers in bold were estimated by multiplying the rate by 30 and dividing by 1,000.
[5]Including abortions obtained in the Netherlands.
[6]Including abortions obtained in the United States.
[7]Residents only.
[8]Including abortions obtained in England and Wales.
[9]Includes estimates for two of the 26 cantons.
[10]Menstrual regulations.
[11]Based on Irish residents who obtained abortions in England.
[12]Based on surveys of ever-married women aged 20–44 (Korea) and 15–49 (Turkey).
[13]Includes spontaneous abortions.
[14]Excludes an estimated 500,000 private-sector abortions.

SOURCE: Stanley K. Henshaw, Susheela Singh, and Taylor Haas, "Table 2. Measures of Legal Abortion, by Completeness of Data, Country and Data Year," in "The Incidence of Abortion Worldwide," *International Family Planning Perspectives*, vol. 25 (suppl.), January 1999, http://www.guttmacher.org/pubs/journals/25s3099.html (accessed September 20, 2005)

out that the upper category, "Believed to be complete," includes countries for which the abortion statistics are thought to be within 20% of the actual numbers. The lower "Incomplete" category includes countries whose statistics may be inaccurate by at least 20% or whose data may not be complete.

Among countries where abortion is legal and data are believed to be complete, Cuba, Belarus, and Estonia had the highest abortion rates—77.7, 67.5, and 53.8 abortions per one thousand women ages fifteen to forty-four, respectively. The Netherlands (6.5 per one thousand women) and Belgium (6.8 per one thousand women) had the lowest abortion rates, followed by Germany (7.6 per one thousand women) and Switzerland (8.4 per one thousand women). Women in Belarus, Cuba, and Estonia were the most likely to choose to terminate their pregnancies with abortion, as these countries also had the highest abortion ratios. Nearly two-thirds (61%) of all pregnancies ended in abortion in Belarus, followed by 58.6% in Cuba and 56% in Estonia. Only about one in ten women in the Netherlands (10.6%) and Belgium (11.2%) terminated their pregnancies with abortion, and women in Tunisia were least likely to choose abortion (7.8%).

Among countries where abortion is legal but the data are incomplete, the authors surmised that the actual abortion rates are higher than shown in Table 8.3. Henshaw, et al., noted that the actual rates for Vietnam (83.3 per one thousand women) and Romania (78.0 per one thousand women) probably were higher because only public-sector abortion numbers were available in the AGI survey. China's real rate of abortions per one thousand women is more likely to be between thirty and thirty-five abortions, not the official rate of 26.1. Unofficial surveys of women in Japan tend to indicate that the abortion rates probably exceeded twenty abortions per one thousand women rather than the reported 13.4 abortions per one thousand women. Similarly, Bangladesh's and India's reported rates of 3.8 and 2.7 abortions per one thousand women, respectively, are more likely to be several times these numbers.

Of those countries with incomplete or questionable data, the highest estimated proportion (ratio) of pregnancies terminated by abortion occurred in Russia and Romania and were about 63% each. (See Table 8.3.)

In countries where abortion is illegal, the AGI estimated the number of induced abortions, basing their figures on such factors as the proportion of women hospitalized as a result of complications and on surveys conducted by health-care professionals. The authors, however, warned that even in cases where women sought hospitalization, many other factors came into play, including "the extent to which safe abortion is practiced, the probability of complications arising from procedures provided by nonphysicians and the ease of access to a hospital."

Of abortions performed in Western industrialized countries, Australia has the highest rates of abortion, at 22.2 per one thousand. This is followed closely by the United States at 21.3 per one thousand. The Netherlands had the lowest abortion rate, at 6.5 per one thousand.

Abortion Laws and Rates

Worldwide, women have abortions whether laws are restrictive or not, and the rate of abortion is not higher in countries where abortion is permitted. Table 8.4 compares the rate of abortion in six countries with liberal abortion laws to the rate of abortion in eight countries with severely restricted abortion laws. Among these countries, the rate of abortion is much higher in the countries with restrictive laws compared with countries with more permissive laws, in spite of the fact that abortions in countries with restrictive abortion laws are generally illegal and often unsafe.

ABORTION IN SELECTED COUNTRIES

Poland

The collapse of Communism in Poland in 1989 led to the prohibition of abortion, which had been legal since 1956. As soon as Lech Walesa's Solidarity Party gained control of the parliament, it amended the existing abor-

TABLE 8.4

Abortion rates worldwide, various years by country, 1989–2000

Country	Abortion rate per 1,000 women, 15–44
Where abortion is broadly permitted	
Belgium, 1996*	7
England/Wales, 1996	16
Finland, 1996	10
Germany, 1996	8
Netherlands, 1996	7
United States, 1996/2000	23/21
Where abortion is severely restricted	
Brazil, 1991	41
Chile, 1990	50
Columbia, 1989	36
Dominican Republic, 1990	47
Mexico, 1990	25
Nigeria, 1996	25
Peru, 1989	56
Philippines, 1994	25

*Includes abortions obtained in the Netherlands.

SOURCE: Amy Deschner and Susan A. Cohen, "Abortion Laws and Rates," in "Special Analysis: Contraceptive Use is Key to Reducing Abortion Worldwide," *The Guttmacher Report on Public Policy*, The Alan Guttmacher Institute (AGI), October 2003, http://www.guttmacher.org/pubs/tgr/06/4/gr060407.pdf (accessed September 20, 2005)

tion law. Strongly supported by the Roman Catholic Church, the new statute severely restricted access to abortion, requiring a woman requesting a state-funded abortion to present written approval from three physicians and a psychologist from a state-approved list of doctors.

The new abortion provision granted physicians and hospital staffs in public hospitals the right to refuse to perform abortions. As a result, the number of abortions in state-funded hospitals fell from 105,300 in 1988 to about thirty-one thousand in 1991, according to figures provided by the Polish government. In addition, the state stopped funding contraceptives for the poor, and funding was reduced for the Polish affiliate of the International Planned Parenthood Association, resulting in the closing of half of its offices.

In March 1993 a new antiabortion law, granting protection to a fetus from the moment of conception, went into effect. The law allowed abortion only if the pregnancy seriously threatened a woman's life or health, in cases of rape or incest, or if the fetus had irreparable abnormalities. Private clinics were forbidden to perform abortions, and physicians performing illegal abortions could be imprisoned for up to two years. If the woman died of complications, a physician could face up to ten years' imprisonment. Women who had abortions were not punishable.

The new law also required that the Catholic Church be involved in reproductive services and that sex education be based on "family and conceived-life values as well as on methods and means of conscious procreation." "Conscious procreation" meant contraception, but little information on contraception was delivered by health professionals, other than information on withdrawal and rhythm methods, which were accepted by the Catholic Church.

The government reported that 782 legal abortions were performed in 1994 in Poland. Pro-choice organizations, however, estimated that forty thousand to fifty thousand Polish women had abortions abroad or at home illegally.

In November 1995 Lech Walesa lost the presidential election to pro-choice candidate Aleksander Kwasniewski. Although about 90% of Poles are Catholic, a number of surveys have found that most favored liberalization of Poland's restrictive abortion laws.

A year later, in November 1996, the Polish government again legalized abortion. The new law permitted women to obtain an abortion until the twelfth week of pregnancy if they were financially or emotionally unprepared for childbirth. A woman seeking an abortion was required to obtain counseling and wait three days before having the procedure. The new law forbade abortion against a woman's will or after the fetus had become viable (able to survive outside the womb). The law further addressed the abortion issue by providing for government funding of oral contraceptives and sex education.

In May 1997 Poland's highest court, the Constitutional Tribunal, struck down the 1996 abortion law, declaring the provision allowing abortions "for compelling social and financial reasons" unconstitutional. The Tribunal ruled that "the first article of our Constitution names Poland as [a] democratic state based on the rule of law. The highest value in a democracy is human life, which must be protected from its beginning to the end." In December 1997 the newly elected Parliament, dominated by pro-Church legislators, reinstated the strict 1993 antiabortion law. Under this law abortions are allowed only in cases of life endangerment, rape, or incest or if the fetus is damaged irreparably.

During the campaign for the 2001 general election, the Democratic Left Alliance promised to liberalize abortion. Although they won the election, laws were not changed because Poland sought the support of the Roman Catholic Church to join the European Union, which the Church would offer only if the existing abortion law remained in place.

In late 2004 the United Nations Human Rights Committee concluded a review on Poland's compliance with the International Covenant on Civil and Political Rights, demanding that the nation liberalize its abortion laws. In mid-2005 the leader of the ruling Democratic Left Alliance, Wojciech Olejniczak, spoke in favor of amendments to the abortion law, which would reduce the restrictions on a woman's right to choose. Olejniczak commented: "The Polish Left is not antireligious but I want to make one thing absolutely clear: the state must be secular" (BBC Monitoring Service, June 19, 2005).

Romania

During the rule of Communist dictator Nicolae Ceausescu (1967–89), abortion was allowed only when a woman was older than forty-five years and had at least five children. Modern contraception also was severely restricted. Ceausescu had hoped to build his country into a powerful nation based on population growth. Nonetheless, birth rates did not increase. Although the 1967–68 total fertility rate (3.6 lifetime births per woman) nearly doubled the 1966 level, it declined to 2.9 in 1970, fell to 2.1 by 1984, and remained at about 2.3 births per woman from 1985 through the end of Communism and Ceausescu's rule in 1989 ("World Fertility Report 2003," Population Division of the United Nations Department of Economic and Social Affairs, January 2005).

It was only after Ceausescu's regime was overthrown that the situation in Romania was revealed to the world. Without contraception, women resorted to abortion to prevent unwanted births. During Ceausescu's rule an estimated ten thousand women died from illegal abortions, either self-induced or induced by untrained persons. During the ten-year period prior to Ceausescu's fall from power (1979–89), Romania had the highest maternal mortality rate in Europe—ten times higher than any other European country (Patricia Stephenson, et al., "Commentary: The Public Health Consequences of Restricted Induced Abortion—Lessons from Romania," *American Journal of Public Health*, vol. 82, no. 10, October, 1992). Many women also suffered permanent disfigurement.

Romania's interim government after the revolution made abortion available on request through the twelfth week of pregnancy. Abortions up to the twenty-fourth week of pregnancy were permitted in cases of rape, incest, and endangerment of the woman's life if she were to carry her pregnancy to term. After abortion was legalized the total fertility rate declined from 2.3 live births to 1.5 live births per woman (1990–93), whereas the total induced abortion rates doubled, from 1.7 to 3.4 abortions per woman. Also, when abortion became legal in Romania in 1990, abortion-related mortality fell to one-third of its highest level, which had occurred the previous year ("Abortion in Context: United States and Worldwide: Issues in Brief," Alan Guttmacher Institute, 1999 Series, no. 1, May 1999).

With the shift in policy allowing abortion on demand, Romanians have resorted to abortion as a principal method of birth control. According to Glasgow's *Sunday Herald*, in 2002, 70% of pregnancies in Romania ended in abortion. In 2003 Romania had the second-highest abortion rate in Europe (after Russia), according to a February 10, 2004, news report by LifeSiteNews.com. In 2004, for the first time since the fall of the communist regime in 1989, the number of births was higher than the number of abortions (*Iran Daily*, May 3, 2005). The Romanian parliament passed a law in September 2004 guaranteeing women the right to be informed about abortions and their risks.

Russia

In 1970 Russia had 27.5 abortions for every ten live births; this ratio fell somewhat steadily to 17.5 abortions for every ten live births in 1997 (Julie DaVanzo and Clifford Grammich, *Dire Demographics: Populations Trends in the Russian Federation*, Santa Monica, CA: Rand, 2001). In October 2005 *The Guardian*, a London newspaper, reported that Russia still registered more abortions each year than live births.

Abortion law was liberalized in Russia in 1955. Abortions were allowed on demand through the twelfth week of pregnancy and for medical and social reasons through the twenty-second week. Because modern methods of contraception were not available for many years, most women relied on abortion to control childbirth. A Russian woman who did not want more than two children would likely have as many as four or more abortions in her lifetime.

However, in August 2003 the Russian government passed a resolution on abortion, which involves restrictions on women's access to abortion after twelve weeks. Previously, women in Russia could receive an abortion between twelve and twenty-two weeks of pregnancy by meeting one of thirteen special circumstances, including divorce, poverty, and poor housing. The 2003 resolution reduced these to four circumstances: rape, imprisonment, death or severe disability of the husband, or a court ruling removing the woman's parental rights.

In 2005 the Russian parliament (Duma) turned down proposed legislation that would further restrict the conditions under which a woman could obtain an abortion. Legislators declared that the proposed draft runs contrary to the fundamentals of the Russian legislation on protection of health of citizens, which gives a woman the right to decide on motherhood.

Ireland

Ireland is the only western European country that still bans abortion except in cases where the mother's life is threatened. (See Table 8.1.) (Northern Ireland's abortion laws differ; the section here does not address Northern Ireland.) In 1992 the Irish Supreme Court ruled that abortion could be legally performed if there was a threat to the mother's life, including the threat of suicide.

In late 1992 Irish voters approved a law giving women the right to obtain information regarding abortion services abroad and allowing women to travel abroad to get abortions. In May 1995 the Irish Supreme Court ruled constitutional a measure allowing doctors and clinics to provide women with information about foreign abortion clinics. In 1997 an *Irish Times* poll found that 77% of respondents believed abortion should be allowed.

According to the Irish Family Planning Association (http://www.ifpa.ie), slightly more than six thousand Irish women receive abortions annually at clinics in England, where the practice was legalized in 1967. Still more travel to the Netherlands, Spain, and Belgium for abortions. Although abortion is still illegal in Ireland, its abortion rate—as reported by the Irish Family Planning Association—was 7.5 in 2001 (abortions per one thousand women ages fifteen to forty-four).

China

In China abortion is permitted to save the mother's life, to preserve physical health, and to safeguard mental health. Abortion also is permitted in cases of rape, incest, and fetal impairment and for economic or social reasons.

In the 1970s China initiated a stringent family planning program that has resulted in one of the fastest fertility declines in the world. The program promotes one-child families in urban areas and two-child families in rural areas and for ethnic minorities. In "Low Fertility in Urban China," a conference paper presented to the International Union for the Scientific Study of Population (http://eprints.anu.edu.au/archive/00001368/, March 2001), Zhongwei Zhao notes that between 1975 and 1998 the total fertility rate declined by about two children, from 3.57 to 1.49 lifetime births per woman for China countrywide, and declined by about a half child in urban China, from 1.78 to 1.13. In 2005 China's total fertility rate remained low countrywide at 1.60 lifetime births per woman. Nonetheless, in 2005 China was the most populous country in the world with over 1.3 billion inhabitants ("2005 World Population Data Sheet," Population Reference Bureau, http://www.prb.org/pdf05/05WorldDataSheet_Eng.pdf, 2005).

Contraceptives generally are provided free by local family planning services, and the abortion-inducing drug mifepristone, approved in 1988, was used widely for more than a decade. However, in October 2001 the State Drug Administration reaffirmed a ban on unsupervised mifepristone use for abortions because of a rising black market for the drug and concerns that its unsupervised use could be dangerous. The pill cannot be sold at pharmacies, even with a prescription. It can only be given at a hospital under a doctor's supervision.

In some circumstances the government can mandate that an abortion be performed. In 1994 under the provisions of the Maternal Health Care Law, couples planning to marry had to submit to prenatal testing to prevent "inferior births." An abortion would be recommended if the fetus had a severe hereditary disease or was seriously impaired. Critics considered this a "eugenics law," designed to terminate the birth of defective babies.

China amended the law the following year, deleting the controversial language concerning "inferior births." A couple planning to get married was required to undergo a medical examination to determine the presence of genetic disorders. If such disorders were found, they had to agree to long-term contraception or they could not get married. Although the law specified that a woman carrying an imperfect fetus could not be coerced to abort, her physician must advise her to do so.

Critics feel that a pervading cultural preference for boys in China, coupled with the limitation on the number of births per family, endangers females. Every year, many girls are abandoned, killed, aborted, or hidden from family planning authorities.

The World Factbook 2005 (Dulles, VA: Potomac Books, 2005), a publication of the Central Intelligence Agency of the United States, estimates that in late 2005 106 boys were born for every one hundred girls worldwide. This statistic—the "sex ratio at birth"—indicates the number of male births for every one hundred female births. *The World Factbook 2005* also estimates that, for China, the sex ratio at birth in late 2005 was 112 boys per one hundred girls. A July 2001 news release by the Population Council (http://www.popcouncil.org/media-center/newsreleases/pdr27_2chu.html) notes that the reported sex ratio at birth in China was about the same as the worldwide average in the 1960s and 1970s and that the ratio increased after 1980, from 108.5 in 1981 to 111.9 in 1990. The State Family Planning Commission has suggested that women with no or few sons were more likely to underreport female births and to practice selective abortion using ultrasound scans to determine the sex of their fetuses and ensure the birth of boys. Population data from the *The World Factbook 2005* shows that in China men outnumber women by slightly over thirty-nine million.

India

When the Indian government started providing family planning services in 1952, it became the first developing country to promote population control. Overall, the total fertility rate in India has been declining. In 1981 the total fertility rate was 4.9 lifetime births per woman ("World Fertility Patterns 2004," United Nations

Population Division). By 1990 the total fertility rate had decreased to 3.8, and by 2005 it was projected to be 2.8 (U.S. Census Bureau, "Global Population Profile: 2002," http://www.census.gov/ipc/www/wp02.html). Despite these efforts to control population growth, India has seen its population more than double between 1960 (446 million per the U.S. Census Bureau, "Global Population Profile: 2002") and mid-2005 (1.1 billion according to the "2005 World Population Data Sheet" published by the Population Reference Bureau). According to calculations of the Population Reference Bureau, India is expected to become more populous than China—the most populous country in 2005—by 2050.

In 1969 India legalized abortion to help control its population growth, but government facilities have not been able to keep up with the great number of women seeking abortions. In rural areas, where facilities are lacking or inadequate, women obtain abortions from midwives and untrained practitioners. Approximately twenty thousand Indian women die each year from unsafe abortions (Suneeta Mittal, Consortium on National Consensus for Medical Abortion in India, http://www.aiims.ac.in/aiims/events/Gynaewebsite/ma_finalsite/introduction.html). In 1995–96 an estimated 566,500 abortions were reported. (See Table 8.3.) The actual number, however, is believed to be higher.

There is a strong preference for sons in India, as in China. This preference in India is strongly influenced by the custom of providing a suitable dowry (money or property brought by a bride to her husband at marriage), which puts a great financial burden on the bride's parents. In addition, sons customarily live with their parents after marriage, providing both financial and emotional support to them, especially as the parents grow older.

Medical advances have made sex-selective abortions easier. Prenatal testing has become routine among educated middle- and upper-class women, who often terminate their pregnancies if they are carrying a daughter. Modern technology also has reached some rural areas, where vans with ultrasound machines enable expectant mothers to determine the sex of their fetuses. The enactment of laws in 1996 forbidding sex selection has not deterred selective abortion practices. After the 2001 census found that there were 927 females for every one thousand males younger than age six, the Indian Supreme Court in September 2003 ruled that federal and state governments must begin enforcing the ban on sex selection.

Latin America

In most countries of Latin America abortion is illegal except in cases of endangerment of the woman's life, rape, incest, and fetal abnormality. However, women rarely seek legal abortions using these "exceptions" because they do not know they are eligible nor do they know the legal requirements for obtaining an abortion. Hence, abortions have become secret and generally unsafe in Latin America.

According to the Center for Reproductive Rights, of the approximately twenty million unsafe abortions performed each year worldwide, an estimated four million—about one-fifth—are performed (illegally) in Latin America. Unsafe abortion is the cause of as many as 21% of maternal deaths—five thousand women each year—in Latin America ("Abortion in Context: United States and Worldwide: Issues in Brief," The Alan Guttmacher Institute, 1999).

According to the AGI, most of the women having an abortion in Latin America are in their twenties or older and married. Many already have children. Many married women, especially the poor, already have all the children they can afford to raise. Single women might not want to raise a child alone or cannot support a child by themselves. Working women and those with more education may not want additional children. Some women continue to get pregnant because they are not using any contraception or because they are using unreliable methods, such as withdrawal. Others have unwanted pregnancies because they do not know about the likely time of conception or are using contraceptives incorrectly or irregularly.

MEXICO. As in the other Latin American countries, abortion is generally illegal in Mexico. However, abortions in this country are legal in some circumstances in all thirty-one states and the federal district; the law varies by state, however. All states allow abortion in cases of pregnancies resulting from rape. Most states and the federal district allow abortion if the pregnancy endangers the woman's life; in nine states and the federal district, abortion is legal if the woman's health is in serious danger.

The results of one study revealed that poverty was a key factor in leading Mexican women to seek unsafe abortions. Results of another study found that key reasons women sought induced abortions were that they became pregnant at a young age, their partner pressured them to do so, they had economic constraints, and they already had too many children (Davida Becker, Sandra G. Garcia, and Ulla Larsen, "Knowledge and Opinions about Abortion Law among Mexican Youth," *International Family Planning Perspectives*, vol. 28, no. 4, December 2002).

According to the AGI, 533,000 induced abortions occur each year in Mexico, which is 25.1 abortions per one thousand women ages fifteen to forty-nine and a ratio of 17.1 abortions per one hundred live births. More than 40% of women seeking abortions in Mexico are younger than age twenty-four, and 33% are older than age thirty.

Bureaucratic, legal, and medical barriers make it hard for Mexican women to obtain legal abortions. For instance, women seeking legal abortions in Mexico City in the case of rape face burdensome, time-consuming administrative procedures. Also, when a pregnancy threatens a woman's health in Mexico City, physicians are required to get a second opinion before authorizing an abortion. This process may cause a substantial delay; if this occurs, the abortion may be performed at a point in the pregnancy when it is less safe.

Provider attitudes and knowledge also affect women's ability to obtain legal abortion services. Conservative providers may refuse services and may treat poorly those women they suspect of having had induced abortions. Political and religious groups in Mexico create barriers to abortion services by trying to limit access and campaigning against efforts to liberalize abortion laws.

In September and October 2000 the Population Council's regional office for Latin America and the Caribbean, in collaboration with a Mexican market research firm, carried out a household survey in Mexico to gather information about the public's knowledge of and opinions on abortion and emergency contraception. Table 8.5 shows characteristics of the 907 respondents and their opinions about emergency contraception and abortion.

Most study participants (70–83%) felt that women should have access to legal abortion when a pregnancy is the result of a rape, when the woman's life is at risk, or when her health is in danger. All of the states from which study participants were selected permit abortion when a pregnancy results from rape, and 84% do so when a pregnancy poses a risk to a woman's life. (See Table 8.6.) A woman can obtain a legal abortion in 36% of states if a pregnancy is dangerous to her health or if the fetus is found to have severe birth defects.

Survey results released in 2005 revealed that poor Mexican youth ages thirteen to nineteen years had confusion about contraceptives and little understanding of their use. The survey, sponsored by a research center of the National Autonomous University of Mexico, showed that of the 15,488 participating teenagers, 12.9%, or close to two thousand, said that they had had sexual intercourse. Of those, fifty-seven said that their relations had resulted in an unwanted pregnancy, and 46.2% terminated the pregnancy with an abortion.

South Africa

In South Africa under apartheid (1948–91—the system of racial segregation that involved discrimination against nonwhites), abortion was illegal except in cases where the pregnancy threatened the woman's mental health. The government, fearing that black people would outnumber white people, used tax credits to encourage white women to have children. Nonetheless, many upper- and middle-income women with unwanted pregnancies sought abortions in private physicians' offices or abroad.

TABLE 8.5

Knowledge and opinions about emergency contraception and abortion among Mexican youth, 2000

Characteristic	% (Population=907)
Sex	
Male	47
Female	53
Age	
15–17	33
18–24	67
Marital status	
Never-married	77
Consensual union	5
Married	17
Divorced/separated	1
Parity[a]	
0	78
1	14
≥2	7
Missing	1
Education	
≤Complete elementary	13
Some/complete middle school	27
Some/complete technical high school	5
Some/complete preparatory high school	32
>High school	23
Is employed	
Yes	87
No	13
Region	
Pacific North	8
North Central Gulf	14
Bajio	16
Central	19
Mexico City	20
Southeast	22
Residence	
Urban	76
Rural	24
Total	**100**
Attendance at religious services	
≥Once a week	41
<Once a week	59
Religious identification	
Catholic	73
Other	8
Not religious	19
Registered to vote	
Yes	54
No	14
Not eligible	33
Political party identification	
PAN[b]	28
Other	21
None	16
Not eligible to vote	33
Missing	3

Characteristic	% (Population=907)
Knows someone who has had an abortion	
Yes	20
No	79
Knows someone who has used emergency contraceptive pills	
Yes	8
No	92
Missing	1
Prior knowledge about emergency contraceptive pills	
Yes	37
No	63
Knows the legal status of abortion	
Yes	46
No	54
Attitude toward emergency contraceptive pills	
Liberal	91
Conservative	9
Total	**100**

[a]Parity means the number of children ever born to a woman.
[b]PAN is the National Action Party.

SOURCE: Davida Becker, Sandra G. Garcia, and Ulla Larsen, "Table 1. Percentage Distribution of Respondents to Survey on Knowledge and Opinions About Emergency Contraception and Abortion, by Selected Characteristics, Mexico, 2000," in "Knowledge and Opinions About Abortion Law Among Mexican Youth," *International Family Planning Perspectives*, The Alan Guttmacher Institute (AGI), vol. 28, no. 4, December 2002, http://www.guttmacher.org/pubs/journals/2820502.pdf (accessed September 20, 2005)

Many poor women with unwanted pregnancies, however, either terminated their own pregnancies or used the services of unqualified abortionists.

In 1975, reacting to pressures from the medical profession and women's groups, the legislature enacted the Abortion and Sterilization Act, which legalized abortion.

Nonetheless, because of the stringent provisions of the law, such as requiring the approval of two physicians and a psychiatrist, many women continued seeking illegal abortions.

In November 1996 South Africa's first democratically elected Parliament passed a new abortion law—the most liberal abortion law in Africa—The Choice of Termination of Pregnancy Act. Under the law, women and adolescents could get state funding for abortions up to the twelfth week of pregnancy. From the thirteenth up to and including the twentieth week of pregnancy, abortion is legal in cases of danger to the mother's physical or mental health, rape, incest, and fetal defect. The law also allows abortion if continuing the pregnancy would affect the woman's social or economic circumstances. Abortion after twenty weeks of pregnancy also is allowed if a physician or trained midwife finds that continuation of the pregnancy would threaten the woman's health or result in fetal abnormality. Although adolescents are counseled to consult their parents, the law allows them to have an abortion without parental knowledge. Research after the implementation of the new abortion law suggests that the act has increased availability, but access to an abortion is still elusive for certain groups, especially women from rural areas and younger women.

TABLE 8.6

Percentage of Mexican states allowing abortion in various circumstances, and support for legal abortion in each circumstance, by region, 2000

Circumstance	States allowing abortion (N=25)[4]	Respondents supporting legal abortion						
		All regions (N=907)	Pacific North (N=75)	North Central Gulf (N=131)	Bajio (N=148)	Central (N=168)	Mexico City (N=182)	Southeast (N=203)
Pregnancy is the result of a rape	100	70	76	58	65	79	80	64
Woman's life is at risk	84	83	95	75	82	86	84	81
Woman's health is in danger	36	77	85	73	73	77	76	78
Fetus has birth defects	36	50	63	43	42	48	61	46
Economic reasons	4	19	11	21	11	21	30	14
Woman is single	0	13	10	9	8	10	21	13
Woman is a minor	0	22	15	21	14	22	27	26
Pregnancy resulted from contraceptive failure	0	11	10	13	5	10	17	10
On request	0	20	14	18	13	24	28	20

*Excludes the six states not represented in the sample; includes the federal district.

SOURCE: Davida Becker, Sandra G. Garcia, and Ulla Larsen,"Table 3. Percentage of States Allowing Abortion in Various Circumstances, and Percentage of Respondents Supporting Legal Abortion in Each Circumstance, by Region," in "Knowledge and Opinions About Abortion Law Among Mexican Youth," *International Family Planning Perspectives*, The Alan Guttmacher Institute (AGI), vol. 28, no. 4, December 2002, http://www.guttmacher.org/pubs/journals/2820502.pdf (accessed September 20, 2005)

In mid-2005 Parliament put forth an amendment to the 1996 law—The Choice of Termination of Pregnancy Amendment Bill. This proposed legislation sought to designate facilities that can provide abortion services to women, decentralize and improve the efficiency of the abortion process, and allow registered nurses and midwives who have undergone appropriate training to perform abortions. However, the bill encountered a massive groundswell of public opinion against abortion, which became evident after the 1996 legislation went into effect.

In an effort to quantify public sentiment on this issue, the Human Sciences Research Council questioned 4,980 adults in the South African Social Attitudes Survey. Results of the survey were released in full in 2004 and revealed two key findings. One was that more than two-thirds (70%) of the South African adult respondents were opposed to abortion, even if the family concerned is poor and cannot afford more children. The other key finding was that more than half (56%) were against ending the pregnancy of a woman whose child may be "deformed."

CROSS-BORDER ABORTIONS

Abortion laws in Europe run the gamut from a total ban in Ireland (see the subheading "Ireland") to the twenty-four-week gestation limit in Great Britain and the Netherlands. Women who wish to terminate an early pregnancy can travel to countries such as France, Great Britain, and Sweden and have a medical abortion with the help of the abortion-inducing pill mifepristone. As expected, women of means are more able to avoid their country's abortion laws by going to a country that suits their situation. According to Heather Boonstra in "Voi-

TABLE 8.7

Countries that have approved the use of mifepristone, 1988–2002

Austria	(1999)	The Netherlands	(1999)
Belgium	(1999)	New Zealand	(2001)
China	(1988)	Norway	(2000)
Denmark	(1999)	Republic of South Africa	(2001)
Finland	(1999)	Russia	(1999)
France	(1988)	Spain	(1999)
Georgia	(2000)	Sweden	(1992)
Germany	(1999)	Switzerland	(1999)
Greece	(1999)	Taiwan	(2000)
India	(2002)	Tunisia	(2001)
Israel	(1999)	Ukraine	(2000)
Latvia	(2002)	United Kingdom	(1991)
Luxembourg	(1999)	United States	(2000)

SOURCE: Compiled by Sandra Alters for Thomson Gale using data from The Alan Guttmacher Institute and various other sources

cing Concern for Women, Abortion Foes Seek Limits on Availability of Mifepristone" (*The Guttmacher Report on Public Policy*, vol. 4, no. 2, April 2001), abortion rates declined in the 1990s in countries that approved mifepristone. (See Table 8.7 and Figure 8.2.)

DEATHS FROM ABORTION

Abortion is one of the safest medical procedures. As with most medical procedures, however, it becomes unsafe if it is performed by untrained providers in unsanitary conditions. For many women with unwanted pregnancies, a safe abortion can be too expensive, unavailable, or illegal. Because of these limitations, a woman may delay getting an abortion until later in her pregnancy when the risk of complications increases.

FIGURE 8.2

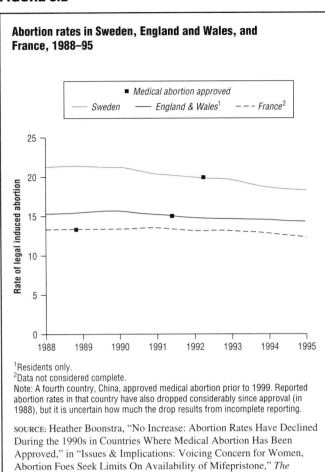

Abortion rates in Sweden, England and Wales, and France, 1988–95

■ Medical abortion approved

—— Sweden ——— England & Wales[1] – – – France[2]

[axis label] Rate of legal induced abortion

[1]Residents only.
[2]Data not considered complete.
Note: A fourth country, China, approved medical abortion prior to 1999. Reported abortion rates in that country have also dropped considerably since approval (in 1988), but it is uncertain how much the drop results from incomplete reporting.

SOURCE: Heather Boonstra, "No Increase: Abortion Rates Have Declined During the 1990s in Countries Where Medical Abortion Has Been Approved," in "Issues & Implications: Voicing Concern for Women, Abortion Foes Seek Limits On Availability of Mifepristone," *The Guttmacher Report on Public Policy*, The Alan Guttmacher Institute (AGI), April 2001 http://www.guttmacher.org/pubs/tgr/04/2/gr040203 .pdf (accessed September 20, 2005)

WHO estimated that in 2000 approximately 67,900 women worldwide died due to unsafe abortions. (See Table 8.8.) This accounts for 13% of maternal deaths worldwide. Most deaths due to unsafe abortions occur in the developing world. It is primarily these countries in which abortion is illegal, and thus women there have the majority of the illegal, generally unsafe abortions that occur worldwide each year. For example, according to the WHO, 140 women died due to unsafe abortions per one hundred thousand live births in 2000 in eastern Africa compared to less than one death per one hundred thousand live births due to unsafe abortions in eastern Asia, northern Europe, western Europe, and northern America.

Up to half of all women who undergo unsafe abortions have complications. The most common complications include incomplete abortion, tears in the cervix, perforation of the uterus, fever, infection, septic shock, and severe hemorrhaging. Other serious long-term health consequences also may affect women who have unsafe abortions. These problems may include chronic pelvic pain, problems getting and staying pregnant, infertility, blockage of a fallopian tube, and ectopic pregnancy.

A WORLDWIDE PLAN FOR REPRODUCTIVE HEALTH

At the landmark International Conference on Population and Development (ICPD) in Cairo, Egypt, in September 1994, 179 nations reached consensus on a twenty-year plan to achieve "reproductive health and rights for all." The plan was wide-ranging and included ideas about increased contraceptive services, fewer maternal deaths, better education for girls, and greater equality for women. The Cairo conference was the first in which the pervasiveness of abortions throughout the world was discussed openly.

The international community agreed on a common position regarding abortion (quoted in "Background Information on Key International Agreements," UNFPA: United Nations Population Fund, http://www.unfpa.org/mothers/concensus.htm), which states:

> In no case should abortion be promoted as a method of family planning. All Governments and relevant inter-governmental and non-governmental organizations are urged to strengthen their commitment to women's health, to deal with the health impact of unsafe abortion as a major public health concern and to reduce the recourse to abortion through expanded and improved family planning services. Prevention of unwanted pregnancies must always be given the highest priority and every attempt should be made to eliminate the need for abortion. Women who have unwanted pregnancies should have ready access to reliable information and compassionate counseling.

In July 1999 179 countries met to assess the progress of the "Programme of Action." The five-year review process, known as ICPD+5, found that nations implementing the Programme recommendations had improved conditions in their countries. For example, more than forty countries had introduced reproductive health services, and nearly half the countries had addressed the issue of adolescent reproductive health needs. Almost all Latin American countries had introduced policies or laws to safeguard women's rights, and more than half the Asian countries and some African countries had protected women's rights in such areas as inheritance, property, and employment. Nonetheless, the delegates agreed that much work still needed to be done.

In 2004 a ten-year review of the Programme of Action took place. Progress toward goals was seen to be impressive; however, there was also mixed results. For example, although the United Nations Population Fund (UNFPA) reported that contraceptive use had increased by 11% since 1994, nevertheless, birth rates remained high in some parts of the world, particularly sub-Saharan

TABLE 8.8

Estimates of annual incidence of unsafe abortion and mortality due to unsafe abortion, 2000

	Unsafe abortion incidence			Mortality due to unsafe abortion		
	Number of unsafe abortions (thousands)	Unsafe abortions to 100 live births	Unsafe abortions per 1000 women aged 15–44	Number of maternal deaths due to unsafe abortion	Percent (%) of all maternal deaths	Unsafe abortion deaths to 100,000 live births
World	19,000	14	14	67,900	13	50
Developed countries[a]	500	4	2	300	14	3
Developing countries	18,400	15	16	67,500	13	60
Africa	4,200	14	24	29,800	12	100
Eastern Africa	1,700	16	31	15,300	14	140
Middle Africa	400	9	22	4,900	10	110
Northern Africa	700	15	17	600	6	10
Southern Africa	200	16	17	400	11	30
Western Africa	1,200	13	25	8,700	10	90
Asia[a]	10,500	14	13	34,000	13	40
Eastern Asia*	b	b	b	b	b	b
South-central Asia	7,200	18	22	28,700	14	70
South-eastern Asia	2,700	23	21	4,700	19	40
Western Asia	500	10	12	600	6	10
Europe	500	7	3	300	20	5
Eastern Europe	400	14	6	300	26	10
Northern Europe	10	1	1	b	4	b
Southern Europe	100	7	3	<100	13	1
Western Europe	b	b	b	b	b	b
Latin America and the Caribbean	3,700	32	29	3,700	17	30
Caribbean	100	15	12	300	13	40
Central America	700	20	21	400	11	10
South America	2,900	39	34	3,000	19	40
Northern America	b	b	b	b	b	b
Oceania[a]	30	12	17	<100	7	20

Note: Figures may not exactly add up to totals because of rounding.
[a]Japan, Australia and New Zealand have been excluded from the regional estimates, but are included in the total for developed countries.
[b]No estimates are shown for regions where the incidence is negligible.

SOURCE: "Table 3. Global and Regional Estimates of Annual Incidence of Unsafe Abortion and Mortality Due to Unsafe Abortion, by United Nations Region, Around the Year 2000," in *Unsafe Abortion: Global and Regional Estimates of the Incidence of Unsafe Abortion and Associated Mortality in 2000, 4th ed.*, World Health Organization, 2004, http://www.who.int/reproductive-health/publications/unsafe_abortion_estimates_04/estimates.pdf (accessed September 20, 2005)

Africa and parts of Asia. (A high birth rate is often due to a lack of affordable contraception.) In another example, although only twenty-four deaths occur per one hundred thousand live births in Europe, nevertheless, 920 women die for every one hundred thousand live births in sub-Saharan Africa. Despite these setbacks, the attendees at the ICPD+10 meetings declared the need to continue addressing major issues such as gender equality, reproductive health and family planning, safe motherhood, and safe abortion.

CHAPTER 9

PUBLIC ATTITUDES TOWARD ABORTION

Like all statistics, public opinion polls should be viewed cautiously. The way a question is phrased influences the respondents' answers. Many other factors may also influence a response in ways that are difficult to determine. For instance, a respondent might never have thought of the issue until asked, or he or she might be giving the pollster the answer he or she thinks the pollster wants to hear. Organizations that survey people's opinions do not claim absolute accuracy; their findings are approximate snapshots of the attitudes of the nation at a given time. The surveys presented here have been selected from numerous polls taken on abortion. A typical, well-conducted survey claims accuracy to about plus or minus three percentage points.

WHEN DOES LIFE BEGIN?

A Fox News/Opinion Dynamics poll conducted in July 2003 asked, "Do you believe that human life begins at conception, or once the baby may be able to survive outside the mother's womb with medical assistance, or when the baby is actually born?" Of all respondents, 55% believed life began at conception; 23% felt life began when the fetus could survive outside the womb, 13% believed it began "at birth," and 9% were "not sure."

The Harris Interactive Election 2000 survey, conducted April 4–10, 2000, asked adults who had previously identified themselves as being pro-choice or pro-life, "When does life begin?" A vast majority (88%) of the pro-life group responded that life begins at conception. The pro-choice group's opinions about when life begins were much more divided than the opinions of the pro-life group. For instance, the largest proportion of pro-choice respondents (38%) said that life begins when the fetus can survive outside the mother's uterus (after the point of viability). Only 23% of those identifying themselves as pro-choice felt that life begins at conception. In addition, 15% of pro-choice respondents

said that life begins at birth; 8% were not sure; and 14% responded that life begins "once brainwaves or motion are observed from the fetus." Just 7% of the pro-life group agreed with this final statement.

SHOULD ABORTION BE LEGAL?

In 1973, a few months after the *Roe v. Wade* Supreme Court decision, a Harris Poll asked, "In 1973, the Supreme Court decided that state laws which made it illegal for a woman to have an abortion up to three months of pregnancy were unconstitutional, and that the decision on whether a woman should have an abortion up to three months of pregnancy should be left to the woman and her doctor to decide. In general, do you favor or oppose this part of the U.S. Supreme Court decision making abortions up to three months of pregnancy legal?" Half (52%) of the respondents favored the decision, whereas 42% opposed it. The remaining persons were unsure or refused to respond. In 1998, on the twenty-fifth anniversary of *Roe*, the Harris Poll asked the same question. The proportion of those who supported the decision was higher, 57%, while the proportion of those against the decision was about the same, 41%. In recent years support for *Roe* has declined. In a 2005 Harris poll the percentage of those favoring the ruling dropped to 1973 levels at 52%, and the proportion who opposed the ruling rose to 47%. Only 1% were unsure.

A 2005 Gallup poll yielded a slightly different result than did the Harris Poll when it asked this question: "Would you like to see the Supreme Court overturn its 1973 Roe versus Wade decision concerning abortion, or not?" An overwhelming majority of respondents—63%—would not like to see the Supreme Court overturn its decision. Only 28% would.

Each year or two from 1975 to 2005, Gallup Poll researchers asked Americans this question: "Do you

FIGURE 9.1

Public opinion on whether abortion should be legal, 1975–2005

Numbers shown in percentages based on yearly averages from 1975–1005

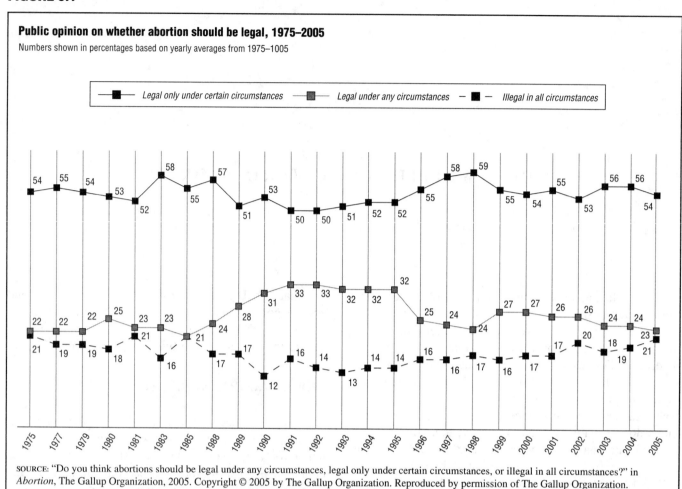

■— Legal only under certain circumstances   ■— Legal under any circumstances   – ■ – Illegal in all circumstances

SOURCE: "Do you think abortions should be legal under any circumstances, legal only under certain circumstances, or illegal in all circumstances?" in *Abortion*, The Gallup Organization, 2005. Copyright © 2005 by The Gallup Organization. Reproduced by permission of The Gallup Organization.

think abortions should be legal under any circumstances, legal only under certain circumstances, or illegal in all circumstances?" Over this thirty-year span, American opinions about abortion have vacillated somewhat. (See Figure 9.1.) In 1975 about 22% of Americans thought abortions should be legal under any circumstances. After peaking at 33% in 1991 and 1992, support for this idea fell to about the 1975 level at 23% in 2005. In 1975 about half (54%) thought abortions should be legal only under certain circumstances. In 1995 59% supported this idea, but support fell after that. In 2005 54% of Americans thought abortions should be legal only under certain circumstances—the same proportion as in 1975. In 1975 21% of respondents thought abortions should never be legal. After vacillating between that high of 21% and a low of 16% over three decades, in 2005 the "never" response returned to the 1975 level of 21%.

During Which Stage of Pregnancy Should Abortion Be Legal?

The Supreme Court's decision in *Roe v. Wade* permits abortion throughout pregnancy, but it allows restrictions to be put on its use in the second and third

trimesters. In 2000 the Harris Poll surveyed Americans to find out when they thought abortions should be illegal. Respondents had identified themselves as pro-life or pro-choice. They all were asked the question, "In general, at which of the following points, if any, do you believe abortions should be illegal or not allowed?" Most respondents—both pro-choice and pro-life—felt that there should be some restrictions on abortion. Of the pro-choice respondents, 24% felt abortion should be legal in all circumstances, with no restrictions.

Three-quarters of people identifying themselves pro-life felt that abortion should be illegal "anytime after conception," whereas only 3% of people identifying themselves as pro-choice agreed. The pro-choice group was more likely to consider abortion an illegal act the closer it occurred to the full term of the pregnancy. Of pro-choice respondents, 15% felt that abortion should be illegal "after motion or brainwaves" have been observed in the fetus, and 48% said that abortion should be illegal at the stage in which the fetus would be likely to survive outside the womb.

In Harris polls in 1998 and 2005 respondents (not separated as to pro-choice or pro-life) were asked, "In general, do you think abortion should generally be legal or generally illegal during the following stages of pregnancy?" In February 2005 60% responded that abortion should be legal during the first three months of pregnancy. A similar proportion of those surveyed in 1998 (63%) responded the same way. A much smaller percentage of respondents in both polls felt that abortion should be legal during the second trimester of pregnancy—26% in both 2005 and 1998. Only 12% in 2005 and 13% in 1998 felt that abortion should be legal in the last trimester of pregnancy. This is comparable to the percentage reported in a 2003 ABC News/*Washington Post* poll: only 11% felt that abortion should be legal once a woman is at least six months pregnant.

Under What Specific Situations Should Abortion Be Legal?

For many people abortion is a difficult issue—permissible in some situations but not in others. Several questions in a Gallup Poll repeated over the years address the issue of certain exceptions that would make abortion permissible or illegal in the respondents' view. In the 2003 poll 88% of respondents reported that abortion should be legal "to save [the] woman's life"; 82% said they support abortion "to save [the] woman's health"; and 81% support it "in cases of rape and incest." These ideas had slightly less support in the 2000 Gallup poll. Most of those polled in 2000 agreed that abortion should be legal when the pregnant woman's life (84%), physical health (81%), or mental health (64%) is in danger or when the pregnancy is the result of rape or incest (78%). In 2003 and 2000 about half (54% and 53%, respectively) agreed that abortion should be legal when there is evidence that the baby may be physically or mentally impaired. However, a June 2003 Gallup Poll revealed that approval often depends on when in pregnancy the abortion would be performed.

OPINIONS ON ABORTION POLICY OF THE GEORGE W. BUSH ADMINISTRATION

One of the first items on the presidential agenda of George W. Bush when he took over the office in January 2001 was to reinstate the "Mexico City Policy," which had been reversed by the previous president, Bill Clinton. The Mexico City Policy, put into action by President Ronald Reagan, had been enforced by executive order for almost a decade prior to Clinton rescinding it. It was a policy that the United States would no longer support private family planning groups overseas that performed or promoted abortion. With that action, Bush made his stance on abortion clear. (See Chapter 3.)

In the following month (February 2001) the Gallup Organization asked Americans, "How important a priority do you think abortion will be for the Bush administration?" (They chose top, high, or low priority or not a priority at all.) The results showed that 14% thought abortion would be a "top" priority, and 34% thought it would be a "high" priority. Despite Bush's action to reinstate the "Mexico City Policy," the largest proportion of respondents (38%) thought abortion would be a "low" priority during Bush's presidency. When asked what is most likely to happen to abortion laws during the Bush administration, 65% felt abortion laws would be made more strict, 26% thought the laws would not be more strict, and 6% felt that all abortions would be made illegal.

A May 2004 Gallup Poll revealed that "abortion views in the United States are strongly related to one's politics and level of religious commitment. Bush's political allies—self-identified conservatives and regular church-goers—tend to favor limited (if any) abortion rights, while those in the middle and left of the political spectrum have more permissive views on abortion."

A January 2003 Gallup/CNN/*USA Today* poll asked those surveyed if abortion was a top legislative priority to them. Sixty percent responded that it was "moderately, not that important." By December 2004 the same percentage of respondents thought abortion *was* a legislative priority. At that time a Gallup poll asked those surveyed how important it was to them that the president and Congress deal with the issue of abortion in the next year. Nineteen percent of Americans thought it was extremely important and 41% thought it was extremely/very important.

OPINIONS ON "PARTIAL BIRTH" ABORTION

In October 2003 the Gallup researchers asked Americans if the U.S. government should make the partial-birth abortion (late abortion) procedure illegal or keep it legal. (For background, see "Partial-Birth Abortion" in Chapter 2.) Of respondents, 68% said it should be illegal and 25% said it should be legal. The results of a January 2003 Gallup poll and a July 2003 ABC News poll varied little: 70% and 62%, respectively, would support a ban on the procedure, and 25% and 20%, respectively, felt it should be legal.

The 2003 poll results show a slight but steady increase from previous years in support for banning partial-birth abortion. Three years prior, in October 2000, Gallup researchers asked Americans how they would vote, if it were possible to do so, on a law that would make partial-birth abortion illegal (except when necessary to save the life of the mother). Sixty-four percent responded that they would vote against the procedure. In 1996 57% of Americans supported making partial-birth abortions illegal.

On November 5, 2003, President George W. Bush signed the Partial-Birth Abortion Ban Act into law. However, legal challenges to the law's constitutionality have postponed its implementation. As of mid-2005, the Bush administration planned to ask the Supreme Court to uphold the partial-birth abortion ban.

ABORTION STANCE BASED ON PERSONAL CHARACTERISTICS

Age and Attitude toward Abortion

Older Americans are more likely than younger Americans to support restrictions on legal abortion, according to the 2003 ABC News/*Washington Post* poll. A Gallup poll conducted from January 2000 to May 2001 revealed the same fact. In the Gallup poll 62% of those age sixty-five and older supported major restrictions on abortion, while only 55% of those in the eighteen to twenty-nine age bracket and 54% of those in the thirty to sixty-four age bracket did. Thus, young Americans appear to have more liberal attitudes toward abortion, while those sixty-five and older appear to have more conservative attitudes.

Education Level and Attitude toward Abortion

Better-educated Americans are more likely to support legal abortion than less-well-educated Americans, according to the 2003 ABC News/*Washington Post* poll. A 2003 Gallup/CNN/*USA Today* poll got similar results. This poll showed that college graduates (35%) are more likely than noncollege graduates (24%) to say that abortion should be legal. In addition, a Gallup poll conducted from January 2000 to May 2001 reached a similar conclusion. It showed that as education increases, support for major restrictions on abortion decreases. While 62% of those with a high school education or less supported major restrictions on abortion, only 40% with post-graduate degrees supported major restrictions.

Religious Beliefs/Affiliation and Attitude toward Abortion

According to the 2003 ABC News/*Washington Post* poll, Americans who profess no religious affiliation are more likely to support legal abortion than Americans who identify themselves as belonging to a spiritual group. Gallup, in describing the results of a May 2001 poll, calls the difference in attitude toward abortion between religious and nonreligious Americans "sharp." Results of that poll found that more than two-thirds of "very religious" Americans (68%) think legal abortion should be limited to a few cases or none at all. This is almost exactly the same as the percentage of nonreligious Americans who think abortion should be legal in all or most cases (71%). Gallup continues: "Previous research by Gallup on this subject shows that this difference in abortion opinion among people of various levels of religious

commitment holds true whether looking at Catholics, Protestants, or born-again Christians. The most deeply religious people in each faith are always much more inclined to the pro-life position than those who are less devout."

Protestants and Catholics express similar views on abortion. In an April 2005 Gallup poll Catholics who attended church weekly and Protestants who did the same were asked if they found abortion morally wrong. About three-quarters of each group answered "yes" to that question: 74% of Catholics and 78% of Protestants. The general population of Catholics and non-Catholics (neither of whom necessarily attend church weekly) express similar views on abortion as well. When asked if they find abortion morally acceptable, 37% of the Catholics responded "yes" as did 39% of the non-Catholics.

Political Affiliations and Attitude toward Abortion

A May 2004 Gallup poll determined that 77% of those who identify themselves as politically conservative believe abortion should be legal in only a few (52%) or in no (25%) circumstances. At the same time nearly half (47%) of those who identify themselves as liberal believe abortion should be legal in all circumstances. A 2003 Gallup/CNN/*USA Today* poll also reports that more Democrats (a group usually identified as liberal) than Republicans (a group usually identified as conservative) think that abortion should be legal.

A Gallup poll conducted from January 2000 to May 2001 reveals data consistent with these findings. Support for major abortion restrictions were higher among respondents who identified themselves as moderate rather than liberal: 70% of moderates supported major restrictions, compared with 33% of liberals. Likewise, the results of the poll show that a smaller percentage of Democrats (49%) favor major restrictions on abortion while a larger percentage of Republicans (68%) favor such restrictions.

A May 2005 Gallup poll asked a question about the "moral acceptability" of abortion. Less than one-third of Republicans (29%) found abortion morally acceptable, while half (51%) of Democrats found this practice morally acceptable.

Gender and Attitude toward Abortion

A person's age, education level, religious beliefs, and political affiliation play a major role in their opinions about abortion. Those who are older, less educated, devoutly religious, and politically conservative are more likely to believe that abortion should be restricted. Differences in opinions between men and women about abortion are not as clear cut.

According to both a 2003 ABC News/*Washington Post* poll and a 2003 Gallup poll, gender seems to have a small effect on opinion regarding abortion. A slightly greater percentage of women (58%) than men (54%) supported abortion being legal in almost all cases. Men and women also agreed on the various conditions in which abortion should or should not be legal. However, these polling results were not supported by an April 2004 poll—"Abortion a More Powerful Issue for Women"—conducted by the Pew Research Center for the People & the Press. According to the Pew poll, "33% of women say they strongly oppose more restriction on abortion, compared with 26% of men. On the other side of the issue, 19% of women strongly favor greater restrictions, compared with 15% of men. Taken together, the majority of women (52% overall) feel strongly about the issue one way or the other, while only 41% of men say the same."

Pro-Choice/Pro-Life Identification

In examining trends from 1996 to 2005 within Gallup polls and with the consistent question, "With respect to the abortion issue, would you consider yourself to be pro-choice or pro-life?," those identifying themselves as pro-choice range from a low of 47% in October 2000 to a high of 55% in February of 2001—only months apart. Those identifying themselves as pro-life during that same time span range from a low of 37% in March 1996 to a high of 45% in October 2000.

Although percentages fluctuate over the years, those identifying themselves as pro-choice always made up a greater percentage of survey respondents in the Gallup polls than did those identifying themselves as pro-life. The difference in percentage points between the two groups, from 1996 to 2005, ranges from a low of only two percentage points (in October 2000) to a high of nineteen percentage points (in March 1996).

IT SHOULD BE ILLEGAL FOR MINORS TO CROSS STATE LINES FOR AN ABORTION WITHOUT THE PARENTS' CONSENT

The "Child Custody Protection Act," later known as the "Child Interstate Abortion Notification Act," criminalizes the act of transporting a minor across a state line with the intent that she obtain an abortion and in order to avoid the parental notification law of her home state. Also, in regard to states that do not have a parental notification requirement, the bill mandates that a physician performing an abortion must provide twenty-four-hour notice to a parent of a minor before the abortion is performed. This bill passed the House in June 1999, but the Senate did not act on the bill. It then was reintroduced in the House as H.R. 476 on September 6, 2001, but the Senate still did not act on it. The bill was reintroduced in the Senate (S. 851) and the House (H.R. 1755) in 2003. Again, the bill was passed in the House, but no action was taken in the Senate. In 2005 the bill was introduced in the House as the "Child Interstate Abortion Notification Act" H.R. 748, and on April 27, 2005, it passed. On July 11, 2005, it was placed on the calendar of the Senate as S. 403, but no action had been taken as of mid-September, 2005.

STATEMENT OF CONGRESSMAN PATRICK MCHENRY (R), 10TH DISTRICT OF NORTH CAROLINA, INTRODUCING THE 2005 VERSION OF THE CHILD INTERSTATE ABORTION NOTIFICATION ACT (H.R. 748), APRIL 27, 2005

Madam Speaker, America as a Nation must defend life from the moment of conception to natural death. Later today, the House will take up, the Child Interstate Abortion Notification Act, introduced by my good friend, the gentlewoman from Florida (Ms. Ros-Lehtinen). This bill will protect minors and their parents from inconsistent State abortion laws.

Currently, 23 States require a parent to be involved in a child's abortion decision, while 27 do not. This bill would prosecute anyone who transports a minor to a State without parental consent laws with the purpose of under-mining parental rights. It requires that any time a minor goes for an abortion, the physician must at least try to notify the parents.

Madam Speaker, we need to make sure that we have serious parental involvement in these difficult and potentially dangerous decisions. I urge my colleagues on both sides of the aisle to support this reasonable measure and vote "yes" on H.R. 748 later today.

STATEMENT OF CONGRESSMAN PHIL GINGREY, M.D. (R), 11TH DISTRICT OF GEORGIA, SUPPORTING THE 2005 VERSION OF THE CHILD INTERSTATE ABORTION NOTIFICATION ACT (H.R. 748), APRIL 27, 2005

...Mr. Speaker, I fear that the opponents of this bill will demagogue it as an assault on a woman's right to choose, but this bill has absolutely nothing, let me repeat, nothing to do with a woman's right to choose. Rather, this bill ensures that no minor is deprived of any protection according to not only her but also her parents under the laws of her State....

Having practiced as an OB-GYN for nearly 30 years, I am uniquely qualified to discuss the medical and legal obligations of a physician to his or her patient. And this law not only ensures the protection of minors but it also clarifies the responsibility of the physician to make sure that he or she is not inappropriately performing an abortion on a minor without the legally mandated consent of her parents.

This bill also affirms the principles of federalism and it prevents the circumvention and violation of laws passed by State legislatures. Over 30 States have passed parental notification laws, Mr. Speaker. In fact, in my home State of Georgia, the legislature just recently passed a new abortion notification law in an overwhelming and bipartisan fashion, and this Congress has the responsibility to defend that federalism and the integrity of State laws in interstate matters....

Mr. Speaker, this legislation recognizes this fundamental bond between parents and child and it recognizes the obligation of a parent to be involved and to assist in making important decisions affecting both the life and the health of a minor. Children cannot even be given aspirin at school without their parents' permission, so I cannot comprehend how anyone could possibly justify that administering an abortion is less traumatic or potentially dangerous than taking an aspirin. Yet, Mr. Speaker, that is exactly what the opponents of this bill are saying through their opposition to H.R. 748.

During this debate, I encourage my colleagues to remain focused on the matter at hand and remember that this legislation seeks to uphold the legislatively guaranteed rights of parents and their minor children. Let us not allow this debate to be bogged down with the same tired rhetoric about a woman's right to choose.

I ask my colleagues to support the rule and the underlying bill for final passage.

STATEMENT OF CONGRESSWOMAN ILEANA ROS-LEHTINEN (R), 18TH DISTRICT OF FLORIDA, SUPPORTING THE 2005 VERSION OF THE CHILD INTERSTATE ABORTION NOTIFICATION ACT (H.R. 748), APRIL 27, 2005

. . . I am so proud to stand here in favor of House Resolution 748, the Child Interstate Abortion Notification Act. This bill will incorporate all of the provisions previously contained in the previous legislation that we had filed, the Child Custody Protection Act, making it a Federal offense to transport a minor across State lines to circumvent that State's abortion parental notification laws.

In addition, this year's bill will require that in a State without a parental notification requirement, abortion providers are required to notify a parent. It will protect minors from exploitation from the abortion industry, it will promote strong family ties, and it will help foster respect for State laws. Similar but not identical legislation has had the support of the overwhelming majority of the Members of Congress who have voted in favor of it, not only in 1998 and in 1999, but also in 2002.

I am extremely hopeful that this commonsense pro-family legislation will pass both the House, the Senate, and will be signed into law by our President. . . .

STATEMENT OF CONGRESSMAN J. GRESHAM BARRETT (R), 3RD DISTRICT OF SOUTH CAROLINA, SUPPORTING THE 2005 VERSION OF THE CHILD INTERSTATE ABORTION NOTIFICATION ACT (H.R. 748), APRIL 27, 2005

Mr. Speaker, I rise today in support of H.R. 748 and the rule that we have in front of us this afternoon. I commend the sponsor of the legislation, the gentlewoman

from Florida (Ms. Ros-Lehtinen), for introducing this legislation, legislation of which I am a proud cosponsor.

Mr. Speaker, I find it unacceptable that under the current law any person in this country can take a pregnant minor to another State for the purpose of having an abortion without parents' knowledge and/or consent. . . .

When it comes to such a serious medical procedure being performed on a minor, we cannot leave that notification up to a scared child. Every parent or legal guardian has a right to know, and this legislation ensures that right. I urge my colleagues to support the rule on H.R. 748 which ensures that right.

STATEMENT OF CONGRESSWOMAN MELISSA HART (R), 4TH DISTRICT OF PENNSYLVANIA, SUPPORTING THE 2005 VERSION OF THE CHILD INTERSTATE ABORTION NOTIFICATION ACT (H.R. 748), APRIL 27, 2005

. . . I am just shocked at some of the debate I hear on the other side of the aisle opposing this legislation. The whole point here is to support the family. The whole point here is to prevent the person who may even be a sexual predator or the person who is exploiting this minor from transporting this child across a State line to obtain an abortion and basically get rid of his problem.

It is outrageous that we would not support this legislation. A minor needs parental consent to engage in sports in school, to get a tattoo or a body piercing; yet we are allowing people to take a child across State lines for an abortion.

Mr. Speaker, it is important that we pass this bill. It is important to preserve families. . . .

STATEMENT OF CONGRESSMAN STEVE KING (R), 5TH DISTRICT OF IOWA, SUPPORTING THE 2005 VERSION OF THE CHILD INTERSTATE ABORTION NOTIFICATION ACT (H.R. 748), APRIL 27, 2005

Mr. Speaker, I rise today in support of the rule and the underlying bill, the Child Interstate Abortion Notification Act [CIANA].

Mr. Speaker, eight in 10 Americans favor parental notification laws, and 44 States have recognized the important role of parents in a minor child's decision to have an abortion by enacting a parental involvement statute. Even so, many of these laws are being circumvented by people who simply transport girls across State lines to States without parental notification laws for the purpose of getting an abortion.

All too often these other adults are grown men who sexually preyed upon the young girls, and they used the abortions to cover up their crimes. CIANA returns parental rights to parents.

Despite the strong deference it gives to abortion rights, even the U.S. Supreme Court recognizes that parents' rights to control the care of their children is among the most fundamental of all liberty interests. The Supreme Court has consistently recognized that parents have a legal right to be involved in their minor daughter's decision to seek medical care, including abortion.

The court has consistently affirmed a State's right to restrict the circumstances under which a minor may obtain an abortion in ways that adult women seeking abortion are not restricted. The Supreme Court has also observed that "the medical, emotion, and psychological consequences of an abortion are serious and can be lasting," and that "it seems unlikely that a minor will obtain adequate counsel and support from an attending physician at an abortion clinic where abortions for pregnant minors frequently take place."

The Supreme Court has also stated that "minors often lack the experience, perspective, and judgment to recognize and avoid choices that could be detrimental to them."

No one has the child's best interest at heart more than her parents. Minors have to have parental permission to be given an aspirin by the school nurse. Twenty-six States have laws requiring parental consent before minors can get body piercings or tattoos, and in fact some States prohibit tattooing of minor children even with parental consent. Parents must be able to play a role.

The public, State statutes, and Supreme Court precedent all support parental involvement in a minor's life decision. Please support the rule and the underlying bill.

STATEMENT OF CONGRESSMAN RANDY NEUGEBAUER (R), 19TH DISTRICT OF TEXAS, SUPPORTING THE 2005 VERSION OF THE CHILD INTERSTATE ABORTION NOTIFICATION ACT (H.R. 748), APRIL 27, 2005

Mr. Speaker, I rise today in support of H.R. 748, the Child Interstate Abortion Notification Act of 2005, and the rule. I want to thank the gentlewoman from Florida (Ms. Ros-Lehtinen) for leading the charge on this important piece of legislation.

Let us talk about what this piece of legislation does. It does three things: one, it upholds the democratic process that has taken place in 44 States; it respects the rights of parents to be involved in the medical decisions for their children; and, most importantly, it protects the health of young daughters.

When someone takes their child to get their teeth cleaned, if they are underage today, they have to have a parent's permission. We should have parents involved in this very important decision in a young woman's life and protect them from those who do not have their best interests at heart.

I encourage the Members of this body to do the right thing today. Let us protect these young women and make sure that this important decision is with a parent's involvement and not with someone who does not have their best interests.

TESTIMONY OF TERESA STANTON COLLETT, PROFESSOR OF LAW, UNIVERSITY OF ST. THOMAS SCHOOL OF LAW, MINNEAPOLIS, HEARING ON THE CHILD INTERSTATE ABORTION NOTIFICATION ACT BEFORE THE SUBCOMMITTEE ON THE CONSTITUTION, HOUSE JUDICIARY COMMITTEE, MARCH 3, 2005

... I am honored to have been invited to testify on H.R. 748, the "Child Interstate Abortion Notification Act" (the "Act"). My testimony represents my professional knowledge and opinion as a law professor who writes on the topic of family law, and specifically on the topic of parental involvement laws. It also represents my experience in assisting legislators across the country in evaluating parental involvement laws during the legislative process and defending parental involvement laws in the courts. I have served as a member of the Texas Supreme Court Subadvisory Committee charged with proposing court rules implementing the judicial bypass of parental notification in that state. I testified before the House and Senate Judiciary Committees in 1998, 2001, and 2004 in support of "the Child Custody Protection Act" which is the predecessor to H.R. 748....

It is my opinion that the Child Interstate Abortion Notification Act will significantly advance the state's interest in promoting the health and safety of young girls experiencing an unplanned pregnancy, as well as the interests of parents seeking to provide support and guidance to their minor daughters during this difficult time. In the cases where the pregnancy results from unlawful conduct by adult men, the Act will provide greater assurances that unlawful acts will come to the attention of law enforcement officials so that the perpetrators can be prosecuted.

... The United States Supreme Court has described parents' right to control the care of their children as "perhaps the oldest of the fundamental liberty interests recognized by this Court." In addressing the right of parents to direct the medical care of their children, the Court has stated: Our jurisprudence historically has reflected Western civilization concepts of the family as a unit with broad parental authority over minor children.

Our cases have consistently followed that course; our constitutional system long ago rejected any notion that a child is "the mere creature of the State" and, on the contrary, asserted that parents generally "have the right, coupled with the high duty, to recognize and prepare [their children] for additional obligations." Surely, this includes a "high duty" to recognize symptoms of illness and to seek and follow medical advice. The law's concept of the family rests on a presumption that parents possess what a child lacks in maturity, experience, and capacity for judgment required for making life's difficult decisions. It is this need to insure the availability of parental guidance and support that underlies the laws requiring a parent is notified or gives consent prior to the performance of an abortion on his or her minor daughter. The national consensus in favor of this position is illustrated by the fact that there are parental involvement laws on the books in forty-four of the fifty states. Only six states in the nation have not attempted to legislatively insure some level of parental involvement in a minor's decision to obtain an abortion. Of the forty-four states that have enacted laws, ten statutes have been determined to have state or federal constitutional infirmities. Therefore the laws of thirty-four states are in effect today. Ten of these remaining states have laws that empower abortion providers to decide whether to involve parents or allow notice to or consent from people other than parents or legal guardians. These laws are substantially ineffectual in assuring parental involvement in a minor's decision to obtain an abortion. However, parents in the remaining twenty-four states are effectively guaranteed the right to parental notification or consent in most cases....

There is widespread agreement that as a general rule, parents should be involved in their minor daughter's decision to terminate an unplanned pregnancy. This agreement even extends to young people, ages 18 to 24. To my knowledge, no organizations or individuals, whether abortion rights activists or pro-life advocates, dispute this point. On an issue as contentious and divisive as abortion, it is both remarkable and instructive that there is such firm and long-standing support for laws requiring parental involvement....

In addition to improving the medical care received by young girls dealing with an unplanned pregnancy, parental notification will provide increased protection against sexual exploitation of minors by adult men....

In those few cases where it is not in the girl's best interest to disclose her pregnancy to her parents, state laws generally provide the pregnant minor the option of seeking a court determination that either involvement of the girl's parent is not in her best interest, or that she is sufficiently mature to make decisions regarding the continuation of her pregnancy. This is a requirement for parental consent laws under existing United States Supreme Court cases, and courts have been quick to overturn laws omitting adequate bypass....

The Child Interstate Parental Notification Act has the unique virtue of building upon two of the few points of agreement in the national debate over abortion: the desirability of parental involvement in a minor's decisions about an unplanned pregnancy, and the need to protect the physical health and safety of the pregnant girl. I urge members of this committee to vote for its passage.

CHAPTER 11

IT SHOULD NOT BE ILLEGAL FOR MINORS TO CROSS STATE LINES FOR AN ABORTION WITHOUT THE PARENTS' CONSENT

TESTIMONY OF WARREN SEIGEL, M.D., DIRECTOR OF ADOLESCENT MEDICINE, CHAIRMAN OF PEDIATRICS, CONEY ISLAND HOSPITAL, HEARING ON THE CHILD INTERSTATE ABORTION NOTIFICATION ACT BEFORE THE SUBCOMMITTEE ON THE CONSTITUTION, HOUSE JUDICIARY COMMITTEE, MARCH 3, 2005

... I am submitting testimony today as a resident of New York State, an experienced health care provider, a leader in the American Academy of Pediatrics and the Society for Adolescent Medicine, and a member of Physicians for Reproductive Choice and Health, known as PRCH....

I submit this testimony to you today on behalf of the PRCH Board of Directors and our more than 6,500 physician and non-physician members to express our opposition to H.R. 748, known as the "Child Interstate Abortion Notification Act," or CIANA. This bill puts young women's lives at risk, makes criminals out of caring physicians, and affects the care of all patients.

I recognize that parents ideally should be—and usually are—involved in health decisions regarding their children. However, the Child Interstate Abortion Notification Act does nothing to promote such communication. Instead, CIANA places incredible burdens on both young women and physicians; infringes on the rights of adolescents to health care that does not violate their safety and health; makes caring family, friends and doctors criminals; and could be detrimental to the health and emotional well-being of all patients.

As a pediatrician, I believe CIANA will create insurmountable obstacles for adolescents. Young women seeking abortions in a state other than their home state will be forced to comply with the parental notification laws in both states. They will also have to navigate through the complex and emotionally draining judicial bypass procedure in both states. This will cause delays that may be harmful to the young woman's health by forcing her to undergo a later-term procedure. The American Medical Association states that a delay in receiving care will "increase the gestational age at which the induced pregnancy termination occurs, thereby also increasing the risk associated with the procedure." Requiring adolescents to comply with laws in more than one state will certainly increase the delay in receiving care.

CIANA also requires parental notification for young women receiving abortions in states where they are not permanent residents. Young women who are not trying to circumvent parental notification laws but are, in fact, living temporarily in a state for college, boarding school or other reasons will need to seek the care that is closest to them. CIANA would prohibit these women from the most available health care.

Women from states with no parental notification legislation face an additional burden. Even if a young woman is not subject to any parental notification laws in either the state where she is from or the state where she is accessing care, CIANA will require parental notification. Judicial bypass procedures only exist in states with parental notification laws in place. Thus, in states with no parental notification legislation, young women will not have access to the judicial bypass option.

When judicial bypass is available, the delays it may cause are compounded by a mandatory delay period of at least 24 hours, which is required by CIANA.... Additionally, young women as a population are already more likely to be seeking abortion later in their pregnancy. The Centers for Disease Control have shown that adolescents obtain 30% of all abortions performed after the first trimester, and younger women are more likely to obtain abortions at 21 weeks or more gestation. Mandatory delays will only serve to increase these trends. CIANA also requires a mandatory delay even if a parent is present and consenting. If this legislation is about parental notification, then what is the purpose of this delay if not to keep young women from accessing the care that they need in a timely manner?

I am also concerned that CIANA places extreme and unreasonable burdens on physicians and the other patients they treat. Physicians will be required to have detailed knowledge of the parental notification laws in the 49 states where they do not practice.…

Physicians will be required in some cases to travel to the home state of the young woman to give notification in person to the parents.… What becomes of all the other patients seeing their physician for other health care issues during this time? This requirement will not only increase the delay for the procedure but is simply impossible for a physician to carry out, thereby denying a young woman her right to an abortion.…

This legislation contains an inadequate exception to protect a young woman's life and no exception to protect her health.…

Although this legislation is supposedly aimed at increasing parent-child communication, the government cannot mandate healthy families and, indeed, it is dangerous to attempt to do so.… The American Academy of Pediatrics, a national medical organization representing the 60,000 physician leaders in pediatric medicine—of which I am a member and leader—has adopted the following statement regarding mandatory parental notification: "Adolescents should be strongly encouraged to involve their parents and other trusted adults in decisions regarding pregnancy termination, and the majority of them voluntarily do so. Legislation mandating parental involvement does not achieve the intended benefit of promoting family communication, but it does increase the risk of harm to the adolescent by delaying access to appropriate medical care."

It is important to consider why a minority of young women cannot inform their parents. The threat of physical or emotional abuse upon disclosure of the pregnancy to their parents or a pregnancy that is the result of incest make it impossible for these adolescents to inform their parents. Under CIANA, young women would be forced to put themselves in dangerous situations in order to receive medical care.

Young women have many reasons for needing to travel out of state to have an abortion. Eighty-seven percent of U.S. counties have no abortion provider. In some states, there is only one provider available. In cases like these, the nearest abortion provider may be in another state. Financially, an abortion may be more affordable at a facility in another state. As I mentioned before, an adolescent may be temporarily residing in another state and need local care. CIANA penalizes young women for seeking the closest and most affordable health care.…

Physicians for Reproductive Choice and Health is in absolute agreement with leading medical organizations on this issue. The American Medical Association, the American College of Obstetricians and Gynecologists, the American College of Physicians and the American Public Health Association all oppose mandatory parental-involvement laws because they endanger the health of adolescents and pose undue burdens on physicians. Additionally, the American Academy of Pediatrics and the Society for Adolescent Medicine have opposed similar legislation, entitled the Child Custody Protection Act, currently under consideration in the Senate as S. 8, because of the harm it may cause adolescents.

It is for all of these reasons that we must protect the rights of young women to access safe, affordable and appropriate health care. We must make it easier for physicians to provide needed services, not more difficult. As a physician, I believe that this legislation represents bad medicine and places politics before the health of our youth. Practicing physicians and scientific evidence overwhelmingly agree that this legislation would negatively impact the health of adolescents. It is for this reason that I appear in opposition to H.R. 748.

STATEMENT OF CONGRESSWOMAN LOUISE M. SLAUGHTER (D), 28TH DISTRICT OF NEW YORK, OPPOSING THE 2005 VERSION OF THE CHILD INTERSTATE ABORTION NOTIFICATION ACT (H.R. 748), APRIL 27, 2005

…This bill is another invasion into the private lives of American families making the decisions for themselves, and it is an invasion into the legal rights afforded all women in this country. I am talking about the legal right for women to choose, which is protected by the Constitution of the United States.

We have a duty in this body to consider legislation which will maximize our freedom and equality, values which are the very fabric of our society. Our job here is to protect the legal rights of those we serve and not to take them away, and I urge a "no" vote on this bill.…

STATEMENT OF CONGRESSWOMAN SHEILA JACKSON LEE (D), 18TH DISTRICT OF TEXAS, OPPOSING THE 2005 VERSION OF THE CHILD INTERSTATE ABORTION NOTIFICATION ACT (H.R. 748), APRIL 27, 2005

…The Child Interstate Abortion Notification Act (CIANA), while good in its intention, was written with several areas of vagueness, overly punitive nature, and constitutional violations that very much deserve debate in order to save lives and to obviate the need for piles upon piles of legal pleadings.

The mandatory parental-involvement laws already create a draconian framework under which a young woman loses many of her civil rights. My state, Texas, is one of 23 states (AL, AZ, AR, GA, IN, KS, KY, LA, MA, MI, MN, MS, MO, NE, ND, PA, RI, SD, TN, UT, TX, VA, WY) that follows old provisions of the "Child Custody Protection Act" which make it a federal crime for an adult to accompany a minor across state lines for abortion services if a woman comes from a state with a strict parental-involvement mandate. There are 10 states (CO, DE, IA, ME, MD, NC, OH, SC, WI, WV) that are "non-compliant," or require some parental notice but other adults may be notified, may give consent, or the requirement may be waived by a health care provider in lieu of the parental consent. Finally, there are 17 states (AK, CA, CT, DC, FL, ID, IL, MT, NV, NH, NJ, NM, NY, OK, OR, VT, WA) that have no law restricting a woman's access to abortion in this case. The base bill, if passed, would take away the States' rights to make their own determination as to legislating the abortion issue for minors with respect to parental notification.

My amendment to the Child Interstate Abortion Notification Act, would change the prohibitions to exempt grandparents of the minor or clergy persons. This must be done because some minors want the counsel of a responsible adult, and are unable to turn to their parents. . . .

H.R. 748, as drafted, will not improve family communication or help young women facing crisis pregnancies. We all hope that loving parents will be involved when their daughter faces a crisis pregnancy. Every parent hopes that a child confronting a crisis will seek the advice and counsel of those who care for her most and know her best. In fact, even in the absence of laws mandating parental involvement, many young women do turn to their parents when they are considering an abortion. One study found that 61 percent of parents in states without mandatory parental consent or notice laws knew of their daughter's pregnancy.

Unfortunately, some young women cannot involve their parents because they come from homes where physical violence or emotional abuse is prevalent or because their pregnancies are the result of incest. In these situations, the government cannot force healthy family communication where it does not already exist—and attempts to do so can have tragic consequences for some girls.

Major medical associations—including the American Medical Association, the American College of Obstetricians and Gynecologists, the American College of Physicians, and the American Public Health Association—all have longstanding policies opposing mandatory parental-involvement laws because of the dangers they pose to young women and the need for confidential access to physicians. These physicians see young ladies on a daily basis and hear their stories. They would not protest this law unless they felt there were severe stakes.

CIANA criminalizes caring adults—including grandparents of the minor, who attempt to assist young women facing crisis pregnancies. In one study, 93 percent of minors who did not involve a parent in their decision to obtain an abortion were still accompanied by someone to the doctor's office. If CIANA becomes law, a person could be prosecuted for accompanying a minor to a neighboring state, even if that person does not intend, or even know, that the parental-involvement law of the state of residence has not been followed. Although legal abortion is very safe, it is typically advisable to accompany any patient undergoing even minor surgery. Without the Jackson Lee-Nadler Amendment, a grandmother could be subject to criminal charges for accompanying her granddaughter to an out-of-state facility—even if the facility was the closest to the young woman's home and they were not attempting to evade a parental involvement law. . . .

STATEMENT OF CONGRESSWOMAN MAXINE WATERS (D), 35TH DISTRICT OF CALIFORNIA, OPPOSING THE 2005 VERSION OF THE CHILD INTERSTATE ABORTION NOTIFICATION ACT (H.R. 748), APRIL 27, 2005

Mr. Speaker, I rise in strong opposition to the bill and to the proposed rule for this bill.

The two amendments made in order under the proposed rule, the Scott amendment and the Jackson-Lee/Nadler amendment are very important amendments. At the same time, it is instructive to note that many of the nine Democratic amendments that were not made in order seek to protect the people most directly affected by the bill: the young girls who wish to exercise their constitutional right to end their pregnancy.

For example, I offered an amendment before the Committee on Rules to create an exception to the criminal penalties and a civil suit imposed on a person transporting a young girl across State lines in cases where the minor is a victim of incest. Because the bill lacks a judicial bypass procedure in circumstances where the Federal notification requirements apply, under this bill a young girl could be required to notify a parent who impregnated her before obtaining an abortion even though it would be inappropriate, traumatic, and potentially dangerous to require her to do so.

Mr. Speaker, if a young girl is required to notify a parent who has molested her that she is pregnant before traveling to another State to seek an abortion, I fear that some girls may seek to end their pregnancy without help, whether they do so by traveling alone to another State for the procedure, or even worse, through a self-induced or illegal back-alley abortion. However, the Republican members on the Committee on Rules refused to make this amendment in order on a party-line vote.

Mr. Speaker, the gentleman from New York (Mr. Nadler) and I also offered a commonsense amendment barring a parent who has molested his daughter and caused her to be pregnant from any relief under this bill.

However, this too was rejected on a party-line vote.

Mr. Speaker, this bill should be considered under an open rule that would allow consideration of amendments to protect the young girls who choose to seek an abortion. In its current form, the bill gives rights to a parent who has victimized his daughter.

I urge my colleagues to reject the rule.

CHAPTER 12

THE *ROE V. WADE* DECISION SHOULD BE RECONSIDERED

TESTIMONY OF M. EDWARD WHELAN, ESQ., PRESIDENT, ETHICS AND PUBLIC POLICY CENTER BEFORE THE SENATE JUDICIARY SUBCOMMITTEE ON THE CONSTITUTION, CIVIL RIGHTS, AND PROPERTY RIGHTS, HEARING ON SUPREME COURT ABORTION CASES, JUNE 22, 2005

Good afternoon, Chairman Brownback and Senator Feingold, and thank you very much for inviting me to testify before you and your subcommittee on this important subject.

I am Edward Whelan, president of the Ethics and Public Policy Center. The Ethics and Public Policy Center is a think tank that for three decades has been dedicated to exploring and explaining how the Judeo-Christian moral tradition and this country's foundational principles ought to inform and shape public policy on critical issues.

The Ethics and Public Policy Center's program on The Constitution, the Courts, and the Culture, which I direct, explores the competing conceptions of the role of the courts in our political system. This program focuses, in particular, on what is at stake for American culture writ large—for the ability of the American people to function fully as citizens, to engage in responsible self-government, and to maintain the "indispensable supports" of "political prosperity" that George Washington (and other Founders) understood "religion and morality" to be.

Why re-examine *Roe v. Wade*? Why are we here today addressing a case that the Supreme Court decided 32 years ago, that it ratified 13 years ago, and that America's cultural elites overwhelmingly embrace? The answer, I would submit, is twofold.

First, *Roe v. Wade* marks the second time in American history that the Supreme Court has invoked "sub-stantive due process" to deny American citizens the authority to protect the basic rights of an entire class of human beings. The first time, of course, was the Court's infamous 1857 decision in the *Dred Scott* case (*Dred Scott v. Sandford*, 60 U.S. 393 [1857]). There, the Court held that the Missouri Compromise of 1820, which prohibited slavery in the northern portion of the Louisiana Territories, could not constitutionally be applied to persons who brought their slaves into free territory. Such a prohibition, the Court nakedly asserted, "could hardly be dignified with the name of due process."...Thus were discarded the efforts of the people, through their representatives, to resolve politically and peacefully the greatest moral issue of their age. Chief Justice Taney and his concurring colleagues thought that they were conclusively resolving the issue of slavery. Instead, they only made all the more inevitable the Civil War that erupted four years later.

Roe is the *Dred Scott* of our age. Like few other Supreme Court cases in our nation's history, *Roe* is not merely patently wrong but also fundamentally hostile to core precepts of American government and citizenship. *Roe* is a lawless power grab by the Supreme Court, an unconstitutional act of aggression by the Court against the political branches and the American people. *Roe* prevents all Americans from working together, through an ongoing process of peaceful and vigorous persuasion, to establish and revise the policies on abortion governing our respective states. *Roe* imposes on all Americans a radical regime of unrestricted abortion for any reason all the way up to viability—and, under the predominant reading of sloppy language in *Roe*'s companion case, *Doe v. Bolton*, essentially unrestricted even in the period from viability until birth. *Roe* fuels endless litigation in which pro-abortion extremists challenge modest abortion-related measures that state legislators have enacted and that are overwhelmingly favored by the public—provisions, for example, seeking to ensure informed consent and parental involvement for minors and barring atrocities like partial-birth abortion. *Roe* disenfranchises the millions and millions of patriotic American citizens who believe that the self-evident truth proclaimed in the Declaration of Independence—that all men are created equal and are endowed by their Creator with an unalienable right to life—warrants significant governmental protection of the lives of unborn human beings.

So long as Americans remain Americans—so long, that is, as they remain faithful to the foundational principles of this country—I believe that the American body politic will never accept *Roe*.

The second reason to examine *Roe* is the ongoing confusion that somehow surrounds the decision. Leading political and media figures, deliberately or otherwise, routinely misrepresent and understate the radical nature of the abortion regime that the Court imposed in *Roe*. And, conversely, they distort and exaggerate the consequences of reversing *Roe* and of restoring to the American people the power to determine abortion policy in their respective States. The more that Americans understand *Roe*, the more they regard it as illegitimate.

Reasonable people of good will with differing values or with varying prudential assessments of the practical effect of protective abortion laws may come to a variety of conclusions on what abortion policy ought to be in the many diverse states of this great nation. But, I respectfully submit, it is well past time for all Americans, no matter what their views on abortion, to recognize that the Court-imposed abortion regime should be dismantled and the issue of abortion should be returned to its rightful place in the democratic political process....

Myths about *Roe* abound, and I will not strive to dispel all of them here. One set of myths dramatically understates the radical nature of the abortion regime that *Roe* invented and imposed on the entire country. *Roe* is often said, for example, merely to have created a constitutional right to abortion during the first three months of pregnancy (or the first trimester). Nothing in *Roe* remotely supports such a characterization.

A more elementary confusion is reflected in the commonplace assertion that *Roe* "legalized" abortion. At one level, this proposition is true, but it completely obscures the fact that the Court did not merely legalize abortion—it constitutionalized abortion. In other words, the American people, acting through their state legislators, had the constitutional authority before *Roe* to make abortion policy. (Some States had legalized abortion, and others were in the process of liberalizing their abortion laws.) *Roe* deprived the American people of this authority.

The assertion that *Roe* "legalized" abortion also bears on a surprisingly widespread misunderstanding of the effect of a Supreme Court reversal of *Roe*. Many otherwise well-informed people seem to think that a reversal of *Roe* would mean that abortion would thereby be illegal nationwide. But of course a reversal of *Roe* would merely restore to the people of the States their constitutional authority to establish—and to revise over time—the abortion laws and policies for their respective States.

This confusion about what reversing *Roe* means is also closely related to confusion, or deliberate obfuscation, over what it means for a Supreme Court Justice to be opposed to *Roe*. In particular, such a Justice is often mislabeled "pro-life." But Justices like Rehnquist, White, Scalia, and Thomas who have recognized that the Constitution does not speak to the question of abortion take a position that is entirely neutral on the substance of America's abortion laws. Their modest point concerns process: abortion policy is to be made through the political processes, not by the courts. These Justices do not adopt a "pro-life" reading of the Due Process Clause under which permissive abortion laws would themselves be unconstitutional....

TESTIMONY OF PROFESSOR RONALD D. ROTUNDA OF THE UNIVERSITY OF ILLINOIS LAW SCHOOL, CHAMPAIGN, IL, BEFORE THE SUBCOMMITTEE ON THE CONSTITUTION, FEDERALISM, AND PROPERTY RIGHTS, SENATE JUDICIARY COMMITTEE, HEARING ON "*THE 25TH ANNIVERSARY OF ROE V. WADE: HAS IT STOOD THE TEST OF TIME?*" JANUARY 21, 1998

The Supreme Court issued its first abortion opinion on January 22, 1973. That opinion, *Roe v. Wade*...has ushered in a quarter century of criticism by many academic commentators. In so doing, the Supreme Court created a right to abortion (essentially abortion on demand) that was broader than the abortion rights granted by almost any other western nation. It also federalized the abortion issue, an issue that had been left in the custody of the states for nearly two centuries.

Though a fragmented Court itself later backtracked on *Roe* in *Planned Parenthood of Southeastern Pennsylvania v. Casey*...it did not overrule all of *Roe* because, as the O'Connor-Kennedy-Souter plurality candidly stated, it was important to respect precedent....

Our Constitution respects and protects privacy in many ways, but the Court normally derives this right to privacy from various clauses in the text, such as the privacy rights that derive from the First and Fourth Amendments. The Court has also been protective of activity that occurs in the home, but abortions, which occur in the hospital or in medical clinics, are not private in that sense.

Indeed, the analysis of *Roe* specifically does not rely on any interpretation of the text of the Constitution.... Instead, the *Roe* Court announced that it simply "agree[d]" with the proposition that "the right of privacy, however based, is broad enough to cover the abortion decision," although this right is "not absolute." ...

What is the true rationale of *Roe*? It is often described as a women's rights case. Supporters have argued that a woman should have the right to control her own body. However, Justice Blackmun's majority opinion specifically rejected that contention.... The opinion states quite emphatically: "In fact, it is not clear to us that the claim ... that one has an unlimited right to do with one's body as one pleases bears a close relationship to the right of privacy previously articulated in the Court's decisions...."

...It is popularly understood that Justice Harry Blackmun's majority opinion in *Roe* stated that the state has no right to regulate abortion prior to the end of approximately the first trimester. That is when the state's interest reaches, in Blackmun's words, "a compelling point." During the second and third trimesters, the state has more power.

But this is not what Blackmun actually held. He wrote the opinion as if it were a doctor's rights case, not a women's rights case. Consider this strange sentence in his opinion: "For the period of pregnancy prior to this 'compelling' point, the attending physician, in consultation with his patient, is free to determine, without regulation by the state, that, in his medical judgment, the patient's pregnancy should be terminated...."

Under *Roe* and similar abortion decisions that rely on it, the woman does not have the right to choose; she does not have a right to abortion. It is the doctor (whom the *Roe* opinion assumed to be a man) who has that right. In a small bow to women's rights, Justice Blackmun noted that the doctor should consult with his patient, the woman on whom the abortion is to be performed. And when the patient consults with the doctor, the doctor has a constitutional right to be free of "regulation by the state."

Two years after *Roe*, *Connecticut v. Menillo* upheld a Connecticut law making it a crime for "any person" to attempt an abortion. The Court ruled that this criminal statute—although it seemed to go far beyond what *Roe* allowed—was constitutional as applied to an attempted abortion performed by someone other than a licensed physician.... A woman has no right to choose a non-doctor to perform an abortion, even though a non-doctor might be just as safe and even though a woman can choose a non-doctor, such as a midwife, to deliver a full-term baby.

Later cases have confirmed that *Roe* was primarily drafted to protect doctors, not their patients. Thus, the Court has said, in *Colautti v. Franklin* ... that "neither the legislature nor the courts" can define viability objectively, "be it weeks of gestation, or fetal weight, or any other single factor," because the judgment of the doctor must control.

Planned Parenthood of Central Missouri v. Danforth struck down a section of a law that forbade the use of saline amniocentesis as a method of abortion after the first trimester because the Court ruled that the law was not necessary to protect maternal health. However, the state specifically found that this technique "is deleterious [harmful] to maternal health," and the lower court findings supported this conclusion....

Even though the Court majority admitted that other techniques were safer for women, it simply concluded that saline abortions were "an accepted medical procedure" in the view of doctors ... and thus were constitutionally protected from state regulation. Women are the victims of this decision....

Those people who insist that no statute should limit *Roe* in any way, those who believe that we must follow *Roe* without change ... those advocates should read that decision and the others that follow in its wake. The decision is not about protecting women; it is about protecting doctors.

TESTIMONY OF STEVE CALVIN, M.D., SPECIALIST IN MATERNAL–FETAL MEDICINE, BEFORE THE SUBCOMMITTEE ON THE CONSTITUTION, FEDERALISM, AND PROPERTY RIGHTS, SENATE JUDICIARY COMMITTEE, HEARING ON *"THE 25TH ANNIVERSARY OF ROE V. WADE: HAS IT STOOD THE TEST OF TIME?"* JANUARY 21, 1998

...The subspecialty of maternal–fetal medicine is only two decades old and is unique in that we care for two patients in the mother and her unborn child.... Only on very rare occasions are the medical interests of the mother and unborn baby in conflict.

During the last 25 years, progress in the area of obstetrics and maternal–fetal medicine has been astonishing. By 1973, obstetrics had made great strides in making pregnancy and birth a relatively safe experience for women. Since the beginning of this century, developments in antibiotics, transfusion, and anesthesia caused the risk of maternal death to decrease by 50- to 100-fold. Attention was then turned to improving the outcome for the baby....

The new focus on the baby was achieved by development of fetal ultrasound imaging technology. Prior to

1973, the anatomic development and activities of the fetus were invisible.

...At the time of the *Roe v. Wade* decision, ultrasound during pregnancy was largely experimental. During the '70s and '80s, the beneficial uses of ultrasound in pregnancy multiplied....

Current ultrasound imaging techniques reveal the marvelous complexity of prenatal growth and development....However, the use of this wonderful window on the womb has become increasingly disconcerting for some who would rather view the fetus as pregnancy tissue or the product of conception....

In the last two and one-half decades, our ability to obtain clear images of the fetus has expanded the concept of the fetus as a patient....

Unborn babies can be treated with medications for dangerously irregular heart rhythms and can receive blood transfusions if they are anemic. On rare occasions, surgical procedures can be performed before birth....

We are clearly in a new era of obstetrics because of ultrasound and the expanding concept of treatment of the fetus as a patient. Yet there is an inescapable schizophrenia when modern medicine works under ethical rules which say that a fetus is a patient only when the mother has conferred this status. The trouble is that this status can be withheld or withdrawn. The combination of current unrestricted legal abortion and our increasing abilities to diagnose fetal abnormalities and diseases prenatally is a very dangerous two-edged sword.

In many ways, modern obstetrics is becoming an impersonal techno specialty dedicated to the concept of the perfect baby. Prenatal diagnosis can benefit the mother and baby when treatment options are available, but much of prenatal diagnosis is designed to detect fetal abnormalities so that the choice of abortion is available. The majority of these abnormalities, such as Down Syndrome, are not usually fatal. Even abortion supporters are horrified by the possibility of abortions based only on the sex of the unborn child. But why is abortion for the most sexist of reasons any worse that abortion for any other reason?

So far we do not have an overtly eugenic social policy but we are certainly encouraging family-based eugenics [selective breeding]. This use of abortion will gradually weaken society's commitment to the inclusion and care of the disabled in our human community.

In 1973, *Roe v. Wade* shattered the issue of abortion into sharp fragments. We are still dealing with the medical, social, and political fallout of the Supreme Court's willingness to go far beyond the traditional boundaries of medical ethics and practice. The tenets of Hippocratic medicine have served us well for more than 2,000 years.

But our 25-year experiment with unrestricted abortion has caused the practice of medicine to become increasingly inconsistent. The tension between valuable ethical traditions and currently legal medical practice is untenable (cannot be maintained).

STATEMENT OF JEAN A. WRIGHT, M.D., M.B.A, BEFORE THE SUBCOMMITTEE ON THE CONSTITUTION, FEDERALISM, AND PROPERTY RIGHTS, SENATE JUDICIARY COMMITTEE, ON *"THE 25TH ANNIVERSARY OF ROE V. WADE: HAS IT STOOD THE TEST OF TIME?"* JANUARY 21, 1998

...I would like to focus my remarks on the changes we have seen in the field of pediatrics, particularly the areas of neonatology, surgery, anesthesia, and intensive care. Medical knowledge in those areas provide a new standard of science, upon which a very different conclusion might be reached if *Roe v. Wade* were decided in 1998, rather than the limited information that was available in 1973....

In 1973, the scientific discussion heavily focused on the issues of fetal viability. At that time, the common understanding was that infants born before 28 weeks could not survive. Today, that age of viability has been pushed back from 28 weeks to 23 and 24 weeks. And some investigators are working on an artificial placenta to support those even younger.

In fact, while the number of children that are born and survive at 23–28 weeks gestation [is] still a minority of the infants in a NICU [Neonatal Intensive Care Unit], they are common enough that the colloquial term "micro-preemie" has been coined to describe them, and an additional body of neonatal science has grown to support the care of the very premature infant. So in 25 years, we have gone from a practice in which those infants, once thought to be non-viable, are now beneficiaries of medical advances in order to provide them with every opportunity to survive.

...Very pre-term neonates [newborns] have the neuroanatomic substrate and functional physiologic and chemical processes in the brain responsible for mediating pain or noxious stimuli (known as nociception)....

Anatomic studies have shown that the density of cutaneous nociceptive nerve endings in the late fetus and newborn infant equal or exceed that of adult skin.

...A controlled study of intrauterine blood sampling and blood transfusions in fetuses between 20 and 34 weeks of gestation showed hormonal responses that were consistent with fetal perception of pain....

Pre-term neonates born at 23 weeks gestation show highly specific and well-coordinated physiologic and behavioral responses to pain, similar to those seen in full-term neonates, older infants, and small children....

All of the scientific references I have just made are from research breakthroughs in the last 10 years. This information was not available in 1973. As a result of this newly emerging understanding of fetal pain development, Anand and Craig, in a 1996 editorial in the journal PAIN, called for a new definition of pain, a definition that is not subjective and that is not dependent on the patient's ability to provide a self-report.

...Today, we are the beneficiaries of an enormous fund of new medical knowledge, and I believe we should incorporate that into our approach to protecting the life of the unborn.

Furthermore, places such as the University of California, with its Fetal Surgery Center, are doing just that. Exciting surgical advances, which allow for the surgeon to partially remove the fetus through an incision in the womb, fix the congenital defect, and then slip the "pre-viable" infant back into the womb, should make us reconsider the outcome and viability of many pre-term infants, particularly those with challenging congenital defects.

...Today we are hearing evidence, both medical and legal, that was not available to our counterparts in 1973. We cannot change the ramifications of their decision, but we can make better and more informed decisions today. Just as the incoming tide raises the level of the water in the harbor, and in doing so, all the boats rise to the same new level; so should we allow the tide of new medical and legal information serve as a tide to raise both our medical and legal understanding of the unborn. And in doing so, lead us to making better decisions for this vulnerable population.

STATEMENT OF REPRESENTATIVE HELEN CHENOWETH (R-ID), NOVEMBER 21, 1997

Twenty-four years ago, the Supreme Court removed a God-given, unalienable right from unborn babies, a right it has the duty to secure and protect. In doing so, it elevated a "judge-made" right, the right of a person's privacy, above the God-given right to life.

It has always been my belief that unborn children should be cherished, and abortion for the convenience of the mother is contrary to the convictions that mean a great deal. I believe the life of an unborn child is to be respected as truly as the life of a newborn.

It grieves my heart that each day more and more lives are lost because of abortion. I think it is unfortunate that the courts have decided to abandon basic principles of the Constitution and of science by legalizing the senseless taking of human life by abortion. What is even more tragic is that many groups, which have termed themselves

as "advocates for women," have promoted abortion rights as the premiere principle of women's rights. I find it further appalling that the federal government is forcing states to fund abortions with taxpayer funds by justifying abortion as a necessary function for the reproductive health of women.

I believe that if the Supreme Court continues to uphold the wrong decision made in *Roe v. Wade*, Congress should enact laws that would disallow abortion, except in very extreme circumstances. At the very least, Congress should prohibit the government from funding abortion. However, before we can pass laws forbidding abortion, we must change the dynamic of the debate by educating the American public to favor the protection of life at its natural beginning—the point of conception. I think that when all Americans, including many women who are confused about the issue, begin to realize the serious ramifications of abortion, they will strongly support the need to protect the sanctity of life.

My position in representing the people of Idaho has always been, and will continue to be, guided by the conviction that abortion is wrong and should only be considered in cases of criminal rape, incest, or when the mother's life is in imminent danger.

STATEMENT OF SENATOR JOHN P. EAST (R-NC), JANUARY 16, 1986

Regarding abortion, the source of the current controversy over abortion, of course, is the 1973 *Roe v. Wade* decision of the United States Supreme Court. The *Roe* ruling made two principal determinations. First, *Roe* recognized a federal constitutional right to an abortion throughout pregnancy for virtually any reason. Second, *Roe* determined that the unborn child is not a "person" under the Fourteenth Amendment to the U.S. Constitution, which guarantees a right to life. I disagree with both of these aspects of the *Roe* decision.

The Constitution does not make any explicit or implicit reference to abortion, much less guarantee a right to it. Hence, the *Roe* decision, which invalidated the duly enacted abortion laws of all 50 states, was an unconstitutional act on the part of the Court. It is incumbent upon the Court to recognize its error and overrule the *Roe* recognition of a right to abortion....

Legislative history reveals that the framers of the Fourteenth Amendment clearly intended for its provisions to protect all human beings. Since unborn children are human beings, I believe that the Fourteenth Amendment protects their right to live. The Court ought to overrule *Roe* in this regard as well. Until it does so, I will continue to support congressional initiatives to provide unborn children with a constitutionally guaranteed right to life.

STATEMENT OF SENATOR STROM THURMOND (R-SC), BEFORE THE SUBCOMMITTEE ON THE CONSTITUTION, SENATE JUDICIARY COMMITTEE, FEBRUARY 28, 1983

...First, whatever one's personal views about abortion, the plain fact is that *Roe v. Wade* represented one of the most blatant exercises in judicial activism in the history of this country. In one fell swoop, seven men on the Court reinterpreted what had been the law of the land for nearly two centuries and overturned the laws adopted by the legislatures in every one of the 50 states.

Second, in *Roe v. Wade*, seven men on the Court established as a new law of the land in the area of abortion a policy significantly more permissive of abortion than the policy that had been freely adopted by the legislatures in every one of the 50 states.

Third, in *Roe v. Wade*, seven men on the Court established as a new law of the land a policy on abortion as liberal and permissive of abortion as any law in the entire world. There are absolutely no serious legal or constitutional barriers to a person obtaining an abortion for any reason, at any stage of her pregnancy.

Fourth, since *Roe v. Wade*, we have had a national policy on abortion bitterly opposed by large numbers of individuals in this country who are totally without any recourse to their elected representatives. This is not how public policy is developed in a free society on issues of this bitterness and divisiveness.

Fifth, *Roe v. Wade*, itself, amended the Constitution of the United States in reading in a policy of abortion at odds with its language, at odds with its legislative history, and at odds with the long-standing practices of the states in this country.

STATEMENT OF PROFESSOR LYNN WARDLE, BRIGHAM YOUNG UNIVERSITY SCHOOL OF LAW, BEFORE THE SUBCOMMITTEE ON THE CONSTITUTION, SENATE JUDICIARY COMMITTEE, FEBRUARY 28, 1983

I appear before the subcommittee today to recommend that it propose and the Senate pass an amendment to the Constitution that would reverse *Roe v. Wade*....

I would like to rephrase the issue. I think the question is whether the right of the people to protect human life is to be abridged. A decade has passed since *Roe v. Wade* was decided, a decade in which federal courts have faced a flood of abortion litigation, in which Congress has faced a deluge of abortion proposals, and in which the number of abortions performed annually has reached in excess of 1.5 million, a total approaching 15 million since *Roe v. Wade*.

Moreover, as many commentators had predicted, since *Roe*, there has been a profound and appalling increase in the kinds of inhumane acts that manifest a disregard for and involve even the destruction of other forms of unwanted, defenseless human life. Not only are human beings who bear the stigma of being labeled defective because of some potential physical or mental condition being ruthlessly destroyed before birth, but since *Roe*, they have increasingly become the victims of infanticide and selective nontreatment, to use the euphemism.

...While these practical and doctrinal excesses are approaching shocking extremes, the Supreme Court has refused to reconsider *Roe v. Wade*. Thus, at this time, 10 years after that disaster, I feel the sentiments of the English statesman and orator, Edmund Burke, who is reported to have said, "An event is happening about which it is difficult to speak, but about which it is impossible to remain silent." I believe the time has come for Congress to restore the right of the people to protect all human life.

It is now painfully apparent that the constitutionalization of abortion is a slippery slope, leading ever downward into increasingly more detailed technical questions. As the courts have become increasingly more involved in supervising the enactment and enforcement of abortion regulations, the fundamental question keeps reappearing—why should the courts, rather than state legislatures, be deciding these issues? The answer, of course, is that they should not.

The exercise of judicial power to invalidate legislation affects the relationship between the coequal branches of government. The assumption by the judiciary of a major role in supervising abortion regulation represents a substantial shift in the delicate balance of power.

I believe that the issue of abortion is the type of issue that should appropriately be left to legislative resolution. When employed unwisely or unnecessarily, the Supreme Court's power to declare legislative acts unconstitutional constitutes a threat to the continued effectiveness of the federal courts as well as to the stability of our democratic system. After all, there is some irony that a people who are self-governing cannot establish the laws dealing with such a fundamental question as the regulation and legality of abortion....

CHAPTER 13

THE *ROE V. WADE* DECISION SHOULD NOT BE RECONSIDERED

REMARKS DELIVERED BY SENATOR DIANNE FEINSTEIN (D-CA) AT THE LOS ANGELES COUNTY BAR ASSOCIATION AND PUBLIC COUNSEL LUNCHEON AT THE BILTMORE HOTEL, LOS ANGELES, CA, AUGUST 24, 2005

...In 1992, I was elected as a Democratic pro-choice woman to represent the State of California. In poll after poll, Californians are consistently and overwhelmingly pro-choice. In fact, the most recent Field Poll, conducted in May, 2004, 71 percent of California voters support maintaining the current level of access to abortion services, or lessening existing restrictions. So do a majority of all Americans.

It would be very difficult for me to vote to confirm someone to the Supreme Court whom I knew would overturn *Roe*, and return our country to the days of the 1950s.

I remember what it was like then, when abortion was illegal. When I was a college student, I watched the passing of the plate to collect money so young women could go to Tijuana for an abortion. I knew a woman who ended her life because she was pregnant.

In the 1960s I served on the California Women's Board of Terms and Parole. California had an indeterminate sentence law then, and we actually sentenced women convicted of felonies in the State, and I sentenced women who were convicted of the crime of performing an illegal abortion. I saw what they did. I saw how they did it. And I saw the morbidity they left in their wake. I don't want to go back to those days.

Today we are faced with a divided court and a polarized country. It's clear the American people are divided about the course this country has taken. However, it is also clear, that Americans overwhelmingly believe that the government should not interfere with personal family decisions—especially decisions about life and death.

These are private matters. They represent the most personal, moral, and spiritual choices an individual or family must make. It may be fruitful for some on the extremes to reduce these issues to rhetorical slogans for their own political advantage, but how the Court decides future cases could determine whether both the beginning-of-life and the end-of-life decisions remain private, or whether they could be subject to expensive litigation or perhaps the risk of prison.

I believe the choice is clear. Government should not be allowed to interfere in personal family decisions and overrule the most difficult choices a family can make. The question I have, is how John Roberts will react to these real life dilemmas when, and if, they come before him....

STATEMENT OF SENATOR THOMAS HARKIN (D-IA) REGARDING A RESOLUTION TO THE PARTIAL-BIRTH ABORTION BAN ACT, WHICH HE SPONSORED WITH SENATOR BARBARA BOXER (D-CA), APRIL 25, 2000

...Last October 21, during debate on the so-called partial-birth abortion bill in the Senate, I, along with Senator Boxer, offered a resolution to this so-called partial-birth abortion bill. Our resolution was very simple. It stated that it was the sense of the Senate that *Roe v. Wade* was an appropriate decision and should not be repealed....

Our amendment barely passed, 51-47. Fifty-one said yes, *Roe v. Wade* was a good decision, it should not be overturned. Forty-seven Senators voted against that resolution, basically saying they did not agree with *Roe v. Wade* and that it should be overturned.

... Every time the so-called partial-birth abortion bill, or any other antichoice legislation, comes to the Senate floor, I will offer my amendment, and there will be another vote on the *Roe v. Wade* resolution. People in the leadership know that. That is why they have not bothered to bring up any of their antichoice legislation since the last vote on October 21. They know I will offer my amendment every single time to lift their veil of moderation. So today I am challenging the House Republican leadership to allow a vote on our amendment. Let's let people know where their representatives stand on the basic issue of choice, the basic issue of *Roe v. Wade*. Because *Roe v. Wade* is the moderate, mainstream policy on which American women have come to rely. The *Roe v. Wade* vote in the Senate should send a wakeup call to all Americans that this policy is in jeopardy. They need to act to maintain it.

In this most personal of decisions, we need to trust women, not politicians, to make the choice. ... Whether it is the case in front of the Supreme Court or whether it is the vote in the Senate, the issue is simply this: Do you trust politicians, whether they are in a State government or in the Federal Government, to make this decision for women or do you trust women?

... The bottom line is this: *Roe v. Wade* was an enlightened decision. It is moderate. It puts the basic decisions on reproductive health where it belongs, with the woman and not with the Government.

Today, as the Supreme Court, across the street, listens to the arguments on the Nebraska partial-birth abortion law, let us resolve that we are going to maintain a woman's basic right to choose, that we will not let the politicians take it over, that we will not return to the dark days of back-alley abortions and the criminalization of a woman's own right to choose her reproductive health.

That is what this issue is about.

STATEMENT OF REPRESENTATIVE PETE STARK (D-CA) REGARDING THE TWENTY-SIXTH ANNIVERSARY OF *ROE V. WADE*, FEBRUARY 9, 1999

Friday, January 22nd, 1999, marked the twenty-sixth anniversary of the Supreme Court decision in *Roe v. Wade*, which ensured the right of all women to make decisions concerning their reproductive health. For millions of women, *Roe v. Wade* has secured the constitutional right to seek access to safe and legal family planning and abortion services. Its impact on the health and safety of the lives of women cannot be overstated.

It is an outrage that, despite the Supreme Court's ruling, women still face barriers to seeking abortion without danger. States continue to find ways to restrict access by law, and even more troubling is the recent trend of clinic violence and the harassment of doctors and workers by anti-choice activists. I would like to highlight some cases from this past year of violence and threatening behavior in my home state of California.

In February, a bombing attempt was made on a family planning clinic in Vallejo. The briefcase that contained the alleged bomb was later discovered to be empty.

In April, a firebomb was thrown at a Planned Parenthood family planning clinic in San Diego, causing $5,000 in damages. ...

In July, a San Mateo family planning clinic worker was accused of physical assault by three anti-choice protestors. The protestors' injuries were not found by the police to warrant charges.

In San Diego, a clinic was vandalized, the buildings covered with the words "baby killer."

In September, the new Planned Parenthood headquarters in Orange County faced over thirty chanting anti-choice protestors.

In Fairfield, a physician was harassed by anti-choice protestors as he arrived for work one morning.

These events are mirrored by others across the country and show that the fight for reproductive choice did not end with the *Roe v. Wade* decision. Twenty-six years ago, the Supreme Court held up the right to reproductive choice for women, yet it is still debated on the floor of the House of Representatives on a near daily basis. We must keep up the fight for a woman's right to choose. I remain committed to do all I can to preserve that choice.

STATEMENT OF RONALD M. GREEN, JOHN PHILIPS PROFESSOR OF RELIGION, DARTMOUTH COLLEGE, AND DIRECTOR OF DARTMOUTH'S ETHICS INSTITUTE, BEFORE THE SUBCOMMITTEE ON THE CONSTITUTION, HOUSE JUDICIARY COMMITTEE, APRIL 22, 1996

In considering the question of abortion more than twenty-three years ago, the Supreme Court had to face an extremely difficult set of questions. Among these were the question[s] of how we are to assess the legal and moral claims of prenatal life, and how we are to balance the claims of the embryo or fetus against a woman's rights of autonomy and privacy in reproductive decision-making.

The issue of the moral or legal status of prenatal human life is particularly difficult. In approaching this issue, the court noted the wide diversity of philosophical and religious views on when life begins.

... Obviously the Court could not privilege any one position ... and chose instead to look at the discernible interests of women and society in the matter of state involvement in regulating abortion and protecting prenatal life.

...The Court also acted in the best positive American traditions of separation of church and state by allowing individuals and religious groups the freedom to determine how they themselves view and will decide to treat prenatal human life.

...The justices...made the decision...that questions affecting the basic rights of women and involving a determination of the moral and legal status of prenatal life could not be left to the jurisdiction of local communities or the state. It is unthinkable that one state could come to a ruling on this matter, for example, not to protect the fetus, while another could rule differently.

The Court ruled properly, I believe, when it concluded that during the early phases of a pregnancy, maternal privacy and autonomy should take priority over any state interests in prenatal life.

...[Some people] argue that even if the early embryo or fetus lacks many of the qualities we normally associate with full humanness, it possesses a unique genetic identity and potential and should be respected for this. However...it is now known that, following conception, the embryo can spontaneously fission into two distinct persons, each having an identical genome or genetic blueprint. This is the way that identical twins develop in nature. More surprisingly, during the early phases of development, two distinct embryos can fuse together to create a single individual, with each genetic cell line integrating itself successfully in the resulting bodily structure.... So it is not true that a unique human genetic identity is forged at conception or that we can unambiguously speak of individual persons as beginning at this time.

After the time of viability, when a fetus can live on its own in the world as a distinct and recognizable human being, the justices believed that it is reasonable to place greater restrictions on a woman's autonomy and privacy in the name of this growing human potential. [But] in cases of conflicts between the life and health of the mother and the life of the fetus, her well-being, as determined by competent medical authority, must come first.

...After more than two decades the basic framework of *Roe* still makes sense.

As a society we will continue to argue about the specifics of abortion law and policy within this reasonable framework. My own personal view is that we should continue to adhere to the lines drawn by the Court in *Roe*, including the specific application of the trimester approach adopted there. I hold this view because I believe that nothing has happened since 1973 that compels us to change this approach. The age of viability has not changed dramatically during this period and medical technology has not advanced to the point that we can avoid the occasional need for tragic later-term decisions about the woman's health or the health of her child.

STATEMENT OF WALTER DELLINGER, PROFESSOR OF LAW, DUKE UNIVERSITY SCHOOL OF LAW, DURHAM, NC, BEFORE THE SUBCOMMITTEE ON CIVIL AND CONSTITUTIONAL RIGHTS, HOUSE JUDICIARY COMMITTEE, OCTOBER 2, 1990

There is no doubt that a woman's right to decide whether or not to terminate a pregnancy is, at a minimum, a liberty interest protected by the due process clause. Any other conclusion would require the Court to overrule *Griswold v. Connecticut* protecting the right of married couples to use birth control.... Restrictive abortion laws give the state control over a woman's basic choices about reproduction and family planning, an intrusion utterly incompatible with any meaningful concept of individual liberty.

It is no exaggeration to say...that mandatory childbearing is a totalitarian intervention into a woman's life.

Congress could, moreover, conclude that restrictive abortion regulations have a clearly disproportionate impact on the equality and liberty interest of poor women, young women, and women of color. The kinds of restrictions that states are enacting even now, while *Roe* still hangs by a thread, are restrictions that have devastating consequences for women who are hostage to youth, poverty, and geography.

...The fact is that in a federal system of open borders and freedom of interstate travel, no state can, in fact, enforce its restrictive abortion policy against its affluent and well-educated residents. What states may do is to enforce restrictive policy against those many of its residents who are vulnerable.

The notion of returning the abortion issue to the states would not actually result in different rules for residents of different states, as much as it would functionally produce different abortion policies for different economic and social classes.

The Congress can clearly take into account the fact that separate state policies would produce a national double standard for rich and poor, wholly incompatible with basic principles of justice. A woman's right to choose would be determined by the fortuitous happenstance of where she lived and whether she had the information and money to travel elsewhere, sometimes to a distant location, to obtain an abortion.

STATEMENT OF SENATOR BOB PACKWOOD (R-OR) BEFORE THE SUBCOMMITTEE ON THE CONSTITUTION, SENATE JUDICIARY COMMITTEE, FEBRUARY 28, 1983

I would urge this committee to recall that, by and large, constitutional amendments are designed to confirm consensus, not create it.... I know those who share my view on abortion cite the polls indicating that by a margin of 2-to-1, people in this country think that a woman ought to have the right to choose whether or not she wants to have an abortion....

There is no...consensus in this country for a constitutional amendment to reverse *Roe v. Wade*....

I am hard-pressed to understand how those who are very strongly opposed to the right to choose, who are convinced that abortion is murder...how they can vote for a states' rights amendment, which says in essence that murder is OK in some states and not in others.

...I think we are all aware that a constitutional amendment would not actually prohibit abortion. Abortion was illegal in most places in this country—and in a few states—prior to *Roe v. Wade*. The difference is that many more women died, because the abortions were... done under the most unsanitary conditions.

Any constitutional amendment we pass may make abortion illegal, but it will not make it impossible, and it will be a sorry day for women in this country if we force them back into the situation that we forced them into prior to *Roe v. Wade*.

STATEMENT OF RHONDA COPELON, CENTER FOR CONSTITUTIONAL RIGHTS, BEFORE THE SUBCOMMITTEE ON THE CONSTITUTION, SENATE JUDICIARY COMMITTEE, MARCH 7, 1983

No decision of the Supreme Court of the United States has meant more to the lives, the health, the well-being, the freedom and the dignity of women in this country than the decisions in *Roe v. Wade*.

Roe v. Wade ranks with other landmark decisions that have moved this nation on the path toward liberty and equality....

Roe v. Wade is not...a departure from constitutional tradition, rather it applied to women some of the basic concepts upon which this nation was founded, and that is one of the reasons it is so difficult to undo.

It repudiated the historic disregard for the dignity and full personhood of women and the relegation of women to a separate sphere and second class citizenship. It brought legal theory, developed by and for men, closer to encompassing the existence of women.

Consider for a moment the relation of some of our most fundamental constitutional principles to the issue of compulsory pregnancy and childbearing.

We all hold as sacred the physical privacy of our homes. If we guard so jealously our physical environment and possession from intrusion by the state, how can we accord lesser status to the dominion and control over the physical self?

The First Amendment protects our thoughts, our beliefs, our verbal as well as symbolic expression. We can neither be restrained from speech nor forced to break silence. The Constitution protects these rights not only because of a utilitarian view that a marketplace of ideas served the public good but also because of the place of expression in the development of individual identity and the fulfillment of human aspirations.

Is not the commitment to bring a child into the world and to raise it through daily love, nurture and teaching an awesome form of expression, a reflection of each individual's beliefs, thoughts, identity, and the notion of what is meaningful? Men and women speak with their bodies on picket lines and in demonstrations. Women likewise speak in childbearing.

The First Amendment also demands that the state respect diverse beliefs and practices that involve worship, ritual, and decisions about everyday life. We recognize as religious, matters of life and death and of ultimate concern. The decision whether or not to bear a child—like objection to military service—is a matter of conscientious dimension.

The religions and the people of this country are deeply divided over the propriety and, indeed, the necessity of abortion. While for some, any consideration of abortion is a grave evil, others hold that a pregnant woman has a religious and moral obligation to make a decision and to consider abortion rather than sacrifice her well-being, that of her family, or that of the incipient life. The right to abortion is thus rooted in the recognition that women, too, make conscientious decisions.

We deem fundamental also the principle enshrined in the Thirteenth Amendment that no person should be forced into involuntary servitude as a result either of private conspiracy or public law. Does this right not extend to women entitling her to say "no" to the unparalleled labor demanded by pregnancy, childbirth, and childbearing—to say "no" to the expropriation of her body and service for the sake of another? If we strip away the sentimentalism that has rendered invisible the work of childbearing and childrearing, forced pregnancy must surely be recognized as a form of involuntary servitude.

What of the equality of women? Not to apply the foregoing fundamental constitutional principles to the question of the liberty to choose abortion is to deny women equal personhood and dignity in the most fundamental sense.

At the same time, to deny the right to abortion ensures that women will be excluded from full participation in society. Unexpected pregnancy and involuntary motherhood can preclude education, shatter work patterns and aspirations, and make organizational and political involvement impossible. A woman is no more biologically required to remain pregnant than a cardiac patient is to die of a treatable condition.

In sum, the criticism of *Roe v. Wade* has less to do with judicial excess than it does with a view of woman as less than a whole person under the Constitution, as someone whose self and aspirations can and should be legally subordinated to the service of others. The criticism reflects a failure to understand the gravity with which women view the responsibility of childbearing and the violence of forced pregnancy to human dignity.

CHAPTER 14
CERTAIN TYPES OF LATE-TERM ABORTIONS SHOULD BE ILLEGAL

On October 2, 2003, the House voted 281–142 to approve a bill that would ban certain types of late-term abortions—those that proponents of the measure term "partial-birth" abortions. The bill defines partial-birth abortion as a procedure in which a fetus is partially delivered alive and a physician performs "an overt act that the person knows will kill the partially delivered living fetus." The ban, which does not include a health exception, would apply when the "entire fetal head is outside the body of the mother or, in the case of breech presentation, any part of the fetal trunk past the navel is outside the body of the mother." Doctors who perform the procedure could face fines and prison sentences of up to two years. On October 21, 2003, the U.S. Senate voted 64–34 to approve the bill (known as S. 3). The version passed by the House and the Senate omits a nonbinding resolution expressing support for the *Roe v. Wade* decision, which was included in the original Senate version of the bill. The measure was signed by President George W. Bush on November 5, 2003, making it the first federal law criminalizing an established abortion procedure.

Hours after the President signed the bill, however, a federal judge in Nebraska placed a temporary restraining order on it, preventing the Justice Department from enforcing the new law. The next day, two more judges in San Francisco and New York City followed, questioning the bill's constitutionality. Three organizations that support a woman's right to choose—the American Civil Liberties Union, the National Abortion Federation, and Planned Parenthood Federation—filed the lawsuits, seeking an injunction to bar its enforcement, relying in part on the legislation's failure to allow such an abortion to protect a woman's health, as required by earlier court decisions (such as *Stenberg v. Carhart*). The lawsuits challenged the constitutionality of the Partial-Birth Abortion Ban Act of 2003.

The federal judge in San Francisco, the first to render a decision, ruled that the Act was unconstitutional in three ways: it places an undue burden on women seeking abortions, its language is vague, and it lacks a required exception for medical actions needed to preserve the woman's health. In 2004 federal judges in all three states ruled the legislation as unconstitutional. In July 2005 a Federal appeals court in St. Louis upheld the Nebraska ruling. At that time, the Bush administration planned to ask the Supreme Court to uphold the partial-birth abortion ban.

STATEMENT OF SENATOR RICK SANTORUM (R-PA), INTRODUCING THE PARTIAL-BIRTH ABORTION BILL ON THE SENATE FLOOR, MARCH 10, 2003

Mr. President, we are now on a piece of legislation known as the partial-birth abortion bill. It is a bill we have debated in the Senate in two previous Congresses on four different occasions. We debated it the first time and passed it. It was vetoed by the President, President Clinton at the time, back in 1996. Then we attempted to override the President's veto and fell just a few votes short.

We came back the next session, went through the same process, sent the bill to the President, he vetoed it again, and we came closer but we still failed in overriding the President's veto.

Subsequently, there were a whole series actually, concurrent with that debate of States, over half the States in the Union, that passed bans on this horrific partial-birth abortion procedure. That is the procedure where the baby is delivered—this is a baby at over 20 weeks gestation; in other words, halfway through the pregnancy. The gestational period is 40 weeks. This procedure is only performed on babies in utero after 20 weeks. So these are late-term abortions.

The process is as follows: A woman shows up and decides she wants to have an abortion after 20 weeks. A doctor decides to use this methodology. The woman is given a drug to dilate her cervix. She is sent home. Two days later she returns, and the baby is then delivered in a breech position. Under the definition of this act as currently constituted, the baby has to be alive when it is brought in through the birth canal, the baby has to be in a breech position, has to be outside the mother at least past the navel, and be alive. Then the baby is killed in a fashion that I will describe in more detail later.

That procedure, as I said, was banned by over 25 States. It was brought, obviously, to the courts by many in those States. There were a couple of circuit courts that found this to be constitutional, one that did not. The Supreme Court took one of those cases, the Nebraska case that was appealed to the circuit, and made a decision which I think was in error. It was a horrible decision, but a decision I think we need to contemplate here. It is a decision that said that an abortion past 20 weeks of a child that would otherwise be born alive is now encompassed by Roe v. Wade.

You hear a lot of comments about Roe v. Wade, that Roe v. Wade only allows legal abortions within the first trimester and under limited circumstances in the second trimester. These are babies in the second and third trimester, where the courts have basically said, as many of us who have been studying this issue for a long time have said, that there is no limitation on the right to abortion. Abortion is a right that is absolute in America. There are no limitations, as a result of court decisions, on the right to an abortion.

So they held, in this case, that the language of the statute was too vague and that the description of the procedure was too vague, and that there needed to be a health exception to this procedure; in other words, to preserve the health of the mother.

We have responded to that with a bill we introduced last year, in the last session of Congress. In the last session of Congress, we introduced a piece of legislation in the House that was passed. Steve Chabot, at the time chairman of the Constitution Subcommittee on the Judiciary Committee, passed a piece of legislation in the House that banned this procedure. It is identical to the bill that is on the floor today....

We believe the issues the Supreme Court brought up with respect to the infirmities in the Nebraska statute have been addressed by this legislation. First, we have gone into much greater detail in describing this procedure, and either later tonight or tomorrow I will read the text of the bill and I will provide graphic illustration as to how this procedure is conducted.

Second, we dealt with the issue of health. Roe v. Wade requires a health exception when the health of the mother is potentially in danger. We have included in this legislation a voluminous amount of material that shows clearly, without dispute, in my mind without dispute, period, not just in my mind without any medical dispute, that there are no reasons this procedure has to be available for the health of the mother because there are no instances in which this procedure is required for the health of the mother. There is no medical organization out there that believes that to be the case.

While some do not support the legislation or have a neutral position, nobody has come forward and said this is medically necessary to protect the health of the mother, much less, by the way, the life of the mother.

So, since there is no reason for a health exception because there are no instances where a health exception is needed, then Roe does not apply. So we have laid that out very clearly in this legislation. We believe as a result of that, Congress has the right because we do a heck of a lot more exhaustive study, in our deliberations with hearings and other testimony, than the Supreme Court can. They have to rely on the record of the lower court and the arguments made to that lower court.

In the case of Nebraska, frankly, the arguments were not particularly well put and the evidence was not particularly robust for either side. It was a very weak record, and the court made a decision based on that record. They will have a different record before them in this case when it is brought up to the court, and I believe the record will be clear and dispositive that no health exception is necessary. We have dealt with the constitutional issues. Now we are back to the focus of this legislation. Do you want to allow a horrific procedure that is not medically necessary, never medically indicated, not taught in any medical school in this country, not recommended, and which, in fact, major health organizations of this country have said is bad medicine, contra-indicated, that is so brutal in the way it is administered to a baby that otherwise would be born alive?

Let me emphasize that it is a baby fetus—some will refer to it as the child in utero—that would otherwise be born alive. You don't want to allow this child to be brutally killed by thrusting a pair of scissors into the back of its skull and suctioning its brains out.

This goes on in America thousands of times a year. The number of partial-birth abortions has tripled, according to the abortion industry that doesn't keep very good records. They admit that. It has tripled, they say, to 2,200. Oddly enough, back in 1997 when we were debating this, the Bergen County Record took the bother of asking the local abortion clinic how many they did just in Bergen County. The partial-birth abortion national number at that time was 600. In Bergen County, they did 1,500. I guess they dismissed that.

The bottom line is that this goes on an enormous amount of times and they call it a rare procedure. If we had a procedure that killed 2,200 children in America every single year, we would not be saying it is a rare procedure in America. If we had a disease that affected 2,200 little babies every year, we wouldn't say this is a rare thing when we know, by the way, that the number is multiples of that. The people we have to rely on for that information are the people who want this to be legal and who don't tell us about the abortions they perform.

This is something that needs to be done. I am hopeful that we can deal with this issue in an expeditious fashion, get this over in the House of Representatives and have them pass it, and have the President sign it, because he will sign it.

I think there is broad bipartisan support for this legislation as there has been in the past. It is overwhelmingly supported by the American people. A very large majority support this legislation. Even those who do not consider themselves pro-life believe that at some point we have to draw the line on the brutal killing of a child literally inches from constitutional protection—inches from being born and being completely separated from the mother, being held in the birth canal and executed, having scissors thrust into the base of its skull and then to have a suction catheter inserted and the "cranial content" removed.

Just to describe it here sends chills down your back. Yet people will defend this procedure and say that a civilized nation such as America believes this is proper medicine. Medicine, healing? I, frankly, don't know who is healed in that situation. I do not know who is protected in that situation when every credible medical core organization says it is not medically necessary; in fact, it is "bad medicine," and it is harmful to the woman. I have just described how harmful it is to the little child.

I ask my colleagues to join me in passing this piece of legislation and ending this outrageous procedure.

STATEMENT OF MARK G. NEERHOF, M.D., BEFORE THE SENATE COMMITTEE ON THE JUDICIARY, SUBCOMMITTEE ON THE CONSTITUTION, MARCH 25, 2003

Mr. Chairman and committee members, Thank you for the opportunity to come and speak with you today.

My name is Mark Neerhof. I am an associate professor of Obstetrics and Gynecology at Northwestern University Medical School. I am an attending physician in the Department of Obstetrics and Gynecology, Division of Maternal-Fetal Medicine at Evanston Northwestern Healthcare in Evanston, Illinois. I have been practicing Maternal-Fetal Medicine for 14 years. I am very familiar with fetal anomalies of all sorts, and am familiar with the options available for termination of pregnancy. I have done many deliveries at the gestational ages where an intact D&X [the medical term for a so-called partial-birth abortion] is performed, and as a consequence, I am very familiar with the mechanism of delivery, including at these early gestational ages. I came here today to express my support for a ban on intact D&X. I will divide my reasons into 3 categories: maternal, fetal, and ethical.

Maternal Considerations

There exist no credible studies on intact D&X that evaluate or attest its safety. The procedure is not recognized in medical textbooks. Intact D&X poses serious medical risks to the mother. Patients who undergo an intact D&X are at risk for the potential complications associated with any surgical mid-trimester termination, including hemorrhage, infection, and uterine perforation. However, intact D&X places these patients at increased risk of 2 additional complications. First, the risk of uterine rupture may be increased. An integral part of the D&X procedure is an internal podalic version, during which the physician instrumentally reaches into the uterus, grasps the fetus' feet, and pulls the feet down into the cervix, thus converting the lie to a footling breech. The internal version carries risk of uterine rupture, abruption, amniotic fluid embolus, and trauma to the uterus.

The second potential complication of intact D&X is the risk of iatrogenic laceration and secondary hemorrhage. Following internal version and partial breech extraction, scissors are forced into the base of the fetal skull while it is lodged in the birth canal. This blind procedure risks maternal injury from laceration of the uterus or cervix by the scissors and could result in severe bleeding and the threat of shock or even maternal death. These risks have not been adequately quantified.

None of these risks are medically necessary because other procedures are available to physicians who deem it necessary to perform an abortion late in pregnancy. As ACOG [American College of Obstetricians and Gynecologists] policy states clearly, intact D&X is never the only procedure available. Some clinicians have considered intact D&X necessary when hydrocephalus is present. However, a hydrocephalic fetus could be aborted by first draining the excess fluid from the fetal skull through ultrasound-guided cephalocentesis. Some physicians who perform abortions have been concerned that a ban on late abortions would affect their ability to provide other abortion services. Because of the proposed changes in federal legislation, it is clear that only intact D&X would be banned. It is my opinion that this legislation will not affect the total number of terminations done in this country, it will simply eliminate one of the procedures by which termination can be accomplished.

Fetal Considerations

Intact D&X is an extremely painful procedure for the fetus. The majority of intact D&X are performed on periviable fetuses. Fetuses or newborns at these gestational ages are fully capable of experiencing pain. The scientific evidence supporting this is abundant. If one still has a question in one's mind regarding this fact, one simply needs to visit a Neonatal Intensive Care Unit, and your remaining doubts will be short-lived. When infants of similar gestational ages are delivered, pain management is an important part of the care rendered to them in the intensive care nursery. However, with intact D&X, pain management is not provided for the fetus, who is literally within inches of being delivered. Forcibly incising the cranium with a scissors and then suctioning out the intracranial contents is certainly excruciatingly painful. I happen to serve as chairman of the Institutional Animal Care and Use Committee at my hospital. I am well aware of the federal standard regulating the use of animals in research. It is beyond ironic that the pain management practiced for an intact D&X on a human fetus would not meet federal standards for the humane care of animals used in medical research. The needlessly inhumane treatment of periviable fetuses argues against intact D&X as a means of pregnancy termination.

Ethical Considerations

Intact D&X is most commonly performed between 20 and 24 weeks and thereby raises the question of the potential viability of the fetus. Recent unpublished data from my institution indicates an 88% survival rate at 24 weeks. These numbers will undoubtedly continue to improve over time.

Beyond the argument of potential viability, many pro-choice organizations and individuals assert that a woman should maintain control over that which is part of her own body (i.e., the autonomy argument). In this context, the physical position of the fetus with respect to the mother's body becomes relevant. However, once the fetus is outside the woman's body, the autonomy argument is invalid. The intact D&X procedure involves literally delivering the fetus so that only the head remains within the cervix. Based on my own experience, I can tell you that if the fetal head remains in the cervix, insertion of scissors into the base of the skull is, by necessity, a blind procedure, and consequently, potentially hazardous. If, as I suspect, the head is out of the cervix and in the vagina, that fetus is essentially delivered because there is nothing left to hold the fetal head in. At this juncture, the fetus is merely inches from being delivered and obtaining full legal rights of personhood under the US Constitution. What happens when, as must occasionally occur during the performance of an intact D&X, the fetal head inadvertently slips out of the mother and a live infant is fully delivered? For this reason, many otherwise pro-choice individuals have found intact D&X too close to infanticide to ethically justify its continued use.

In summary, the arguments for banning this procedure are based on maternal safety, fetal pain, and ethical considerations. I regret the necessity to support the development of legislation which will regulate medical care because, in general, that is not desirable. However, in this case, it is born out of the reluctance of the medical community to stand up for what is right....

STATEMENT OF STEVE CHABOT, CONGRESSMAN (R), 1ST DISTRICT OF OHIO, BEFORE THE HOUSE JUDICIARY COMMITTEE, SUBCOMMITTEE ON THE CONSTITUTION, MARCH 25, 2003

We have convened this afternoon to receive testimony on H.R. 760, the Partial-Birth Abortion Ban Act of 2003.

On February 13, on behalf of over 100 original co-sponsors, I introduced H.R. 760, the Partial-Birth Abortion Ban Act of 2003 which will ban the dangerous and inhumane procedure during which a physician delivers an unborn child body until only the head remains inside the womb, punctures the back of the child skull with a sharp instrument, and sucks the child brains out before completing delivery of the dead infant. An abortionist who violates this ban would be subject to fines or a maximum of two years imprisonment, or both. H.R. 760 also establishes a civil cause of action for damages against an abortionist who violates the ban and includes an exception for those situations in which a partial-birth abortion is necessary to save the life of the mother. On March 13, 2003, the Senate approved S. 3, which is virtually identical to H.R. 760, by a 64 to 33 vote.

A moral, medical, and ethical consensus exists that partial-birth abortion is an inhumane procedure that is never medically necessary and should be prohibited. Contrary to the claims of those who proclaim the medical necessity of this barbaric procedure, partial-birth abortion is, in fact, a dangerous medical procedure that can pose serious risks to the long-term health of women. As testimony received by the Subcommittee on during the 107th Congress demonstrates, there is never any situation in which the procedure H.R. 760 would ban is medically necessary. In fact, ten years after Dr. Martin Haskell presented this procedure to the mainstream abortion community, partial birth abortions have failed to become the standard of medical practice for any circumstance under which a woman might seek an abortion.

As a result, the United States Congress voted to ban partial birth abortions during the 104th, 105th, and 106th Congresses and at least 27 states enacted bans on the procedure. Unfortunately, the two federal bans that reached President Clinton's desk were promptly vetoed.

To address the concerns raised by the majority opinion of the United States Supreme Court in *Stenberg v. Carhart*, H.R. 760 differs from these previous proposals in two areas.

First, the bill contains a new, more precise definition of the prohibited procedure to address the Court concerns that Nebraska's definition of the prohibited procedure might be interpreted to encompass a more commonly performed late second trimester abortion procedure. As previous testimony indicates, H.R. 760 clearly distinguishes the procedure it would ban from other abortion procedures.

The second difference addresses the majority opinion that the Nebraska ban placed an "undue burden" on women seeking abortions because it failed to include an exception for partial-birth abortions deemed necessary to preserve the "health" of the mother. The *Stenberg* court based its conclusion on the trial court factual findings regarding the relative health and safety benefits of partial-birth abortions' findings which were highly disputed. The Court was required to accept these findings because of the highly deferential, "clearly erroneous" standard that is applied to lower court factual findings.

Those factual findings, however, are inconsistent with the overwhelming weight of authority regarding the safety and medical necessity of the partial-birth abortion procedure—including evidence received during extensive legislative hearings during the 104th, 105th, and 107th Congresses, which indicates that a partial-birth abortion is never medically necessary to preserve the health of a woman, poses serious risks to a woman health, and lies outside the standard of medical care.

Under well settled Supreme Court jurisprudence, the United States Congress is not bound to accept the same factual findings that the Supreme Court was bound to accept in Stenberg under the "clearly erroneous" standard. Rather, the United States Congress is entitled to reach its own factual findings—findings that the Supreme Court consistently relies upon and accords great deference—and to enact legislation based upon these findings so long as it seeks to pursue a legitimate interest that is within the scope of the Constitution and draws reasonable inferences based upon substantial evidence. Thus, the first section of H.R. 760 contains Congress's extensive factual findings that, based upon extensive medical evidence compiled during congressional hearings, a partial birth abortion is never necessary to preserve the health of a woman.

H.R. 760's findings are not "false" as its opponents have charged. They are based upon the very opinions of doctors, medical associations, and a review of the practices of the medical profession as whole. Thus, they are "legislative facts" drawn from reasonable inferences based upon substantial evidence. The fact that the abortion lobby disagrees with these inferences only demonstrates how out of step they are with public opinion and the mainstream medical community.

Despite overwhelming support from the public, past efforts to ban partial birth abortion were blocked by President Clinton. We now have a President who has promised to stand with Congress in its efforts to ban this barbaric and dangerous procedure. It is time for Congress to end the national tragedy of partial-birth abortion and protect the lives of these helpless, defenseless, little babies....

STATEMENT OF CURTIS COOK, M.D., BEFORE THE HOUSE JUDICIARY COMMITTEE, SUBCOMMITTEE ON THE CONSTITUTION, JULY 9, 2002

My name is Dr. Curtis Cook and I am a board-certified Maternal–Fetal Medicine specialist (perinatologist) practicing and teaching in the state of Michigan. I provide care exclusively to women experiencing complicated pregnancies. These include women with preexisting medical conditions such as diabetes, hypertension and even cardiac disease and cancer. This group of complicated pregnancies also entails those with suspected fetal abnormalities including lethal fetal anomalies such as anencephaly (absent brain) and renal agenesis (absent kidneys). Additionally, this group of complicated pregnancies includes those women who have developed obstetrical complications during the course of their gestation. This would include situations such as the premature onset of labor or early leaking of the amniotic fluid.

Never in the ten years I have been providing perinatal care to women with complicated pregnancies have I ever experienced a clinical situation where the late-term abortion procedure being considered before this committee (partial-birth abortion [PBA]) has ever been required or even considered as a clinically superior procedure to other well-known and readily available medical and surgical options. This includes the clinical situations where this technique has been used by some physicians, and even the theoretical situations proposed by zealous advocates of this rogue procedure. Additionally, I have queried many colleagues with decades of clinical experience and have yet to find one individual who has experienced a clinical situation that would require this procedure. This procedure has been discussed very publicly for more than five years and yet we have not seen it embraced by the medical community simply for its lack of merit in modern obstetrics.

As part of my professional responsibilities, I also teach medical students and residents the clinical management of pregnant women. This includes the various medical and surgical options for facilitating a birth or emptying a uterus in all three trimesters of pregnancy. I have never encountered teaching materials on this technique (PBA) except for the information presented by Dr. Haskell at a National Abortion Federation seminar. I am also a fellow of both the American College of Obstetricians and Gynecologists and the Society of Maternal-Fetal Medicine as well as a member of the Association of Professors of Gynecology and Obstetrics. I am not aware of any educational materials from any one of these groups discussing the specific technique of partial-birth abortion (or D&X/intact D&E), the appropriate clinical use of this procedure or even clinical reports of its use. This also leads me to believe this is a rogue procedure with no role in modern obstetrics.

Frankly, I am appalled that any physician is providing such "services" given the gruesome nature of this inhumane procedure. By their own admission these procedures are being performed primarily between 20–28 weeks gestation and sometimes beyond on mostly healthy mothers carrying healthy babies. The current survivability of infants born at 23 weeks is greater than 30% and at 24 weeks it is almost 70%. By 28 weeks the survival rate exceeds 95%! Many of these infants are literally inches away from enjoying the full rights afforded any American citizen including the rights to life, liberty and the pursuit of happiness.

Every argument brought forth by the zealous advocates of this procedure has been summarily dismissed in the light of the medical facts. This includes even early arguments that this procedure was never being performed. Later the argument proposed was that this procedure was rarely performed and when it was performed it was provided only to mothers or infants with severe medical problems. We know now by the independent investigations of the Washington Post, the New Jersey Bergen Record, the American Medical Association News and others that these procedures are being performed by the thousands on mostly healthy mothers carrying healthy babies as admitted to by high profile providers of this technique. It was even preposterously proclaimed that the anesthesia provided the mother during the procedure was responsible for killing the fetus rather than the act of puncturing the base of the skull and suctioning out the brain contents. This was roundly criticized by all legitimate medical bodies putting to rest the concerns of thousands of other women undergoing indicated surgical procedures during the course of their pregnancy. Indeed several pediatric pain specialists and obstetrical anesthesiologists have stated that there is good evidence to support that this procedure would generate excruciating pain for the partially born infant. In fact, this technique would not even be allowed for the purpose of euthanizing research laboratory animals.

Again I speak from the experience of providing medical and surgical care to infants at the same point in pregnancy at which these abortions are being performed. I also regularly care for women with same diagnoses as those undergoing partial-birth abortion and have been able to safely deliver these women without having to resort to these brutal techniques. This procedure does not protect the life nor preserve the health of pregnant women. It also does not enhance the ability of women to have successful pregnancies in the future and may even hinder such efforts. I am at a loss to think of any benefit of this procedure other than the guarantee of a dead baby at the time of the completed delivery.

In summary, I feel this procedure (PBA) is unnecessary, unsavory and potentially unsafe for women. Unfortunately it is still being perpetuated upon thousands of innocent partially-born children in this country every year. As I did before this committee five years ago, again I urge you to act quickly to prohibit this abomination of American medicine. . . .

CHAPTER 15
NO NEW LIMITATIONS SHOULD BE PLACED ON LATE-TERM ABORTION PROCEDURES

OPINION OF RICHARD G. KOPF, CHIEF UNITED STATES DISTRICT JUDGE, IN THE DECISION FOR *CARHART V. ASHCROFT*, UNITED STATES DISTRICT COURT FOR THE DISTRICT OF NEBRASKA, SEPTEMBER 8, 2004, AFFIRMED BY *CARHART V. GONZALES*, UNITED STATES COURT OF APPEALS FOR THE 8TH CIRCUIT, JULY 8, 2005

... Like giving birth to a child, when a woman ends her pregnancy during or after the second trimester, she confronts a serious problem. Her cervix will frequently be too small to allow the skull of the human fetus to pass through it. Although terminating a pregnancy in America is safer than childbirth, this "skull-is-too-large" difficulty makes the abortion of a human fetus, like the birth of a human baby, potentially very dangerous to both the life and health of the woman. Our elected representatives have decided that it is *never* necessary to use a specific surgical technique—"partial-birth abortion"—to deal with this concern during an abortion. On the contrary, they have banned the procedure.

After giving Congress the respectful consideration it is always due, I find and conclude that the ban is unreasonable and not supported by substantial evidence. In truth, "partial-birth abortions," which are medically known as "intact D&E" or "D&X" procedures, are sometimes necessary to preserve the health of a woman seeking an abortion. While the procedure is infrequently used as a relative matter, when it is needed, the health of women frequently hangs in the balance.

Four examples, out of many, illustrate this point:

- During the 17th week of gestation, before many physicians are comfortable inducing fetal death by injection prior to beginning a surgical abortion, one of Mr. Ashcroft's expert witnesses conceded that it would be consistent with the standard of care at the University of Michigan Medical School, where she practices, to crush the skull of the living fetus when the body was delivered intact outside the cervix and into the vaginal cavity if the skull was trapped by the cervix and the woman was hemorrhaging. (Tr. 1598–1602, Test. Dr. Shadigian.)

- Another of Mr. Ashcroft's expert witnesses, the head of obstetrics and gynecology at Yale, testified on direct examination, and confirmed again on cross-examination, that there are "compelling enough arguments as to [the banned technique's] safety, that I certainly would not want to prohibit its use in my institution." (Tr. 1706 & 1763, Test. Dr. Lockwood.)

- Another physician, Dr. Phillip D. Darney, the Chief of Obstetrics and Gynecology at San Francisco General Hospital, a major metropolitan hospital that performs 2,000 abortions a year, provided Congress with two very specific examples of abortions at 20 weeks and after (one case presenting with a bleeding placenta previa and clotting disorder and the other with a risk of massive hemorrhage) "in which the 'intact D&E' technique was critical to providing optimal care" and was the "safest technique of pregnancy termination" in those situations. (Ct.'s Ex. 9, Letter to Sen. Feinstein from Dr. Darney, at 100–01.)

- Still another doctor, who had served on the committee of physicians designated by the American College of Obstetricians and Gynecologists (ACOG) to look into this issue and who holds certifications in biomedical ethics, obstetrics and gynecology, and gynecologic oncology, Dr. Joanna M. Cain, testified that in the case "of cancer of the placenta often diagnosed in the second trimester," where "the least amount of instrumentation possible of the uterine wall is desirable[,] ... it is much safer for the woman to have an intact D&X to remove the molar pregnancy." (Pls.' Ex. 115, Dep. Dr. Cain, at 177.)

Therefore, I declare the "Partial-Birth Abortion Ban Act of 2003" unconstitutional because it does not allow, and instead prohibits, the use of the procedure when necessary to preserve the health of a woman. In addition, I decide that the ban fails as a result of other constitutional imperfections. As a result, I will also permanently enjoin enforcement of the ban. Importantly, however, because the evidence was sparse regarding postviability, I do not decide whether the law is unconstitutional when the fetus is indisputably viable.

STATEMENT OF SENATOR BARBARA BOXER REGARDING THE SENATE'S PASSAGE OF S. 3, THE PARTIAL-BIRTH ABORTION BAN ACT OF 2003, SEPTEMBER 15, 2003

...Now, what does *Roe* guarantee to women?

In the decision of the Supreme Court, the Court found that a woman's reproductive decisions are a privacy right guaranteed by the Constitution. But I have to say that even though this right was granted to women, it was not an unbalanced decision. It was a very moderate decision. That is why, in my opinion, the majority of Americans support it.

In the early stages of a pregnancy, the Government cannot intervene with a woman's right to choose. That is it, plain and simple. Guess what. We are not going to be big brother or sister, as the case may be. We are going to allow a woman, her doctor, and her God to make that decision.

But in the later stages of pregnancy, *Roe* found that the Government can intervene, that it can regulate, that it can restrict abortion. We all support that. All of us support that. But there is one caveat—always, always, always. Any law that a State may pass to restrict abortion rights has to have an exception to protect the life of the woman or to protect her health.

This is important because, I have to tell you, *Roe*, before 1973—and I remember those years—life for women was very different. Before *Roe*, up to 1.2 million women each year resorted to dangerous illegal abortions. According to one estimate, at least 5,000 women a year died as a result of botched illegal abortions. Thousands of others nearly died, became infertile, or suffered other health complications....

So the point is that when the Court made this historic decision called *Roe v. Wade*, women were dying, maybe 5,000 a year. And you ask me, why would people, lawmakers, want to see us go back to those days? I will tell you right now, I don't understand it. It isn't right. It isn't right for the women of this country. It isn't right for the families of this country. *Roe v. Wade* was a balanced decision.

Then you have a situation where we wish we had more family planning funds because then we would be in a situation where we would not have these unwanted pregnancies. The same people who want to outlaw abortion are not interested in family planning funds. And interestingly, the same people who want to go back to the days when abortion was illegal, who will fight for the right of the fetus over the right of a woman, where are they, sometimes, on preschool programs, afterschool programs, caring for our children, helping our children? A lot of times they do not vote for it. As a friend of mine once said, he sometimes thinks that some of our colleagues who take this position, and then don't help the kids, are all for the kids between conception and birth; and then where are they?

So the reason we are here tonight is because the House is so radical on the point that they will not accept our language, that simply says: The decision of the Supreme Court in *Roe* was appropriate and secures an important right, and such decision should not be overturned.

Imagine, they say they want S. 3 so badly, they want to outlaw this medical procedure, which is the first time an accepted medical procedure is outlawed by politicians, but yet they cannot accept this language, which has no force of law. That is the incredible thing. It is a sense of the Senate. It does not even have the force of law, but it shows you that the goal here is not simply outlawing this one procedure; it is overturning *Roe*. I cannot say that enough because that is absolutely true, even when 80 percent of the people said that whether to have an abortion is a decision to be made between a woman and her doctor.

This debate is very serious. It is very serious because the underlying bill, S. 3, which bans this procedure, makes no exception for the health of the woman, and we tried every which way to do that. We said: *Roe* is the law of the land. Under *Roe*, the life and the health of a woman must always be protected. So in order to be constitutional, we are willing to walk hand in hand with you, and we will ban this procedure, even though some of us believe we should not get into playing doctor—that is not our role. There is no OB/GYN in this body. People don't come to us when they are sick. They come to us when they are sick and tired of politics, but they don't come to us when they are physically ill.

We were willing—those of us who are very pro-choice—to say: We will accept this if you will have an exception for the life and the health of a woman. Oh, no. They would not do it. That is why our language on *Roe*, that we attached to this bill, is so important. Because, folks, this bill, when it becomes law—and it will become law—is going straight to the Court.

We want the Court to understand we stood firmly for *Roe*. When they take a look at the outlawing of this procedure, and when they see there is no exception for the health of a woman, they will realize maybe some people voted for it who would have preferred a health exception. By showing them we have the votes to sustain a sense of the Senate in favor of *Roe*, we will be sending a strong signal on behalf of the women of this Nation to the courts. . . .

TEXT OF A MARCH 25, 2003, LETTER FROM LYNN EPSTEIN, M.D., PRESIDENT OF THE AMERICAN MEDICAL WOMEN'S ASSOCIATION, INC., TO JERROLD NADLER (D-NY), HOUSE OF REPRESENTATIVES, EXPRESSING OPPOSITION TO THE PARTIAL-BIRTH ABORTION BAN ACT OF 2003

The American Medical Women's Association (AMWA) strongly opposes HR 760, the "Partial-Birth Abortion Ban Act of 2003." While the Association has high respect for each member and their right to hold whatever moral, religious and philosophical beliefs his or her conscience dictates, as an organization of 10,000 women physicians and medical students dedicated to promoting women's health and advancing women in medicine, we believe HR 760 is unconscionable.

AMWA has long been an advocate for women's access to reproductive health care. As such, we recognize this legislation as an attempt to ban a procedure that in some circumstances is the safest and most appropriate alternative available to save the life and health of the woman. Furthermore, this bill violates the privilege of a patient in consultation with her physician to make the most appropriate decisions regarding her specific health circumstances.

AMWA opposes legislation such as HR 760 as inappropriate intervention in the decision-making relationship between physician and patient. The definition of the bill is too imprecise and it includes non-medical terminology for a procedure that may ultimately undermine the legality of other techniques in obstetrics and gynecology used in both abortion and non-abortion situations. At times, the use of these techniques is essential to the lives and health of women. The potential of this ban to criminalize certain obstetrics and gynecology techniques ultimately interferes with the quality of health and lives of women. Furthermore, the current ban fails to meet the provisions set forth by the Supreme Court in *Stenberg v. Carhart*, a ruling that overturned a Nebraska statute banning abortion because it contained no life and health exception for the mother.

AMWA's position on this bill corresponds to the position statement of the organization on abortion and reproductive health services to women and their families.

AMWA believes that the prevention of unintended pregnancies through access to contraception and education is the best option available for reducing the abortion rate in the United States. Legislative bans for procedures that use recognized obstetrics and gynecological techniques fails to protect the health and safety of women and their children, nor will it improve the lives of women and their families. . . .

TEXT OF A MARCH 31, 2003, LETTER FROM GEORGE C. BENJAMIN, M.D., EXECUTIVE DIRECTOR OF THE AMERICAN PUBLIC HEALTH ASSOCIATION, TO THE U.S. HOUSE OF REPRESENTATIVES URGING OPPOSITION TO THE PARTIAL-BIRTH ABORTION BAN ACT OF 2003

On behalf of the American Public Health Association (APHA)[,] the largest and oldest organization of public health professionals in the nation, representing more than 50,000 members from over 50 public health occupations, I write to urge your opposition to H.R. 760, the Partial-Birth Abortion Ban Act of 2003.

APHA has long-standing policy regarding the sanctity of the provider-patient relationship and has long advocated for a [woman's] right to choose from a full range of reproductive health options. We believe that a physician in consultation with the patient should make the decision regarding what method should be used to terminate a pregnancy.

We are opposed to H.R. 760 because we believe this and other legislative and judicial restrictions to safe, medically accepted abortion procedures severely jeopardize women's health and well-being. APHA also opposes the bill because it fails to include adequate health exception language in instances where certain procedures may be determined by a physician to be the best or most appropriate to preserve the health of the woman. We urge members of the House of Representatives to oppose this legislation.

Thank you for your attention to our concerns regarding the negative effect this legislation would have to a woman's right to a safe, legal abortion.

TEXT OF A MARCH 5, 2003, LETTER TO SENATOR BARBARA BOXER FROM FELICIA H. STEWART, M.D., A PHYSICIAN MEMBER OF PHYSICIANS FOR REPRODUCTIVE CHOICE AND HEALTH, REGARDING SENATE ACTION ON THE PARTIAL-BIRTH ABORTION BAN ACT OF 2003

I understand that you will be considering Senate S. 3, the ban on abortion procedures, soon and would like to offer some medical information that may assist you in your efforts. Important stakes for women's health are involved: if Congress enacts such a sweeping ban, the result could effectively ban safe and common, pre-viability abortion procedures.

...The criminal ban being considered is flawed in a number of respects: it fails to protect women's health by omitting an exception for women's health; it menaces medical practice with the threat of criminal prosecution; it encompasses a range of abortion procedures; and it leaves women in need of second trimester abortions with far less safe medical options: hysterotomy (similar to a cesarean section) and hysterectomy.

The proposed ban would potentially encompass several abortion methods, including dilation and extraction (d&x, sometimes referred to as "intact d&e"), dilation and evacuation (d&e), the most common second-trimester procedure. In addition, such a ban could also apply to induction methods. Even if a physician is using induction as the primary method for abortion, he or she may not be able to assure that the procedure could be effected without running afoul of the proposed ban. A likely outcome if this legislation is enacted and enforced is that physicians will fear criminal prosecution for any second trimester abortion—and women will have no choice but to carry pregnancies to term despite the risks to their health. It would be a sad day for medicine if Congress decides that hysterotomy, hysterectomy, or unsafe continuation of pregnancy are women's only available options. Williams Obstetrics, one of the leading medical texts in Obstetrics and Gynecology, has this to say about the hysterotomy "option" that the bill leaves open: "Nottage and Liston (1975), based on a review of 700 hysterotomies, rightfully concluded that the operation is outdated as a routine method for terminating pregnancy." Cunningham and McDonald, et al, Williams Obstetrics, 19th ed., (1993), p. 683.

Obviously, allowing women to have a hysterectomy means that Congress is authorizing women to have an abortion at the price of their future fertility, and with the added risks and costs of major surgery. In sum, the options left open are less safe for women who need an abortion after the first trimester of pregnancy.

I'd like to focus my attention on that subset of the women affected by this bill who face grievous underlying medical conditions. To be sure, these are not the majority of women who will be affected by this legislation, but the grave health conditions that could be worsened by this bill illustrate how sweeping the legislation is.

Take for instance women who face hypertensive disorders such as eclampsia—convulsions precipitated by pregnancy-induced or aggravated hypertension (high blood pressure). This, along with infection and hemorrhage, is one of the most common causes of maternal death. With eclampsia, the kidneys and liver may be affected, and in some cases, if the woman is not provided an abortion, her liver could rupture, she could suffer a stroke, brain damage, or coma. Hypertensive disorders are conditions that can develop over time or spiral out of control in short order, and doctors must be given the latitude to terminate a pregnancy if necessary in the safest possible manner.

If the safest medical procedures are not available to terminate a pregnancy, severe adverse health consequences are possible for some women who have underlying medical conditions necessitating a termination of their pregnancies, including: death (risk of death higher with less safe abortion methods); infertility; paralysis; coma; stroke; hemorrhage; brain damage; infection; liver damage; and kidney damage.

Legislation forcing doctors to forego medically indicated abortions or to use less safe but politically-palatable procedures is simply unacceptable for women's health....

TEXT OF A MARCH 10, 2003, LETTER TO SENATOR BARBARA BOXER FROM NATALIE E. ROCHE, M.D., AND GERSON WEISS, M.D., REGARDING THE PARTIAL-BIRTH ABORTION BAN ACT OF 2003

We are writing to urge you to stand in defense of women's reproductive health and vote against S. 3, legislation regarding so-called "partial birth" abortion.

We are practicing obstetrician-gynecologists, and academics in obstetrics, gynecology and women's health. We believe it is imperative that those who perform terminations and manage the pre- and post-operative care of women receiving abortions are given a voice in a debate that has largely ignored the two groups whose lives would be most affected by this legislation: physicians and patients.

It is misguided and unprincipled for lawmakers to legislate medicine. We all want safe and effective medical procedures for women; on that there is no dispute. However, the business of medicine is not always palatable to those who do not practice it on a regular basis. The description of a number of procedures—from liposuction to cardiac surgery—may seem distasteful to some, and even repugnant to others. When physicians analyze and debate surgical techniques among themselves, it is always for the best interest of the patient. Abortion is proven to be one of the safest procedures in medicine, significantly safer than childbirth, and in fact has saved numerous women's lives.

While we can argue as to why this legislation is dangerous, deceptive and unconstitutional—and it is— the fact of the matter is that the text of the bill is so vague and misleading that there is a great need to correct the misconceptions around abortion safety and technique.

It is wrong to assume that a specific procedure is never needed; what is required is the safest option for the patient, and that varies from case to case....

(1) So-called "partial birth" abortion does not exist. There is no mention of the term "partial birth" abortion in any medical literature. Physicians are never taught a technique called "partial birth" abortion and therefore are unable to medically define the procedure.

What is described in this legislation, however, could ban all abortions. "What this bill describes, albeit in non-medical terms, can be interpreted as any abortion," stated one of our physician members. "Medicine is an art as much as it is a science; although there is a standard of care, each procedure—and indeed each woman—is different. The wording here could apply to any patient." The bill's language is too vague to be useful; in fact, it is so vague as to be harmful. It is intentionally unclear and deceptive.

(2) Physicians need to have all medical options available in order to provide the best medical care possible. Tying the hands of physicians endangers the health of patients. It is unethical and dangerous for legislators to dictate specific surgical procedures. Until a surgeon examines the patient, she does not necessarily know which technique or procedure would be in the patient's best interest. Banning procedures puts women's health at risk.

(3) Politicians should not legislate medicine. To do so would violate the sanctity and legality of the physician-patient relationship. The right to have an abortion is constitutionally-protected. To falsify scientific evidence in an attempt to deny women that right is unconscionable and dangerous.

The American College of Obstetricians and Gynecology, representing 45,000 ob-gyns, agrees: "The intervention of legislative bodies into medical decision making is inappropriate, ill advised, and dangerous."

The American Medical Women's Association, representing 10,000 female physicians, is opposed to an abortion ban because it "represents a serious impingement on the rights of physicians to determine appropriate medical management for individual patients."...

We know that there is no such technique as "partial birth" abortion, and we believe this legislation is a thinly-veiled attempt to outlaw all abortions. Those supporting this legislation seem to want to confuse both legislators and the public about which abortion procedures are actually used. Since the greatest confusion seems to center around techniques that are used in the second and third trimesters, we will address those: dilation and evacuation (D&E), dilation and extraction (D&X), instillation, hys-terectomy and hysterotomy (commonly known as a c-section).

Dilation and evacuation (D&E) is the standard approach for second-trimester abortions. The only difference between a D&E and a more common, first-trimester vacuum aspiration is the cervix must be further dilated. Morbidity and mortality studies indicate that this surgical method is preferable to labor induction methods (instillation), hysterotomy and hysterectomy.

From the years 1972–76, labor induction procedures carried a maternal mortality rate of 16.5 (note: all numbers listed are out of 100,000); the corresponding rate for D&E was 10.4. From 1977–82, labor induction fell to 6.8, but D&E dropped to 3.3. From 1983–87, induction methods had a 3.5 mortality rate, while D&E fell to 2.9. Although the difference between the methods shrank by the mid-1980s, the use of D&E had already quickly outpaced induction, thus altering the size of the sample.

Morbidity trends indicate that dilation and evacuation is much safer than labor induction procedures, and for women with certain medical conditions, e.g., coronary artery disease or asthma, labor induction can pose serious risks. Rates of major complications from labor induction were more than twice as high as those from D&E. There are instances of women who, after having failed inductions, acquired infections necessitating emergency D&Es, which ultimately saved her fertility and, in some instances, her life. Hysterotomy and hysterectomy, moreover, carry a mortality rate seven times that of induction techniques and ten times that of D&E.

There is a psychological component which makes D&E preferable to labor induction; undergoing difficult, expensive and painful labor for up to two days is extremely emotionally and psychologically draining, much more so than a surgical procedure that can be done in a few hours under general or local anesthesia. Furthermore, labor induction does not always work: Between 15 and 30 percent of cases require surgery to complete the procedure. There is no question that D&E is the safest method of second-trimester abortion.

There is also a technique known as dilation and extraction (D&X). D&X is merely a variant of D&E. There is a dearth of data on D&X as it is an uncommon procedure. However, it is sometimes a physician's preferred method of termination for a number of reasons: it offers a woman the chance to see the intact outcome of a desired pregnancy, thus speeding up the grieving process; it provides a greater chance of acquiring valuable information regarding hereditary illness or fetal anomaly; and there is a decreased risk of injury to the woman, as the procedure is quicker than induction and involves less use of sharp instruments in the uterus, providing a lesser chance of uterine perforations or tears and cervical lacerations.

It is important to note that these procedures are used at varying gestational ages. Neither a D&E nor a D&X is equivalent to a late-term abortion. D&E and D&X are used solely based on the size of the fetus, the health of the woman, and the physician's judgment, and the decision regarding which procedure to use is done on a case-by-case basis. . . .

Because this legislation is so vague, it would outlaw D&E and D&X (and arguably techniques used in the first-trimester). Indeed, the Congressional findings—which go into detail, albeit in non-medical terms—do not remotely correlate with the language of the bill. This legislation is reckless. The outcome of its passage would undoubtedly be countless deaths and irreversible damage to thousands of women and families. We can safely assert that without D&E and D&X, that is, an enactment of S. 3, we will be returning to the days when an unwanted pregnancy led women to death through illegal and unsafe procedures, self-inflicted abortions, uncontrollable infections and suicide.

The cadre of physicians who provide abortions should be honored, not vilified. They are heroes to millions of women, offering the opportunity of choice and freedom. We urge you to consider scientific data rather than partisan rhetoric when voting on such far-reaching public health legislation. We strongly oppose legislation intended to ban so-called "partial birth" abortion.

TESTIMONY OF SENATOR OLYMPIA SNOWE (R-ME) IN OPPOSITION TO S. 3, THE PARTIAL-BIRTH ABORTION BAN ACT OF 2003, OCTOBER 22, 2003

In 1973—26 years ago now—the Supreme Court affirmed for the first time a woman's right to choose. This landmark decision was carefully crafted to be both balanced and responsible while holding the rights of women in America paramount in reproductive decisions. It is clear that the underlying Santorum bill does not hold the rights of women paramount—instead, it infringes on those rights in the most grievous of circumstances.

Indeed, S. 3 undermines basic tenets of *Roe v. Wade*, which maintained that women have a constitutional right to an abortion, but after viability—the time at which it first becomes realistically possible for fetal life to be maintained outside the women's body—States could ban abortions only if they also allowed exceptions for cases in which a woman's life or health is endangered. And the Supreme Court reaffirmed their support for exceptions for health of the mother just 3 years ago.

In *Stenberg vs. Carhart*, a case involving the constitutionality of Nebraska's partial birth abortion ban statute,

the Supreme Court invalidated the Nebraska statute because it lacks an exception for the performance of the D&X dilation and extraction procedure when necessary to protect the health of the mother, and because it imposes an undue burden on a woman's ability to have an abortion. This case was representative of 21 cases throughout the Nation. Regrettably, however, Senator Santorum's legislation disregards both Supreme Court decisions by not providing an exception for the health of the mother and providing only a narrowly defined life exception.

And let there be no mistake I stand here today to reaffirm that no viable fetus should be aborted—by any method—unless it is absolutely necessary to protect the life or health of the mother. Period.

During the Senate consideration of this bill earlier this year, I once again cosponsored Senator Durbin's amendment which specifies that postviability abortions would only be lawful if the physician performing the abortion and an independent physician certified in writing that continuation of the pregnancy would threaten the mother's life or risk grievous injury to her physical health. It mirrors laws already on the books in 41 States, including my home State of Maine, which ban postviability abortions while at the same time including life and health exceptions mandated by the Supreme Court under *Roe v. Wade*.

This amendment, which was tabled during the Senate's debate, would have lowered the number of abortions because it bans all postviability abortions. S. 3, in contrast, will not prevent a single abortion. Sadly, it will force women to choose another, potentially more harmful procedure.

Is this what we really want? To put women's health and lives at risk? And shouldn't these most critical decisions be left to those with medical training—not politicians?

The findings in S. 3 would have you believe that this procedure is never necessary to preserve the life or health of the mother and that in fact it poses significant health risks to a woman. This is simply not true. Let me explain why there must be a health exception for "grievous physical injury" in two circumstances.

First, the language was to apply in those heart-wrenching cases where a wanted pregnancy seriously threatens the health of the mother. The language would allow a doctor in these tragic cases to perform an abortion because he or she believes it is critical to preserving the health of a woman facing: peripartal cardiomyopathy, a form of cardiac failure which is often caused by the pregnancy, which can result in death or untreatable heart disease; pre-eclampsia, or high blood pressure which is caused by a pregnancy, which can result in kidney failure, stroke or death; and uterine ruptures which could result in infertility.

Second, the language also applied when a woman has a life-threatening condition which requires life-saving treatment. It applies to those tragic cases, for example, when a woman needs chemotherapy when pregnant, so the families face the terrible choice of continuing the pregnancy or providing life-saving treatment. These conditions include: breast cancer; lymphoma, which has a 50 percent mortality rate if untreated; and primary pulmonary hypertension, which has a 50 percent maternal mortality rate.

Now, I ask my colleagues, who could seriously object under these circumstances?

I cosponsored this amendment because I believed that it was a commonsense approach to a serious problem for American women and a contentious issue for the United States Congress. Unfortunately, the omission of this or any other exemption from this ban in cases when the life of the mother is threatened poses a significant and likely a constitutional problem, and without such an exception, I could not support this conference report.

IMPORTANT NAMES AND ADDRESSES

Alan Guttmacher Institute
120 Wall St., 21st Fl.
New York, NY 10005
(212) 248-1111
1-800-355-0244
FAX: (212) 248-1951
E-mail: info@guttmacher.org
URL: http://www.agi-usa.org

American Association of University Women (AAUW)
1111 Sixteenth St. NW
Washington, DC 20036
1-800-326-2289
FAX: (202) 872-1425
E-mail: info@aauw.org
URL: http://www.aauw.org

American Civil Liberties Union (ACLU)
125 Broad St., 18th Fl.
New York, NY 10004
(212) 549-2500
1-888-567-2258
E-mail: aclu@aclu.org
URL: http://www.aclu.org

American College of Obstetricians and Gynecologists
409 12th St. SW
P.O. Box 96920
Washington, DC 20090-6920
(202) 638-5577
E-mail: resources@acog.org
URL: http://www.acog.org

American Life League
P.O. Box 1350
Stafford, VA 22555
(540) 659-4171
FAX: (540) 659-2586
URL: http://www.all.org

American Medical Association (AMA)
515 N. State St.
Chicago, IL 60610

1-800-621-8335
URL: http://www.ama-assn.org

Catholics for a Free Choice
1436 U St. NW, Suite 301
Washington, DC 20009-3997
(202) 986-6093
FAX: (202) 332-7995
E-mail: cffc@catholicsforchoice.org
URL: http://www.catholicsforchoice.org

Center for Reproductive Rights
120 Wall St.
New York, NY 10005
(917) 637-3600
FAX: (917) 637-3666
E-mail: info@reprorights.org
URL: http://www.reproductiverights.org

Centers for Disease Control and Prevention (CDC)
Division of Reproductive Health
4770 Buford Hwy. NE, Mail Stop K-20
Atlanta, GA 30341-3717
(770) 488-5200
E-mail: ccdinfo@cdc.gov
URL: http://www.cdc.gov/reproductivehealth/index.htm

Christian Coalition of America
P.O. Box 37030
Washington, DC 20013-7030
(202) 479-6900
FAX: (202) 479-4260
E-mail: Coalition@cc.org
URL: http://www.cc.org

Concerned Women for America
1015 Fifteenth St. NW, Suite 1100
Washington, DC 20005
(202) 488-7000
FAX: (202) 488-0806
URL: http://www.cwfa.org

Family Research Council
801 G Street NW

Washington, DC 20001
(202) 393-2100
FAX: (202) 393-2134
URL: http://www.frc.org

Feminist Majority Foundation
1600 Wilson Blvd., Suite 801
Arlington, VA 22209
(703) 522-2214
FAX: (703) 522-2219
URL: http://www.feminist.org

Henry J. Kaiser Family Foundation
2400 Sand Hill Rd.
Menlo Park, CA 94025
(650) 854-9400
FAX: (650) 854-4800
URL: http://www.kff.org

Human Life International
4 Family Life Ln.
Front Royal, VA 22630
(540) 635-7884
1-800-549-5433
FAX: (540) 622-6247
E-mail: hli@hli.org
URL: http://www.hli.org

Institute of Medicine (National Academy of Sciences)
500 Fifth St. NW
Washington, DC 20001
(202) 334-2352
FAX: (202) 334-1412
E-mail: iomwww@nas.edu
URL: http://www.iom.edu

International Planned Parenthood Federation (IPPF)
4 Newhams Row
London, SE1 3UZ
United Kingdom
44 (0) 20 7939 8200
FAX: 44 (0) 20 7939 8300
E-mail: info@ippf.org
URL: http://www.ippf.org

Medical Students for Choice
P.O. Box 70190
Oakland, CA 94612
(510) 238-5210
FAX: (510) 238-5213
E-mail: msfc@ms4c.org
URL: http://www.ms4c.org

NARAL Pro-Choice America (Formerly National Abortion and Reproductive Rights Action League [NARAL])
1156 15th St. NW, Suite 700
Washington, DC 20005
(202) 973-3000
FAX: (202) 973-3096
URL: http://www.prochoiceamerica.org

National Abortion Federation (NAF)
1755 Massachusetts Ave. NW, Suite 600
Washington, DC 20036
(202) 667-5881
Hotline: 1-800-772-9100
FAX: (202) 667-5890
E-mail: naf@prochoice.org
URL: http://www.prochoice.org

The National Campaign to Prevent Teen Pregnancy
1776 Massachusetts Ave. NW, Suite 200
Washington, DC 20036
(202) 478-8500
FAX: (202) 478-8588
E-mail: campaign@teenpregnancy.org
URL: http://www.teenpregnancy.org

National Center for Health Statistics
Metro IV Building
3311 Toledo Rd.
Hyattsville, MD 20782
(301) 458-4000
1-866-441-6247
E-mail: nchsquery@cdc.gov
URL: http://www.cdc.gov/nchs

National Institutes of Health (NIH)
9000 Rockville Pike
Bethesda, MD 20892
(301) 496-4000
E-mail: nihinfo@od.nih.gov
URL: http://www.nih.gov

National Organization for Women (NOW)
1100 H Street NW, 3rd Floor

Washington, DC 20005
(202) 628-8669
FAX: (202) 785-8576
E-mail: now@now.org
URL: http://www.now.org

National Right to Life Committee
512 10th St. NW
Washington, DC 20004
(202) 626-8800
E-mail: nrlc@nrlc.org
URL: http://www.nrlc.org

National Women's Health Network
514 10th St. NW, Suite 400
Washington, DC 20004
(202) 347-1140
FAX: (202) 347-1168
E-mail: nwhn@nwhn.org
URL: http://www.womenshealthnetwork.org

National Women's Political Caucus
1634 I St. NW, Suite 310
Washington, DC 20006
(202) 785-1100
FAX: (202) 785-3605
E-mail: info@nwpc.org
URL: http://www.nwpc.org

Planned Parenthood Federation of America, Inc.
434 W. 33rd St.
New York, NY 10001
(212) 541-7800
1-800-230-7526
FAX: (212) 245-1845
E-mail: communications@ppfa.org
URL: http://www.plannedparenthood.org

Population Action International
1300 19th St. NW, 2nd Fl.
Washington, DC 20036
(202) 557-3400
FAX: (202) 728-4177
E-mail: pai@popact.org
URL: http://www.populationaction.org

Population Council
1 Dag Hammarskjold Plaza
New York, NY 10017
(212) 339-0500
FAX: (212) 755-6052

E-mail: pubinfo@popcouncil.org
URL: http://www.popcouncil.org

Population Reference Bureau
1875 Connecticut Ave. NW, Suite 520
Washington, DC 20009-5728
(202) 483-1100
FAX: (202) 328-3937
1-800-877-9881
E-mail: popref@prb.org
URL: http://www.prb.org

Pro-Life Action Ministries
P.O. Box 75368
St. Paul, MN 55175-0368
(651) 771-1500
URL: http://www.plam.org

The Religious Coalition for Reproductive Choice
1025 Vermont Ave. NW, Suite 1130
Washington, DC 20005
(202) 628-7700
FAX: (202) 628-7716
E-mail: info@rcrc.org
URL: http://www.rcrc.org

United Nations Population Fund (UNFPA)
220 E. 42nd St.
New York, NY 10017
(212) 297-5000
URL: http://www.unfpa.org

United States Conference of Catholic Bishops
Committee for Pro-Life Activities
3211 4th St. NE
Washington, DC 20017-1194
(202) 541-3070
URL: http://www.nccbuscc.org/prolife

World Health Organization (WHO)
Regional Office for the Americas
525 23rd St. NW
Washington, DC 20037
(202) 974-3000
FAX: (202) 974-3663
E-mail: postmaster@paho.org
URL: http://www.who.int/en/
URL: http://www.paho.org

RESOURCES

Two major sources of abortion statistics are available in the United States—the Centers for Disease Control and Prevention (CDC) in Atlanta, Georgia, and the Alan Guttmacher Institute (AGI) in New York. The CDC annually publishes its "Abortion Surveillance." The most current information on abortion data from the CDC used in the preparation of this book was "Abortion Surveillance—United States, 2001" (*Morbidity and Mortality Weekly Report, Surveillance Summaries*, vol. 53, no. SS-09, November 26, 2004).

The CDC also published "Births: Preliminary Data for 2003," *National Vital Statistics Reports*, National Center for Health Statistics, vol. 53, no. 9, November 23, 2004; "Births: Final Data for 2002," *National Vital Statistics Reports*, National Center for Health Statistics, vol. 52, no. 10, December 17, 2003; "Estimated Pregnancy Rates for the United States, 1990–2000: An Update," *National Vital Statistics Reports*, vol. 52, no. 23, June 15, 2004; "Teenage Births in the United States: State Trends, 1991–2000, an Update," *National Vital Statistics Reports*, National Center for Health Statistics, vol. 50, no. 9, May 30, 2002; "QuickStats: Pregnancy, Birth, and Abortion Rates for Teenagers Aged 15–17 Years—United States, 1976–2003," *Morbidity and Mortality Weekly Report*, vol. 54, no. 4, National Center for Health Statistics, February 4, 2005; "Trends in Sexual Risk Behaviors among High School Students—United States, 1991–2001," *Morbidity and Mortality Weekly Report*, vol. 51, no. 38, September 27, 2002; "Youth Risk Behavior Surveillance—United States, 2003," *Morbidity and Mortality Weekly Report*, vol. 53, no. SS-2, May 21, 2004; and "Assisted Reproductive Technology Surveillance, United States, 2002," *Morbidity and Mortality Weekly Report Surveillance Summaries*, vol. 54, no. SS02, June 3, 2005.

Other government publications used in this book include "Funding History FY 1971–2005," U.S. Department of Health and Human Services, Office of Popula-tion Affairs, Office of Family Planning; and "Fertility of American Women: June 2002, Population Characteristics," in *Current Population Reports*, U.S. Census Bureau, U.S. Department of Commerce, Economics and Statistics Administration, October 2003.

The AGI, which strongly supports abortion as an option, is the major nongovernment source of abortion statistics in the world. The AGI publishes the results of its abortion surveys in its bimonthly journal, *Family Planning Perspectives*, a primary resource for any study of abortion, family planning, and pregnancy. One of the *Family Planning Perspectives* articles used in this publication was "Abortion Training in U.S. Obstetrics and Gynecology Residency Programs, 1998," by Rene Almeling, Laureen Tews, and Susan Didley (vol. 32, no. 6, November/December 2000).

The AGI publishes many reports and fact sheets on family planning issues. Among the AGI publications that provided helpful information were "Induced Abortion in the United States: Facts in Brief," May 18, 2005; *Teenage Sexual and Reproductive Behavior in Developed Countries: Can More Progress Be Made?* by Jacqueline E. Darroch, Jennifer Frost, and Susheela Singh, 2001; *Public Funding for Contraceptive, Sterilization and Abortion Services, FY 1980–2001: National and State Tables and Figures*, by Adam Sonfield and Rachel Benson Gold, 2005; and *Estimates of U.S. Abortion Incidence in 2001 and 2002*, by Lawrence B. Finer and Stanley K. Henshaw, May 18, 2005.

The Guttmacher Report on Public Policy, a bimonthly review by AGI's policy analysts, furnished current information on the political aspects of abortion. The AGI public policy reports used in this volume include: "Countries with Dedicated Products Approved for Emergency Contraception," in "Emergency Contraception: The Need to Increase Public Awareness," by Heather Boonstra, October 2002; "Special Analysis: Contraceptive

Use Is Key to Reducing Abortion Worldwide," by Amy Deschner and Susan A. Cohen, October 2003; and "Issues & Implications: Voicing Concern for Women, Abortion Foes Seek Limits on Availability of Mifepristone," Heather Boonstra, April, 2001.

The AGI also publishes a quarterly journal, *International Family Planning Perspectives*, with articles on family planning, contraception, and abortion around the world. Articles used in this publication include "Knowledge and Opinions about Abortion Law among Mexican Youth," by Davida Becker, Sandra G. Garcia, and Ulla Larsen (vol. 28, no. 4, December 2002); and "The Incidence of Abortion Worldwide," by Stanley K. Henshaw, Susheela Singh, and Taylor Haas (vol. 25 [supplement], 1999).

Additional information on international abortion statistics was provided by the World Health Organization (WHO) in *Unsafe Abortion: Global and Regional Estimates of the Incidence of Unsafe Abortion and Associated Mortality in 2000*, 4th ed., 2004. *The Anti-Abortion Law in Poland: The Functioning, Social Effects, Attitudes, and Behaviors*, edited by Wanda Nowicka (September 2000), which is published by the Polish Federation for Women and Family Planning, provided information on abortion in Poland. The Population Reference Bureau provided "Total Fertility Rates in Different World Regions" (2001). Charles F. Westhoff and ORC Macro collected information on abortion in Russia (DHS Analytical Studies #1, *The Substitution of Contraception for Abortion in Kazakhstan in the 1990s*, Calverton, MD, 2001). Victoria A. Velkoff and Arjun Adlakha of the International Programs Center of the Bureau of the Census provided information on Indian women in "Women's Health in India" (Washington, DC, 1998).

The National Abortion Federation (NAF), a national association of abortion providers and a strong abortion advocate, tabulates statistics on incidents of violence against abortion providers. NAF publishes a wide range of consumer education materials on abortion and operates a nationwide toll-free consumer hotline to answer questions and make referrals to qualified abortion providers throughout the United States and Canada. "NAF Violence and Disruption Statistics: Incidents of Violence & Disruption against Abortion Providers in the U.S. & Canada" (Washington, DC, July 2005) was particularly helpful.

NARAL Pro-Choice America (formerly National Abortion and Reproductive Rights Action League), also an abortion advocate, publishes information on the status of abortion in the individual states in "Who Decides? A State-by-State Review of Abortion and Reproductive Rights," 14th ed. (Washington, DC, 2004). The National Campaign to Prevent Teen Pregnancy provides a wealth of information on teen pregnancy, including "Teen Sexual Activity, Pregnancy and Childbearing among Latinos in the United States" (*Fact Sheet*, August 2003) and *Just the Facts: Data on Teen Pregnancy, Childbearing, Sexual Activity, and Contraceptive Use* (April 2004).

Louis Harris and Associates Inc. (New York) and the Gallup Organization Inc. (New Jersey) publish surveys on American attitudes toward abortion, as do various news media. The Henry J. Kaiser Family Foundation (California) also provides information on abortion in several publications, including "National Survey of Adolescents and Young Adults: Sexual Health Knowledge, Attitudes and Experiences" (2003) and "National Surveys of Women's Health Care Providers and the Public: Views and Practices on Medical Abortion" (September 2001).

INDEX

Page references in italics refer to photographs. References with the letter t *following them indicate the presence of a table. The letter* f *indicates a figure. If more than one table or figure appears on a particular page, the exact item number for the table or figure being referenced is provided.*

A

AAFP (American Academy of Family Physicians), 46–48

ABC News/*Washington Post* poll, 111, 112, 113

Abortion

abortion providers, availability of, 43, 46–48

abortion providers and percentage of counties/women without an abortion provider, by state, 55*t*

abortion ratio, by age group of women who obtained legal abortion, selected years, 46*f*

abortion ratio, by age group of women who obtained legal abortion, selected states, 43*f*

abortion ratio, by age group of women who obtained legal abortion, state of occurrence, 44*t*–45*t*

American experience, 6–7

in ancient times, 1–2

ART outcomes, by procedure type, 93*t*

attitudes about, 7

British tradition, 5

characteristics of women seeking, 38–40

characteristics of women who obtained legal abortions, 41*t*

Child Interstate Abortion Notification Act, 115–122

Christian position on, 2–4

collection of abortion data, 37

cost of, 48–50

deaths, number of, and fatality rates for abortion-related deaths reported to CDC, by type of abortion, 58*t*

definition of, 1

ethical questions, 89–92, 94

fertility indicators, by age, race, Hispanic origin, 49*t*

fetal rights, 94

genetic testing and, 92

health and, 87–89

Islamic position on, 4

Jewish position on, 4

legal abortions, by demographic characteristics, selected states, 42*t*

legal abortions, by ethnicity of women, state of occurrence, selected states, 48*t*

legal abortions, by length of gestation, demographic characteristics of women who obtained abortions, 57*t*

legal abortions, by number of previous abortions, 51*t*

legal abortions, by race of women, 47*t*

location of, 42

methods of, 2*t*, 50–53

mifepristone, percent of physicians surveyed who provide or will likely provide it in coming year, 59*f*

mifepristone, percent of physicians surveyed who say they are familiar with, 58*f*

multiple births and, 92, 94

number of abortions, 37–38

number of abortions, selected years, 40*f*

number, ratio, rate of legal abortions, 39*t*

number, ratio, rate of legal abortions, by state, percentage of legal abortions obtained by out-of-state residents, 52*t*–53*t*

number, ratio, rate of legal abortions performed, selected years, 38*f*

Partial-Birth Abortion Ban Act, statements against, 141–147

Partial-Birth Abortion Ban Act, support of, 135–140

percentage distribution of obstetrics, gynecology residency programs, by availability of first-trimester abortion training, 56*t*

percentage distribution of women obtaining abortions, by contraceptive method used in month of conception, 50*t*

practices among physicians surveyed, 60*f*

public opinion about, 109–113, 110*f*

reasons for, 40

Roe v. Wade, reconsideration of, 123–128

Roe v. Wade, testimony on upholding, 129–133

stem cell research and, 90–91

teen pregnancy outcomes, 64

time of performance, 50

timing of abortions, 56*f*

timing, percentage of women who obtained early/late abortions, by age group, selected states, 42*f*

waiting periods, mandatory state, and biased counseling for abortion, 54*f*

women speak out, 7–8

"Abortion a More Powerful Issue for Women" (Pew Research Center), 113

Abortion Act of 1967, 5

"Abortion among Adolescents" (Adler, Ozer, and Tschann), 78

"Abortion and Its Health Effects" (David and Lee), 88

Abortion and Sterilization Act (South Africa), 105

Abortion bans

state, 14*t*

states with, 13

See also Partial-Birth Abortion Ban Act

Abortion clinics

abortion clinic violence, by state, 84*f*

abortion counseling by, 12–13
abortions performed in, 40
actions against, 82, 84
family planning funding through Title X, 27, 29–31
Freedom of Access to Clinic Entrances Act, 84–86
incidents of violence/disruption against abortion providers in U.S. and Canada, 83t
protesters at, court cases on, 17–18
quality of abortion services, 81–82
violent incidents at, 130
"Abortion Clinics: Information on the Effectiveness of the Freedom of Access to Clinic Entrances Act" (Government Accountability Office), 85
Abortion Control Act, 19–20
"Abortion in Context: United States and Worldwide: Issues in Brief" (Alan Guttmacher Institute), 101, 104
"Abortion Incidence and Services in the United States in 2000" (Henshaw and Finer), 43
"Abortion, Informed Consent, and Mental Health" (Russo and Rubin), 88
Abortion laws
 abortion law worldwide, 33f
 abortion rates and, 100
 of China, 102–103
 countries changing their abortion laws since initial imposition of "Global Gag Rule," 33t
 levels of abortion restriction worldwide, 97f
 of Mexico, 104
 of Poland, 100–101
 of Russia, 102
 worldwide, 95, 97–98
 See also Legislation and international treaties
Abortion politics
 abortion law worldwide, 33f
 anti-choice legislation considered by states, 24f
 choice positions, 21
 choice positions of state governments, 25f
 choice positions of state governors, 26f
 choice positions of state legislatures, 27f
 family planning, contraception, funding for, 27, 29–31
 family planning, contraception, international U.S. aid for, 31–33
 federal funding and abortion, 21, 23–24
 funding for Office of Family Planning, 32t
 "Global Gag Rule," countries changing their abortion laws since initial imposition of, 33t
 low-income women's access to abortion, 28t

military personnel, abortion services for, 26–27
percentage of births to unmarried women, by state and territory, 35t
positions of state Democratic, Republican parties on woman's right to choose abortion, 22t
public funding for abortion services, 29t–30t
state anti-choice legislation, 23f
state funding and abortion, 24–26
Unborn Victims of Violence Act, 34
welfare reform and, 33–34
Abortion providers
 availability of, 43, 46–48
 number of, and percentage of counties/women without an abortion provider, 55t
 percentage distribution of obstetrics, gynecology residency programs, by availability of first-trimester abortion training, 56t
 quality of abortion services, 81–82
 See also Abortion clinics; Physicians
Abortion rate
 number of abortions, selected years, 40f
 number of legal/illegal induced abortions worldwide, 98t
 number of reported abortions, abortion rate, abortion ratio, 78t
 number, ratio, rate of legal abortions, 39t
 number, ratio, rate of legal abortions performed, selected years, 38f
 pregnancy, birth, abortion rates for teens, 77f
 pregnancy rate, birth rates, abortion rates among teenagers in U.S., other developed countries, 62 (f5.2)
 of Romania, 101, 102
 of Russia, 102
 in Sweden, England and Wales, and France, 107f
 of teens, 61, 71–72
 trends in, 37–38
 worldwide statistics comparison, 98–100
 worldwide, various years by country, 100t
Abortion ratio
 by age group of women, 39–40
 by age group of women who obtained legal abortion, 2001, 78f
 by age group of women who obtained legal abortion, selected years, 46f
 by age group of women who obtained legal abortion, selected states, 43f
 by age group of women who obtained legal abortion, state of occurrence, 44t–45t

of Mexico, 104
number of legal/illegal induced abortions worldwide, 98t
number of reported abortions, abortion rate, abortion ratio, 78t
number, ratio, rate of legal abortions, 39t
number, ratio, rate of legal abortions performed, selected years, 38f
of Russia, 102
of teens, 73–74
trends in, 37
"Abortion Services and Military Medical Facilities" (University of Maryland School of Law, Thurgood Marshall Law Library), 26–27
"Abortion Surveillance—United States, 2001" (Centers for Disease Control and Prevention)
 abortion timing, 1
 number of abortions, 16, 37–38
 on teen abortion, 72
 women seeking abortion, characteristics of, 38–40
Abortion, teenage
 abortion rates, 71–72
 abortion ratio, by age group of women who obtained legal abortion, 2001, 78f
 abortion ratios, 72–73
 abortions by race/ethnicity, 72
 factors that affect pregnancy and, 74–75
 induced abortion rates by age, race, Hispanic origin, 77t
 knowledge about abortion, 75–77
 number of reported abortions, abortion rate, abortion ratio, 78t
 pregnancy, birth, abortion rates for teens, 77f
 relinquishment for adoption, 74
 state restrictions on minors' access to abortion, 79t
"Abortion Training in U.S. Obstetrics and Gynecology Residency Programs, 1998" (Almeling, Tews, and Dudley), 43, 46
Abortion, U.S. Supreme Court decisions
 abortion cases, chronology of major, 10t–11t
 abortion clinics, protesters at, 17–18
 Doe v. Bolton, 12
 fetus rulings, 18–19
 government support/nonsupport of abortion, 12–13
 judicial appointments, politics, 9
 Roe v. Wade, 9, 11, 19–20
 state abortion bans, 14t
 state restrictions on abortion, 13, 15–17
Abortion worldwide
 abortion rates in Sweden, England and Wales, and France, 107f

abortion rates worldwide, various years by country, 100t
in China, 102–103
cross-border abortions, 106
deaths from abortion, 106–107
in India, 103
in Ireland, 102
in Latin America, 103–104
laws, 95, 97–98
levels of abortion restriction worldwide, 97f
measures of legal abortion worldwide, by completeness of data, country, and data year, 99t
Mexican states allowing abortion in various circumstances, and support for legal abortion in each circumstance, 106 (t8.6)
Mexican youth, knowledge, opinions about emergency contraception/abortion among, 105t
mifepristone, countries that have approved use of, 106 (t8.7)
number of legal/illegal induced abortions worldwide, 98t
in Poland, 100–101
Programme of Action, 107–108
in Romania, 101–102
in Russia, 102
in South Africa, 104–106
statistics, comparison of, 98–100
statistics on, 95
unsafe abortion, estimates of annual incidence of, mortality due to unsafe abortion, 108t
world abortion laws, 96t
Abstinence
effective sex education programs, 68
for teen pregnancy prevention, 65
teen pregnancy rate decline and, 62–63
Abstinence-only education, 68
Abstinence-plus education, 68
"Abstinence Promotion and Teen Family Planning: The Misguided Drive for Equal Funding" (Dailard), 67
Accreditation Council for Graduate Medical Education (ACGME), 46
ACLU (American Civil Liberties Union)
on mifepristone, 53
Partial-Birth Abortion Ban Act and, 135
"ACLU Hails FDA Approval of Safe, Early-Option Abortion Pill" (American Civil Liberties Union), 53
ACOG (American College of Obstetricians and Gynecologists), 137, 145
Addresses/names, organization, 149–150
Adler, Nancy E.
"Abortion among Adolescents," 78
on post-abortion stress syndrome, 88

"Adolescent Knowledge and Attitudes about Abortion" (Stone and Waszak), 75–77
Adolescents
age of women seeking abortion, 39
family planning services for, 30
welfare reform and abortion, 33
See also Abortion, teenage; Teenage pregnancy; Teenagers
Adoption, 74
"Adoption, Adoption Seeking, and Relinquishment for Adoption in the United States" (Centers for Disease Control and Prevention), 74
Advance Data from Vital and Health Statistics (Centers for Disease Control and Prevention), 74
Advice and Consent: The Politics of Judicial Appointments (Segal and Epstein), 9
Advocates for Life Ministries, 85–86
AFDC (Aid to Families with Dependent Children), 33
Africa
abortion statistics of, 98
birth rates, 107–108
Age
abortion ratio, by age group of women who obtained legal abortion, 2001, 78f
abortion ratio, by age group of women who obtained legal abortion, selected years, 46f
abortion ratio by age group of women who obtained legal abortion, selected states, 43f
abortion ratio, by age group of women who obtained legal abortion, state of occurrence, 44t–45t
abortion stance and, 112
fertility indicators, by age, race, Hispanic origin, 49t
number of abortions, selected years, 40f
percentage of women who obtained early or late abortions, by age group, selected states, 42f
teen pregnancy rate and, 62
teen pregnancy rates, by age group, 63f
of women seeking abortion, 38–40
Agency for International Development, Planned Parenthood Federation of America v., 32
AGI. See Alan Guttmacher Institute
Aid, foreign, 31–33
Aid to Families with Dependent Children (AFDC), 33
Akron Center for Reproductive Health, Akron v., 15–16
Akron Center for Reproductive Health, Ohio v., 15
Akron (OH), 15–16
Akron v. Akron Center for Reproductive Health, 15–16

Alan Guttmacher Institute (AGI)
abortion data collection by, 37
on abortion in Latin America, 104
on availability of abortion providers, 43
cost of abortion, 48–50
family planning funding through Title X, 27, 29
number of abortions, 38
on reasons for abortion, 40
Romania's abortion-related mortality, 101
on sex education, 67
"Sexuality Education: Facts in Brief," 65
"State Facts about Abortion," 21
on state funding and abortion, 25–26
on teen pregnancy/abortion, factors that affect, 74–75
on teen pregnancy rates, 61–62
worldwide abortion data collection, 95
worldwide abortion statistics comparison, 98–100
Alaska, abortion laws in, 7, 8
Alexandria Women's Health Clinic, Bray v., 17–18
Allocution to Midwives (Pope Pius XII), 3
Almeling, Rene, 43, 46
"An Almost Absolute Value in History" (Noonan), 2–3
AMA. See American Medical Association
American Academy of Family Physicians (AAFP), 46–48
American Academy of Pediatrics, 120
American Bar Association, 7
American Civil Liberties Union (ACLU)
on mifepristone, 53
Partial-Birth Abortion Ban Act and, 135
American Coalition of Life Activists, 85–86
American College of Obstetricians and Gynecologists (ACOG), 137, 145
American Indians and Alaska Natives, 70
American Journal of Public Health, 101
American Law Institute, 7
American Medical Association (AMA)
abortion in nineteenth century and, 6
attack of "gag rule," 31
liberalization of abortion laws, 7
American Medical Women's Association (AMWA), 143, 145
American Psychological Association (APA), 88
American Psychologist, 78
American Public Health Association (APHA), 143
American Religious Identification Survey (Graduate Center of the City University of New York), 2, 4
American Society for Reproductive Medicine (ASRM), 91–92

Amniocentesis
 ban of saline, 125
 gender selection and, 91
AMWA (American Medical Women's
  Association), 143, 145
Ancient times, abortion in, 1–2
Anencephaly, 92
Angelo, E. Joanne, 89
Anti-choice legislation
 considered by states, 24f
 number of measures, 21
 state anti-choice legislation, 23f
Antiabortion laws, 6–7
APA (American Psychological
  Association), 88
Apartheid, 104
APHA (American Public Health
  Association), 143
Apostolicae Sedis (Pope Pius IX), 3
Aquinas, St. Thomas, 3
Archer, William, 31
Aristotle, 1
Arizona State Supreme Court, 7
Arson-related fires, in abortion
  clinics, 82
ART (assisted reproductive technology)
 methods of, 92
 outcomes of assisted reproductive
   technology, by procedure type,
   93t
Ashcroft, Carhart v., 141–142
Ashcroft, John, 141–142
*Ashcroft, Planned Parenthood
  Assn. v.*, 16
Asia, abortion statistics of, 98
Asian and Pacific Islander Americans
 fertility rate for, 40
 teen birth rates, 70
ASRM (American Society for
  Reproductive Medicine), 91–92
Assisted reproductive technology (ART)
 methods of, 92
 outcomes of assisted reproductive
   technology, by procedure type,
   93t
"Assisted Reproductive Technology
  Surveillance—United States, 2002"
  (Centers for Disease Control and
  Prevention), 92
Augustine, St., 3
Australia, abortion rate of, 100

B

"Background Information on Key
  International Agreements" (United
  Nations Population Fund), 107
Baird, Bellotti v., 13
Balanced Budget Act, 25
Bangladesh, abortion rate of, 100
Barrett, J. Gresham, 116
BBC Monitoring Service, 101

Beal v. Doe, 12
Becker, David, 104
Beckman, Linda J., 81–82
Belarus, abortion rate of, 99
Belgium, abortion rate of, 99
Bellotti v. Baird, 13
Benedict XVI, Pope, 3
Benjamin, George C., 143
BET (Black Entertainment
  Television), 70
Biased counseling, 42, 54f
Birth control
 abortion rate decrease and, 38
 abstinence education and, 66
 for teen pregnancy prevention, 65
 teen pregnancy rate and, 61
Birth defects
 reasons for abortion, 7
 screening for, 92
Birth rate
 contraception and, 107–108
 induced abortion rates by age, race,
   Hispanic origin, 77t
 per 1,000 girls age 15–19 by racial/
   ethnic group, 74f
 pregnancy, birth, abortion rates for
   teens, 77f
 pregnancy rate, birth rates, abortion
   rates among teenagers in U.S.,
   other developed countries, 62
   (f5.2)
 of Romania, 101
 teen, 70–71, 72
 teen birth rates, 75t
 teen, U.S., 61–62
 teenage birth rates in U.S., other
   developed countries, 72f
 for teenagers, percent decline in, 76f
 for women under age 20, 73 (t5.3)
Births
 with assisted reproductive technology,
   92
 percentage of births to unmarried
   women, by state and territory, 35t
 See also Nonmarital births
"Births to Teenagers in the United States,
  1940–2000" (Centers for Disease
  Control and Prevention), 70
Black/African Americans
 abortion ratio for, 40
 teen birth rates, 70, 71
 teen pregnancy rate for, 62
Black Entertainment Television (BET), 70
Blackmun, Harry
 *Planned Parenthood of Southeastern
   Pennsylvania v. Casey*, 20
 on *Roe v. Wade*, 125
 Rust v. Sullivan statement, 13
 Webster v. Reproductive Health Services
   statement, 19
Blackstone, William, 5

Bolton, Doe v., 12, 123
Bombings, of abortion clinics, 82
Bone marrow stem cells, 91
Boonstra, Heather, 106
Bourne, Aleck, 5
Bourne, Rex v., 5
Boxer, Barbara
 Global Gag Rule and, 33
 letters about Partial-Birth Abortion
   Ban Act, 143–146
 on Partial-Birth Abortion Ban Act,
   129, 142–143
Bracton, Henry de, 5
Bradshaw, Zoe, 88–89
Bray v. Alexandria Women's Health Clinic,
  17–18
Breyer, Stephen, 17
Burke, Edmund, 128
Bush, George H. W.
 fetal tissue research and, 90
 "gag rule," 31
 overturning of Comstock Law, 7
Bush, George W.
 abortion policy of, public opinion on,
   111
 Mexico City Policy reinstated by, 32
 Partial-Birth Abortion Ban Act and,
   135
 Partial-Birth Abortion Ban Act signed
   by, 17, 112
 stem cell research and, 90–91
 Title X funding and, 31
 U.S. funds for family planning and, 33
Butyric acid attacks, 82

C

Cain, Joanna M., 141
California
 abortion clinic incidents in, 82, 130
 abortion laws in, 7
 abortion rates in, 42
 Partial-Birth Abortion Ban Act
   lawsuit in, 17
 voters as pro-choice, 129
California Women's Board of Terms and
  Parole, 129
"Call to Action to Promote Sexual Health
  and Responsible Sexual Behavior"
  (Satcher), 67
Calvin, Steve, 125–126
"Can More Progress Be Made? Teenage
  Sexual and Reproductive Behavior in
  Developed Countries" (Alan
  Guttmacher Institute), 61
Carhart, Stenberg v.
 Partial-Birth Abortion Ban Act and,
   139, 143, 146
 ruling on, 16–17
Carhart v. Ashcroft, 141–142
Carhart v. Gonzalez, 141

Carter, Jimmy, 30

Casey, Planned Parenthood of Southeastern Pennsylvania v., 19–20, 124

Casey, Robert, 19–20

Catholics, 112

See also Roman Catholic Church

CDC. *See* Centers for Disease Control and Prevention

Ceausescu, Nicolae, 101

Center for Population Options, 75–77

Center for Reproductive Rights

on abortion in Latin America, 104

on abortion limitations, 97

on worldwide abortion laws, 95, 97

Centers for Disease Control and Prevention (CDC)

abortion data collection by, 37

on abortion methods, 50

on abortion timing, 1

assisted reproductive technology, 92

federal funding for abortion, 23

number of abortions, 16, 37–38

pregnancies ending in abortion, 64

sexual risk behaviors of teens, 70

teen abortion, 72

teen birth rates, 70–71

teen relinquishment for adoption, 74

women seeking abortion, characteristics of, 38–40

Central Intelligence Agency, 103

Chabot, Steve, 136, 138–139

Channel One News, 70

Chemotherapy, 147

Chenoweth, Helen, 127

Child Custody Protection Act, 115

Child Interstate Abortion Notification Act (CIANA)

opposition to, 119–122

support of, 115–118

Childbirth, death from, 88

Children. *See* Minors; Teenagers

China

abortion in, 100, 102–103

UNFPA funding cut for, 32

CHIP (State Children's Health Insurance Program), 25

"Choice of and Satisfaction with Methods of Medical and Surgical Abortion among U.S. Clinic Patients" (Harvey, Beckman, and Satre), 81–82

Choice of Termination of Pregnancy Act, 105–106

Choice of Termination of Pregnancy Amendment Bill, 106

Choice positions

choice positions of state legislatures, 27f

of state Democratic, Republican parties on woman's right to choose abortion, 22t

of state governments, 21, 25f

of state governors, 26f

See also Pro-choice groups; Pro-life groups

Christianity, position on abortion, 2–4

Chukwu octuplets, 92, 94

CIANA (Child Interstate Abortion Notification Act)

opposition to, 119–122

support of, 115–118

Circuit Courts of Appeals, 9

Clark, Leslie F., 69

Clinic blockades, 84

Clinical Policy Guidelines (National Abortion Federation), 81

Clinics. *See* Abortion clinics

Clinton, Bill

abortion provision in act signed by, 25

abortion services for military personnel and, 27

fetal tissue research and, 90

Global Gag Rule and, 32

Mexico City Policy and, 111

Partial-Birth Abortion Ban Act vetoed by, 17, 135, 138, 139

repeal of "gag rule," 31

welfare reform and, 33

Code of Assyria, 1

Code of Canon Law, 3

Coke, Edward, 5

Colautti v. Franklin, 18–19, 125

Collett, Teresa Stanton, 117–118

Colorado, abortion laws in, 7

Colorado, Hill v., 18

Commentaries on the Laws of England (Blackstone), 5

"Commentary: The Public Health Consequences of Restricted Induced Abortion Lessons from Romania" (Stephenson et al.), 101

Comstock, Anthony, 6

Comstock Law, 6–7

Conception, life beginning at, 109

Condoms

abortion rates and, 38

media influences on teen sex, 69

in sex education program, 68

teen condom use, 70

teen pregnancy rate and, 62

use prior to pregnancy, 40

Confidentiality, 30

Connecticut, abortion law of, 6

Connecticut, Griswold v., 131

Connecticut v. Menillo, 15, 125

Connecticut Welfare Department, 12

"Conscious procreation," 101

Consent. *See* Parental consent

Conservative Judaism, position on abortion, 4

Consortium on National Consensus for Medical Abortion in India, 103

Constitution Tribunal (Poland), 101

Contraception

abortion rate decrease and, 38

birth rates and, 107–108

in China, 102–103

Comstock Law and, 6–7

funding through Title X, 27, 29–31

in Latin America, 104

Mexican youth, knowledge, opinions about emergency contraception/abortion among, 105t

percentage distribution of women obtaining abortions, by contraceptive method used in month of conception, 50t

in Poland, 100, 101

in Romania, 101

in Russia, 102

teen condom use, 70

teen pregnancy rate and, 61, 62, 63

U.S. aid for family planning, contraception, 31–33

use prior to pregnancy, 40

"Contraceptive Use among U.S. Women Having Abortions in 2000–2001" (Jones, Darroch, and Henshaw), 40

Cook, Curtis, 139–140

Copelon, Rhonda, 132–133

Cost, of abortion, 48–50

Council of Vienne, 3

Court cases

abortion cases, chronology of major, 10t–11t

Akron v. Akron Center for Reproductive Health, 15–16

Beal v. Doe, 12

Bellotti v. Baird, 13

Bray v. Alexandria Women's Health Clinic, 17–18

Carhart v. Ashcroft, 141–142

Carhart v. Gonzalez, 141

Colautti v. Franklin, 18–19, 125

Connecticut v. Menillo, 15, 125

Doe v. Bolton, 12, 123

Dred Scott v. Sandford, 123

Griswold v. Connecticut, 131

H. L. v. Matheson, 13, 15

Harris v. McRae, 12

Hill v. Colorado, 18

Hodgson v. Minnesota, 15

Madsen v. Women's Health Center, 18

Maher v. Roe, 12

Miller v. Zbaraz, 12

NOW v. Scheidler, 18

Ohio v. Akron Center for Reproductive Health, 15

Planned Parenthood Assn. v. Ashcroft, 16

Planned Parenthood Association of Utah v. Matheson, 30

Planned Parenthood Federation of America v. Agency for International Development, 32

Planned Parenthood of Central Missouri v. Danforth, 13, 125

Planned Parenthood of Northern New England, et al. . . . v. Peter Heed, Attorney General of the State of New Hampshire, 15

Planned Parenthood of Southeastern Pennsylvania v. Casey, 19–20, 124

Poelker v. Doe, 12

Rex v. Bourne, 5

Roe v. Wade, 8, 9, 11

Roe v. Wade, Protestantism and, 4

Roe v. Wade, reconsideration of, 123–128

Roe v. Wade, testimony on upholding, 129–133

Rust v. Sullivan, 12–13, 31

Schenck, et al., v. Pro-Choice Network of Western New York, et al., 18

state restrictions on abortion, 13, 15–17

Stenberg v. Carhart, 16–17, 139, 143, 146

United States v. Zbaraz, 12

Webster v. Reproductive Health Services, 19

Williams v. Zbaraz, 12

Crafting an Abortion Law That Respects Women's Rights: Issues to Consider (Center for Reproductive Rights), 97

Cross-border abortions, 106

Cuba, abortion rate of, 99

Curettage, 50

D

Dailard, Cynthia, 67

Danforth, Planned Parenthood of Central Missouri v., 13, 125

Darney, Phillip D., 141

Darroch, Jacqueline E.

on contraceptive use, 40

on teen pregnancy rates, 61–62

DaVanzo, Julie, 102

David, Henry P., 88

De Legibus Angliae (Bracton), 5

Death threats, to abortion providers, 82

Deaths

from abortion, 50–51, 88

from abortion in Latin America, 104

from abortion in Romania, 101

from abortion, worldwide, 106–107

of Indian women from abortion, 103

number of, and fatality rates for abortion-related deaths reported to CDC, by type of abortion, 58t

pregnancy-related *vs.* abortion, 78

Dellinger, Walter, 131

Democratic Left Alliance, 101

Democratic Party

abortion stance and, 112

choice positions of state Democratic, Republican parties on woman's right to choose abortion, 22t

Department of Defense (DOD), 26–27

Department of Health, Education, and Welfare (HEW), 21, 23

See also U.S. Department of Health and Human Services

Departments of Labor and Health and Human Services, and Education, and Related Agencies Appropriations Act, 25

Departments of Labor and Health, Education, and Welfare Appropriations Act, 23

Didache (*Teachings of the Lord through the Apostles* or *The Doctrine of the Twelve Apostles*), 2

Dire Demographics: Populations Trends in the Russian Federation (DaVanzo and Grammich), 102

Diseases, prenatal testing for, 92

District Courts, 9

Doctor–patient relationship, 31

DOD (Department of Defense), 26–27

Doe, Beal v., 12

Doe, Poelker v., 12

Doe v. Bolton, 12, 123

Down syndrome, 92

Drazen, Jeffrey M., 91

Dred Scott v. Sandford, 123

Drugs

sale of in nineteenth century U.S., 6

thalidomide, 7

See also Mifepristone

Dudley, Susan

on abortion medical training, 43, 46

"Safety of Abortion," 88

Due process

Roe v. Wade and, 11, 123, 124

Roe v. Wade support and, 131

E

Early-abortion pill. *See* Mifepristone

East, John P., 127–128

Eastern Orthodox Church, 2, 4

Echevarria, Laura, 52

Eclampsia, 144

Education

abortion stance and, 112

abstinence education, 65–67

teen pregnancy/abortion and, 74

"The Effects of Induced Abortion on Emotional Experiences and Relationships: A Critical Review of the Literature" (Bradshaw and Slade), 88–89

Embryo

Roe v. Wade support and, 131

stem cell research, 90–91

in vitro fertilization, 90

"Emerging Answers—Research Findings on Programs to Reduce Teen Pregnancy" (National Campaign to Prevent Teen Pregnancy), 63

"The Emotional Effects of Induced Abortion" (Planned Parenthood Federation of America), 88

Emotions, 88–89

Encyclopedia of Women and Gender (Worrell), 88

England

abortion rates in Sweden, England and Wales, and France, 107f

abortion tradition of, 5

English common law, 5

Ensoulment, 3, 4

Epstein, Lee, 9

Epstein, Lynn, 143

"Estimated Pregnancy Rates for the United States, 1990–2000: An Update" (Centers for Disease Control and Prevention), 72

Estonia, abortion rate of, 99

Ethical questions

about abortion, 94

fetal rights, 94

fetal tissue transplantation research, 89–90

genetic testing, 91–92

infertility treatments, 92, 94

of partial-birth abortion, 138

stem cell research, 90–91

in vitro fertilization, 90

Ethics, 89

Ethics and Public Policy Center, 123–128

Ethics Committee of the American Society of Reproductive Medicine, 91–92

Ethnicity. *See* Race/ethnicity

Europe, 98–99

See also specific countries

Evangelium Vitae (Pope John Paul II), 3

EWTN Catholic Network, 3

Excommunication, 3

Expectations for future, 74

Exposure, 1

F

FAA (Foreign Assistance Act), 31

FACE. *See* Freedom of Access to Clinic Entrances Act

"Facts" (National Campaign to Prevent Teen Pregnancy), 63–64

Fairfield (CA), 130

Family planning

in China, 102

funding through Title X, 27, 29–31

Office of Family Planning, funding for, 32*t*

U.S. aid for family planning, contraception, 31–33

Family Planning Perspectives

abortion training article, 46

sexual and reproductive behavior article, 61–62

teenagers and abortion article, 75–77

Family Planning Program, 27, 29–31

Fatality rates

from abortion procedures, 50

for abortion-related deaths reported to CDC, by type of abortion, 58*t*

"F.D.A. Approves Sale of Abortion Pill" (National Right to Life), 52

Federal government

federal funding and abortion, 21, 23–24

Unborn Victims of Violence Act and, 94

Federal judges, 9

Feinstein, Dianne, 129

Feldt, Gloria, 52–53

Feminist Majority Foundation (FMF), 85

Fertility

indicators by age, race, Hispanic origin, 49*t*

infertility treatments, 92, 94

by race/ethnicity, 40

Fertility rate

in China, 102

in India, 103

in Romania, 101

Fetal remains, 15–16

Fetal rights, 94

Fetal viability, 18–19, 20, 126

Fetus

British statutes on abortion, 5

court rulings on, 18–19

fetal rights, 94

fetal tissue transplantation research, 89–90

Islamic position on abortion and, 4

Partial-Birth Abortion Ban Act, statements against, 141–147

Partial-Birth Abortion Ban Act, support of, 135–140

Poland's antiabortion law, 100

public opinion on beginning of life, 109

Roe v. Wade and, 11, 125–127, 130–131

Roman Catholic Church's views on abortion, 3

states with laws regarding fetuses as victims, 36*f*

Unborn Victims of Violence Act, 34

Fifth Amendment, 11

Finer, Lawrence B., 43

Finkbine, Sherri, 7

First Amendment

abortion protestors and, 18

Roe v. Wade and, 132

Rust v. Sullivan and, 12–13

First trimester, 11

Florida

abortion rates in, 42

attacks on abortion clinics in, 82

FMF (Feminist Majority Foundation), 85

Foreign Affairs Authorization Act, 33

Foreign aid, 31–33

Foreign Assistance Act (FAA), 31

Fourteenth Amendment, 11, 127–128

Fox News/Opinion Dynamics poll, 109

France

abortion rates in Sweden, England and Wales, and France, 107*f*

cross-border abortions, 106

Franklin, Colautti v., 18–19, 125

Freedom of Access to Clinic Entrances Act (FACE)

clinic blockades and, 84

effectiveness of, 85

function of, 84

Internet and, 85–86

opponents/proponents of, 85

protections of, 18

Friends (television show), 69

"From the Patient's Perspective: Quality of Abortion Care" (Henry J. Kaiser Family Foundation), 81

Frost, Jennifer J., 61–62

"Fulfilling the Promise: Public Policy and U.S. Family Planning Clinics" (Alan Guttmacher Institute), 27, 29

Funding

for abortions, court cases on, 12–13

for family planning, contraception, 27, 29–31

federal funding and abortion, 21, 23–24

funding for Office of Family Planning, 32*t*

public funding for abortion services, 29*t*–30*t*

state funding for abortion, 24–26

G

Gag rule, 31

Gag Rule, Global, 32–33, 33*t*

Gallup/CNN/*USA Today* poll, 111, 112

Gallup Poll

abortion stance based on characteristics, 112, 113

public opinion on George W. Bush's abortion policy, 111

public opinion on legality of abortion, 109–110

on specific abortion situations, 111

GAO (U.S. Government Accountability Office), 85

Garcia, Sandra G., 104

Gaudium Et Spes (EWTN Catholic Network), 3

Gender, abortion stance and, 112–113

Gender selection

in China, 103

ethical questions of, 91–92

in India, 103

"General Facts and Stats" (National Campaign to Prevent Teen Pregnancy), 64

Genetic testing

in China, 103

ethical question of, 91–92

Genetics and I.V.F. Institute, 91

Genetics and Public Policy Center of Johns Hopkins University, 92

Georgia, 12

Germany, abortion rate of, 99

"Get 'In the Know': Questions about Pregnancy, Contraception and Abortion—Cost of Abortion" (Alan Guttmacher Institute), 48–50

Gingrey, Phil, 115–116

Global Gag Rule, 32–33, 33*t*

"Global Population Profile: 2002" (U.S. Census Bureau), 103

Gonzalez, Carhart v., 141

Government, 12–13

See also Federal government; State governments

"Government-Mandated Parental Involvement in Family Planning Services Threatens Young People's Health" (NARAL Pro-Choice America Foundation), 30

Graduate Center of the City University of New York, 2

Grammich, Clifford, 102

Grandparents, 121

Great Britain

abortion tradition of, 5

cross-border abortions, 106

Greece, abortion in, 1

Green, Ronald M., 130–131

Griffin, Michael, 82

Griswold v. Connecticut, 131

The Guardian (newspaper), 102

Gunn, David, 17, 82

The Guttmacher Report on Public Policy (Alan Guttmacher Institute), 106

Gynecologists. See Obstetricians/gynecologists

Gynecology residency programs, 43, 56*t*

H

H. L. v. Matheson, 13, 15

Haas, Taylor, 98–100

Harkin, Thomas, 129–130

Harris Interactive Election 2000 survey, 109

Harris Poll
    on abortion timing restrictions,
        110–111
    on legality of abortion, 109
Harris v. McRae, 12
Hart, Melissa, 116
Harvard University John F. Kennedy
    School of Government, 68
Harvey, S. Marie, 81–82
Haskell, Martin, 138, 140
Hawaii, abortion laws in, 7
Health
    abortion and, 87
    deaths from abortion worldwide,
        106–107
    morbidity/mortality from abortion,
        87–88
    Partial-Birth Abortion Ban Act and,
        136, 137, 141–142
    post-abortion stress syndrome, 88–89
    Roe v. Wade and, 125–126
    women's health, Partial-Birth
        Abortion Ban Act and, 144, 146–
        147
Health care, 12
Health insurance, 50
Heart and Soul magazine, 70
Henry J. Kaiser Family Foundation
    media influences on teen sex, 69
    on quality of abortion care, 81
    sex education survey, 68
    "Sex on TV: Content and Context," 69
    survey on teen sexuality, 61
    surveys on medical abortions, 51–52
    teen pregnancy rate decline, 62–63
    on teen sexual activity, 65
Henshaw, Stanley K.
    abortion providers, availability of, 43
    on contraceptive use, 40
    on unintended pregnancy, abortion, 88
    worldwide abortion statistics
        comparison, 98–100
Hereditary diseases, 92
HEW. *See* Department of Health,
    Education, and Welfare
HHS. *See* U.S. Department of Health and
    Human Services
Hill v. Colorado, 18
Hippocrates, 1–2
Hippocratic Oath, 1–2
Hispanic Americans
    abortion ratio for Hispanic women, 40
    teen birth rates, 70–71
    teen pregnancy rates, 62
HIV (Human Immunodeficiency Virus),
    67, 68
Hodgson v. Minnesota, 15
Holocaust, 4
Homicide laws, 36f
Hominization, of fetus, 3

Hospitals
    abortion costs, 50
    abortions performed in, 40, 43
    abortions worldwide and, 100
    court decisions on abortion and, 12,
        15, 16
    military hospitals, 26
Human embryo. *See* Embryo
Human Immunodeficiency Virus (HIV),
    67, 68
Human life, 109
Human Science Research Council, 106
Humanae Vitae (Pope Paul VI), 3
Hyde Amendment
    constitutionality of, 12
    passage of, challenges of, 23–24
Hyde, Henry, 23, 24–25
Hylomorphism, 3
Hypertensive disorders, 144
Hysterectomy
    mortality rate of, 145
    Partial-Birth Abortion Ban
        Act and, 144
    percentage of abortions performed
        by, 50
Hysterotomy
    mortality rate of, 145
    Partial-Birth Abortion Ban Act and,
        144
    percentage of abortions performed by,
        50

I

Iatrogenic laceration, 137
ICPD (International Conference on
    Population and Development), 107
Idaho, abortion rates in, 42
In vitro fertilization (IVF), 90, 92
Incest
    Child Interstate Abortion Notification
        Act, opposition to, 120, 121–122
    legal abortion in case of, 97, 111
    teen abortion in case of, 76
    worldwide abortion laws and, 101,
        102, 105
"The Incidence of Abortion Worldwide"
    (Alan Guttmacher Institute), 98–100
India
    abortion in, 103
    abortion rate of, 100
Indian Supreme Court, 103
Induced abortion
    induced abortion rates by age, race,
        and Hispanic origin, 77t
    morbidity/mortality rate, 145
    Partial-Birth Abortion Ban Act and, 144
    See also Abortion
"Induced Abortion in the United States:
    Facts in Brief" (Alan Guttmacher
    Institute), 40, 87

"Induced Abortion Worldwide:
    Facts in Brief" (Alan Guttmacher
    Institute), 95
Infant Life Preservation Act, 5
Infanticide, 2
Infertility treatments
    description of, ethics of, 92, 94
    outcomes of assisted reproductive
        technology, by procedure
        type, 93t
Informed consent, 13
Instillation, 50
Institute of Medicine, 87
The Institutes of the Laws of England
    (Coke), 5
Intact dilation and extraction (D & X).
    See Partial-birth abortion
International community
    abortion law worldwide, 1999, 33f
    countries changing their abortion laws
        since initial imposition of "Global
        Gag Rule," 33t
    teen birth rates, 70
    teenage abortion rate in, 61–62
    teenage birth rates in U.S., other
        developed countries, 72f
    U.S. aid for family planning,
        contraception, 31–33
    See also Abortion worldwide
International Conference on Population
    and Development (ICPD), 107
International Family Planning Perspectives,
    98, 104
International Planned Parenthood
    Federation (IPPF)
    funding cut, 31
    Global Gag Rule, 32–33
    Polish affiliate, 100
Internet, 85–86
Interstate abortion
    Child Interstate Abortion Notification
        Act, opposition to, 119–122
    Child Interstate Abortion Notification
        Act, support of, 115–118
IPPF. *See* International Planned Parenthood
    Federation
Iran Daily, 102
Ireland, abortion in, 102
Irish Canons, 3
Irish Family Planning Association, 102
Irish Supreme Court, 102
Irish Times, 102
"Is the Fetus a Person? The Bible's View"
    (Ward), 2
Islam, 4
IVF (in vitro fertilization), 90, 92

J

Jackson Lee, Sheila, 120–121
Japan, abortion rate of, 100

Jews, position on abortion, 1, 4
John Paul II, Pope, 3
Jones, Rachel K., 40
Judaism, position on abortion, 4
Judicial appointments, 9
Judicial bypass
    for abortion, 77
    Child Interstate Abortion Notification
        Act and, 119
    court cases on, 15

K

Kaeser, Lisa, 33
King, Steve, 116–117
Kirby, Douglas
    on abstinence-only programs, 66
    on consequences of teen
        pregnancy, 63
    sex education survey findings, 68–69
Kiwibox.com, 70
"Knowledge and Opinions about Abortion
    Law among Mexican Youth" (Becker,
    Garcia, and Larsen), 104
Koop, C. Everett, 87, 88
Kopf, Richard G., 141–142
Kopp, James, 82
Koran (Qur'an), 4
Kwasniewski, Aleksander, 101

L

Larsen, Ulla, 104
Late-term abortion
    Partial-Birth Abortion Ban Act,
        statements against, 141–147
    Partial-Birth Abortion Ban Act,
        support of, 135–140
Latin America
    abortion in, 103–104
    abortion statistics of, 98
Law enforcement, 85
Lee, Ellie, 88
Legalized Abortion and the Public Health
    (Institute of Medicine), 87
Legislation and international treaties
    Abortion Act of 1967, 5
    Abortion and Sterilization Act, 105
    abortion cases, chronology of major,
        10t–11t
    Abortion Control Act, 19–20
    abortion laws worldwide, 95, 97–98
    anti-choice legislation considered by
        states, 24f
    Balanced Budget Act, 25
    "Bonus to Reward Decrease in
        Illegitimacy Ratio," 33–34
    British statutes on abortion, 5
    Child Custody Protection Act, 115
    Child Interstate Abortion Notification
        Act, opposition to, 119–122

Child Interstate Abortion Notification
    Act, support of, 115–118
Choice of Termination of Pregnancy
    Act, 105–106
Comstock Law, 6–7
Departments of Labor and Health and
    Human Services, and Education,
    and Related Agencies
    Appropriations Act, 25
Departments of Labor and Health,
    Education, and Welfare
    Appropriations Act, 23
Foreign Affairs Authorization
    Act, 33
Foreign Assistance Act, 31
Freedom of Access to Clinic Entrances
    Act, 18, 84–86
Hyde Amendment, 12, 23–24
Infant Life Preservation Act, 5
Maternal Health Care Law, 103
Miscarriage of Women Act of
    1803, 5
Model Penal Code, 7
National Defense Authorization
    Act, 27
National Institutes of Health
    Revitalization Act, 90
Offences against the Person Act, 5
Partial-Birth Abortion Ban Act, 17,
    112, 129–130
Partial-Birth Abortion Ban Act,
    statements against, 141–147
Partial-Birth Abortion Ban Act,
    support of, 135–140
Personal Responsibility and Work
    Opportunity Reconciliation Act
    of 1998, 33, 65–66
Racketeer Influenced and Corrupt
    Organizations Act, 18, 86
Responsible Education about Life
    Act, 67
state anti-choice legislation, 23f
Title X of the Public Health Service
    Act, 27, 29–31
Unborn Victims of Violence Act, 34,
    94
Uniform Abortion Act, 7
Welfare Reform Extension Act of
    2003, 66
world abortion laws, 96t
Life consequences, of teen pregnancy,
    63–64
Life, public opinion on beginning of, 109
LifeSiteNews.com, 102
"Living the Gospel of Life: A Challenge
    to American Catholics" (National
    Conference of Catholic Bishops of
    the United States), 3
Lockwood, Dr., 141
Low birth weight, 64
"Low Fertility in Urban China"
    (Zhao), 102

Low-income people
    family planning funding through
        Title X, 27, 29–30
    low-income women's access to
        abortion, 28t

M

MacNaghten, Justice, 5
Madsen v. Women's Health Center, 18
Maher, Edward, 12
Maher v. Roe, 12
Maimonides, Moses, 4
Males
    family planning involvement of, 30
    preference for sons in China, India,
        103
Managed care, abortion funding and,
    24–25
Marital status, 74
Marshall, Thurgood, 15
Martin, Bob, 69
Massachusetts, 13
Maternal-fetal medicine
    Partial-Birth Abortion Ban Act and,
        137–138, 139–140
    Roe v. Wade and, 125–126
Maternal Health Care Law (China), 103
Matheson, H. L. v., 13, 15
*Matheson, Planned Parenthood Association
    of Utah v.*, 30
McCaughey septuplets, 92, 94
McCorvey, Norma, 9, 11
McHenry, Patrick, 115
McRae, Harris v., 12
The Meaning of the Glorious Qur'an
    (Pickthall), 4
Media, influences on teen sex, 69–70
Medicaid
    federal funding and abortion, 21,
        23–24
    funding for nontherapeutic
        abortions, 12
    funding of abortions, 50
    state funding for abortion, 24–26
    teen pregnancy/abortion and, 75
Medical abortions
    cost of, 49
    cross-border abortions, 106
    mifepristone, countries that have
        approved use of, 106 (t8.7)
    percentage of abortions performed
        by, 50
    physicians' offering of, 51–53
    safety of, 88
    satisfaction with abortion method,
        81–82
Medical questions
    about abortion, 87–89
    outcomes of assisted reproductive
        technology, by procedure type, 93t

Medicare, 24
Medicine, legislation of, 144–145
Men, abortion attitudes of, 112–113
Menillo, Connecticut v., 15, 125
Mental health, 7, 95
Methotrexate abortion, 81, 82
Mexico
    abortion in, 104
    Mexican states allowing abortion in
        various circumstances, and
        support for legal abortion in
        each circumstance, 106 (*t*8.6)
    Mexican youth, knowledge, opinions
        about emergency contraception/
        abortion among, 105*t*
Mexico City Policy
    Global Gag Rule, 32–33
    public opinion on George W. Bush's
        abortion policy, 111
Midwives, 6
Mifepristone
    in China, 102–103
    cost of medical abortions, 49
    countries that have approved use of,
        106 (*t*8.7)
    cross-border abortions, 106
    for medical abortions, 5
    opponents/proponents of, 52–53
    percent of physicians surveyed who
        provide or will likely provide it in
        coming year, 59*f*
    percent of physicians surveyed
        who say they are familiar with,
        58*f*
    physicians' offering of medical
        abortions, 51–52
Military personnel, abortion services
    for, 26–27
Miller, Kim S., 69
Miller v. Zbaraz, 12
Minnesota, 15
Minnesota, Hodgson v., 15
Minors
    Child Interstate Abortion Notification
        Act, opposition to, 119–122
    Child Interstate Abortion Notification
        Act, support of, 115–118
    parental consent/notification rulings
        and, 13, 15
    state restrictions on minors' access to
        abortion, 79*t*
    See also Adolescents; Teenagers
Miscarriage, 1
Miscarriage of Women Act of 1803, 5
Mishnah, 4
Missouri
    abortion restrictions of, 19
    *Planned Parenthood of Central Missouri
        v. Danforth*, 13
Missouri Compromise of 1820, 123
Mittal, Suneeta, 103

Money. *See* Funding
Morbidity, 87–88
Morbidity and Mortality Weekly Report
    (Centers for Disease Control and
    Prevention), 70, 72
*Morbidity and Mortality Weekly Report,
    Surveillance Summaries* (Centers for
    Disease Control and Prevention), 37
Mortality
    abortion and, 87–88
    maternal mortality rate in Romania,
        101
    rate, abortion methods and, 145
    unsafe abortion, estimates of annual
        incidence of, mortality due to
        unsafe abortion, 108*t*
Mother
    abortion, changing attitudes toward, 7
    maternal mortality rate in
        Romania, 101
    Partial-Birth Abortion Ban Act
        and, 137
Multiple births, 92, 94
Multipotent cells, 89
Murder
    abortion attitudes, 6, 76
    abortion debate, 2, 3
    of abortion doctors, clinic
        workers, 82
    abortion law and, 5
    of abortion providers, 85
    protests at abortion clinics, 84
    Roe v. Wade controversy and, 132

N

Nadler, Jerrold, 143
NAF. *See* National Abortion Federation
Names/addresses, organization, 149–150
NARAL Pro-Choice America
    Foundation
    on abortion measures, 21
    on FACE, 85
    on parental notification, 30
National Abortion Federation (NAF)
    clinical policies guidelines of, 81
    Partial-Birth Abortion Ban Act and,
        135
    "Safety of Abortion," 88
    survey on abortion training, 43, 46
    on violence against abortion clinics,
        82, 84
National Autonomous University of
    Mexico, 104
National Campaign to Prevent Teen
    Pregnancy
    life consequences of teen pregnancy,
        63–64
    sex education survey findings, 68–69
    teen birth rates, 70–71
    teen pregnancy outcomes, 64

"2002 National Clinic Violence Survey
    Report" (Feminist Majority
    Foundation), 85
National Conference of Catholic Bishops
    of the United States, 3
National Defense Authorization Act, 27
National Family Planning and
    Reproductive Health Association, 31
National Institutes of Health, 90
National Institutes of Health
    Revitalization Act, 90
National Organization for Women
    (NOW), 18
National Public Radio, 68
National Right to Life Committee
    (NRLC), 52
"National Survey of Adolescents and
    Young Adults: Sexual Health
    Knowledge, Attitudes and
    Experiences" (Henry J. Kaiser
    Foundation), 61, 63, 68
"National Survey of Women's Health
    Care Providers on Reproductive
    Health: Views and Practices on
    Medical Abortion" (Henry J. Kaiser
    Family Foundation), 51–52
"A National Survey: Views of Women's
    Health Care Providers on Abortion"
    (Henry J. Kaiser Family
    Foundation), 51
National Vital Statistics Reports (Centers
    for Disease Control and Prevention)
    on teen abortion, 72
    on teen birth rates, 70
Nature Cell Biology journal, 91
Nature journal, 91
Nebraska
    Partial-Birth Abortion Ban Act and,
        135, 136, 139
    partial-birth abortion court case, 16–17
    Stenberg v. Carhart, 146
Neerhof, Mark G., 137–138
Netherlands
    abortion rate of, 99, 100
    cross-border abortions, 106
Neugebauer, Randy, 117
New England Journal of Medicine, 91
New Hampshire, 15
New York
    abortion laws, 6, 7
    abortions in, 8
    Partial-Birth Abortion Ban Act
        lawsuit in, 17
New York City (NY)
    abortion rates in, 42
    abortion training in, 46
New York State Department of Health, 8
New York Times, 6
Nixon, Richard
    Comstock Law and, 6–7
    federal funding for abortion, 21

Nonmarital births
    births to unmarried teenagers, 70
    births to unmarried women, 73 (t5.4)
    percentage of births to unmarried
        women, by state and territory, 35t
    welfare reform and abortion, 33–34
Nontherapeutic abortions, 12
Noonan, John T., 2–3
North America, abortion
    statistics of, 98
North Carolina, abortion laws in, 7
North Dakota, abortion rates in, 42
"Not Just Another Single Issue"
    (National Campaign to Prevent Teen
    Pregnancy), 64
NOW (National Organization for
    Women), 18
NOW v. Scheidler, 18
"Nuremburg Files" Web site, 85–86

O

Obstetricians/gynecologists
    abortion medical training, 43
    maternal-fetal medicine, 125–126
    medical abortions offered by, 51–53
    Partial-Birth Abortion Ban Act and,
        143–146
    percentage distribution of obstetrics,
        gynecology residency programs,
        by availability of first-trimester
        abortion training, 56t
Oceania, abortion statistics of, 98
O'Connor, Sandra Day, 16
Offences against the Person Act, 5
Office of Family Planning, 32t
Ohio, 15–16
Ohio v. Akron Center for Reproductive
    Health, 15
Olejniczak, Wojciech, 101
Operation Save America, 84
Organization names/addresses, 149–150
Orthodox Judaism, 4
Out-of-wedlock births. See Nonmarital
    births
Ozer, Emily J., 78

P

Packwood, Bob, 132
Pain
    partial-birth abortion and, 138
    pre-term neonates and, 126–127
Paltrow, Lynn M., 94
Parental consent
    for abortion, 77–78
    for abortion, teens' views about, 76
    court cases on, 13
    for sex education, 67–68
Parental notification
    for abortion, 77–78

Child Interstate Abortion Notification
    Act, opposition to, 119–122
Child Interstate Abortion Notification
    Act, support of, 115–118
confidential family planning services
    for adolescents, 30
Supreme Court rulings on, 13, 15
Parents
    abortion decisions, involvement in,
        77–78
    sex education and, 67–68
    sex on television and, 69
Parents' rights, 94
Partial-birth abortion
    court cases on, 16–17
    Partial-Birth Abortion Ban Act,
        statements against, 141–147
    Partial-Birth Abortion Ban Act,
        support of, 135–140
    public opinion on, 111–112
Partial-Birth Abortion Ban Act
    constitutionality of, 112
    passage of, 17
    statements against, 141–147
    support of, 135–140
    Thomas Harkin on, 129–130
Paul VI, Pope, 3
Pediatrics, 69
Pennsylvania
    Abortion Control Act of, 19–20
    fetus ruling, 18–19
Pennsylvania Department of Public
    Welfare, 12
Personal Responsibility and Work
    Opportunity Reconciliation Act of
    1998
    money for abstinence education, 65–66
    TANF program through, 33
Perspectives on Sexual and Reproductive
    Health, 40
Peter Heed, Attorney General of the State of
    New Hampshire, Planned Parenthood of
    Northern New England, et al. . . . v., 15
Pew Research Center, 113
PGD (preimplantation genetic diagnosis),
    92
Physicians
    abortion medical training, 43, 46–48
    abortion practices among physicians
        surveyed, 60f
    abortion providers, number of, and
        percentage of counties/women
        without an abortion provider, 55t
    abortion restrictions court case and,
        15–16
    Child Interstate Abortion Notification
        Act and, 119–120
    court rulings on fetus and, 18–19
    medical abortions offered by, 51–53
    mifepristone, percent of physicians
        surveyed who provide or will

likely provide it in coming year,
    59f
mifepristone, percent of physicians
    surveyed who say they are
    familiar with, 58f
number of abortions performed by, 37
Partial-Birth Abortion Ban Act and,
    135, 139–140, 141, 143–145
Roe v. Wade and, 125
Physicians for Reproductive Choice and
    Health (PRCH), 119–120
Physicians' offices, abortions performed
    in, 40
Picker Institute, 81
Picketing, against abortion clinics, 84
Pickthall, Mohammed M., 4
Pill, abortion
    mifepristone controversy, 52–53
    physicians' offering of medical
        abortions, 51–52
    use prior to pregnancy, 40
    See also Mifepristone
Pius IX, Pope, 3
Pius XII, Pope, 3
Planned Parenthood
    abortion clinic incidents in California,
        130
    "gag rule," 31
    "Nuremburg Files" Web site and,
        85–86
Planned Parenthood Assn. v. Ashcroft, 16
Planned Parenthood Association of Utah v.
    Matheson, 30
Planned Parenthood Federation of
    America
    on effects of abortion, 88
    on mifepristone, 52–53
    Partial-Birth Abortion Ban Act
        and, 135
    on state abortion laws, 15
Planned Parenthood Federation of America
    v. Agency for International
    Development, 32
Planned Parenthood of Central Missouri v.
    Danforth, 13, 125
Planned Parenthood of Northern New
    England, 15
Planned Parenthood of Northern New
    England, et al. . . . v. Peter Heed, Attorney
    General of the State of New Hampshire, 15
Planned Parenthood of Southeastern
    Pennsylvania v. Casey, 19–20, 124
Plato, 1
Pluripotent cells, 89, 90
Poelker v. Doe, 12
Poland, abortion in, 100–101
Politics
    judicial appointments and, 9
    political affiliations, abortion stance
        and, 112
    See also Abortion politics

Poll, 109
Population
    abortion in Romania and, 101
    abortion laws worldwide and, 95
    of China, 102
    of India, 103
Population Crisis Committee, 32
Population Reference Bureau, 103
Portland Feminist Women's Health
    Center, 85–86
Post-abortion stress syndrome, 88–89
Poverty, 104
PRCH (Physicians for Reproductive
    Choice and Health), 119–120
Preconception gender selection, 91–92
Pregnancy
    abortion during, 1
    contraceptive use prior to, 40
    fetal rights and, 94
    "gag rule," 31
    infertility treatments, 92, 94
    legal abortions, by length of gestation,
        demographic characteristics of
        women who obtained abortions, 57t
    public opinion on abortion and, 110–111
    public opinion on beginning of life, 109
    Roe v. Wade and, 11
    state pregnancy rates among
        teenagers, 65f
    state restrictions on abortion, 13
    timing of abortions, 50, 56f
    worldwide number of pregnancies, 95
    See also Teenage pregnancy
Pregnancy rate
    pregnancy, birth, abortion rates for
        teens, 77f
    pregnancy rate, birth rates, abortion
        rates among teenagers in U.S.,
        other developed countries, 62 (f5.2)
    state pregnancy rates among
        teenagers, changes in, 66f
    teen pregnancy rate trends, 61–63
    teen pregnancy rates, by age group, 63f
    teen pregnancy rates, by racial/ethnic
        subgroups, 64f
    of teens, 72
Preimplantation genetic diagnosis
    (PGD), 92
Prenatal testing
    in China, in India, 103
    ethical question of, 91–92
    for fetal abnormalities, 126
Presbyterian Church, 4
President's Commission on Population
    Growth and the American Future, 7
President's Council on Bioethics, 91
Private family planning clinics, 30–31
Pro-choice groups
    anti-choice legislation and, 21
    Freedom of Access to Clinic Entrances
        Act and, 85

identification with, 113
    mifepristone and, 52–53
    public opinion on abortion timing
        restrictions, 110–111
    public opinion on beginning of
        life, 109
    religion and, 112
    Roe v. Wade, support of, 129–133
    state funding for abortion and,
        24–25
Pro-choice legislation, 21
Pro-Choice Network of Western New York,
    et al., Schenck, et al., v., 18
Pro-Life Action Ministries, 89
Pro-Life Direct Action League, 18
Pro-life groups
    Freedom of Access to Clinic Entrances
        Act and, 85–86
    identification with, 113
    mifepristone and, 52
    public opinion on abortion timing
        restrictions, 110–111
    public opinion on beginning of life,
        109
    religion and, 112
    Roe v. Wade and, 124
    state funding for abortion and,
        24–25
    views of, 21
    violence against abortion clinics,
        82, 84
"Programme of Action," 107–108
Project Rachel, 89
Protestantism, 2, 4
Protestants, 112
Protests, at abortion clinics, 17–18, 84
Psychological problems, from abortion,
    87, 88–89
Public funding
    for abortion services, 29t–30t
    for nontherapeutic abortions, 12
Public Health Service Act, Title X of, 27,
    29–31
Public opinion
    on abortion policy of George W. Bush
        administration, 111
    abortion stance based on
        characteristics, 112–113
    about sex education, 68
    on beginning of human life, 109
    on legality of abortion, 109–111
    on "partial birth" abortion, 111–112
    South African attitudes about
        abortion, 106
    teens on abortion, 75–77
    on whether abortion should be legal,
        110f
"Punishing Women for Their Behavior
    during Pregnancy: An Approach That
    Undermines the Health of Women and
    Children" (Paltrow), 94

Q
Quacks, 6
Quickening, 5, 6
"QuickStats: Pregnancy, Birth, and
    Abortion Rates for Teenagers Aged
    15–17 Years—United States, 1976–
    2003" (Centers for Disease Control
    and Prevention), 72
Qur'an (Koran), 4

R
Race/ethnicity
    birth rates for teenagers, by racial/
        ethnic group, 74f
    fertility indicators, by age, race,
        Hispanic origin, 49t
    legal abortions, by ethnicity of women,
        state of occurrence, selected
        states, 48t
    legal abortions, by race of
        women, 47t
    teen abortion by, 72
    teen birth rates by, 70–71
    teen pregnancy/abortion and, 75
    teen pregnancy rate and, 62
    teen pregnancy rates, by racial/ethnic
        subgroups, 64f
    of women seeking abortion, 40
Racketeer Influenced and Corrupt
    Organizations Act (RICO), 18, 86
RAND Corporation, 69
Rape
    British abortion laws and, 5
    legal abortion in case of, 97, 111
    legal abortion in Mexico and, 104
    teen abortion in case of, 76
    worldwide abortion laws and, 101,
        102, 105
Reagan, Ronald
    clinics and abortion counseling, 30
    "gag rule," 30–31
    Mexico City Policy and, 111
    study on health effects of abortion,
        87, 88
    Title X funding and, 31
    U.S. foreign aid for family planning/
        contraception, 31–32
"Reconceptualizing Adolescent Sexual
    Behavior: Beyond Did They or
    Didn't They?" (Whitaker, Miller, and
    Clark), 69
Reform Judaism, position on abortion, 4
Rehnquist, William H.
    Roe v. Wade and, 124
    Rust v. Sullivan statement, 13
    Webster v. Reproductive Health Services
        statement, 19
Reid, Harry, 85
Religion
    abortion and, 131, 132
    abortion stance and, 112

Christian position on abortion, 2–4
Islamic position on abortion, 4
Jewish position on abortion, 4
Religious Coalition for Reproductive Choice, 2
"Remarks by the President on Stem Cell Research" (White House), 91
"Reproductive Decisions" (American Academy of Family Physicians), 46–48
Reproductive Genetic Testing: What America Thinks (Genetics and Public Policy Center), 92
Reproductive Health Services, Webster v., 19
Reproductive health, worldwide plan for, 107–108
The Republic (Plato), 1
Republican Party
    abortion stance and, 112
    choice positions of state Democratic, Republican parties on woman's right to choose abortion, 22t
Resources, 151–152
Responsible Education about Life Act, 67
Rex v. Bourne, 5
RICO (Racketeer Influenced and Corrupt Organizations Act), 18, 86
Rideout, Victoria, 69
Right-to-life groups. *See* Pro-life groups
Roche, Natalie E., 144–146
Rockefeller, John D., III, 7
Roe, Maher v., 12
Roe v. Wade
    abortion politics and, 21
    Akron v. Akron Center for Reproductive Health and, 16
    federal funding for abortion and, 23
    fetal tissue transplantation research and, 89
    fetus rulings and, 18–19
    Harris v. McRae ruling and, 12
    historic decision, 8
    history of, 11
    overview of, 9
    Partial-Birth Abortion Ban Act and, 135, 136, 142
    Protestant positions on abortion and, 4
    public opinion on, 109–110
    reconsideration of, testimony in support of, 123–128
    state restrictions on abortion and, 13
    teens' abortion knowledge and, 76
    upheld, 19–20
    upholding, testimony on, 129–133
Roman Catholic Church
    Poland's abortion prohibition and, 100–101
    position on abortion, 2, 3
Romania
    abortion in, 101–102
    abortion rate of, 100

Rome, 1, 2
Ros-Lehtinen, Ileana, 115, 116
Rotunda, Ronald D., 124–125
Rubella (German measles), 7
Rubin, Lisa, 88
Rudolf, Eric, 82
Russia
    abortion in, 102
    abortion rate of, 100
Russo, Nancy Felipe, 88
Rust v. Sullivan, 12–13, 31

S

Safe sex, 69–70
"Safety of Abortion" (National Abortion Federation), 87, 88
St. Augustine, 3
St. Louis, Missouri, 12
St. Thomas Aquinas, 3
Saline amniocentesis, 125
San Diego (CA), 130
San Mateo (CA), 130
Sandford, Dred Scott v., 123
Santorum, Rick, 135–136, 146
Satcher, David, 67
Satre, Sarah J., 81–82
Scalia, Antonin
    Roe v. Wade and, 124
    Webster v. Reproductive Health Services statement, 19
Scheidler, Joseph, 18
Scheidler, NOW v., 18
Schenck, et al., v. Pro-Choice Network of Western New York, et al., 18
Second trimester, 11
Second Vatican Council, 3
Segal, Jeffrey A., 9
Seigel, Warren, 119–120
Seventeen magazine, 62–63
"Sex and STD/HIV Education" (Alan Guttmacher Institute), 67
"Sex Education in America" (Henry J. Kaiser Family Foundation), 68
"Sex on TV: Content and Context" (Kaiser Family Foundation), 69
Sex ratio, 103
Sex selection. *See* Gender selection
Sexual activity
    media influences on teen sex, 69–70
    prevention of teen pregnancy, 65
    sexual education/abstinence education and, 65–67
    teens, attitudes among adolescents/ young adults about relationships, sexual activity, 67t
Sexual education
    abstinence education, 65–67
    characteristics of effective, 68–69
    parents and, 67–68

in Poland, 100–101
Sexual risk behaviors
    percentage of high school students who reported, 71t–72t
    of teens, trends in, 70
"Sexuality Education: Facts in Brief" (Alan Guttmacher Institute), 65
Sexually transmitted disease (STD), 67–68
Shadigian, Dr., 141
Singh, Shusheela
    on teen pregnancy rates, 61–62
    worldwide abortion statistics comparison, 98–100
Skinner v. Oklahoma, 11
Slade, Pauline, 88–89
Slaughter, Louise M., 120
Smith, Christopher, 32
Snowe, Olympia, 33, 146–147
"Socioeconomic Disadvantage and Adolescent Women's Sexual and Reproductive Behavior: The Case of Five Developed Countries" (Alan Guttmacher Institute), 61
Socioeconomic status
    abortion based on, 95, 97
    teen pregnancy/abortion and, 74
Solidarity Party, 100
South Africa, abortion in, 104–106
South Dakota
    abortion rates in, 42
    state funding for abortion, 24
Southern Baptist Convention, 4
"A Special Word to Women Who Have Had an Abortion" (Angelo), 89
Sperm sorting, 91
Spina bifida, 92
Spontaneous abortion, 1
Sports Illustrated, 70
Spousal consent, 13
Stalking, 82, 84
Stark, Pete, 130
A State-by-State Review of Abortion and Reproductive Rights (NARAL Pro-Choice America Foundation), 21
State Children's Health Insurance Program (CHIP), 25
"State Facts about Abortion" (Alan Guttmacher Institute), 21
State governments
    choice positions of, 21
    choice positions of state Democratic, Republican parties on woman's right to choose abortion, 22t
    choice positions of state governments, 25f
    choice positions of state governors, 26f
    choice positions of state legislatures, 27f
State governors, choice positions of, 26f
State legislatures, choice positions of, 27f

State lines
  Child Interstate Abortion Notification Act, opposition to, 119–122
  Child Interstate Abortion Notification Act, support of, 115–118
State Policies in Brief (Alan Guttmacher Institute), 67
States
  abortion bans, 14*t*
  abortion clinic violence, by state, 84*f*
  abortion laws in, 7–8
  abortion providers, availability of, 43
  abortion providers, number of, and percentage of counties/women without an abortion provider, 55*t*
  abortion rates of, 42
  abortion ratio, by age group of women who obtained legal abortion, state of occurrence, 44*t*–45*t*
  anti-choice legislation, 23*f*
  anti-choice legislation considered by, 21
  anti-choice legislation considered by states, 24*f*
  birth rates for teenagers, percent decline in, 76*f*
  Doe v. Bolton ruling and, 12
  fetal rights in, 94
  funding for abortion, 24–26
  with laws regarding fetuses as victims, 36*f*
  legal abortions, by ethnicity of women, state of occurrence, selected states, 48*t*
  legal abortions, by number of previous abortions, 51*t*
  legal abortions, by race of women, 47*t*
  number, ratio, rate of legal abortions, by state, percentage of legal abortions obtained by out-of-state residents, 52*t*–53*t*
  parental consent for abortion in, 77–78
  percentage of births to unmarried women, by state and territory, 35*t*
  pregnancy rates among teenagers, 65*f*
  pregnancy rates among teenagers, changes in, 66*f*
  public funding of nontherapeutic abortions, 12
  restrictions on abortion, 13, 15–17
  teen birth rates, state-specific, 71
  waiting periods, mandatory state, and biased counseling for abortion, 54*f*
Statistical information
  abortion clinic violence, by state, 84*f*
  abortion law worldwide, 33*f*
  abortion, measures of legal abortion worldwide, by completeness of data, country, and data year, 99*t*
  abortion practices among physicians surveyed, 60*f*

abortion providers, number of, and percentage of counties/women without an abortion provider, 55*t*
abortion rates in Sweden, England and Wales, and France, 107*f*
abortion rates worldwide, various years by country, 100*t*
abortion ratio, by age group of women who obtained legal abortion, 2001, 78*f*
abortion ratio, by age group of women who obtained legal abortion, selected years, 46*f*
abortion ratio, by age group of women who obtained legal abortion, selected states, 43*f*
abortion ratio, by age group of women who obtained legal abortion, state of occurrence, 44*t*–45*t*
abortions, number of legal/illegal induced abortions worldwide, 98*t*
anti-choice legislation considered by states, 24*f*
birth rates for teenagers, percent decline in, 76*f*
birth rates for teenagers, by racial/ethnic group, 74*f*
birth rates for women under age 20, 73 (*t5.3*)
births to unmarried women, 73 (*t5.4*)
characteristics of women who obtained legal abortions, 41*t*
choice positions of state Democratic, Republican parties on woman's right to choose abortion, 22*t*
choice positions of state governments, 25*f*
choice positions of state governors, 26*f*
choice positions of state legislatures, 27*f*
deaths, number of, and fatality rates for abortion-related deaths reported to CDC, by type of abortion, 58*t*
fertility indicators, by age, race, Hispanic origin, 49*t*
funding for Office of Family Planning, 32*t*
Global Gag Rule, countries changing their abortion laws since initial imposition of, 33*t*
incidents of violence/disruption against abortion providers in U.S. and Canada, 83*t*
induced abortion rates by age, race, Hispanic origin, 77*t*
legal abortions, by demographic characteristics, selected states, 42*t*
legal abortions, by ethnicity of women, state of occurrence, selected states, 48*t*
legal abortions, by length of gestation, demographic characteristics of

women who obtained abortions, 57*t*
legal abortions, by number of previous abortions, 51*t*
legal abortions, by race of women, 47*t*
levels of abortion restriction worldwide, 97*f*
low-income women's access to abortion, 28*t*
Mexican states allowing abortion in various circumstances, and support for legal abortion in each circumstance, 106 (*t8.6*)
Mexican youth, knowledge, opinions about emergency contraception/abortion among, 105*t*
mifepristone, countries that have approved use of, 106 (*t8.7*)
mifepristone, percent of physicians surveyed who provide or will likely provide it in coming year, 59*f*
mifepristone, percent of physicians surveyed who say they are familiar with, 58*f*
number of abortions, selected years, 40*f*
number of reported abortions, abortion rate, abortion ratio, 78*t*
number, ratio, rate of legal abortions, 39*t*
number, ratio, rate of legal abortions, by state, percentage of legal abortions obtained by out-of-state residents, 52*t*–53*t*
number, ratio, rate of legal abortions performed, selected years, 38*f*
obstetrics, gynecology residency programs, percentage distribution of, by availability of first-trimester abortion training, 56*t*
percentage distribution of women obtaining abortions, by contraceptive method used in the month of conception, 50*t*
percentage of births to unmarried women, by state and territory, 35*t*
pregnancy, birth, abortion rates for teens, 77*f*
pregnancy outcomes among teenagers, 67*f*
pregnancy outcomes among teenagers, selected years, 68*f*
pregnancy rate, birth rates, abortion rates among teenagers in U.S., other developed countries, 62 (*f5.2*)
public funding for abortion services, 29*t*–30*t*
public opinion on whether abortion should be legal, 110*f*
sexual risk behaviors, percentage of high school students who reported, 71*t*–72*t*

state abortion bans, 14*t*

state anti-choice legislation, 23*f*

state pregnancy rates among teenagers, 65*f*

state pregnancy rates among teenagers, changes in, 66*f*

state restrictions on minors' access to abortion, 79*t*

states with laws regarding fetuses as victims, 36*f*

teen birth rates, 75*t*

teen pregnancies, number of, 62 (*f*5.1)

teen pregnancy rates, by age group, 63*f*

teen pregnancy rates, by racial/ethnic subgroups, 64*f*

teenage birth rates in U.S., other developed countries, 72*f*

teens, attitudes among adolescents/ young adults about relationships, sexual activity, 67*t*

timing of abortions, 56*f*

timing, percentage of women who obtained early/late abortions, by age group, selected states, 42*f*

unsafe abortion, estimates of annual incidence of, mortality due to unsafe abortion, 108*t*

waiting periods, mandatory state, and biased counseling for abortion, 54*f*

world abortion laws, 96*t*

STD (sexually transmitted disease), 67–68

Stem cells
fetal tissue transplantation research, 89–90

research, ethical questions of, 90–91

Stenberg v. Carhart
Partial-Birth Abortion Ban Act and, 139, 143, 146

ruling on, 16–17

Stephenson, Patricia, 101

Stevens, John Paul, 15, 20

Stewart, Felicia H., 143–144

Stone, Rebecca, 75–77

"Study Finds Sex Getting Safer on American TV" (Martin), 69

Sullivan, Louis, 90

Sullivan, Rust v., 12–13, 31

Summa Theologica (St. Thomas Aquinas), 3

Sunday Herald (Glasgow), 102

Surgical abortions
safety of, 87

satisfaction with abortion method, 81–82

Survey, accuracy of, 109

Sweden
abortion rates in Sweden, England and Wales, and France, 107*f*

cross-border abortions, 106

Switzerland, abortion rate of, 99

T

Taney, Roger B., 123

TANF (Temporary Assistance for Needy Families) program, 33–34

Teen People magazine, 70

"Teen Sexual Activity" (Henry J. Kaiser Family Foundation), 65

"Teen Sexual Activity, Pregnancy and Childbearing among Latinos in the United States" (National Campaign to Prevent Teen Pregnancy), 70–71

Teen Summit show, 70

Teenage pregnancy
abortion decisions, parental involvement in, 77–78

abortion ratio, by age group of women who obtained legal abortion, 2001, 78*f*

abortion, teens' knowledge of, 75–77

attitudes among adolescents/young adults about relationships, sexual activity, 67*t*

birth rates, 70–71

birth rates for teenagers, percent decline in, 76*f*

birth rates for teenagers, by racial/ ethnic group, 74*f*

birth rates for women under age 20, 73 (*t*5.3)

births to unmarried women, 73 (*t*5.4)

induced abortion rates by age, race, Hispanic origin, 77*t*

life consequences of, 63–64

number of reported abortions, abortion rate, abortion ratio, 78*t*

number of teen pregnancies, 62 (*f*5.1)

outcomes, 64

pregnancy, birth, abortion rates for teens, 77*f*

pregnancy outcomes among teenagers, 67*f*

pregnancy outcomes among teenagers, selected years, 68*f*

pregnancy rate, birth rates, abortion rates among teenagers in U.S., other developed countries, 62 (*f*5.2)

prevention of, 65–70

rates, 61–63

sexual risk behaviors, percentage of high school students who reported, 71*t*–72*t*

sexual risk behaviors, trends in, 70

state pregnancy rates among teenagers, 65*f*

state pregnancy rates among teenagers, changes in, 66*f*

state restrictions on minors' access to abortion, 79*t*

teen abortion, 71–75

teen birth rates, 75*t*

teen pregnancy rates, by age group, 63*f*

teen pregnancy rates, by racial/ethnic subgroups, 64*f*

teenage birth rates in U.S., other developed countries, 72*f*

Teenagers
knowledge about abortion, 75–77

Mexican youth and abortion, 104

Mexican youth, knowledge, opinions about emergency contraception/ abortion among, 105*t*

See also Abortion, teenage

"Teens Lean Conservative on Abortion" (Gallup Organization), 75

Television, influences on teen sex, 69–70

Temporary Assistance for Needy Families (TANF) program, 33–34

Tews, Laureen, 43, 46

Texas
abortion rates in, 42

attacks on abortion clinics in, 82

Roe v. Wade lawsuit, 9, 11

Thalidomide, 7

"Therapeutic" abortions, 6, 7

Third trimester, 11

Thirteenth Amendment, 132

Thomas, Clarence, 17

Thurmond, Strom, 128

Timing, abortion
early abortions, age and, 38–39

legal abortions, by length of gestation, demographic characteristics of women who obtained abortions, 57*t*

percentage of women who obtained early/late abortions, by age group, selected states, 42*f*

percentage of women who obtained early or late abortions, by age group, selected states, 42*f*

public opinion on abortion timing restrictions, 110–111

statistics on, 50

timing of abortions, 56*f*

Title X of the Public Health Service Act, 27, 29–31

Training
abortion medical training, 43, 46–48

percentage distribution of obstetrics, gynecology residency programs, by availability of first-trimester abortion training, 56*t*

"Trends in Sexual Risk Behaviors among High School Students—United States, 1991–2001" (Centers for Disease Control and Prevention), 70

Trimesters
Planned Parenthood of Southeastern Pennsylvania v. Casey, 20

public opinion on abortion legality and, 110–111

Roe v. Wade on, 11
Webster v. Reproductive Health Services and, 19
Tschann, Jeanne, 78

U

Ultrasonography
    gender selection and, 91
    Roe v. Wade and, 125–126
Unborn Victims of Violence Act
    fetus as victim of crime, 94
    requirements of, 34
UNFPA (United Nations Fund for Population Activities), 31–32
Uniform Abortion Act, 7
"Unintended Pregnancy and Abortion: A Public Health Perspective" (Henshaw), 88
United Nations Fund for Population Activities (UNFPA), 31–32
United Nations Human Rights Committee, 101
United Nations Population Division, 103
United Nations Population Fund (UNFPA), 107
United States
    abortion rate of, 100
    aid for family planning, contraception, 31–33
    American abortion experience, 6–7
    state abortion bans, 14*t*
    teen birth rates in, 70
    teenage abortion rate in, 61–62
    teenage birth rates in U.S., other developed countries, 72*f*
United States v. Zbaraz, 12
University of Maryland School of Law, Thurgood Marshall Law Library, 26–27
Unmarried females
    births to teenagers, 70
    births to unmarried women, 73 (*t*5.4)
    See also Nonmarital births
Unsafe abortion
    deaths from, worldwide, 106–107
    in Latin America, 104
    unsafe abortion, estimates of annual incidence of, mortality due to unsafe abortion, 108*t*
Upjohn Company, 52
U.S. Agency for International Development (USAID), 31
U.S. armed forces, 26–27
U.S. Census Bureau, 103
U.S. Constitution
    Fifth Amendment, 11
    Fourteenth Amendment, 127–128
    Partial-Birth Abortion Ban Act and, 135
    Roe v. Wade and, 124–125, 132–133

Rust v. Sullivan and, 12–13
Stenberg v. Carhart and, 17
U.S. Department of Health and Human Services (HHS)
    fetal tissue transplantation research moratorium, 90
    "gag rule," 30–31
U.S. Government Accountability Office (GAO), 85
U.S. House of Representatives
    Child Interstate Abortion Notification Act, opposition to, 119–122
    Child Interstate Abortion Notification Act, support of, 115–118
    Partial-Birth Abortion Ban Act and, 135, 138–140, 143
U.S. president, 9
U.S. Senate
    Child Interstate Abortion Notification Act and, 115
    judicial appointments and, 9
    Partial-Birth Abortion Ban Act and, 135–138
    Roe v. Wade, reconsideration of, 123–128
    Roe v. Wade, testimony on upholding, 129–133
U.S. Supreme Court
    abortion cases, chronology of major, 10*t*–11*t*
    abortion clinics, protesters at, 17–18
    Doe v. Bolton, 12
    fetal rights and, 94
    fetus rulings, 18–19
    government support/nonsupport of abortion, 12–13
    judicial appointments, politics, 9
    on parents' rights, 117
    Partial-Birth Abortion Ban Act and, 135, 136
    Roe v. Wade, 8, 9, 11
    Roe v. Wade, not overturned, 19–20
    Roe v. Wade, reconsideration of, 123–128
    Roe v. Wade, testimony on upholding, 129–133
    Rust v. Sullivan, 31
    state abortion bans, 14*t*
    state restrictions on abortion, 13, 15–17
USAID (U.S. Agency for International Development), 31

V

Vallejo (CA), 130
Vandalism, of abortion clinics, 82
"Viable fetus," 18–19, 20
Vietnam, abortion rate of, 99–100
Violence
    abortion clinic violence, by state, 84*f*
    against abortion clinics, 82, 84

Freedom of Access to Clinic Entrances Act and, 84–85
    incidents of violence/disruption against abortion providers in U.S. and Canada, 83*t*
"Voicing Concern for Women, Abortion Foes Seek Limits on Availability of Mifepristone" (Boonstra), 106

W

Waagner, Clayton, 82
Wade, Henry B., 9
Wade, Roe v. See Roe v. Wade
Waiting period
    mandatory state waiting periods, and biased counseling for abortion, 54*f*
    states that require, 42
Wales, 107*f*
Walesa, Lech, 100, 101
Ward, Roy Bowen, 2
Wardle, Lynn, 128
Washington, abortion laws in, 7, 8
"Washington Memo" (Kaeser), 33
Washington Post, 91
Waszak, Cynthia, 75–77
"Watching Sex on Television Predicts Adolescent Initiation of Sexual Behavior" (Rand Corporation), 69
Waters, Maxine, 121–122
Webster v. Reproductive Health Services, 19
Weiss, Catherine, 53
Weiss, Gerson, 144–146
Welfare reform, abortion and, 33–34
Welfare Reform Extension Act of 2003, 66
"What They Won't Tell You at the Abortion Clinic" (Pro-Life Action Ministries), 89
Whelan, M. Edward, 123–124
Whitaker, Daniel J., 69
White Americans
    abortion ratio for, 40
    teen pregnancy rate for, 62
White, Byron, 124
WHO. *See* World Health Organization
Williams Obstetrics, 144
Williams v. Zbaraz, 12
Woman's life
    abortion in Ireland to save, 102
    worldwide abortion laws and, 95
Women
    abortion attitudes of, 112–113
    abortion in Latin America, 104
    abortion ratio, by age group of women who obtained legal abortion, selected years, 46*f*
    abortion ratio, by age group of women who obtained legal abortion, selected states, 43*f*

abortion ratio, by age group of women who obtained legal abortion, state of occurrence, 44t–45t

characteristics of women who obtained legal abortions, 41t

deaths from abortion worldwide, 106–107

family planning funding through Title X, 27, 29–30

fertility indicators, by age, race, Hispanic origin, 49t

fetal rights *vs.* parents' rights, 94

legal abortions, by demographic characteristics, selected states, 42t

legal abortions, by ethnicity of women, state of occurrence, selected states, 48t

legal abortions, by race of women, 47t

low-income women's access to abortion, 28t

number of abortions, selected years, 40f

percentage distribution of women obtaining abortions, by contraceptive method used in the month of conception, 50t

percentage of births to unmarried women, by state and territory, 35t

reasons for abortion, 40

seeking abortion, characteristics of, 38–40

speak out about abortion, 7–8

Women's Health Center, Madsen v., 18

Women's right to choose abortion

Child Interstate Abortion Notification Act and, 120

choice positions of state Democratic, Republican parties on woman's right to choose abortion, 22t

Partial-Birth Abortion Ban Act and, 142, 146

Roe v. Wade, reconsideration of, 125, 127

Roe v. Wade, support of, 129–133

worldwide protection of, 107

The World Factbook 2005 (Central Intelligence Agency), 103

"World Fertility Patterns 2004" (United Nations Population Division), 103

"World Fertility Report 2003" (Population Division of the United Nations Department of Economic and Social Affairs), 101

World Health Organization (WHO)

on abstinence programs, 66

deaths from abortion worldwide, 107

worldwide abortion data collection, 95

"2005 World Population Data Sheet" (Population Reference Bureau), 103

"The World's Abortion Laws" (Center for Reproductive Rights), 95, 97

Worldwide community. *See* Abortion worldwide; International community

Worrell, J., 88

Wright, Jean A., 126–127

Z

Zbaraz, Miller v., 12

Zbaraz, United States v., 12

Zbaraz, Williams v., 12

Zhao, Zhingwei, 102

—